EPIC TRADITIONS OF AFRICA

EPIC
TRADITIONS
OF
AFRICA

STEPHEN BELCHER

INDIANA UNIVERSITY PRESS
BLOOMINGTON AND INDIANAPOLIS

This book is a publication of

Indiana University Press
601 North Morton Street
Bloomington, IN 47404-3797 USA

http://www.indiana.edu/~iupress

Telephone orders   800-842-6796
Fax orders   812-855-7931
Orders by e-mail   iuporder@indiana.edu

The paper used in this publication meets the minimum requirements of American National
Standard for Information Sciences—Permanence of Paper for Printed Library Materials,
ANSI Z39.48-1984.

Manufactured in the United States of America

Library of Congress Cataloging-in-Publication Data

Belcher, Stephen Paterson, date
Epic traditions of Africa / Stephen Belcher.
p.   cm.
Includes bibliographical references and index.
ISBN 0-253-33501-9 (cl : alk. paper). — ISBN 0-253-21281-2 (pbk : alk. paper)
1. Epic literature, African—History and criticism.   I. Title.
PL8010.B44   1999
896'.09—DC21   98-55990

1 2 3 4 5   03 02 01 00 99

CONTENTS

❖

——————————

ILLUSTRATIONS

❖
_____

PREFACE

In a sense, this book had its beginnings around 1977, while I was a graduate student hoping to work some aspects of the living African oral tradition into what was then to be a dissertation involving medieval studies. I happened upon Christiane Seydou's edition of *Silâmaka et Poullôri* in the stacks of the Brown University library and realized with delight and wonder that I had found the aspect I wished to investigate. My delight has been easy to sustain, as I went on to locate and study the available material; the purpose of this book is in some sense to share what I felt and what I found. This book presents the work of other scholars and researchers, spread through time and space, and its merit would be to present that work usefully, honestly, and equitably, and to encourage others to wander down the paths others have traced.

I have also been very fortunate in support and encouragement from other scholars. Some have gone far beyond the norms of collegiality and deserve special recognition and thanks for opening their homes or studies and sharing their work with me. This list (in rough chronological order) would begin with Charles Bird, whom I first met in Bamako and who later tolerated a month-long invasion by an alien student in his office in Bloomington. Tom Hale greeted me on my arrival at Penn State and has proved a wonderful friend, mentor, and colleague whose well-stocked library I plundered while re-acclimating after a stint in Mauritania with the Peace Corps, and whose experience continues to be a resource. Ralph Austen in Chicago has shared work, ideas, conference sessions, and his home, allowing me to explore the wonders of the Africana collection at Northwestern University. My thanks to Lilyan Kesteloot and Bassirou Dieng at the Institut Fondamental d'Afrique Noire (IFAN) in Dakar, whose help made a short research trip in 1994 professionally and personally rewarding. I am deeply grateful to Lilyan for according me the freedom of her office—and her company—during my visit; I would also like to record my respect not only for her own work (and she is a pioneer in this field), but for the work she has stimulated among her students. David Conrad has shared unpublished material and personal experiences growing out of an almost unparalleled exploration of West African oral historical traditions. He has also read a first version of this book and has guided it toward improvements. His assistance and encouragement in the project have been immeasurably valuable. I hope he will forgive the errors that have persisted and take pride in his contribution to the work.

Many others deserve thanks. I shall not try to list the individuals to whom I feel a debt of gratitude. I should, however, acknowledge the financial support of the Research and Graduate Study Organization at The Pennsylvania State University, as well as the Department of Comparative Literature, which provided travel funds for trips to Dakar in 1994 and for brief visits to Paris and Brussels in 1996. To friends and colleagues who have guided the book toward greater clarity and usefulness, I would like to express my thanks. To my wife Lee, I owe a special debt.

❖
————————————————

INTRODUCTION

FEW READERS HAVE discovered the treasures of African oral epic. These cultural monuments deserve wider recognition for their complex images of a rich past and for their poetic force, especially since they have become far more accessible through published editions and translations. While oral epic traditions once existed only in the ephemeral interaction of specialized performers with their audiences and patrons in a variety of modes and social settings, a massive collection effort has now resulted in an accumulation of recordings and publications. The barriers of language, distance, and unfamiliarity are becoming surmountable, and the challenge now stems rather from the volume and diversity of material from many regions and cultures. This study is a contribution to the classification and analysis of this body of literature. It is hoped that it will encourage readers to explore this newly available material and to seek a greater appreciation of the particular qualities of this African form of verbal art.

The epic traditions of Africa speak of empires and peoples, heroes and hunters, kings and warriors. Readers may know of Sunjata, the thirteenth-century founder of the empire of Mali. His story is told as an epic throughout the territory of his old empire, in the modern West African states of Mali, Guinea, the Gambia, Senegal, and others. An influential French prose version by the Guinean historian Djibril Tamsir Niane has made Sunjata almost the archetype of West African historical oral epic for readers around the world.[1] Readers may also have encountered Mwindo, the preternatural "Little-One-Just-Born-He-Walks" of the far smaller group of the BaNyanga of eastern Congo; his story leads one deep into the ethnographic and environmental intricacies of a small population largely engaged in the subsistence activities of hunting, gathering, and fishing.[2]

Sunjata and Mwindo may be the best-known examples of their genre among English speakers.[3] But they represent only two among a dozen or more distinct

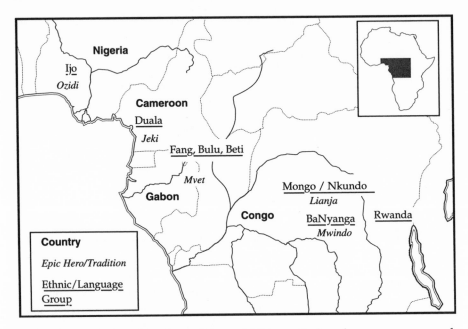

Map 1. Approximate locations of Central African ethnic or language groups and their associated epic heroes.

linguistic and historical traditions, now documented in hundreds of textualized versions. In Central Africa (particularly in Congo and the coastal regions of the Cameroon and Gabon) there are Lianja of the Mongo, Jeki la Nzambe of the Duala, and the complex mythical world of the Fang *mvet* performances (the Fang name for their version of the epic genre), which recount the never-ending struggles of mortal and immortal clans in a magical landscape. West Africa gives us, along with Sunjata, the Soninke legend of Wagadu, the cycle of epics dealing with the Bamana state of Segou, and the adventures of the Fula heroes Hambodedio (Hama the Red) and Silamaka; in the Gambia there is the ill-fated Kelefa Sane, who chose to meet death in battle, or Janke Wali, who destroyed himself along with an invading army at the fall of the city of Kansala. Each of these traditions has its own flavor, its own set of conventions and expectations, its own construction of the past.

This diversity is both the challenge and the appeal of African epic traditions for the student of epic. The range of possibilities developed by different cultures, separate or contiguous, within the boundaries of a given form teaches much about the relations of art and society. To single out one hero, one tradition (as is done most often with Sunjata), is to pull a single thread from a rich tapestry and to lose both its distinctive character and its relation to its matrix. A fundamental premise of this study is that a primary understanding of the distinctive traits and character of African epic traditions and their heroes should start in Africa, with an examination of the documented range of performance and narrative possibilities. A second premise posits that knowledge of the social and historical context and the artistic conventions of an epic text are crucial to an initial understanding and appreciation of what is for most readers probably a foreign art form. This logic calls on readers to resist the temptation to look outside Africa for conceptual models and narrative parallels and to ground their initial approach instead on description and comparison of African traditions. The grandeur of Sunjata's image emerges in contrast to the ignoble kings of Segou; the creative polish of the cycle of Segou contrasts with the somewhat static Soninke traditions of Wagadu; and the courtly or aristocratic tinge to all these examples marks their difference from the more popular hunters' epics.

Defining Terms

The proposed focus on African materials does require some definition and discrimination among terms in order to effect the transition into an African frame of reference. The purpose here is to clarify a quasi-technical use or to identify for the reader significant differences from presumedly familiar contexts; perhaps it is best to begin with the central term. The word "epic" carries a considerable charge. It evokes monuments of the written literary tradition, a larger-than-life scale of narrative that may be tinged with divine inspiration. These associations persist even when the term is given the technical qualifier "oral epic," as has happened in this century to acknowledge the similarities of a wide body of performed narratives spread through Europe and Asia. Students of oral epic may feel that their topic becomes valuable to others only when it elucidates aspects of the literary tradition. Implicit in the term "oral epic" is the notion of a certain fundamental similarity of materials within a Eurasian literary corpus: from the now written texts of Homer and the epics of medieval Europe to the still living oral traditions of Arabic, Turkic, Persian, and Slavic epic.

Controversy has affected application of the word "epic" to African traditions owing to largely stylistic differences between those traditions and the recognized Eurasian corpus.[4] Such differences are to be expected: African cultures are distinct from the historically connected cultures of Europe and western Asia, and the settings and nature of the performance-events are quite different. Concern over equivalence is better expressed by asking whether it is possible to reach an understanding of African oral epic traditions that is in harmony with approaches to other traditions; the answer is most certainly yes.

In this study, the term "epic" refers to an extended narrative on a historical topic, delivered in public performance, most often with musical accompaniment, by a specialized performer. A large number of texts derived more or less directly from such performances have now been published, and these published texts constitute the central corpus of this study.

The critical elements of this definition are the notions of narrative, public performance, and the specialized performer. Each of these elements involves further distinctions: between narrative and the panegyric poetry that in Africa is a significant component of the art of the specialized performer (known in West Africa as a *griot;* no general term applies in Central and Southern Africa); between the public account presented in performance and the private narratives offered by individuals (often of greater historical value); and between the trained and the untrained performer, in which the notion of a performer's authority is also embedded. These three dimensions—performers, the distinction between narrative or praise poetry, and modes of oral history—will be more fully presented in chapter 1 and addressed expressly in the discussions of specific cultural traditions.

Notions of heroism and poetic form are often cited as characteristics of epic but are not used here. Heroism is a culture-bound concept. Heroes act within value-systems and narrative conventions, and the reader must beware of importing concepts. The feudal propensity for violence reflected in medieval epics has quite a different effect when associated with an African past that includes slave-raiding (as raider or as victim).[5]

The question of poetic form often cited in definitions of epic is more problematic because the standard literary concepts of poetics are based upon written material. The primary African materials consist of oral performances with substantial musical accompaniment. The complex interplay of voice and music can be compounded when the language involved is tonal (i.e., the words have rising and falling inflections). These features raise possibilities unforeseen in most handbooks of prosody and still insufficiently analyzed in the field. The poetic aspects of the verbal element, as delivered with music, are still unclear, and so it seems safest not to insist upon this criterion, despite the Eurasian expectation of metered regularity that is probably born of the long-standing influence of written forms on oral texts.[6]

Use of the word "tradition" also requires some explication. The term is used here in two specific and qualified senses: "historical tradition" implies a body of knowledge about some form of history, handed down through a variety of means; this knowledge is taken to include variants of all sorts, as well as the public and private expressions of this knowledge, with no assumption of uniformity or coherence across the sources. This knowledge may include mythical as well as political history. The second qualified use is that of the "performance tradition," which is intended to evoke not only the manner of delivery and continuities in style from one performer to another but also some notion of performance repertoire. In theory, any historical (or other) narrative might be presented in performance; in practice, however, it usually appears that only a distinct subset of the available historical information is so presented; and even that is transformed. Further corollaries of this notion of "performance tradition" are the ideas that the material presented in performance is polished and rehearsed, and that insofar as it may be historical, it represents an accepted public version of history in which "truth" may be subordinated to local consensus.

Both qualified uses of the word point to elements of continuity that may be discerned in different examples of epic or historical narrative, whether they are continuities of information from one individual to another (mediated, quite possibly, by other individuals), or continuities in style and repertoire from one performer to another. The term is used to identify a common property, as distinct from individual invention. While the notion of tradition thus transcends any specific individual, it should not be seen as a superorganic force governing those individuals.

Throughout this study, I have used the word "text" to refer only to a document (transcription, translation, retelling) derived from an oral performance, or to the verbal element of that performance as opposed to the musical. The word "text" does not imply that performers work from memorized material or in reference to some conceptual, unrealized master performance.

Cautions on Methods and Approach

The primary materials of this study come from the oral tradition. Nevertheless, neither the orality nor the performative aspect of these narratives is the primary focus of this study.[7] Those dimensions are treated as necessary background, but the focus is on questions relating to the historical and cultural content of the epics and on the information that members of the culture might possess and bring to their appreciation of any given performance. Some issues are obvious and straightforward: What is the history behind the stories? Who are the principal characters, and how are they to be seen? What other stories might be known about them? Is the story considered true (and by whom)? Other questions may involve research in the fields of history, ethnography, and religion.

Questions of performance are fundamental, comparable to questions of textual history and bibliography for written material. Performance is used here as an initial, almost hidden criterion; it provides evidence that the performer's output is being shaped for artistic purposes (although social purposes, such as the desire to flatter a member of the audience, may intervene). It is at an elementary level a sign of artistic control over the material. But while there is a literature on performance in Africa,[8] specific information on the content and background of the various African epic traditions themselves is less readily available.

Nevertheless, the oral provenance of the material does entail some methodological precautions and warnings. It is axiomatic in the study of oral literatures that no single performance is ever identical to another, although the "information" conveyed may well be the same as that provided elsewhere. This applies equally to different performances by the same performer or group of performers (when different versions are available, comparison can be instructive). The choice of a single version for study, or the reconciliation of different and even contradictory accounts, is problematic. The artistic authority of a given performance may even seem diluted by knowledge of multiforms: Doesn't the existence of a dozen transcribed versions of the epic of Sunjata reduce one's confidence in any specific version?

Such doubts can be resolved. Where there are multiple versions, one must study them. Appreciation and understanding of a tradition grow with awareness of the possible and accepted range of variants, since understanding of a performance is enhanced by knowledge of the choices available to the performer. One method of illustrating this performative range is to publish a set of variants, as Gordon Innes has done for Sunjata (1974) and for later Gambian traditions (1976, 1978). Another is the detailed, comparative annotation of the published text, for which David Conrad's edition of the *Epic of Bamana Segu According to Tayiru Banbera* is a model. But such models of presentation are rare; usually the student must make the effort to locate and study the variant versions.

Not every performance requires comparative analysis. Some stand alone: Hamma Diam Bouraima provides a rich account of the hero Hambodedio's quest for "his" musical tune, Saïgalare.[9] There are other versions of the story (in other languages, even), but this virtuoso account can easily stand alone. The story of Mariheri of Jonkoloni, one of the rebellious kings defeated by the forces of Segou, exists in several published versions, but there is no need to examine all of them to see that the lengthier compound version by Sissoko Kabine is a masterpiece.[10]

Still, the underlying principle is to recognize a variety of versions for any given story. In the supplementary material at the end of this book (the appendix, notes, and list of references), the goal has been to provide useful references to variant versions of the principal stories; these variants include the available historical information, especially when it is based on statements by identified informants, as well as folktales. Ethnographic information is introduced in discussion as specifically relevant to the analysis of a story or incident. Much of the secondary material is in French, a legacy of the colonial division of Africa, but an increasing amount represents the efforts of African scholars to describe and define their own traditions.

Plan of the Work

Aspects of African oral tradition that might be called the building blocks of the epic traditions are explored in greater detail in chapter 1. It offers general descriptions of the modes of oral historiography and the complexities attaching to performers (griots and others) and to the praise poetry traditions that serve as a backdrop to the epic narratives. It is particularly intended to familiarize readers not versed in African studies with some of the underlying concepts. Subsequent chapters will readdress the same issues within specific cultures.

The sequence of chapters 2 through 8 necessarily requires explanation. It is neither a geographic progression (east to west, south to north) nor a strict chronological sequence—and it should be noted here that the simultaneity of oral tradition ensures that all moments of the past are brought into synchrony through their performance in the present. The Soninke empire of Ghana may be the earliest Sahelian state on record (Arab travelers described visits in the ninth century), but the Soninke oral traditions recited today exist along with accounts of eighteenth- and nineteenth-century events. Nor is the sequence intended as an "evolutionary" scheme for African epic.

One underlying thread in this book is the relation of epic and historical tradition. The sequence of chapters begins with a general group of mythical and ahistorical narratives (e.g., the Mwindo epics of Congo and the hunters' traditions of Mali) and ends with strongly historicized and particular accounts, such as that of the death of the Senegalese king Lat Dior while fighting the French in 1886. Chapter 2 thus presents an array of narratives from Central Africa (Congo, Cameroon, Nigeria) united through the figure of the protagonist and his function as a culture hero, a figure of mythical rather than political history. Chapter 3 examines narrative traditions from West African hunting groups. Hunters are the subject of narratives and myths throughout Africa. In the Manden and neighboring regions, however, these narratives are performed as epics, in a manner closely related to that of historical tradition.

The progression then is from ahistorical to historical traditions, and chapters 4 through 7 observe a rough chronology of the states and kingdoms of the western Sahel: the Soninke traditions of Ghana and successor states (ninth to eleventh centuries); the Manden traditions of Sunjata and his successors (thirteenth to sixteenth centuries); the cycle of epics dealing with Bamana Segou (eighteenth to early nineteenth century); and then the less historical, but related, Fula traditions. Chapter 8 represents the anomaly in this sequence: Songhay-Zarma traditions, which deal with the Songhay empire and later events (fifteenth to nineteenth centuries); later material from the Gambia (Gambian traditions also make reference to Sunjata); and the Wolof epic cycle, which covers the fifteenth to nineteenth centuries through a selection of kings. Chapter 8 thus presents material from east and west of the central region covered by the four preceding chapters. This grouping is the consequence of two factors of varying importance. The first, minor factor is that of bulk: the available material from these areas does not require a full chapter for a treatment comparable to that given to other regions. The second, and more interesting, consideration is the relationship of the traditions. For the Songhay-Zarma and for the Wolof, epic traditions seem to be of recent vintage and show the influence or inspiration of other peoples and traditions. Adoption of the genre of oral epic would have been facilitated by the contacts and free movement of peoples through the large colonial territory of French West Africa.

Each chapter begins with a general introduction to the linguistic/cultural group, its history, performance tradition, and the available corpus of epics. This is followed by discussion of major narratives and heroes through the use of synopses, which are followed by analysis and comments on salient comparative features.

Sources: A Caution on Textual Questions

Steering a middle course among disciplinary shoals, this book assembles some of the available information as a stimulus to understanding, appreciation, and further study of African oral epic traditions. Different sorts of texts provide different sorts of information. All of that information may be relevant to an understanding of a given narrative, although the nature of the source (a reliably transcribed recording or colonial-era jottings) will naturally affect the assessment of its contribution and value.

The principle of fieldwork and folkloristics in general is that the ideal "oral

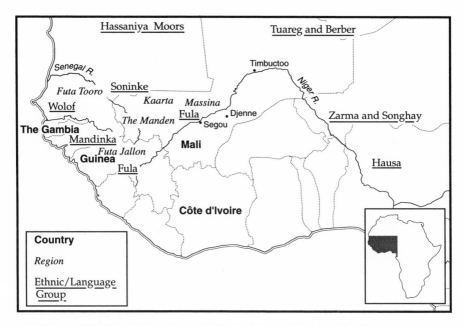

Map 2.   Approximate locations of West African ethnic and language groups.

text" should be a faithful transcription, translation, and description of a performance (however defined) recorded in a natural context. It should document a "typical" event for the culture, free of foreign intrusions, and the analysis should reflect a comparative awareness of multiple events of the same kind.[11] The concern is for authenticity and the minimizing of interference by the collector. Practical experience, however, has modified the imperative. To ensure successful recording, it now seems permissible to stage an event, keeping it as close as possible to its normal course. Such an occasion is known as an "induced natural context." In traditional Africa, almost any large social gathering might serve as the occasion for epic performance: a wedding, naming ceremony, funeral, or an occasion of conspicuous consumption by a local notable. The music and singing provide the entertainment for the occasion.

Few of the texts examined meet the ideal collection criteria of folkloristics. The texts do offer other claims to some form of authority or credibility, and they respond to other concerns. Over the past century, the principal interest in West African traditions in particular has come from historians concerned with content and with the testimony of performers for the historical record rather than with the nuances of performances themselves. Colonial-era sources rarely identify their informant or the conditions of the "performance," such as it may have been.

Further, especially in Francophone scholarship, there is a sense that the performer or informant is an essentially passive vehicle for a communal burden of historical knowledge. Personal control of the information is thus secondary to the larger, collective charge, although the traditionalist, as a possessor of knowledge, is still imbued with some reverence. An American folklorist might observe that such a conception was exploded some generations ago; it is impossible to separate the transmitter from the knowledge. But this objection fails to recognize the particularities of the cultural dynamics involved. Since 1960, when Niane published *Soundiata* and the Senegalese Cheikh Anta Diop (father of Afrocentric studies) defended his doctorate on the continuities of Egyptian culture in Africa at the Sorbonne, faith in the content of historical oral tradition has remained a cornerstone of modern national consciousness throughout Francophone West Africa and beyond. It serves as a rebuttal of the charge that Africans have no history. As an element of disciplinary sociology, it should be recalled that in America, the emphasis on performance arose only after the compilation of massive archives of folktales and the elaboration of monuments of classification such as the *Types of the Folktale* and the *Motif-Index of Folk-Literature*. Africa does not yet have such reference works.

It is important to observe the differences in perspective and purpose. And other factors must be brought into the balance: circumstances of collection, authority of the collector, and the nature of the event and the information. But besides ideology or method, there is the issue of material working conditions. The early stenciled, bilingual texts produced by the Centre d'Etudes Linguistique et Historique par la Tradition Orale (Center for Linguistic and Historical Study by Oral Tradition) of Niamey, Niger, command respect for the commitment and effort they represent, regardless of their lack of performance data. Their contribution to the common store of knowledge should not be disregarded. At the other end of the scale, no English-language series of publications has yet matched the accomplishment of the Paris-based Classiques Africains series, which routinely includes a sound-recording along with its elegantly presented and expensive bilingual texts (recent publications include CDs).

We now have a great deal of material for use in examining the relationship of epic to other forms of tradition. Travelers and colonial administrators of the nineteenth and early twentieth centuries have left behind reports, in varying degrees of fullness, of narratives that have been recorded in modern times as oral epics. Among these early collectors, Leo Frobenius, who traveled throughout Africa in the years before World War I, deserves mention and praise: his massive collection of African traditional literature, *Atlantis,* contains much material that is valuable for present comparative purposes.[12] None of his texts is an exact transcription; he presents only German translations on the basis of dictation by the performer (he seems to have paid them rather well, which may explain the quality of his harvest), but he often includes local language terms which help to establish a context for his material. Another collector was Gilbert Vieillard, a French administrator who specialized in Fula and collected his materials in the original language (they have now been reworked by other scholars) in the years 1928–1929.

There are also a number of written local sources from that same era. Arabic histories of the region were written in Timbuctoo in the seventeenth and eighteenth centuries (the *Tarikh es-Soudan* and the *Tarikh el-Fettach*), and the tradition was continued by others. From the town of Nioro du Sahel in Mali, there is a group of accounts, written around 1895 and published early on,[13] intended as background to the history of the great Muslim leader of the nineteenth century, al-Hajj Umar Tall. In Senegal, the learned Cheikh Moussa Kamara wrote massive histories of the region in Arabic; they are now being translated. He also wrote an early history of Segou (ca. 1900?), which has interesting echoes in modern oral tradition.

And there is more modern work whose reliability is enhanced by the use of tape recorders. The collectors include folklorists, anthropologists, linguists, historians, and students of literature, and they have provided what might be considered the primary texts: documents reliably recorded in oral performance and published in a bilingual format. In almost all cases, the "performances" represent something like an "induced natural context" that make possible the recording process. In a number of cases, special circumstances surrounding the event affect an appreciation of the resulting text. When the Gambian *jali* (singer) Bamba Suso performs the epic of Sunjata for a school audience,[14] or when Kanku Mady Jabaté of Kela recites an "official" version of the epic of Sunjata for a delegation sent down from Bamako to collect such an official version for nation-building purposes,[15] or when Wa Kamissoko speaks in answer to questions from an audience of professional historians,[16] the value of the information may well be independent of its value as a representative "performance-event."

Modern technology and marketing forces are now complicating the situation. Modern music competes with traditional forms; modern tastes may prefer more lively dance music. The radio may have replaced the nobles as a source of patronage; performers no longer aim to become the pampered dependents of the local chief but to become jet-setting rock stars. But epics have found a niche: they circulate widely in cassette form as a sort of cottage industry. It may be premature to explore the generic boundaries of the thirty-minute cassette epic as opposed to the ninety-minute version, but that time may come.

The bottom line is that the texts are taken as they come, their value weighed according to the content, the reliability of the editorial work, and any other pertinent factors. Some texts offer evidence for performance practice, others for narrative content, others for poetic features. The student of oral traditions may work with fewer certainties than the average student of literature, and the challenges may at times seem greater. But the sense of discovery and the excitement of novelty are correspondingly more acute.

EPIC TRADITIONS OF AFRICA

ELEMENTS OF EPIC TRADITIONS

THE INTRODUCTION IDENTIFIED a number of features considered critical for understanding African epic and defined it as an extended historical narrative delivered in public performance by a specialized performer. The introduction also identified some of the oppositions implicit in that definition: narrative as opposed to panegyric, public as opposed to private performance, specialized rather than casual performers. This chapter will define those features and oppositions within the wider context of African oral tradition. Since subsequent chapters will be most concerned with the historical backgrounds to specific traditions, the discussion begins by exploring modes of history and historiography. It then turns to the function of the performers, who are the repositories and transmitters of their traditions, and to the composition of praise poetry, which is the most widespread poetic evocation of the past attested in Africa, and which is intimately involved in the composition of most forms of African oral epic.

History and Narrative Traditions

In Africa, history and oral tradition are intimately linked; much of the continent's past is recoverable only through the use of oral sources. The past thirty-five years have seen growth and refinement in the methods and interpretations of oral history. However, like the word *griot* (the West African musician and lore-master, discussed below), the notion of oral history sometimes leads to misleading assumptions about the nature and possibilities of the oral transmission of history. At times, discomfort with the results of Eurocentric historical studies has led researchers to neglect the rigor and methods of historical analysis that are associated with written sources but that are, as Jan Vansina, Mamadou Diawara, and others have so well demonstrated, fully possible and equally necessary when dealing with oral sources.[1]

The task is neither easy nor always rewarding. Donald Wright's work, published over a twenty-year span, on the history of Niumi, a nineteenth-century kingdom at the mouth of the Gambia River, offers a sense of the hopes, the difficulties, and finally the disappointments encountered in this process. At the other end of the spectrum of confidence in oral sources there is the work of Amadou Hampaté Bâ and J. Daget on the history of the nineteenth-century Fula *dina* (Islamic state) of Massina, a history that was reconstructed from extensive interviews with descendants of the principals; or the collection of royal historical narratives of Rwanda, which constitute an official record of sorts, still dependent on the memory and talent of the human repository.[2]

The historical record derived from oral tradition is variable and particular. It changes with every teller; every narrator has a point of view and possibly an interest in the presentation of the story. Rarely is history codified into a stable narrative recognized by, or imposed on, the community at large; the need for such a "master" narrative is minimal except under specific political and cultural conditions. Centralized monarchies might have a vested interest in their version of the past because it defines their legitimacy. There is evidence that royal courts made some effort to establish an official tradition. Melville and Frances Herskovits, who wrote a groundbreaking study of the kingdom of Dahomey (in the modern republic of Benin), reported that twice (ca. 1720 and again ca. 1850), a king of Dahomey assembled the traditionalists, or clan-genealogists, of the kingdom to promulgate his changes to their genealogical lore. The attempted manipulation of the records has become part of the record.[3] Elsewhere, and perhaps more often, the accuracy of a past record is tacitly subordinate to the needs and interests of the present—and there is no difference between this and the collective historical practices of literate cultures.

When it seems desirable to establish a record of the past, a number of methods may be used. The simplest, perhaps, involves genealogy. To recall ancestors is to move into the past with relative assurance: the chain of transmission involves a relatively small number of links, and family history usually provides the opportunity for multiple tellings of the story. Indeed, it would appear that the most reliable results of oral history derive from studies looking back no more than four or five generations (one to two hundred years).

Genealogy also structures royal narratives: king-lists, with some commentary on the relations and successions, are a staple historical tool used around the world. In Africa, they take a number of forms, from the family list recalled by descendants and retainers, to elaborate drum sequences that replay the praises and themes of each king, to various material objects used as mnemonic devices.[4] Such lists are perhaps less trustworthy than might be desired; the historian David Henige has pointed out the difficulties in connecting king-lists with chronology.[5]

Still, they do function to organize a culture's past, and they provide the underpinnings for at least two epic traditions (the cycle of Segou and the epics of the Wolof), although in other cases they seem absent.

The topic of genealogy leads to a classic illustration of the problems for oral history in the absence of a central ruling tradition. The Tiv of northern Nigeria use genealogy to resolve social disputes.[6] Determining the family relationships of the disputants clarifies their respective obligations and thus helps to settle their divisions. The process, as described by anthropologist Laura Bohannon, involves lengthy discussions, by all parties involved, in which the issues of the dispute are defined. The question is translated into one of relationships and obligations, and then family trees are reconstructed to resolve the issue. The appropriate evidence is identified and then adduced. In the early colonial era, however, when these genealogies were brought into court proceedings (under the British policy of "indirect rule," which attempted respect for local institutions), the genealogies were recorded because their importance was apparent. Decades later, when colonial officers attempted to use this written judicial record to settle cases, it was found that the contemporary Tiv oral genealogies and the older tribunal records no longer agreed. The Tiv genealogies had evolved along with the families they reflected; they remained functional insofar as they related to current family relations and were relevant to immediate problems. There was no value for the Tiv in an objective record; in fact, such a record would have precluded the obvious negotiation process that was critical to settling the disputes.

The Tiv constituted an acephalous or stateless society that placed a premium on consensus and collective action; as such they are quite distinct from most of the peoples with epic traditions (one exception might be the Fang), who are marked by a strong royal or aristocratic tradition. But the Tiv provide a lesson, valued especially by anthropologists, on the contemporary orientation of societies: the present defines the past. This presumption goes back to Bronislav Malinowski's notion of the chartering function of myths and other narratives,[7] which exist to ratify the present state of affairs. Where information preserved from the past is no longer reflected in the actual configuration of society, it is discarded, and other narratives are constructed to reflect the changes.

An image sometimes used to describe the most stable areas of coverage in oral historical traditions is that of an hourglass: a wide top half tapering to a narrow middle and swelling again at the base. The image suggests the way in which knowledge of the recent past (the previous generations) is relatively full but begins to fade beyond an indefinite point in time, typically beyond the fifth generation. But traditions that recount the origin of the culture (and, often, the world) are also relatively well known; these are the base. The story of creation remains stable down through time to a certain undefined point, typically when direct contact with the divine comes to an end. It is the middle ground, linking these two periods, that proves dispensable. The oral traditions of the Manden, for instance, contain a good deal of information about Sunjata, his ancestors, his generals, and the foundation of the empire of Mali in the thirteenth century, but often very little about his successors and the decline of the empire until, beginning with the eighteenth century, the record begins to fill out again with detail connected to modern families.

Traditions of origin are not quite the same as the history of the recent past, which is recoverable through family memories and other means; and there is some disagreement about their value as history. Origins merge with creation and thus with myths. There is clear common ground or crossover between the two processes. Around the world, the history of a culture often starts as a history of the world, funneling down (so to speak) to the specific people in question. When exactly the story leaves the time of creation to enter the field of human history is often vague, and in some ways it seems useful to consider the hourglass division mentioned above as a convenient marker. Consider, for instance, Yoruba traditions, spread among a multitude of city-states. In general, the Yoruba recognize a descent from heaven and the establishment of divine kingship at the town of Ile-Ife (in the mythological period); the different city-states each have their own dynastic records (of the historical period), which are made to link back somehow to Ife.

Differentiation of myth and history is complicated by the historicization of myths that often follows religious conversion or other major cultural changes; in this process, the creation myths are translated into history and gods become kings. Also, especially in regions influenced by Islam, narratives or references from the Old Testament or Koranic history are incorporated into local tradition. (Muslims are not the only ones to do this: the Yoruba Anglican Bishop Samuel Johnson, in his *History of the Yorubas,* traced Yoruba origins to Christian Ethiopia.) These transformations and adoptions have not been carefully analyzed, although the process deserves close attention. Some of the epic narratives covered in this study, especially those from Central Africa, should clearly be placed at the mythical end of the scale. Others from the Sahelian zone might fit there, and others again certainly do not.

To view traditions of origin as myths may cause discomfort. One trouble spot arose in the 1970s in Central Africa, when an anthropologist of religion, Luc de Heusch, applied structuralist methods of analysis to interpret as myth a narrative found widely in several local traditions of origin. In this story, a sober hunter comes to the court of a drunken king (Ngolo-Ngolo, a name recognizable throughout a number of languages of the Bantu family) and marries his daughters; their children later establish civilization and kingship. De Heusch connected this pattern with creation myths and fertility symbols rather than with historical events, and some historians whose narratives he was using have protested (although when the same narrative occurs through a number of neighboring cultures it would seem appropriate to consider nonliteral interpretations).[8] A similar analysis could almost certainly be applied to a figure such as Sunjata, and the work of scholars such as Mamadou Diawara or Fatimata Mounkaila[9] offers a growing recognition that founders of societies fit a paradigm that may not be strictly factual in its basis.

While creation myths may underlie some historical traditions, they do not necessarily contribute to epic traditions except insofar as mythical patterns may structure narratives. This topic deserves further analysis. Most of the epics are set in a purely human world (although the humans are often experts at magic), and traditions of origin do not appear to be preferred material for development in epic performances. Even among the "mythical" Central African traditions, the stories do not deal explicitly with such themes as the creation of the world.

At the other pole of the temporal range are the stories of migrations and village settlements, often falling within the accepted four- or five-generation range for reliable oral traditions but subject in their own way to forces of distortion: local and individual interests, distrust of authorities, incomplete information, and the like. These traditions are to be handled delicately because they deal not with the origin of social institutions but with questions of property, most usually land rights, but also at times with political power and rights of succession.

A short excerpt of oral testimony from the Gambia may serve as illustration. This story was collected in 1969 by the researchers Sékéné-Mody Cissoko and Kaoussou Sambou during a fairly quick tour through a number of villages and towns along the river. The informant was a clan elder, Bakari Sonko, aged eighty, in the village of Berending. The excerpt below is taken from a collection published in bilingual form (Mandinka and French).

> The masters of the earth are not the Sonko, but the Diamme of Bakindiki.
> The Sonko are warriors, because it was war that gave them the land.
> At the time they came, the Diamme ruled the land but paid taxes to Saloum.
> The duty they paid was thatch to roof the king's huts.
> The Sonko came as warriors, they fought with Saloum, and managed to take
>   hold of the land.

The Diamme came and said that they would give women and cattle.
But the Sonko refused that.
The Sonko proposed to share power by turns.
The Diamme did not accept this proposal.
It came to war between them; the Diamme were driven out of the land.
Finally they agreed to share power by turns.
When the Diamme king died, the Sonko would invest their king.
King Koli settled in Berinding and placed his heir at Bifeti and the youngest
    son at Esso.
The son at Bifeti collects the tax, and then takes it, refusing to send it on to his
    elder king.
Koli said that he would kill him; he fled to the youngest brother at Esso.
Jilinkunda and Mansaringsou are brother houses.
It was the Mane who reconciled the Diamme and the Sonko.
When Koli left the Manding he settled first in Bankire, which today is in
    ruins. . . .[10]

The narrative describes how the Sonko clan came to their present area and how they established their power by conquest. This did require accommodation with the original inhabitants, the Diamme (or Jammeh, in more typical Gambian orthography), who were the "masters of the land": this title points to a ritual function associated with fertility and with prior habitation of the territory (such a division of political and ritual authority is common throughout the Mande world). The Sonko were led by "Koli," often (but wrongly) identified as the Fula leader Koli Tengela from the history of the nearby Futa Tooro; Koli seems to have been adopted in Gambian tradition relatively late.[11] The point is that the Sonko came from the Manden (or Manding), which is a frequent source of royal legitimation in Gambian tradition. A staple coda to the epic of Sunjata narrates the conquest of the Gambia by Tira Makhan Traore, one of Sunjata's generals, and a connection to the Manden is a point of pride for many Gambian families.

When the Sonko arrived, the Diamme who already lived there were subject to Saloum, a Wolof state in what is now Senegal; having established themselves, the Sonko then led the region into autonomy. The story concludes with an account of the segmentation of the clan through family tensions, in a not unfamiliar pattern of family disputes over inheritance and property. This observation is a reminder that this history is not primarily that of the village, Berending, but rather that of a subgroup, the Sonko lineage. Reconstructing the history of the entire community requires collecting a variety of narratives, which must then be combined into a whole.[12] The task of reconciling possibly conflicting accounts is necessarily delicate. In the Sahel, this task is part of the function of griots as interpreters of historical traditions. The versions they present are often accepted because they are consensus versions, acceptable to all, rather than because of their greater authenticity.

Bakari Sonko's narrative of Sonko origins is rather dry, neither full nor well developed as a story (this may be due to the method of transcription). He strings together three or four major events in summary form, none of them presented with enough dramatic effect to involve the reader. What matters is that the events occurred and that their consequences (the different placement of clan branches) can still be felt today. His words, however, possess authority: he is the elder of the clan, empowered to speak for it. Based on the terminology already introduced, his account can be classified as a private narrative, not a public performance.

Such dryness characterizes many purely historical oral narratives and many migration legends. Events occur without explication; actors move without perceptible motivation. Supplementary information and explanation can be obtained with further inquiry, especially from private sources, and often the amount of detail elicited is impressive.

As narratives become amplified and structured, as the quality of their telling comes to matter more, they evoke another narrative mode: the folktale, here considered largely as a patterned sequence of recognizable and recurrent actions and motifs. Conceivably, a student might measure the artistic transformation of historical material by observing how that material has been developed along the familiar narrative lines of folktale (e.g., through repeated actions, obvious tests, happy endings, and the like), since some epic plots do agree with known tale types; this task has not yet been undertaken. In other regards, the worlds of epic and folktale can be quite distinct: tales, for instance, are common property throughout a culture, told by anyone; but epic performances come from specialists on far different sorts of occasions.

These are the sorts of historical tradition from which the epic traditions studied here have grown: a mixture of world history (or myth) and detailed local and clan histories. One aspect that should be kept in mind when examining any given epic concerns the visibility of such elements: historical roots are more present in some epics than in others. The crucial difference lies in the skill and artistry brought by the performer to the performed version of the story.

Performers

Musical performers of all sorts go by many names in Africa: *bebom-mvet*, *maabo*, *gewel*, *jeli*, and many others. The most general term, taken into English from French, is *griot*, which in West Africa applies to hereditary musicians and singers. An idealized but misleading picture has attached itself to the concept of the griot, who is seen as a venerable repository of societal traditions and values, embodying through his knowledge a society's past and its human worth. The classic, defining statement of this vision comes from Djibril Tamsir Niane's *Soundiata*, which begins with the words of the griot Mamadou Kouyaté:

> I am a griot. . . . Since time immemorial the Kouyatés have been in the service of the Keita princes of Mali; we are vessels of speech, we are the repositories which harbour secrets many centuries old. The art of eloquence has no secrets for us; without us the names of kings would vanish into oblivion, we are the memory of mankind; by the spoken word we bring to life the deeds and exploits of kings for younger generations.[13]

This statement first appeared in 1960, during the awakening of an independent Africa; and it embodies the aspirations of a new African historiography, of which Niane would be a leader.[14] But this idealized picture hardly represents the complex realities of the performer and of performances in any African society. Some griots are recognized for their knowledge and skill—for example, Kele Monson Diabaté of Kela, Bamba Suso of the Gambia, or Tayiru Banbera of the Bamana traditions (all of them now deceased)—but many others are considered simple or even disreputable musicians.

The very word *griot* deserves a note. Its origin is much discussed but remains unsettled. Whether it comes from Portuguese, a language of the first European traders along the West African coast, or from some African language remains an open question. A recognizable modern form of the word *(guiriot)* occurs in French as early as the sixteenth century. From French, the word has come into English.[15] The term applies to the musicians and singers of many ethnic groups in French West Africa; their functions resemble the combined roles of minstrel and herald in medieval Europe. Music and song are widely seen as their essential activities, but griots also fulfill other purposes. They are widely credited with diplomatic skills (the art of the word) and may serve as intermediaries in negotiations; in the past they were the spokesmen for royalty, protecting the majesty of the ruler by isolating him.

But the term *griot* makes no distinction among the peoples who share the institution. While the word points to a common function, emphasizing the musical element, it disregards the differences of status, training, style, material, and conditions. The term is now being applied ever more widely, within Africa and beyond, as a synonym for the oral performer; and it is being used in contexts that bear no relation to the original usage. In some cases, this extension would seem appropriate. In West African kingdoms such as Abomey, Ashante, or the Yoruba city-states, the functions of the official known as the king's spokesman or "linguist" do seem comparable to the recorded functions of griots in the history of the Sahel. To observe this similarity in royal institutions is to build an understanding of general patterns of West African culture. But caution remains necessary. There are significant differences between the performers of Yoruba *oriki* (clan-praises)[16] and the Mande singers of clan-praises such as *majamu* or *faasa;* and to call an oriki singer a griot would simply be incorrect.

Within the groups covered by this study, a variety of traits distinguish the performers of different regions from one another. A broad, initial division is that between hereditary and nonhereditary performers. In Central Africa and among specialized groups such as the hunters' associations of West Africa, individuals become performers through choice, talent, inspiration, and work. Their musical vocation is often confirmed by a ritual initiation into a cult that serves to ensure their inspiration and to create (and control) the magical forces that may be released through their performances. Ritual initiation matches a longer-term period of training or apprenticeship in the musical skills and narrative techniques of the given genre. The outsider might wonder whether such initiation is symbolic or effective; one observer of Central African mvet performers suggests that the training does result in a fundamental change in the performer's perceptions and perspective—most clearly visible in the mastery of musical and rhythmic complexities—and that performers, caught in their new vision, then become socially marginal.[17]

Incidentally, such ritual elements seem rare among the epic singers of the Sahel, but there are connections with occult powers. Performers may claim to be possessed by spirits during their performance (the phrase "Sing, Goddess" would have a literal meaning for them), and spirits appear frequently in the legends of origin associated with specific instruments or specific tunes. In the world of cults and associations, the ritual connections naturally multiply.

By contrast, where the term *griot* is used, most performers are first defined by birth and then by musical activity. They are members of endogamous status groups or professional lineages, the best known of which are the Mande *nyama-kalaw.*[18] The groups are defined by craft or artisanal activity, and across the Sahel they include specialized blacksmiths, carvers, weavers, fishermen, and griots of different sorts. The listings and configurations vary from culture to culture: Wolof, Tukolor, Maninka, Mandinka, Bamana, Soninke, Fula, and others. The professional groups stand outside the ordinary social stratification of "noble" and "captive" (or slave), and their actual position seems ambiguous. Figures such as blacksmiths, economically central to the community and widely credited with magical powers, are more respected and sometimes feared.[19] Griots as a class are much less respected. They are often associated with shamelessness and greed (in dialectic opposition to the noble's restraint and generosity), and marriage into a griot family brings the risk of loss of status.[20] Nor will a nongriot take on their function. A Malinke or Bamana who is not a *jeli* (griot) by birth will not become a musician or a singer except in very special circumstances (e.g., within an association), nor will such a person sing praises or "perform" epics.

There are varying categories of griots differentiated by their instruments, their claims of origin, and by their status (not all are equal). Traditional instruments such as the *balafon* (wooden xylophone) or the *kora* and the different forms of *ngoni* (all stringed harp-lutes) are subject to traditional constraints. Instrumentalists tend to be men; women specialize in singing the various praise songs.[21] Epic singers are men—no woman's performance of epic has yet been documented—but women may intervene to provide lyric interludes.[22] Modern musical forms involving the use of electric guitars, trumpets, etc., do not correspond to traditional social categories and thus present new opportunities and may be performed by nongriots; but the performer still risks being stigmatized (by nongriots) as a griot.

The old kingdom of Rwanda in Central Africa, established by the Tutsi over the indigenous Twa, had an interesting intermediate category between hereditary and nonhereditary performers: kings were hymned by an "army of poets" (*Umutwe w'Abasize*) whose families benefited from hereditary privileges so long as they preserved the praises of the kings composed by their poet ancestors.[23] This seems to be a form of hereditary entitlement that would set poetic families apart from those they serve.

Another important aspect of the hereditary status of griots in the Sahel involves established relationships between lineages and clans. Two well-known examples from the epic of Sunjata may serve as illustration. Sunjata's griot was Bala Faseke Kouyate (Kuyate), whom he rescued from the sorcerer-king Sumanguru (to complicate the story: Bala Faseke learned to play the balafon from Sumanguru—who had gotten it from spirits—and first used it to sing the praises of Sumanguru). Because of the bond between Sunjata Keita and Bala Faseke, the noble Keita lineage is generally linked to the griot Kouyate lineage (there may be numerous local exceptions). The Kouyates are guardians of the Keita clan traditions, and their knowledge enjoys a special authority within the culture. A Keita noble will feel financial obligations toward a Kouyate; a Kouyate will not hesitate to turn to a Keita for help.

The second example involves the two heroic hunters who, at the start of the epic, slay the Buffalo-Woman of Du and thus win the hand of Sunjata's mother, whom they will pass on to Sunjata's father. They are brothers, members of the Traore lineage. At the moment of crisis, when they must shoot the magic buffalo with a spindle, the older brother falters and the younger performs the task. The older brother then sings the praises of the younger brother and establishes the relations that will thereafter apply between their descendants: his progeny shall become the griot lineage of Jebates (or Jabate, Jobarteh, Diabate, etc.); the younger brother establishes the Traore lineage, which rivals the Keitas for prestige in Mali. The relations of nobles and griots are succinctly described by Masuntu Daraame, a Soninke griot: "The patron is the person to whom we are attached by historical bonds. They are also the social group whom we ask for presents."[24]

The bond between griot and noble is a central element within the more historical Sahelian epic traditions (such bonds do not seem to exist in the Central African sphere). It should be stressed that not every griot was involved in such privileged retainership. Describing the fourteenth-century court of Mali, the Arab traveler Ibn Battuta identified one "griot" named Dougha, who was the king's spokesman, and many other musicians performing as an orchestra; their role was simply to enhance the ruler's pomp. The proportions have probably remained comparable: for one royal intimate, a corps of accompanists. The musicians apparently performed praise songs exalting their semi-sacred king—a phenomenon reported widely across Africa.

The succession of kingdoms in the Sahel, from the Soninke to Mali and Songhay and Segou, through all the principalities, down to the warlord Samory Toure, may well have exhibited a continuity in the use of musicians and praise singers to establish at least the trappings of legitimate political rule (the Islamic Fula states might be the exception). There seem to be echoes of Soninke in the praise songs of Sunjata; Soninke is also used as a language of power in the praise songs of the Songhay. It seems quite probable that new rulers quickly surrounded themselves with the singers whose presence was a recognized sign of a claim to royalty and whose songs echoed those addressed to more established rulers. A similar borrowing sometimes occurs with the content of historical traditions; new dynasties will claim (or forge) a link with such figures as Sunjata in a bid for acceptance and legitimation.

Praise songs are one of the keys to the relations between griots and nobles. Where blacksmiths make real objects used for life-giving and life-taking activities such as agriculture and warfare, the power exercised by griots is that of the Word. They remember and recall the praises, the genealogy, and the history of the clan of their noble patron(s). A gifted griot will not be limited to one family but will know many. The Malian writer Massa Makan Diabaté recalls an occasion in the early 1960s (the funeral of President Modibo Keita's father) when his uncle, the celebrated jeli Kele Monson Diabaté, held members of the government spellbound for seven nights, reciting the genealogies of all the great families of Mali.[25] Griots are thus the repositories of family fame. They control social identities. This power, as well as the bond that entitles them to ask for (or extort) gifts, makes them doubly disquieting. The culturally conditioned response to praise singing is gift giving, perhaps as a form of conspicuous consumption. One celebrated *jelimuso* [griot-woman, griotte] was given an airplane by a wealthy admirer.

But praise songs are not the only link. Mention has already been made of the diplomatic and verbal skills of griots, skills that make them suitable go-betweens and occasionally advisers to kings. It is unwise to place too much trust in the internal evidence of the poems, but they do often show individual griots attached to individual rulers as companions and advisers (e.g., Tinyetigiba Dante, griot of King Da of Segou), and griots are occasionally sent on missions as emissaries. It is easy to imagine that such a position would provide the griot with privileged confidences. The veiled allusions that are such a central feature of praise poetry (see the discussion below) thus serve as an indicator of this insider's knowledge and power. At the same time, the advantage of using a social inferior as agent are obvious: the griot can never hope to supplant the ruler and can only advance through loyal service. This partiality, or venality, again contributes to the public's negative image of griots.

Generalizations about griots are hazardous; throughout the Sahel any number of possibilities are represented. Conditions are changing radically. The old systems of patronage have collapsed, and griots now seek new market opportunities. Whatever the former relations between nobles and singers, they have changed. It seems best to offer some specific examples as an amplification of the composite picture presented above, focusing on the Sahelian performers, and to address the questions thus raised. The first example is Charles Monteil's description of Soninke *geseru* early in this century; the image he created may well have contributed to the idealized pattern that emerged later:

> These *geseru* [Soninke griots] are casted. Those of their children who seem best fitted for the job of lore-keeper take instruction from the oldest and most reputable *geseru*. This "master" normally holds his sessions in the shade of a tree, and nearby a spear is planted in the ground, no doubt to emphasize the epic nature of his teaching. By turn, each student comes forward to declaim what he has learned and then takes hold of the spear. When he has been well enough taught,

the young *gesere* [griot, singular of *geseru*] chooses the family to which he wishes to attach himself. The *geseru* of the *Wago* (sing., *Wage* [the noble clans of the Soninke]) are believed to know the history of all the Soninke in general, of the *Wago* in particular, and more or less some other traditions of other Sudanese tribes. Once he has made his choice, the new *gesere* of the *Wago* travels to Gesene (Guesséné, in the area of Kingi), to the tomb of Dyamera Sokhona Dyaguraga, the most famous of the four *fado* of Wagadu, so as to—in the popular phrase— "open his mouth," meaning to give his first speech as a lore-keeping speaker.[26]

In this first speech, the young aspirant praises a given lineage whose members may then take him on as a retainer. The poetic features of this description are worth noting: the linkage of youth and age beneath a tree (a generational trans- mission of knowledge in a collective, or cosmic, space), the presence of the spear (icon of the warrior's past), travel to a tomb for the public presentation (tribute to ancestors). These features appeal to the imagination and conform to certain stereotypes of youth, valor, and the collective appeal of the village tree. The pic- ture is confirmed in its details by Mamadou Diawara in his wonderful analysis of the sources of oral tradition for the old Soninke kingdom of Jara (near Nioro du Sahel on the Mali-Mauritanian border; the kingdom lasted from the fifteenth to the nineteenth century). Monteil's account shows that the apprenticeship in which the young gesere learns his craft is followed by a form of public examination: the performance at the tomb provides a rite of passage for the individual as well as a collective ratification of the traditions expressed. Further, not all those born to the family become geseru; a first selection of students is based on talent and in- terest, and a second matches the aspirant with the patron family.

Unfortunately, this image does not transfer easily to other groups in the region. The difficulty comes with the notions of a school and a test of the young gesere's mastery, which find no real counterpart in modern conditions. In Mande studies the question of schools for griots (or *jeliw*, in this specific case) is the subject of hot debate. Niane and others have identified regional schools of traditional lore (in the towns of Kela, Fadama, Kankan, Niagassola, and Krina, through the mod- ern states of Mali and Guinea).

Of these, Kela, in Mali, is perhaps the most important because of its associa- tion with a ritual that takes place in the neighboring town of Kangaba (Kela is where the *jelilu*, griots, live). The region claims to be the heart of the Manden, and the ritual is supervised by the Keita lineage, which claims descent from Sunjata. The central activity of the ritual is the replacement of the thatched roof (a prac- tical necessity) on a hut, the *Kama Bloñ* (House of Speech), and the work in- volves refurbishing and repainting the clay walls as well.[27] On the final night of the seven-day ritual, griots come in procession from the neighboring village of Kela to Kangaba, and the night is spent with songs and recitations that recount the history of the world—including, it is said, the epic of Sunjata. Association with this ritual thus gives the griots of Kela (of the Jebate lineage) a certain prestige and authority, buttressed in recent years by the Malian government's acceptance of Kela/Kangaba's claim to be a center of traditional lore and of their version of the Sunjata epic as "authoritative."

Across the border in Guinea, still in the Manden, other "centers" offer other claims. Niagassola is the home of the balafon of Susu Sumanguru, Sunjata's adversary. That balafon is perhaps the first musical instrument of the Sunjata tradition, and the Kouyate lineage that guards it claims descent from Sunjata's griot. Guinean traditions are likely to become better known in the near future, since recent political conditions have been far more favorable to researchers and foreign visitors.

Against the notion of schools of tradition stands the more widely documented model of individual apprenticeship, training, and professional development depending upon talent and opportunity (within the hereditary pool of griots). Clearly, it could be advantageous to the future griot to grow up in an environment of specialists such as a village of griots. The child would acquire familiarity with the material almost by osmosis. What is known of the lives of jeliw of the Mande, such as Kele Monson Diabaté, Fa-Digi Sisókó, and others, supports the notion of individual talent and opportunity. Fa-Digi Sisókó made no claims to special training.[28] He began his career singing to accompany group agricultural work and then began singing Sunjata material. (The same phenomenon is found among the Wolof, where the *gewel* [griot] will challenge the young men who are working in the fields to surpass themselves and withstand the sun.) In the Gambia, Bamba Suso claimed no particular school; his eminence derived from his detailed knowledge of Gambian history. The same is true of a jeli such as Tayiru Banbera and the traditions of Segou.

One performer who illustrates the older style of personal patronage is a Fula *maabo* [lit., weaver, but also singer of epics] of Niger, Boûbacar Tinguidji. This performer, who has left behind a number of excellent epics, exemplifies the changes in the modern career of a court poet.[29] He was born around 1910 in modern Burkina Faso. His parents fled there from Niger to escape a famine. Within his family, his three maternal uncles were musical and taught him their lore (but nothing more: music, he says, was their talent because "they had no head"). Tinguidji jokes that he became a maabo, following his mother's line, because he preferred it to farmwork. He studied in Kounari (a region of Mali, east of Segou) with a maabo whom he called a true wizard of the lute, and he learned enough to become a retainer attached to a noble household. For a time, he lived in Ouagadougou and in Dori (towns of Burkina Faso), in the household of the *amirou* [ruler] of Dori. After that family was imprisoned because of problems with the colonial authorities, he left for another region, the Dargol (now in Niger), and attached himself to the Songhay chief Mossi Gaidou, then to his son and his grandson. Although at the time his epics were recorded (ca. 1970) he was living in Niamey, Niger, he still considered himself a resident of the Dargol, noting with pride that the chief's family paid his taxes for him there. He considers the song he composed for and about Mossi Gaidou the prize piece in his repertoire. He describes his relationship with Mossi Gaidou as follows:

> While my *lamido* [chief] of the Dargol lived, I couldn't travel. For twenty-six years I never left, because he would never have accepted that I turn to another for help: he by himself was enough for me. Anything I asked for, he gave. It was after his death that I went to Niamey. Before, I had been used to saying in conversation, "If I'm lying, may God lead me to Kumasi" [i.e., to Ghana, where many Nigeriens went to look for work]. And when he died, not more than two years later, I went to Kumasi! I had to![30]

Tinguidji's voice and talent, however, were enough for success; he admits that if he had kept all the money he had received, he would want for nothing. But like many other musicians and artists, he was something of a spendthrift. Tinguidji's relationship with his lamido recalls that portrayed in many epics: an intimate and personal bond that goes beyond simple music and performance. It also raises the question of patronage and support: he boasts that his patron's family satisfied his needs. His travel to Kumasi serves as a reminder that patterns of patronage have changed, as have the resources available to patrons. The alleged generosity of former times is no longer feasible; the traditional expectations of the griots, especially in hard economic times such as those now experienced throughout Africa, are seen as a burden by their former providers. Griots have responded by finding new sources of revenue in the broadcast media and recording studios (as well as foreign researchers and universities), but successful griots are only a tiny fraction of those attributed such status by birth and other factors in society.

If the measure of success is popular visibility and income, the most successful griots in Mali nowadays are not the singers of epic, but the women who sing praises. Praise singing is in many ways a preferred genre: it elicits gifts more directly, and the music is livelier. Epic recitations run the risk of monotony and are often broken up with praise singing intervals either by the master singer or sometimes by a woman (often his wife).

The impoverishment of patrons is not the only challenge that griots have had to face. Since the nineteenth century, the Sahel has become more and more Muslim. Conversion to Islam represents a change of eschatology, a different view of the world, its history, and its peoples. It also represents a politically disruptive force, offering opportunities to new men (as happened at the start of the nineteenth century, when the Fula religious leader Cheikou Amadou established an independent Islamic state carved out of the territory of the kingdom of Segou, and continuing today). But griots represent the old, non-Islamic, view of the world (although many are now Muslim), and they are associated with local powers consecrated by traditional belief systems. Griots and Islam can be opposed in ways that go beyond the division of the oral and written that demarcates their respective claims to knowledge. But griots are adjusting. One category of Mande griots, the *funew,* specializes in Islamic praises and is attached to *marabouts,* Muslim teachers and holy men who represent a new wealthy class. Islamic history finds its way into epic narrative, particularly in the form of Old Testament stories. Islamic leaders such as al-Hajj Umar Tall, who conquered Segou around 1859, now appear in epic stories.

Praise Poetry

Praise poetry is also termed panegyric and as such has a complicated relationship with epic. The two genres are rigorously separated in the poetics of the European literary tradition. In Africa the division is less clear. Clan or lineage poems and songs of praise necessarily evoke clan history and the celebrated individuals of the past. The praise song may sometimes tell a story, as would an epic, although allusion and indirect reference are the typical tropes of panegyric. Further, praise songs are incorporated into epics in varying degrees, and they appear inextricable from certain aspects of epic performance. It will be useful to describe the broad features of the genre in Africa before addressing regional peculiarities and the relations of panegyric and epic.

Praise poetry is an almost universal African genre. Praise poems are composed and recited from the Sahara to the Cape of Good Hope, from Dakar to Somalia. Content, context, and mode of performance may vary tremendously: the term is applied to hymns of praise to deities, to the invocations of animals slain in the hunt, to the warrior's shrill proclamation of his deeds, to a bride's description of her beauty and skills, and to the collection of allusive references to the deeds of the ancestors of a given clan. It may seem inappropriate to cover such a variety under one label; further distinctions (recognizing the given local name for each genre mentioned above: *ijala, tige, ikyevugu, rara, jamu*) would seem useful, and the phenomenon deserves comprehensive study.[31]

Praise songs of all varieties share in the creative power of languages. In essence, the praise poem involves the creation and application of names for an individual (or other being) and draws on a repertoire of traditional formulations and allusive references; the genre depends in a sense on the magic (used in the loosest sense) of names and identity.

The Eastern and Southern African tradition of praise singing is relatively well documented and probably the best known to an English-speaking reader. There are many studies on the poetry of the Bahima, the Tswana, the Zulu, the Xhosa, and others, and the list should include less accessible studies on the kingdoms of Rwanda and the Luba. Especially in Southern Africa, a massive amount of material has been collected by researchers documenting oral traditions.[32] The singular "tradition of praise singing" is used advisedly here for Southern and Eastern Africa; while many different languages and polities are involved, the modes of performance are remarkably similar (in at least one case, the same word is used by neighboring peoples), and the groups involved are united by membership in the Bantu-language family as defined by comparative linguistics.

The Southeastern praise poem tradition derives from a social past defined by aristocratic warfare; praise poems are the record of an individual's achievements (or in the case of young men early in their careers, boasts of accomplishments to come). The composition of praise poetry was part of the traditional education of well-born young men, who were expected to be able to produce their own poems. It is thus a very individual or personal genre in its content and as perishable as the generations of men. There are exceptions to this transience. Chiefs were the subject of other men's praise, and the institution of chiefhood was sometimes accompanied by the institution of official praise singers. In this context, praise songs have been preserved beyond an individual life span. Isaac Schapera's collection of Tswana praise songs includes some attributed to chiefs of the eighteenth century, preserved either by "court poets" or by family members; and in Rwanda, the Reverend Alexis Kagame was able to retrieve a considerable corpus of royal praises going back to the eighteenth century at least.

These praise songs are primarily improvisational, employing a repertoire of phrases and images that are available to all but that also allow considerable scope for current, topical, and personal references.[33] The basic technique is allusion—a skillful turn of phrase evokes a range of references and possibly a narrative or historical incident—and allusion leads to other tools of poetic density. Narrative is not desired; clarity is not the aim. The praise poems of chiefs, when preserved, do not recount biography or an institutional history of the chieftaincy. They presume that the audience knows that history, and they exploit that knowledge obliquely and creatively. The concern is to express the idea through effective and adroit phrasing and the most subtle references.

The value of the indirect reference in praise poetry is so central that it seems virtually impossible that the form would transform itself into epic, which is characterized by more explicit narrative and development of events. The same historical material might easily be cast in either form, as panegyric or as epic—it is not a question of the content but of the poetic vision involved. Praise poetry, dependent upon tropes and an insider's knowledge, moves more easily toward greater complications of form than to simplified exposition even when a historical subject might justify clarifications.

This point can be demonstrated in the court poetry of Rwanda, which in many ways occupies a middle ground that combines cultural features of Western and of Southern Africa. Rwandan royal poetry represents a plausible development of the praise poetry tradition characteristic of linguistically related Bantu Africa; it offers a range of forms from the simplest—the spontaneous outcry of the individual, here assumed to be the basic type for the region—to more complex styles governed by rules of sequence and structure. The availability of the wealth of material from Rwanda is the result in particular of the efforts of Father Alexis Kagame, who industriously collected the royal traditions and the court poetry of his homeland and compiled several collections of various genres. He also exploited traditional poetic forms to compose his own version of the biblical creation narrative as a form of proselytizing.[34]

Rwandan historical tradition offers a depth comparable to that of many Sahelian states, going back to the fifteenth century or before, and the depth of this tradition is greater than that of the Zulus and of other groups located to the south. The kingdom of Rwanda developed in relative isolation, at least by contrast with the tumultuous succession of states in West Africa; thus, it can be assumed that the genres of praise poetry that developed there are the fruits of internal development and not of cross-cultural borrowings. There has already been mention of the "Umutwe w'Abasizi," the "army of poets" attached to the king (although in Kagame's time they only numbered nine). Such an institution might well foster competition among poets and push them to refine their poetry. In fact, Kagame credits certain individuals with the invention of specific types of poems.

The following example is from a type of dynastic praise poem that Kagame labels *bisogo* with *impakanizi*; *bisogo* is the general name for a form of dynastic praise poem in which the poet devotes one strophe to each king of the dynasty, introducing each with a brief refrain (the *impakanizi*). The strophe is from a 391-line poem composed by the poet Nyakayonga, son of Musare; it was dedicated to King Mutara, who ruled around 1825. The poet himself seems to have lived somewhat later; another poem of his is dated to 1875. The section translated here deals with one of the earlier kings of the dynasty, Kigeli I Mukobanya, whom Kagame dates to about 1460. At that time, the Tutsi (the rulers of the kingdom of Rwanda) had only recently arrived in the area between the lakes and were still battling it out with indigenous groups.

As Kagame explains the events, Mukobanya's father, Cyilima I (ca. 1430, by Kagame's dates), had been defeated by Murinda, a non-Tutsi king from Bugoyi, a member of the Ba-shi (sing., Mu-shi) group, who demanded of Cyilima his daughter and other tokens of surrender such as the royal drums. Murinda brought his army to celebrate the marriage. Meanwhile, Mukobanya—without his father's knowledge—organized an army of resistance and successfully attacked Murinda by night, thus retrieving the tokens of surrender and preserving royal prestige. Mukobanya and his father ruled jointly after that.

> Mukobanya is too famous,
> I could never block his way!
> > Him also I will beg, I will touch his shoulder.
> > I shall let him speak, and let him begin.
> Let him begin, the Defender of Cows
> Even during his father's lifetime!
> He opposed surrender of the drum,
> He drew his father out of danger.
> He rose for nighttime struggle,
> He is the Battler armed with a lance;
> With it he pierced the savage from Bugoyi,
> Even as the Mushi barred his way with a shield.
> Grant him wide space, let him tell his great deeds!
> Grant him the prize of bravery!
> He did great service to the Dynasty;
> In Bwiyando he held firm
> And broke the resistance of Mugoyi.[35]

The first two lines introduce the king who will be praised in this section; the next two ("Him also") are the impakanizi, the refrain with which the poet introduces each king.[36] Then the poet recalls Mukobanya's claim to fame: he saved the day when his father's defeat had imperiled the kingdom. The "drum" is one of the symbols of royalty; in other poems the king is often hailed with the praise name "Defender of Cows and Drums" or some such phrase. "Battler Armed with a Lance" is another praise name, or what Kagame calls a *cheville*. Here, the conventional praise name merges into the story: it becomes the actual weapon, just as the fight between the forces becomes single combat between the prince and the foreign king.

Once known, the story can be recognized in these lines, but for an outsider the accompanying explanation is vital. The poem is not self-explanatory. This evocation is not a narrative but a précis, a selective presentation of the king's deeds. The lines "He drew his father out of danger. / He rose for the nighttime struggle" might fit a number of situations. Still, the references in Nyakayonga's poem are clearer than in some others. Kagame's collection offers several poems in the same genre, and so it is possible to compare the treatment of Mukobanya by other poets. A twentieth-century poem, addressed to Mutara III, the ruling king when Kagame was writing, offers only two lines of recognizable narrative in the strophe dedicated to Mukobanya:

> He has laid out the adversary, he brought back the maiden
> And also the Reign-cow of Cyilima, which he kept.[37]

The differences here should underline the importance of composition in these poems; each poet handles his material in a slightly different way and brings out a slightly different image of the king while respecting certain rules of form and style. Cattle are a theme in all of the poetry: after the king, the animals represent the highest value besides warfare in traditional Tutsi society. The conventionalized praise names (Battler, Defender of Cows) in Nyakayonga's example are very neatly woven into this strophe so that they hardly seem intrusions or extraneous adornment; they contribute to the matter of the poem. Elsewhere, poems include praise names that are clearly conventional in pattern: "Scion of [attribute: the Favored; the Munificent; the Watering Trough of Morning]" or "Defender/Protector/Pacifier of Cattle." Such phrases stand out as stylized and repetitious notes within the individual composition.

These examples are taken from a more stylized form of poetry than prevails elsewhere in Southeastern Africa and do not necessarily reflect all the poetic dynamics of the genre. But they appear useful as part of the larger argument because they occupy a middle ground between spontaneous lyric praise (the impression, however artfully contrived, of a warrior exulting in his deeds) and such structured historical narratives as king-lists, a narrative mode clearly embedded in the concept of bisogo as a framework and which, as already observed, will appear in certain epic traditions.

There are significant differences between East and West African traditions of praise poetry, although the similarities are strong enough to justify applying the same broad label to the phenomena. One difference lies in the object of the praise. In West Africa, documented praise songs are addressed to individuals and kings, as elsewhere, but also to gods, animals, plants, and inanimate objects. In other words, they have either acquired, or developed from, a ritual and vocative function that is slightly different in emphasis from the individualized panegyric element of Southern Africa. In fact, it seems quite unusual to find self-praise in West Africa, although there are references to such practices among the Wolof (warriors would boast before battle), and among the Yoruba (the new bride will sing of herself).

Another difference is the de-emphasis of the individual. This may seem a paradoxical claim since a praise song is almost always addressed to an individual (especially a wealthy one); but the terms of the address in the praise will often emphasize the individual's social connections: his lineage, the clan, the past. Collective praises, particularly those of clans and lineages, is accorded even greater prominence than has been recorded for Southern Africa.

Collective praises become an element of an individual praise song; they provide verbal material that a performer draws upon in any actualized performance. French scholars use the term *devise* for the praise songs in general, and particularly for the recurrent and semi-fixed elements that may be borrowed. This term has the same use-value as the word "griot" for identifying the common link underlying an institution encountered among many different ethnic groups of West Africa. The French ethnographer Solange de Ganay[38] made one of the first studies of the *devise* while working with the Dogon during the 1930s in the present republic of Mali. Her book, *Les devises des Dogon*, includes a comparative study in which she identifies the phenomenon among many peoples: the *tige* among the Dogon are called *yettode* by the Fulbe, *majamu* among the Malinke and Bambara, *sondre* among the Mossi of Burkina Faso, *santa* among the Wolof, *lamba* among the Susu, *dele* by the Senufo, and from her appendix one might add the *kirari* of the Hausa, as well as various Bantu-family terms of which perhaps the most interesting is *chibongo*, a term that is clearly related to the Zulu *izibongo* (which she also mentions).[39] To this list might be added the Soninke *kuunyi janmu*, the family praises and greetings mentioned by Mamadou Diawara, the Songhay *zamu* described by Thomas Hale,[40] and the Yoruba forms of *ijala*, *rara*, and *oriki*-singing as described by Babalola, Karin Barber, and others. This list of terms is not exhaustive and does not imply absolute identity of the genres, but it does suggest how widespread and generally recognizable this mode of singing may be.

The shift in emphasis from lyric self-expression more typical of the Southern African praise singing tradition to the vocative and quasi-ritual aspects of West African praise singing can be illustrated by examining some of de Ganay's Dogon examples before proceeding to Mande clan praises and their relationship to the epic traditions. The Dogon *tige*, comparable to the Yoruba *ijala*, are salutes or greetings addressed to various entities in an attempt to exercise power or control of some sort. There is a greater range of collected examples for the Dogon and Yoruba traditions than for other groups. It is interesting that in both cases there is a stratum of hunters' songs. Chapter 3 discusses how widespread hunters' narratives can be and how they contribute to the historical epic traditions. Among the Dogon, however, the addresses and salutations go well beyond the world of the hunter: there is a tige for the Dogon people, for subgroups within it, and for the territorial group (the village, the section of the village) as well as individual or lineage tige. There are tige of mockery, occupational tige, social, bodily, funerary, ancestral, war, and ceremonial tige. Many of these are simple names or short phrases; but they can grow in length. Here, for example, is the tige associated with the mask of the *wilu* gazelle:

> Hail, bush-goat!
> Filled with the beans eaten by you,
> A clever man fires at you,
> Blood flows on the ground
> All eyes are on you
> The eyes of the hare are on you
> The eyes of the dove are on you.
> Good bush! shake the legs!
> Good bush! shake the body![41]

The connection with hunting is evident in this short song; the intent of the dance in which the mask is used is apparently to ensure good luck to the hunter, and the gazelle is most interesting to the Dogon in its food-potential. The same interest in food marks the tige of the Fula mask:

> Greetings to you, Fula.
> Your cow's milk—pour it in the calabash
> Your cow is your father's cow
> Your horse is your father's horse
> All men's eyes are on you.[42]

The Fula are the cattle herders of the Sahel (their epic traditions will be considered in chapter 7). This occupation is so closely associated with them that even non-Fula cattle herders, employed to graze a village's cows, become known as the "village Fula." Those of the purest stock are nomadic and live with their cows—hence, one of the two animals in the poem. Since the Islamic wars of the nineteenth century, the Fulbe have taken on another face in the region, as warriors mounted on horses, and this accounts for the second animal associated with them. The Dogon lie between the regions of the Hausa of northern Nigeria and the Fula of the middle Niger valley. Conversion to Islam around 1800 made these groups militant expansionists and caused problems for the peoples around them. The Dogon tige representing the Fula evokes the pacific and militant aspects of these neighbors.

Praising here seems subordinate to naming, perhaps with the goal of compelling obedience to the speaker or asserting control over the entity addressed, or, more humanely, perhaps simply acknowledging the identity of the other being (human, animal, or object). This last social function seems implicit in a category of praises spread over the Sahel and generally associated with clan- or lineage-praise. The names given in the region show a clear relationship—*jamu, majamu,* or *zamu*—and probably derive from the Arabic *ismu* [name]. The implication may be that the single word of the clan name (e.g., Keita, Diarra, Traore) is an abbreviation of a full declamatory utterance that, for the hearer, evokes the glorious past of the lineage to which she or he belongs, and that, from the mouth of a griot, will inspire a frenzy of pride and open-handedness.

The glorious past of the lineage is also related to the world of the epic, and it will be useful to examine some clan praises and then see how they are used in an epic performance. The examples are taken from the Mande world, from a Bamana lineage with connections to the epic of Sunjata.

To my knowledge, no one has made a collection of clan praises for the Manden. The task would be quite delicate and might easily give offense because it necessarily involves the question of relations and legitimacy of clan and lineage branches. Lineages of the same name, in different localities, will have established slightly different praises. Collection in writing would privilege one lineage over another, and this act would no longer be an academic exercise but a political gesture.

Still, some examples are available for study from transcriptions and reports that are scattered through a variety of sources. The French ethnographer Germaine Dieterlen offers two variants of the *devise* of the Diarra (or Jara) lineage associated with the history of Segou (see chapter 6). The Diarra were the second dynasty to rule Segou in the eighteenth century, and they are linked with the Conde lineage of the Maninka who appear in the Sunjata traditions (Sunjata's mother was a Conde). Diarra/Conde praises are thus incorporated into the epic of Sunjata at appropriate moments. First are the praises collected around Segou:

> Diarra,
> Nyaola Zan, Nyaola Yayiri,
> Your grandfather bent the world like a sickle
> He straightened it like a clear path.
> Son of God on earth,
> Diarra!

and:

> Diarra! Kone!
> When there is no Kone among the warriors who will fight,
> The battle is lost beforehand.
> The lion has broken a great bone![43]

Lines from each of these strophes are to be found scattered through the various published selections from the epic cycle of Segou. The second verse also evokes Bakari Jan Kone, the celebrated warrior and servant of the lineage (see chapter 6), while the mention of a lion (*jara* in Bamana) creates a pun on the royal name (Diarra/Jara). But these phrases are not the addresses to the king that appear most frequently within the epics of the Segou cycle. Instead, the epics contain the phrases "Master of water, master of gunpowder, master of iron, master of men." These epithets apply more specifically to the king and not to the lineage. The verses cited above are general purpose lineage praise that could be used in various contexts and probably associated with other elements in a larger praise song. These phrases also differ slightly from the Diarra/Conde praises incorporated in at least one version of the epic of Sunjata.

The epic of Sunjata offers other uses of clan praises for comparison, such as those incorporated in the performance of Tiemoko Kone of Mourdiah, Mali.[44] His version (published in 1970) covers a single early episode of the epic, that of the Buffalo-Woman of Du. A buffalo had been ravaging the town of Du, and no hunter could kill it. Two young men of the Traore lineage go to try their luck (these are the two brothers described above in the section on griots); a diviner tells them that they must be kind to the old woman they will meet at the edge of the village, and so they are. They perform chores for her, although no one realizes that she is in fact the buffalo-woman. She will reward their kindness with the secret of her life; they will win (but not marry) Sogolon, who will become Sunjata's mother. This excerpt comes from the sequence in which they are plying a reluctant old woman with kindness (the editor's unusual line-numbering has been retained here for reference):

320. They put their arms around her, they rubbed and rubbed her, until sleep took her.
321. When she slept, Silanden said to Silanba, "We should not leave until we are sure that Grandmother is asleep."
322. The grandsons of Tuma and Bagi went to bed.
323. The grand-daughter of Bari and Kanidjo remained asleep.
324. Tentu Kanute and Mariba Kanute and Damagana Kanute!
     Rich and powerful Diarra!
     Eye on all and head on all!
     Sigi is not pleasant to take.
     Nguma and Nguma, Nguma and Daba
     When a mouth can eat a hundred,
     Why wonder if it eats fifty?
325. The grand-daughter of Bari and Kanidjo snored.[45]

The patronymics used here are employed repeatedly throughout Tiemoko Kone's performance, as is the praise song in verse 324. The praise song is associated with the Diarra-Conde lineage and thus applies to the old woman (who is related to Sunjata's mother). The pairing of epithets and names (Tuma and Bagi, Bari and Kanidjo, Nguma and Nguma) is a characteristic form that can almost serve to identify praises. The phrase "Rich and powerful Diarra" is encountered in the Diarra praises from Segou, but the others are not.

Humor, irony, and a measure of sincerity are blended in this juxtaposition of terms. The reader might first think of the two hunters, whose actions are in some regards far from manly (they are performing women's work with their cooking and care, an aspect of the epic that deserves further reflection), but the consequences of their deeds will be far-reaching: Sunjata's mother will be delivered to Sunjata's father and the destiny of the Manden will be fulfilled. In that regard, their domestic actions are epic in effect. But the "song," the praise, is actually addressed to (or inspired by) the old woman who has just fallen asleep. She represents the Diarra/Conde lineage at this moment. And it is not absolutely clear here whether the address is satiric or hortatory. When she wakes from her sleep, she will reward the young men for their attentions with the secret of her power. Does the intrusion of the *devise* lead her to that? Or is it intended to magnify the consequences of the situation, to quell any derisive response to an old woman? Does it warn the listener that a great deed is about to occur? All possibilities are open.

Incidentally, there is no evidence that the assorted praise names of a hero, even one so frequently sung as Sunjata, constitute a mnemonic device for the narrative in epic performance. Instead, the inspirational and ennobling effect of the *devise* (whose verbal texture is recognizable even when the actual utterance varies from the established clan names) constitutes a resource to be exploited in different ways and to different extents within the various traditions that will be examined. Praise names are incorporated into the poems to serve a variety of purposes, ranging from filler (as the poet considers what to say next), to confirmation of the "authenticity" of the poet's words, including special emotional effects. The French collector and linguist Gérard Dumestre notes that in a performance by Baba Cissoko, the griot interrupts his narrative only once with praise singing, at the moment of greatest narrative tension. The shift of registers and the intensification of suspense may be more important than the content of the interruption.

In sum, the praise songs in the epics represent a conceptual challenge for their audience. They are not directly connected to the narrative, and they do not dictate or organize its flow. Rather, the praise song disrupts the narrative and creates space for different relationships and perceptions among performer, audience, and performance. The results are no longer simple dualities (performer-audience, narrative-intrusion), but at least a triad (artist, art, and audience), compounded by possible ironies and complexities of tone. When the mix of praise song and narrative is controlled by a master (such as Tiemoko Kone or Kele Monson Diabaté), comprehension requires a greater degree of qualitative evaluation and assessment.

The elements of epic traditions discussed in this chapter provide a background for the discussion of specific epic traditions in the chapters that follow. Not every point will apply directly to every tradition or every epic, but they contribute to a general context. The discussion should thus help to establish an African frame of reference, in which a first distinction is to be made between African epic and other African genres of poetry.

EPICS OF CENTRAL AFRICA

IN GEOGRAPHIC, LINGUISTIC, and historical terms, the epics of Central Africa are the most diverse and problematic. This chapter covers noncontiguous and historically unrelated groups—the Mongo and BaNyanga of the Congo basin, the Fang and Duala populations of Cameroon and Gabon, and the Ijo of Nigeria. While the peoples are disparate, their epic traditions are comparable, sharing as they do a similar style of performance, a focus on the actions of a mythical or ancestral hero, and a lack of reference to recent political history.

In formal terms, these texts are the most difficult to classify as epics in the sense used outside Africa.[1] Transcriptions present a mix of prose and passages of song rather than continuous linear poetry. The narrative line is subordinate to dramatic and musical action in performance, and the performer's behavior is far removed from the impassivity widely associated with epic performance in other traditions. Such sobriety is to be found within this region, for instance, in the recitals of Clément Gakaniisha, narrator of prose Rwandan royal traditions.[2] But the epic narratives are a more collective and popular art form. Performance involves not only words and music but also kinesthetic elements such as dance and mime; the participants include not only the artists but the onlookers.

In this chapter, general discussion of performers and performances is followed by discussion of four specific epic traditions: Lianja of the Mongo, Mwindo of the BaNyanga, Jeki (also Djeki) of the Duala, and the *Ozidi Saga* of the Ijo. These traditions are linked by their dependence on a central hero figure whose biography, composed of multiple and variable episodes, defines the corpus of the tradition. The four examples illustrate possible variations in the configuration of those traditions as well as the common points that bind the heroes.

Discussion of these four traditions is followed by consideration of the mvet performances of the Fang peoples of southern Cameroon and Gabon. The mvet appears to be a special development of the regional epic tradition, exhibiting an established space and roster of characters from a quasi-mythical world but prescribing no set stories: the artist must improvise a complex plot within the accepted parameters and conventions of the traditions.

The chapter will end with a description of materials from other groups reflecting royal or civic poetic traditions that border on epic.

Performers and Performances

The best descriptions of performance contexts come from opposite ends of the regional grouping: from the BaNyanga of Congo and from the Ijo of Nigeria. Some of the salient features of the performance traditions might be summarized as follows:

Talent and interest are the principal qualifications of the performer. The "call" to perform sometimes has shamanic overtones, and training in some instances appears to be a form of initiation with aspects of cultic practice (among the BaNyanga, the performer is in fact a votary of a spirit, *Karisi*) that is meant to link the performer with the spirit of the performance and the hero who will be evoked. In other cases, the training involves observation and imitation of master performers on a formal or informal basis. Performers appear generally to be male, although descriptions of the mvet tradition do occasionally identify female performers and one text from Gabon (the *Epopée Mulombi*) is based on a woman's performance. Gender does not appear to be a determining factor, but so far the vast majority of published texts reflects performances by men.

In performance, the principal narrator may be equipped with a rattle, a bell, or some other object that serves as a prop or symbol (e.g., a spear or a staff); he is accompanied by an instrumentalist or by the group of his apprentices. He does not usually play an instrument himself. Accompanying instruments vary. The instrument called the *mvet* is a four-stringed chordophone made of a shaft of bamboo resembling a bow to which resonating gourds have been attached; other stringed instruments are lyre-shaped. Frequently, accompaniment is provided by drums of various tonalities. The accompaniment may include backup vocals for the songs that frequently punctuate the performance and in which the audience also often participates.

The lead performer's activities differ significantly from the pattern generally encountered in the Sahel and elsewhere, where performance is marked by immobility and an emphasis on the verbal element. By contrast, Central Africa offers a far more animated and dramatic performance event. The singer is not fixed in place but free to move about, and performers exploit this freedom. The story is thus conveyed not only verbally and musically but also kinetically through dance and mime. These supplementary dimensions of the performance are reported in published descriptions, but only one edition, John Pepper Clark-Bekederemo's *Ozidi Saga*, attempts to incorporate this element into the text and to provide the reader with a sense of the fuller experience of the performance event.[3] The problem of translating such elements of a performance into textual form besets studies of oral tradition, and the presence of these elements links such genres as much to drama as to more poetic forms of the Western literary tradition.

The performer thus not only narrates the story but acts it out as well. The performer's animation is matched by that of the audience, which may and often does participate in the dances and songs that are so much part of the occasion. This represents the farthest remove from the performance dynamics of the Sahelian tradition, in which, according at least to the standard view, the static center of the event is the performer, who serves as a prism or a lens through which to experience a diagetic reconstruction of the past. In the Central African tradition, the performer can be viewed as the catalyst uniting the entire community of participants and the constructed world of the performance. The distance between performer and subject collapses; the performer becomes the hero (or his antagonists), and the audience is given an integral role in the event. It seems hardly coincidental that so much of the Lianja cycle, for instance, involves a procession of the hero and his followers that recounts his conquests and the additions to his train: just as the performer becomes the hero in the performance, so the audience, following the performer, becomes what thay actually are: the hero's people.

At one extreme, then, the principal dynamic of this performance tradition would seem to involve the collective experience of a reenacted past rather than the narrator's verbal and narrative reconstruction of it in the telling of the story. This focus on the experience applies generally in oral performance; the text-based notion of a continuous narrative is subordinated here to other considerations, and the effect can be observed in certain aspects of the reported stories.

The subject of the performance is not the "full" story. The anthropologist Daniel Biebuyck reports how one bard, Candi Rureke, commented that he had never performed Mwindo as a continuous whole, and the same observation is made of the Lianja and Jeki cycles.[4] Rather, in each performance selected episodes are presented, drawn from a tradition that can be seen as endless—a bottomless reservoir, an ocean of story from which the performer draws as needed to suit the occasion and his inspiration. The corpus of the tradition breaks down into episodes that may be linked almost arbitrarily. This is particularly noticeable in the hero stories attaching to Lianja and Jeki, less so for Mwindo or Ozidi. Through de Rop and Boelaert's fifty-six versions of *Lianja*, for instance, the story defines itself as a series of episodes of which any single version represents a partial selection and organization. Episodes may be freely transposed, and de Rop comments that performers will improvise and adapt their material to their audience.[5] However, there is a high degree of consistency from version to version in the most common episodes of the performers' documented versions. Elsewhere, Ozidi confronts a series of opponents, much like the Duala hero Jeki; each opponent is treated in a separate episode, the characteristic tone of which is defined by the nature of the antagonist.

Mention has been made of the occasional ritual initiation of performers and the collective experience of the participating community. One possible inference from such an initiation is that performances are overlaid with a quasi-religious quality. Such a quality may pervade the audience's response to the reenactment of traditions that can be seen as defining their collective identity; but this would apply less to the occasions of the performance that in general are public events, organized for the entertainment of the community by some notable. The general tone is one of secular pleasure (an occasion for much drinking, dancing, and song), although Clark-Bekederemo describes, for the Ozidi tradition, some ritual aspects of the production of the drama:

> It begins each day with a round up of seven virgin girls, as special sacrificial offerings are gathered at the compound of the storyteller-protagonist. This sets at once the religious tone of the drama and story. After worshipping before his household and personal gods, the storyteller-protagonist . . . leads a solemn song-procession of the seven virgins to the stream washing the feet of every Ijo village. There, sacrifice is offered in homage to spirits of the water without whose help the enterprise on land cannot prosper. It is well to note here that the prayer is not for art alone but also for life so that the people may have their own fair share of women, children, and money apparently flowing to enrich life elsewhere and without which there can be no real enjoyment of art anywhere.[6]

But Clark-Bekederemo also notes that, "unlike most Ijo festivals and religious occasions, *The Ozidi Saga* observes no distinctions of age, sex, season, and place."[7] This statement might also apply to the performance conditions among the BaNyanga, described by Biebuyck as follows:

> The Nyanga epic is not a text performed only at certain times or on highly esoteric ceremonial occasions. There is nothing secret about it; it is to be heard and enjoyed by all the people. Normally a chief or headman or simply the senior of a local descent group, in order to entertain his people and guests, would invite the bard to perform a few episodes of the epic in the evening, around the men's

hut in the middle of the village. Large crowds of people, male and female, young and old, would come to listen or rather to be participant auditors.[8]

For comparative purposes, the potential religious dimension of the performance, while suggestive and interesting, should not be considered a distinguishing feature of this regional performance style as opposed to the Sahelian group that will be considered later, although at present the Sahel performance tradition clearly appears to be independent of ritual action. But the Sahelian tradition has been overlaid with Islam in recent years, effacing some earlier traditional elements such as the association of praise singing and royalty but leaving sufficient evidence (as, for instance, the institution of the hunters' griot) of non-Islamic belief and practice, and retaining at its core a mystical belief in the power of the spoken word.

Religion is less significant than historical specificity in distinguishing Central African epics from those of the Sahel. Christiane Seydou notes that in the Sahel, traditions are individualized, particularized, and given a specificity of time and place that certainly passes for a form of history.[9] In the Central African traditions, by contrast, the time and place are generally unspecified; the place may be the "here," but the time is the remote past. Historical value is not a consideration in approaching these texts, although they may retain information in cliché form or reflect the past traditions of the groups involved. Rather, the most useful approach is probably to regard many of the narratives as mythical in effect: an exploration of the dimensions of the human condition and the principles of the societies in which people live.

Nsong'a Lianja of the Mongo

Nsong'a Lianja (Lianja of [his sister] Nsongo) serves well to establish the type of hero and narrative characteristic of this grouping. This story (or cycle) is the epic of the Mongo peoples of northeastern Congo, within the great bend of the river, representing a wide variety of lineage and clan segments.[10] The groups constitute a forest-dwelling cultural complex of hunters and low-level agriculturalists (banana plantations) who live in association with Twa pygmies; they migrated into the area from some region across the river to the northeast at some undefined time at least two hundred years ago, according to the collector, G. Hulstaert.[11]

Political organization is minimal; the groups constitute patrilinear segmentary societies in which clan membership (with its network of clients, slaves, and pygmies as specialized hunters) is the principal mode of social identification, although some groups may have adopted such institutions as chiefs and councils from their non-Mongo neighbors, as well as certain religious cults.

State formation or history of conquest are thus not the underlying topics of the Lianja tradition; according to Hulstaert, no common historical traditions are to be found across the different groups. Historical elements might be identified in some of the episodes for some of the localized groups. The story usually concludes (insofar as there is a defined story line that is told continuously) with the progression of Lianja and his sister Nsongo through a succession of peoples whom he subdues in a variety of ways. If analyzed with the tools of philology and toponymy, these episodes might yield some concrete information on the migrations of different groups. The cycle generally ends when Lianja and his sister cross a river, which may reflect the collective experience of the Mongo groups that say they came originally from across the river. Still, the presentation of the material is anything but specific and historical, and it seems far safer to view the story as a collective tradition that owes more to secularized myth and forms of social chartering than to precise history.

Sources

Through the efforts of the Belgian scholars G. Hulstaert, A. de Rop, and E. Boelaert (and their many assistants), more than fifty versions of the story have been published; they vary in length and quality and are presented in bilingual format.[12] Many of these were written documents collected through the mission system; thus, although they do not reflect oral performances, they do give some evidence about the local configurations of the tradition. Wherever possible, the groups of origin are identified. Almost all of the informants reported that the tradition seemed to be dying out.

The cycle covers several generations of the line of Lianja and is clearly set in a mythical time period at the dawn of creation; the extent to which Lianja *is* a generalized and exoteric creation myth (as opposed to the more esoteric versions accessible through initiation societies) has not been discussed in the literature on the subject. However, when Lianja's mother gives birth to what appear to be all the creatures of creation (insects, animals, humans), and when the cycle ends, as it often does, with an ascent into heaven and the capture of the sun, the conclusion that this is the realm of mythical rather than historical time seems inescapable. The creation of the world, however, is not covered by the story; rather, its idiom expresses a concern for social patterning and organization that reflects, in some details, local structures (matriliny, marriage patterns) and economic activities (hunting and farming).

According to Boelaert, the essential theme of the epic is centered in three episodes: the pregnancy of Lianja's mother, during which she suffers from a desire for safou nuts that leads to the death of her husband; the birth of Lianja and his sister and their vengeance on the slayer of their father; and the progression of conquests that follows their victory and that ends when Lianja and his people cross a river and he rises into the sky.[13] But these are the core episodes, and there are many others. Boelaert's 1949 composite version places as many of these different episodes as possible in sequence, beginning with the remote ancestors of Lianja and proceeding down through his conquests. A number of the versions presented by de Rop and Boelaert come close to the length of this compilation, but none goes so far up Lianja's family tree. The following summary presents the various central episodes of the cycle as an illustration of the narrative content of the tradition.

Ancestors of Lianja

A first ancestor travels across the water to steal the sun and to win a bride; the son born to them, Lonkundo, becomes a source of conflict. He would die if given a direct order; nevertheless, his grandmother twice orders him to give her food. The first time he is restored to life by a magical remedy given by his father to his mother; the second time, the grandmother destroys the remedy before the boy is revived. The father, finding his son dead, kills his wife and her family and then revives his son; the son then kills the father and withdraws to the "center of the world," where his father's spirit instructs him in dreams about hunting.

He marries and he and his wife live in the forest. She becomes pregnant and food begins to disappear because the unborn child leaves the womb at night to devour it. They set a trap and the child is caught outside the womb in daylight; they then flee. Itonde, the prodigious and preternatural child, eventually comes after them; he avoids the traps and survives the ordeals that are set to prove that he is his father's son. He is renamed Ilelangonda, which de Rop glosses as "the vine which hangs from the sky without being fastened."[14]

Ilelangonda marries Mbombe, a woman whom he must first defeat in a wrestling match. Their first experience of marriage is something of a comedy of errors involving food. Ilelangonda was given hunting dogs by Mbombe's brother, but he refuses to share the fruits of the hunt with her.

When at last he does, she devours the meat so quickly that the "owner of the forest" warns she should not be allowed to eat meat or the forest will be emptied. In another episode, the wife takes the husband's hunting gear and then catches an animal she cannot master. She calls for help; he comes running and hurls a spear. In the fracas, the animal escapes, and it is unclear if he was aiming for the animal or for his wife. He then runs away, encountering all sorts of animals in his flight and naming them as a means of overcoming his terror.

He comes to a village of women, where he will be eaten unless he can learn their names; with the assistance of an old woman he devises a trick and so learns their names (he breaches the dam on an irrigated field and listens to the women calling each other to come and repair the break). He settles into the village and is eventually joined by his wife, who is pregnant.

The Birth of Lianja

During her pregnancy, Mbombe's appetite is uncertain, until a hornbill drops a safou nut in the courtyard and she tastes it. She then forces her husband into repeated trips to the land of Sausau, where he steals the fruit from a tree guarded by a creature afflicted with yaws. Various animals, servants of Sausau, try to capture the thief but he escapes them. This sequence incorporates many songs, as each animal sings a challenge and Ilelangonda answers them.

Eventually, he makes one trip too many, and the despised turtle succeeds in capturing him. His body is butchered; at first the turtle's deed is not acknowledged, and he receives the excrement for his share. But the excrement turns to meat (and vice versa throughout the village), and so the turtle is recognized as the hero.

Ilelangonda's death is known in his village through signs he had previously announced. Immediately, Mbombe begins to give birth. She does not mourn, as do the other women, because the pangs of labor are on her. "First she gives birth to the red ants, and then the bitter ants and all the insects. Then she gives birth to birds, and then to men of all sorts. She gives birth first to the Balumbe," who sing on emergence and are followed by three or four other clans and then by individuals who will be the helpers of Lianja. Last come Lianja and his sister Nsongo; Lianja causes difficulties because he refuses to emerge by the common exit. He insists on an individual passage, and so his mother's leg is daubed white with kaolin and cut with a knife. His sister may or may not come out this way first; the texts are often unclear. Lianja emerges fully grown and armed (and sometimes with a wife).

He then asks what happened to his father, and his mother lies: she says that he died in a boat or in some other manner. Lianja tests her answers by reenacting the death with the help of the turtle and proving her falsehoods; eventually she tells the truth (and the turtle's legs are permanently shortened in this test): that Ilele died while getting safou nuts for her from Sausau's tree.

Lianja and Nsongo then assemble their army and march against Sausau; sometimes one of the helpers or siblings visits Sausau to learn how things stand. Then the armies join: Lianja himself is preceded in battle as he was preceded in birth by the various insects and clans of humans; generally, the insects are put to flight by smoke bombs, and the humans all kill each other. Only Lianja and Sausau, the chieftain, are left. Sausau's weapons have no effect on Lianja (or else Lianja is able to restore himself; in one or two versions his sister sings as he fights), and Lianja chops off the head of Sausau.

His sister Nsongo then asks him to bring everyone back to life, which he does; sometimes she says that she will marry Sausau and this is why Lianja should spare him. The safou tree is cut down (this often occurs before the battle); to cut it down, the axes must be sharpened with water.

The Marvelous March

Lianja, Nsongo, and their followers then proceed on their way through the forest, conquering all they meet and thus acquiring more followers, some with useful skills such as weaving, fishing, and brewing. These episodes are highly variable and occasionally so elliptical as to be quite obscure and hard to follow; one puzzling motif that recurs frequently is that of a village whose patriarch or elder has a beard that reaches the length of the village. Another encounter involves a wily hunter named Yampunungu, whom Lianja attempts to capture by taking the form of an animal caught in a trap. The hunter, suspecting Lianja, remarks that "if the animal is really a [warthog, bird, whatever] it will do something"; Lianja then does what he has said and so is recognized. Often, Yampunungu is caught because Lianja has changed into a dead antelope; on the second day, Yampunungu fears the meat will rot and risks capture rather than let the meat rot; sometimes he is caught as Lianja transforms himself into some domestic object.

Other exploits include climbing a tree that then carries Lianja into heaven (he runs afoul of the dwellers there and is killed, but Nsongo sends helpers to bring him back to life); an encounter with Indombe, the master serpent, a snake of tremendous weight whom Lianja manages to carry, thanks to a magic bell, and whom Lianja sends into the spirit world; and various encounters with ogres—including a magician whom Lianja defeats by becoming first a child, whom the magician's wife insists on taking along as they flee, and then a fruit, which the magician eats. Lianja calls to the magician from within his belly, and the magician eventually dies.

The action also includes a number of incidents involving Nsongo. Nsongo is the reason for many of Lianja's conquests; she tells him to capture people, and he does. Some of them she takes as lovers or marries; on one occasion, she asks Lianja to bring down darkness in midday so that she may sleep with her lover. He does so grudgingly but refuses to bring back the light until she sends swarms of mosquitoes to sting him.

The adventures conclude (if they ever do) when Lianja, Nsongo, and the others come to a river and cross it. Their followers settle there, while Lianja and Nsongo eventually leave them and rise to heaven.

Performers usually select episodes from this cycle, but there are no precise descriptions indicating what combinations and sequences might be preferred. As a hypothesis, the presence of songs in the narrative may serve as an indication of polish and rehearsal. This criterion identifies several episodes: the flight of Lianja's father through the forest (in which he names, in verse, all the creatures he meets), the safou nut sequence (which offers a similar sequence of naming songs), the birth of Lianja and his companions, and certain later episodes.[15]

An assessment of the significance of the story should not focus only on the nominal hero, despite precedent and expectation. The episodes frequently echo each other and thus lead away from the individual characters and toward the underlying themes that are shared. The theme of food is pervasive; food is seen from a number of perspectives and involves a number of consumers. Grandmother and grandchild, husband and wife, parents and child, all come into conflict in some manner that involves food. Men acquire the technology of hunting (through dreams or as a wedding gift) and are then reluctant to share their gains. Women are portrayed principally as consumers of food, in a manner that threatens the entire environment at one point and causes the death of the husband at another. Children are seen (by their parents) as having ravenous and dangerous appetites. Such imagery reflects not only an adult male point of view but also underlines the centrality of the acquisition of food in a foraging society and the fragility of the balance between population and resources.

The tension lies between the natural resources of the environment and the reproductive potential of women: this is the message of the fearsome appetites displayed on occasion, a warning against the consequences of over-population. But that reproductive potential is also the crucial process for social and human continuity. The generation of children may be frightening in some regards (as in the case of the mobile unborn baby who cleans out the larder nightly), but it is the remedy, so to speak, for death. The central episode of the story juxtaposes the death of the father and the birth of the son so immediately and so dramatically as to make this very point. Lianja's father dies; Lianja is born and takes his place. Continuity is assured; the society will not disappear.

The story of Lianja thus serves as a vehicle for what in this textualized form appears to be a mythological consideration of the foundations of the society. The episodes explore not only the natural processes of increase (food and reproduction), but also questions of social roles (husbands who flee their wives; women who act as men; parents who attempt to kill their children). As often happens in mythology, these explorations involve an inversion of the "normal," or at least contemporary, order: conditions contrary to contemporary fact are presented and then transformed as justification or explanation for present conditions. A curious feature of the narrative sequence is the apparent switch in the central social bond at the end: where the episodes dealing with Lianja's ancestors pit husbands against wives, the final synthesis embodied by Lianja—in the available versions—links brother and sister with little mention of spouses.

The narrative line itself agrees with general models of heroic biography, and it would be a simple matter to align Lianja with any number of other heroes and to interpret his story using established methods of literary analysis. Lianja's father dies, and Lianja must avenge him—countless stories tell the same tale. But a focus on Lianja alone is incomplete and distorts the narrative. For Lianja is not only Lianja, son of Ilelangonda (a title that is never used), he is most visibly Nsong'a Lianja: the Lianja of his sister Nsongo. He does not function alone; he is always accompanied, guided, strengthened, and motivated by his sister; and it is the two of them together who create their people by recruiting for the marvelous march and leading the way to the promised land.

This linkage of the hero and his sister should not be construed as evidence that the society is a matriarchy. Various segments may indeed be matrilineal (although the sources do describe the culture as patrilineal), but the gender relations defined through the other episodes of the cycle are fairly patriarchal and virilocal in their configuration of husband-and-wife relations. Rather, it seems best to view this as a particular definition of an individual: not as a single body, but as a social unit, a dyad. Lianja acts not for himself, as might a traditional European hero, but at the behest of his sister; he is not in conflict with his society but in the process of establishing it. To treat the story of Lianja as a hero myth reduces it by eliminating its sense of balance and duality, its collective rather than individual scope; and it also distorts it by obscuring some of the ethnographic content.

This point is stressed because throughout the traditions examined in this chapter, the hero's ongoing relationship with, and dependence upon, a sister or some other female relative serves as a distinctive identifier for the type. The story of Lofokefoke of the BaMbuli (neighbors to the Mongo) is virtually identical to that of Lianja: after the parents have been united and the father has been killed,[16] the mother demands sau-sau nuts during her pregnancy. The hero's birth is the last of a series, as in Lianja, and once born he departs to avenge his father. One of his praise names terms him *Bonyunga ise Besongo,* which can be glossed as "The one to be feared, brother of the woman Besongo."[17] The names Nsongo and Besongo clearly share the same root.

As a prototype, Lianja displays features that will recur in the presentation of other heroes. His narrative is an open episodic cycle, from which performers select appropriate sequences. The episodes include the actions of ancestors, which appear to govern the hero's own conduct, and a string of adventures in which the hero engages. These various episodes provide the material for comparison with other epics. They also clearly illustrate the folkloric roots of the hero, for similar stories are told in folktales with animal protagonists. The theme of hunting recurs elsewhere, not only in Central Africa. Finally, the importance of the hero's sister in the story, as helper, guide, and companion, seems a distinguishing trait and perhaps a key to certain particularities of the African hero.

The Mwindo Epic of the BaNyanga

There are four published versions and one summary of the Mwindo epic; the first, published in 1969, has been widely anthologized and may be the Central African epic best known to English speakers.[18] The BaNyanga live somewhat to the east of the Mongo, in the Kivu region of Congo. At the time of Daniel Biebuyck's research, in the 1950s, they numbered some twenty-five thousand, and the population was distributed in small chieftainships in which political rule covered a cultural amalgam of Nyanga and associated pygmy groups. The pygmies served as hunters to the chiefs and were also closely associated with the epic tradition in other ways. Food came from a combination of trapping, hunting, fishing, and foraging; the principal cultivated crop (as for the Mongo) was the banana or plantain, although the epics also mention eleusine.

There has already been some description of performance conditions. Performers are often initiated into the cult of the spirit Karisi. They perform on commission for a variety of occasions, contributing to general entertainment and festivities as well as the prestige of their patrons. But another venue, equally important in Biebuyck's descriptions, is the hunting camp, where the narrative tradition truly comes into its own:

> The hunting camp, isolated from the rest of the world in the deep forest, is a setting par excellence where the narrative thrives and the creative imagination operates. There are no large crowds and no diverse musical instruments for big dances; there is no reason for major celebrations, initiations, or rituals. Storytelling is the most effective means of entertainment and relaxation in the camp.[19]

The continuing influence of this second venue may underlie the apparent stylistic and qualitative differences between the published Mwindo texts and the examples from the Lianja tradition. In the Lianja material, the song-and-dance aspect of the performance is clearly manifest through the extended and repetitive lyric interludes (song sequences), which convey a sense of the performance as a collective and participatory experience. In the Mwindo texts, however, such extended and structured repetition is less common. The songs appear to be soliloquies rather than dance music, although it is sometimes unclear whether it is the hero, some other character, or the performer who speaks. In at least one instance, the virtuoso performer of Mwindo, Candi Rureke, introduces a slight personal reference into a song:

> In Ihimbi where dwelt Birori,
> I shall die (today), Mushumo.
> On Ntsuri-hill where dwelt Ruronga,
> (In) Munongo where dwelt Shecara
> Bitumi-hill of Shemene Ndura,
> And the old ones fight because of a wind.[20]

The Mwindo epic tradition, as documented, appears to be the product of a dialectic between two poles: the collective multimodal enthusiasm of the public performance within the village (the conditions under which Candi Rureke performed the first published version of the epic) and the more introspective and purely verbal form of performance of the camp. The result, to judge by the published texts, is a singularly dense and rich tradition in which it seems less appropriate to speak of variants (as would clearly apply to the Lianja episodes) than of individual and separate compositions.

Biebuyck's second volume, *Hero and Chief* (1978), offers a general study of the traditions, the performers, the narratives, and the stylistic features of the published texts. His work is the indispensable introduction to this material and serves as a guide to general narrative patterns. He suggests that the following schema underlies many of the tales: A polygamous husband orders his wives not to bear sons, only daughters. The favorite wife (usually) gives birth to a preternaturally powerful child, who is eventually forced out of the village. He settles nearby and eventually all the people of the father's village, including the father himself, become his subjects.[21] While this pattern is clearly discernible in the first two texts of *Hero and Chief* (versions two and three, in Biebuyck's numbering), it is somewhat more complicated in the others.

An implicit tension between father and son, involving questions of mortality and succession, underlies this pattern, and becomes quite evident in the first and principal Mwindo text, that performed by Candi Rureke. In this extended version the conflict establishes almost the entire action: after Mwindo's birth, he escapes a series of attempts on his life ordered by his father, following which his father flees into the underworld. Mwindo pursues him. Mwindo faces a series of tests in the underworld, which he passes thanks to assistance from Lightning, a sky-divinity who is married to his paternal aunt. He then returns his father to the world of the living, takes his own place as chief, and after a few minor adventures, passes on. In other versions, however, the rivalry with the father is attenuated: in version two, for instance, while Mwindo does bring his father back from the underworld, the principal relationship at the start of the narrative involves Mwindo's sister Nyamitondo, who is married to Lightning, and a monstrous bird whom he and she have accidentally hatched; the end of the story revolves around Mwindo's principal pygmy Shekaruru. In version four, Mwindo becomes an antagonist: the "hero" is Kabutwakenda, Little-one-just-born-he-walked (a praise name usually attributed to Mwindo himself), and while part of their rivalry involves the question of succession to the father, this rivalry involves no hostility toward the father. Only in the summary of Wanowa's epic, which appears as an appendix in *Hero and Chief,* does the familiar Lianja pattern of a dead father recur; but here it is transformed: the son must undertake a voyage to the underworld to obtain the supplies with which he may perform the funeral rituals for his father.

A descent to the underworld of some sort occurs in all five versions, and an ascent to heaven also occurs frequently. Some of the characters he encounters are considered divinities (his uncle Lightning, or Nyamurairi, a god of fire and the underworld). In a number of cases, the hero must perform a structured series of tasks, which he accomplishes either with the assistance of his *conga*-scepter or of some relative. In one of the more striking and unusual processes of this epic tradition, Mwindo's body is forged in heaven and he is given iron clothing.[22]

The local element of the Mwindo tradition is well-translated by the ample ethnographic commentary provided by Biebuyck. Mwindo invites further analysis in terms of regional mythical patterns[23] and the symbolic system of the BaNyanga. But the analysis should start with a comparison of the versions. They are so radically different that it seems dangerous to suggest that there might be a single or basic Mwindo story. There is a character named Mwindo. But the freedom of invention associated with his exploits is vastly different from that of the Lianja corpus, where the various episodes have been normalized and remain recognizably the same from one teller to another. In the Mwindo epic, the differences overpower the similarities. Each version is clearly the product of an individual consciousness expressing itself in a somewhat conventionalized but loose fictional idiom. In this, the BaNyanga traditions echo the conditions described below for the mvet tradition of the Fang.

Biebuyck and Mateene have published one other epic text from the BaNyanga, the "Epic of Kahindo."[24] It tells of a young woman captured by an ogre; she escapes with the help of her "twin," the ogre's daughter. The tone is that of a folktale, and her actions are not portrayed in the heroic dimensions applied to Mwindo.

Lianja and Mwindo come from the eastern Congo, and before considering heroes from well to the west of their territory, the existence of a parallel epic tradition among their neighbors, the Lega, must be acknowledged. N'Sanda Wamenka has published three epic texts that in many regards echo the narrative repertoire of the Lianja and Mwindo traditions.[25] A child is born following the death of his father. He performs prodigious feats of magic and strength, often with the assistance of a sister, and establishes his people. Biebuyck has also promised the publication of a Lega epic text, *Mubila,* and he offers some descriptive parallels of the Lega and BaNyanga traditions.[26]

Jeki la Njambe of the Duala

Jeki is a hero of the Littoral, the coastal region of Cameroon. He appears principally among the Duala but also among neighboring peoples. As a performance tradition, Jeki seems to be dying out. Very few public performers remain active. As a literary tradition, Jeki is developing. Two recent publications offer lengthy versions of the story taken in differing ways from the oral tradition,[27] and Ralph

Austen has published a monograph that includes excerpts from a number of earlier versions.[28]

Recent Duala history principally concerns commerce; the coastal groups served as middlemen and traders rather than as chiefs and warlords. The epic of Jeki la Nzambe offers virtually no history, although Austen presents evidence for reflections of nineteenth-century cultural complexes. Among the Duala, the epic itself is considered something of an anomaly, an incomprehensible legacy from the past whose cultural prestige is independent of its relevance. From a comparative perspective, the story seems less baffling. Jeki's cycle resembles that of Lianja and other regional heroes. It seems plausible to identify him as a culture hero whose story has been preserved well after the passing of the lifestyle that gave it birth.

The story of Jeki is highly episodic; the two published versions present an artificially complete sequence. Bekombo-Priso's published text is based on a night's performance by a recognized virtuoso, Jo Diboko'a Kollo, made at Bekombo-Priso's request. That of Tiki a Koulle a Penda, a virtuoso and retired school administrator, is more of a hybrid, in which the literate performer reviewed the transcriptions of recorded episodes and rerecorded as he felt necessary. Tiki attempts to present a "complete" cycle, a listing of all the principal known episodes (although it is recognized by all, in theory, that such an attempt is impossible); Bekombo-Priso's version limits the number of episodes, but observes a developmental sequence for the hero. This latter version is accompanied by a recording of portions of the performance.

The performance conditions are relatively familiar, and Austen covers them well. A nice feature of Austen's description is his inclusion of home-performances (often by women) as part of the range of venues. Public spectacles feature a leader-narrator accompanied by musicians and a chorus for public performances. Narration is punctuated by frequent songs in a variety of rhythms; the songs are generally simple reflections of the immediate action, as occurs in the Lianja tradition as well. So, immediately after birth the hero sings:

> I am going, I am going!
> I am going, I am going!
> I am walking like father!
> I am walking like mother!
> Now I look like grandfather!
> I am walking like father! . . . [29]

As Jeki sings, he also imitates the gait of the various family members he mentions, and so astounds his mother. This mimicry demonstrates preternatural power and knowledge (and may challenge the performer), but it is not densely poetic.

Performance occasions are hard to specify given the rarity of what Austen terms the virtuoso performers. To some extent, *Jeki* may no longer be a popular art form, but rather an elite entertainment. Austen notes that Tiki is engaged for funerals and wakes, largely because of the need for time-consuming entertainments rather than because the tradition is associated with mortuary practices.[30] Performances are reserved for nighttime, and they are accompanied by elaborate magical and occult precautions, largely to protect the performer from envious sorcery.

Austen has performed the broadest comparison of available versions so far available, and he finds the story line to be stable through the variants; like Lianja, the story of Jeki appears to have consolidated itself and the principal mechanism at work now is preservation rather than generation. Tiki's version provides a wide number of possible variant adventures for the hero, but these are essentially formula narratives in which the detail and the terms of the confrontation may vary but not the essential pattern.

The Story of Jeki

Jeki's father is antisocial, a trait expressed through his sorcerous knowledge, and he leaves his original group. He and his wife settle some distance away. She loses her first child, a daughter, who is stolen by a bush spirit (or a chimpanzee) who has been teaching the mother how to farm, and so the mother becomes the "despised wife." By other wives, Njambe has ninety-nine sons. Finally the despised wife, Jeki's mother, becomes pregnant and gives birth to the hero, who is preceded by retainers and weaponry.

Jeki proves himself to his father and his brothers. They attempt in various ways to kill him, but fail. His father then sets him three tests: to fetch a monstrous crocodile, to capture a monstrous eagle, and to "clean out the cupboard" in his house, which happens to contain a mother leopard and her young. Jeki performs all these tasks easily, with the help of his magical amulet *Ngalo*. By doing so he apparently destroys the sources of his father's occult power.

Jeki then embarks on a series of adventures and confrontations with foreign enemies. His exploits may include a visit to the underworld to rescue the sister who was stolen. Sometimes he gets married; sometimes he is reconciled with his father; sometimes he kills his father and becomes chief. The ending, appropriately enough, is left vague, and it is claimed that the cycle has no end.

As a type, Jeki is clearly related to Lianja and Mwindo. Birth, social function, weaponry, and preternaturally early activity unite the heroes. The hostile opposition to the father is perhaps closer to the pattern visible in Mwindo. Again there is a connection between hero and sister, although here it is attenuated (the hero may rescue the sister, but she is not an active helper).

The connections with aetiologic mythology are less evident than with Lianja, although the case for such a reading would be plausible. Jeki's travels define the cosmology of the human world, and the forces he masters permit subsequent human exploitation. Austen observes that the name of Jeki's father, Njambe or Nyambe, is a general Bantu-family term for the sky-god, and his epithet *Iyono* has the meaning of "eternal." Jeki could thus be seen as the demiurge completing the work of creation started by his father, in a pattern familiar throughout West African mythical systems and beyond. The actions of Jeki, moreover, are restorative, since his father's initial situation is one of moral ambiguity because of his control of witchcraft. Bekombo-Priso dismisses such an identification, but for unconvincing reasons: his presumption seems to be that any identification of Njambe and Jeki as father-and-son divinities necessarily implies a Christian connection.[31] Such is not the case. Comparative mythology provides any number of idle creator gods *(dei otiosi)* whose more active offspring are responsible for shaping the human world.

The Jeki performance tradition is no longer vital at the popular level. It is now being maintained to some extent by the actions of intellectuals; Tiki a Koulle a Penda, for instance, is a retired school administrator who performs *Jeki* out of respect for the tradition. Austen has documented a number of other such "artificial" modes of preservation and appropriation of the epic. It is a new vehicle for Duala and Cameroonian nationalism, and the literary interpretations that express that function are the most interesting modern aspect of the tradition.[32]

The *Ozidi Saga* of the Ijo

The Ijo are a river people of the Niger delta in Nigeria, and their history and culture are somewhat entwined with those of Benin, the delta city celebrated for its bronzes. The Ijo also sing a hero, Ozidi, known so far through a single but massive transcription by the poet John Pepper Clark-Bekederemo.[33] He recorded three performances by different performers and chose the best for publication. This version was not performed in Ijo territory but among the resident Ijo community of Ibadan (the principal university town at the time) by a noted performer, Okabou Ojobolo, over a period of seven nights, which is the prescribed duration of the event.

Isidore Okpewho has made himself the patron and gatekeeper of this epic through a series of essays illuminating the mode of performance, the transcription, and the general poetic content, and his work is certainly the starting point for critical appreciation.[34] The performance style is the familiar one for this unit. It takes place in the open, and the audience participates in the songs, dances, and commentary. This particular version seems, from the annotation, particularly dramatic. Ojobolo clearly put all of himself into the performance.

The principal concern here is the way in which this story line compares with those already encountered, and it is indeed familiar. Although the narrator introduces complexities, the general outline is recognizable.

Ozidi

Ozidi's father is the ruler of the town, but a cabal of plotters assassinates him and places his brother (a coward) on the throne. Ozidi is born after his father's death, and his grandmother Oreame trains him to be a warrior and avenge his father. He proceeds to seek out and challenge the members of the cabal (he begins by killing two of their wives), and he slays them one by one in tempestuous combat. In the course of a fight, he almost invariably gets into trouble and requires the rapid and magical assistance of his grandmother Oreame to regain the upper hand; he nevertheless wins every time. Having wiped out the plotters, he then encounters a series of other adversaries who come to seek him out. Some are monstrous (a half-man, one with twenty limbs, one who walks on his head), some are quasi-comical, such as the Scrotum-King who walks with swinging ballocks (he personifies the disease elephantiasis), and finally the Smallpox King whose arrival evokes images of the colonial conquest: he sails up river in a boat and fires cannons at the town. The grapeshot scars Ozidi as would smallpox, but he recovers. He then gives up fighting after a final song of triumph.

The story line offers an essentially episodic structure spread over the seven nights of the performance. However, Ojobolo complicates the sequence by intertwining episodes. For instance, at the end of the first night Ozidi has prepared his challenge to two of the murderers by killing their wives, but he does not actually come to combat with them; instead, the night ends victoriously with a third victim, Agbogidi, who is suddenly introduced.[35] At the end of the second night, the first of the two selected murderers has been killed, but his corpse is still mobile. At the end of the third, the second murderer has still not been dispatched. Threads carry over from night to night.

The action does escalate; later battles seem more complex than earlier ones. Ozidi and Oreame face paired antagonists (images of themselves?) whose powers rival their own; some enemies are almost divinities. The Smallpox King suggests a number of regional deities (the Yoruba Sakbata, god of smallpox, or the Fon Sagbata, who also rules the earth from underground). The appearance of smallpox is an incidental detail that does link up with previous stories; throughout Central African traditions, there are figures covered with sores or boils. The theme deserves study, as Sunjata's mother is also covered with warts when she first appears. Such a motif may be part of world folklore, but it has a particularly sharp local resonance.

Ozidi differs from previous heroes in some respects. His roster of antagonists is not the same, nor do his exploits involve travel. His enemies come to him in succession once he has purged the town of the plotters. Ozidi's female helper is not his sister but his grandmother Oreame, who seems clearly defined as a witch. This variation is a twist on the previous association of heroes with sisters,[36] but one that might be explained given additional information on kinship patterns and the cultural view of magic. Neither Clark-Bekederemo nor Okpewho indicates whether Oreame should be seen as a lineage elder (with intimations of matriarchy) or, in another aspect of her position as grandmother, as a post-menopausal and nonreproductive woman who controls occult powers.

The *Ozidi Saga* raises the most serious questions of generic definition, and these may justify a short digression. The narrative line classes it with the other stories examined so far. But the performance, as described and published, also leads away from narrative. In the later sections of the text, the audience's rapport with the performer is such that he does not need to give details of the killings, nor of how Ozidi rouses himself for battle. A simple evocation of the appropriate song or narrative phrase cues the moment. Frequently, he does not "step back" to narrate an encounter of two adversaries: he acts it out, playing each part in turn and supplementing the verbal element with the visual and kinetic.

In other words, this performance might equally well be viewed as drama; in fact, from the point of view of performance studies, it should be examined as a collective and participatory drama (this is the principal thrust of Okpewho's readings). But this is not an either/or situation. A reader versed in the European tradition, in which genres have long since differentiated themselves (despite the tendency of creative authors to mix them up again), might wish to distinguish the genres. For an appreciation of *Ozidi,* and for other pieces, such distinctions are more counterproductive than useful. *Ozidi* exists on a plane anterior to such distinctions, and the *Ozidi* tradition comfortably and richly embodies elements of epic and drama without regard to the historical contingencies of European generic terms.

This view of the *Ozidi Saga* is also a reminder that the Ijo lie geographically between the Yoruba and the Igbo, groups celebrated for their ceremonial masked dances and for their rich ritual life. The writer Wole Soyinka, drawing on Yoruba tradition, has chosen drama as his vehicle because he finds the material singularly apt. Yet *Ozidi* is not a ritual drama by its editor's description. It is a heroic narrative that meshes easily with the others considered so far. The conventions of its performance, and the expertise of the artist, carry certain elements that are present elsewhere to a more intense degree, but this does not represent an absolute change of form.

Elements for Interpretation of the Central African Hero

Before considering the distinctive mvet tradition of the Fang, it would seem appropriate to offer some general observations on the heroic narrative pattern illustrated in the four traditions under discussion here. First, none of these traditions bears a close relationship to what could be termed political history. No states or dynasties are founded. They contain little specific information on migration, although migration patterns are probably reflected in the epics. There is little even in the way of wars. When conflicts occur, the victims are often brought back to life—this seems a more desirable outcome. The action takes place mostly on a supernatural or fantastic plane, which suggests the world of the folktale (and the plots come in patterns that conform to recognized folktale types) but more strongly evokes a mythical world of creation. The stories tell how people learned to gather food, of the invention of traps, of the establishment of social relations and gender roles. They tell of the establishment of the relations between the different levels of the world by drawing on the common device of the travels of the hero. They suggest the establishment of natural cycles of death and birth (most pointedly, perhaps, in the Lianja sequence, in which the mother cannot mourn the death of her husband because the pangs of labor are upon her). Interpretations of the stories should therefore not be based on the contingent and accidental events of history. Rather, understanding should be sought through anthropology and folklore, which can elucidate cultural content, or through literature for an appreciation of the narrative qua story.

Interpretations must also be based on the recognition that these are the narratives of communities composed of multiple individuals, interests, and perspectives. This observation serves as a warning against overreliance on "universal" patterns of heroic action like those defined by Otto Rank and Joseph Campbell that are built upon theories of the psychological development of the individual. It is true that the heroes examined here may well agree with the biographical pattern of hero-lives as defined by Archer Taylor, Lord Raglan, Jan de Vries, and others. But it is hardly surprising to find that an African hero conforms to standard hero patterns: the point of such models is that they identify common features. But analysis must include the questions of uncommon and unique features, and it must ask what salient elements should be retained for consideration and whether the human environment of the stories has had some effect as well.

One criticism of interpretive models for literature and folklore based upon psychological theory derives from their premise of a uniform notion of personhood extended across cultures.[37] The stress on individual development in tales reflects a very narrow and developmental view of the person, which may not correspond to the social construction of the individual in Africa. Paul Riesman's essay "Notion of Person in Africa" contains a valuable discussion as well as a valuable survey of the now extensive literature on the subject.[38]

Here, the concern is more with the empirical evidence derived from study of the narratives than with conceptual objections to psychological theory. Narrative patterns do exist and can be detected. But a careful reading of the narratives leads to dissatisfaction with the hero-pattern's reliance upon a single individual as center of the action. These narratives consistently present a male actor supported by female power: Lianja acts with his sister, and occasionally for her. Mwindo derives his power from the matrimonial alliance of his sister (or his father's sister) with Lightning. Ozidi requires the help of his grandmother Oreame to succeed. And even Jeki, in whom the tradition seems much attenuated and somewhat transformed, relies heavily on his mother and on occasion is accompanied by his sister. It could be argued that these female characters fulfill a purely supportive role (a Proppian function, so to speak), but such an argument disregards how essential they are in the stories. They define the heroes' purposes, they guide the heroes—and the pair forms an indivisible unit.

Thus, it seems most fruitful to consider the hero not as an individual but as a social unit, which in this case means a human couple, however constituted. African mythology offers androgynous figures and sibling-spouses from the earliest examples (the Ennead of Egypt) to the Dogon and the Fon. The exact relations of the pair undoubtedly depend upon local marital patterns. The point can be illustrated by French ethnographer Denise Paulme's analysis of a dilemma tale in which a man crosses a river in a canoe with three women: his wife, his sister, and his mother-in-law.[39] When the canoe capsizes, he can save only one woman. Whom shall he save? Paulme found that the answer alternated between wife and sister, depending upon the marriage practices of the groups involved. Where the marriage alliance involved an exchange of women, the sister was saved. Where the alliance involved the payment of a bride-price, the wife was saved. The mother-in-law, unfortunately, always drowned. Thus, uterine bonds, cemented by property and inheritance rights, may be stronger than conjugal unions in certain cases.

But the fundamental point is that isolating the (male) hero disregards an essential dynamic of the stories. While the male hero may possess tremendous powers, he does not always control them and he certainly does not work alone. He acts in a world defined by his predecessors and is to some extent controlled by them. He follows rules established by another; his power derives from another. He furthers a larger social dynamic that begins with parents. The tension between father and son is one of the motivating forces behind the narrative pattern, and it may be expressed either in a positive manner (Lianja and Ozidi avenge their fathers) or negatively, through hostility and attempted infanticide (Shemwindo and Njambe each try to have their offspring done in). This narrative axis clearly supports the potential Freudian reading that Rank and others bring to such stories, but it also leaves open other possibilities. It should be remembered that in the world of Lianja, husbands and wives may be hostile competitors and that mothers may fear their children.

The tension between father and son is not only the psychological experience of the developing child. In the stories, it is exploited as a meditation upon the human condition that is entirely appropriate in mythical thinking. The son may be living evidence of the father's eventual death, and so he inspires negative feelings in the father; but from the point of view of the larger community, the son represents the assurance that the father's role will be continued. The loss of an individual will not lead, through erosion, to the destruction of the community. In this sense, the tension reflects a more positive mechanism, showing how the community recreates and perpetuates itself. This perspective highlights the importance of the paired offspring, who form a new couple. The younger couple replaces the lost older couple. It is hardly coincidental that the hero's adventures so often require a descent to the underworld following the father (or, for Jeki, the sister), for it is the mythical progression through the cycle of life and death and life again that affirms the continuity of the social unit.

Heroes offer other dimensions as well. They are not always presented as positive forces. The analyses of Biebuyck and Austen show how the hero may be antisocial and destructive, proof of the power of unrestrained ambition and egocentrism; both writers suggest that the hero might well be seen as an unreliable trickster figure who evades the normal restrictions of social codes.[40] From this perspective, the heroes examined here may be associated with a widespread body of narratives throughout West Africa known generally as the *enfant terrible* story, in which the protagonist—but again, a pair of figures is involved—travels through the world essentially doing everything backwards until he is either killed or made a ruler.[41] A certain ambivalence about hero figures is evident here. The established story type may deal with repeated violations of the dictates of filial piety, courtesy, and even common sense. But also, especially in those versions that make the miscreant a ruler, they show how the perverse brother has imposed himself on the world by testing himself against it. He has not been found wanting. He has dared to take power, and such daring comes at a social cost.[42]

The tension between parents and children reflects another dimension: economic survival. Children are necessary for the continuity of society. But in the foraging lifestyle that characteristizes groups such as the BaNyanga and the Mongo (and in the past the Duala), the margin of survival is thin. Children may stretch resources, and overpopulation is a real danger for such groups. Colin Turnbull gives a contemporary image of the socially disruptive effects of famine in *The Mountain People;* while he describes a different region (northern Kenya/ Uganda), the lesson remains relevant. Recall how many incidents of the Lianja cycle involve food and competition; the same theme echoes through the other texts. The connection of demographics and food supply is thus an essential part of the background to the stories and points to a real element of the past history of at least some of the peoples involved: the question of migrations and population movements.

Despite the visionary treatment of migrations in books such as Armah's *Two Thousand Seasons,* or the solidarity that results from treks such as those of the Mormons in America, migrations are not necessarily socially constructive activities. In fact, in the case of the probable mechanisms behind the great Bantu diaspora, migrations could be viewed as evidence of social fission and tensions. For in this environment, the migrations emerge from a growing recognition of the inadequacy of the local food supply and the need for the dispossessed portion of the community to split off and establish a new community elsewhere. Migrations occur not out of a spirit of pioneering colonization like that associated by Americans with the Oregon Trail, but out of desperation: out of the need to avoid starvation or to escape danger (and there are accounts of such escapes in the epics). Migrations involve a division of the community; their leaders are great men and women but also destroyers of an established order. This image is replicated in the stories, most clearly in *Lianja,* where the hero and his sister progress with a triumphant and swelling train. It is echoed in *Ozidi,* where the hero acquires a retinue of singers, drummers, and flute-players (these are of course also the mark of a chief). It is found in the Lega epics, where heroes establish their own communities in the wild to escape a tyrannical elder. This narrative mechanism provides a faint reflection of the historical environment of the narrative tradition. It integrates the travels that the group acknowledges must have occurred before the people reached their present site. But because it is transferred to a mythical and ahistorical world, this mechanism avoids the possibly painful recollection of the schism that such movement necessarily entails.

The final observation might be that the standardization of the narrative seems to accompany attenuation of the performance tradition. Among the Mongo, where the Lianja tradition is dying out, the potential variety and creativity of the many episodes is coalescing into a core of relatively stable incidents. The fifty versions collected by Boelaert, de Rop, and Hulstaert are very uneven in length and quality, but the fullest versions show relative agreement on the incidents and their presentation. Jeki would seem to illustrate a later phase of this process of attrition: the story seems out of phase with its current context, and perhaps artificially preserved as a relic. It has lost its innovative vitality. The various episodes are all cut from a pattern, especially in the full version of Tiki. The contrast to these examples might be provided by the Mwindo tradition, whose multiforms argue for a continuing engagement of the performers with their material. This parallel, however, must be set in its time frame: the Mwindo tradition of the 1950s is almost certainly not the tradition of today; Jeki in the 1980s may well not be the Jeki of forty years earlier.

The Mvet Tradition

The term *mvet* refers both to a stringed instrument equipped with resonators and to the genre of narration for which the instrument is the accompaniment. It also serves as the title of various works from Gabon and southern Cameroon that have been published as texts.[43] The mvet tradition differs from those examined so far principally in its content. Narratives do not involve a recurrent central hero such as Lianja, Jeki, or Mwindo but evoke a world of the mythic past, populated by known characters and families in an apparently consistent set of relations,[44] in which the protagonists are created through the choice of the narrator. The stories, in other words, are admittedly a fiction, though they operate within an established and quasi-historical sphere.

The performance conditions are familiar and involve a narrator accompanied by musicians and singers whose performance involves both narrative and dramatic elements.[45] One difference, however, may be observed in the nature of the lyric elements, which generally are extended meditative solos rather than the short occasional songs found elsewhere in this region. Performances occur at night and typically last all night. Performers are self-chosen and are initiated through an apprenticeship with a master; Pascal Boyer offers a valuable study of the training and status of the *bebom-mvet,* as the performer is known. Having left their masters (often with a rupture), they occupy an anomalous niche, caught between their artistic vocation—which does not provide a sufficient livelihood—and an ambiguous status in which other members of society regard them with with some suspicion and a measure of distrust.

Intellectuals, however, have adopted the mvet as the national epic tradition of Gabon and Cameroon, and it is largely as the result of cultural nationalism that transcriptions and other versions are available. In the early 1960s a corpus of mvet performances was recorded at the University of Yaounde; only small portions have been published.[46] The intellectuals' adoption has taken other forms. In Gabon, Tsira Ndong Ndoutoume, who claims to be an initiated mvet performer, has now published three volumes of mvet in French prose. The dynamics of textualization are fascinating.

The mvet tradition is based upon a world in which two clans of humans oppose each other. The clan of Engong, ruled by Akoma Mba, possesses immortality; the clan is known as the people of iron. Opposing them is the clan of Oku, humans who do not possess immortality but who seek on occasion to acquire it. The frictions between the clans are the essential theme of the genre, although the specific cause of the frictions varies as does the cast of characters. Certain figures recur. The principal one is the quasi-divine Akoma Mba, the powerful but withdrawn ruler of the clan of Engong whose intervention in the story usually marks the decisive resolution. Thus, there is less a story line than a system for making stories, and the demands upon the performer's creativity seem to be of a slightly different nature than with the Lianja tradition, for instance, where recall, selection, and linkage are clearly the essential basic skills. Here, each individual piece grows out of the creative imagination of the performer (although certain stories and themes may be sufficiently well established to provide raw material), and the process is far more generative and fertile than other examples that have been discussed. Character, theme, plot—these elements are not provided by tradition but must be elaborated by the performer in a creative act. This is one reason why the work of Ndoutoume must be included in this examination of the tradition. In terms of composition, his role as an author using writing is arguably similar to that of the singer Zwé Nguema,[47] who performed for more than ten hours in one night. The fact that Ndoutoume feels free to adapt the genre to writing, and that his efforts gain acceptance from his compatriots, is a relevant component of the mvet tradition in the modern era.

Brief synopses of story lines can serve to illustrate the discussion. Awona's two excerpts of a longer performance tell how Akoma Mba determined to divide his power in Engong.[48] He summoned (by letter) all the leaders of Engong to recognize Otungu, his brother and heir. One chief, however, refused submission and beat the brother, who fled far into the forests. In the next excerpt, Akoma Mba asks who will go to find his brother, and two heroes are magically born to undertake the quest. One of them goes traveling, crosses a vast water, and then is captured and set to work at forced labor. His namesake (or twin?) realizes that his brother is in trouble and goes after him, retracing his brother's steps. He, too, is captured but manages to send word to Akoma Mba, who mounts a rescue expedition. This excerpt ends with the rescue of the two heroes and with the greater quest for Akoma Mba's brother still to be undertaken: clearly the story has the potential to be expanded. This tale bears an obvious relation to Aarne-Thompson tale-type 303, "The Two Brothers," although the similarity resides principally in the structuring of the story and less in the details.

A text published by Samuel Martin Eno-Belinga, *Mvet-Moneblum* (The blue man),[49] tells of Mekui-Mengomo-Ondo, a young man who dares to challenge his father over his marriage by asking for a wife and is therefore brought before Akoma Mba, where he is judged and exiled to the land of Edeñ-Ndoñ. There he is set to forced labor, building roads for Edeñ-Ndoñ. He also happens to fall in love with the wife of his captor (although she is cast less as an adulterous Guinevere than as the princess who must be rescued from the ogre). Having completed his tasks, he attempts to carry off the woman, who reciprocates his affections, and a sorcerous battle of power ensues between the hero and his captor. The hero eventually summons help from Akoma Mba, who sends an army to his rescue and defeats the captor. Since the initial difference between the son and his father involved the question of the son's marriage, the denouement resolves the problems.

From Gabon, the mvet of Zwé Nguema, presented by Pepper, has a less definite story line. Zong Midzi, a man of Oku (the mortals), declares war against Angone Endong of Engong, who had somehow provoked him. Angone is preparing to punish this mortal when the maiden Nkoudang, a princess, declares that she loves the name Zong Midzi and that she wishes to marry the man. War plans are delayed; she is given a week in which to accomplish her ambition. She leaves with her mother and on the road grants her favors to an insistent (and irresistible) lover named Nsoure Afane, who then accompanies her. Zong Midzi hears about this and comes to meet her, accompanied by his favorite wife, Esone Abeng. Eventually the two couples meet, but the lover misrepresents the situation. In the fog and ensuing confusion, Zong Midzi kills Nkoudang, the maiden who had come seeking him, while the lover Nsoure kills Zong Midzi's wife, Esone Abeng. Open warfare then breaks out between the clan of Engong (which wants to avenge their daughter Nkoudang) and Zong Midzi, the man of power. The lover Nsoure is judged and set aside. Eventually, after being captured and then escaping into the underworld, Zong Midzi is executed by Akoma Mba.

In this tradition, heroes are defined by their control of magical powers; the lover Nsoure Afane, for instance, flies about on a metal ball. Other heroes fly or tunnel through the earth. Weapons and implements are stored inside the body, in the belly, and called upon at need, often through the use of a little bell (performers, incidentally, sometimes use a bell as a prop). Battles are exaggerated contests of power and (for the performer) imagination, in which the changes of the ground rules defy all expectations. The magic, rather than suggesting a lost and mythical world of divine beings, magnifies the scale of the story; its function is much like that of special effects. Much of the magic seems to echo a nineteenth-century vision of European power and the wondering observation of technology; it is similar to Amos Tutuola's transformation of recognizable colonial realities in *The Palm-Wine Drinkard*.

But this vision of the world is not entirely uncritical. If European technology is transmuted into magical powers that the heroes can master, there is surely also a negative image of colonialism and the European presence in the image of forced labor and road building. To be sure, these are presented as tasks that the hero must fulfill, and in this regard they echo the labors of Mwindo with Nyamurairi or those of any fairy-tale hero who wishes to rescue the princess from the ogre's castle. But a text such as *Mvet-Moneblum* clearly evokes the world of colonial servitude, for it details how the labor gang is clothed, housed, and fed before it is sent out to work. These administrative workforce issues clearly suggest colonial procedures and policies.

The not-so-subtle critique of colonialism evident in the performed texts reappears in somewhat different guise in Ndoutoume's written versions. One of his texts tells of a young man of power who is concerned about the evil uses of iron and therefore attempts to eradicate iron from the earth: this necessarily leads him into conflict with the people of Engong, who are the people of iron. The last volume in Ndoutoume's trilogy involves a bridge over the river that separates Oku from Engong; the bridge represents the intrusion of the White Man's world and leads to a showdown debate before the sky-god, which ends in a homiletic indictment of modernization.

In many regards, the mvet tradition is unique in Africa. It is perhaps most readily compared to the medieval romance tradition that flourished around the Mediterranean and beyond. The narrative staple appears to be the traveling couple, but in contrast to the story of the siblings Lianja and Nsongo, the romantic aspect is dominant in the mvet tradition. The genre clearly offers unlimited possibilities for thematic development and thus updates itself freely. It can only be hoped that more examples will be made available.

Royal and Civic Poetry and Possible Additions

The focus in this study on texts that appear to be primarily mythological should not be construed as an indication that historical or dynastic materials are absent in this region. The operative criteria by which materials were selected were public performance in narrative form, and many of the currently documented historical traditions that might be advanced as epic do not meet these criteria—and the collections are admittedly incomplete. The historical traditions of the Luba reported by Jan Vansina, Harold Womersley, and others are congruent with the themes of heroic action and social construction; but de Heusch, writing in 1972, could identify no vernacular versions or transcriptions from the oral tradition in print. And there is no documentation of the performance of a body of narratives by specialists or others. Vansina, reviewing the oral sources of historical tradition in this region, lists corporate groups, clan lineages, ritual priests, and an official called the "keeper of the oral archives"; but he provides no references to performers, poetry, or musical accompaniment.[50] There are, however, collections of the Luba heroic poetry called *kasala*.[51] This poetry is not narrative in nature but allusive and elliptic, and it fits easily with the other Southern African praise-singing traditions.

The kingdom of Rwanda might offer epic. Thanks to the efforts of Alexis Kagame and others (see chapter 1), a wealth of poetic and narrative material relating to the royal court and historical traditions is available. And there is, very clearly identified, the institution of the court poet, or indeed, the "corporation" of poets; but as has been shown, dynastic poetry is essentially nonnarrative. It plays with formalized patterns of allusion and sequence and obeys complex poetic rules. It deserves to be more widely known since it is perhaps the best available illustration of the poetic complexities of an oral courtly tradition. A contrast of prose and poetry is in some ways incorporated into these genres; the *ikyevugu*, for instance—a self-praise poem—incorporates a short prose narrative explication to accompany the allusive references and metaphors of the poem. The contrast carries over into the historical narrative traditions. The editors of the historical narratives, Coupez and Kamanzi, choose to present them as prose, and they describe the performance of Clément Gakaniisha, from whom they recorded their narratives, as follows:

> Unlike the amateur, who will move around and change the tone of his voice, the professional reciter adopts an impassive position and a rapid and monotonous delivery. Should the audience respond with laughter, or express its admiration for a particularly brilliant passage, he will suspend his voice with detachment until silence is restored.[52]

Pending further documentation of the performance aspects of this tradition (something that, unfortunately, seems unlikely at this time), these historical accounts appear to be something other than the epic genre under consideration here.

Nigeria also offers a wealth of historical narratives as well as the *Ozidi Saga:* praises and histories from the many kings and chiefs of Yoruba towns and from other groups. Chukwuma Azuonye is documenting the traditions of the Igbo city of Ohafia with descriptions of performers and their poems, and he considers them to be possibly epic. Two things preclude greater exploration of the Ohafia poems at this time: first, there is no extensive published corpus; and second, the few pieces reproduced by Azuonye are very short. Until more material becomes available in print, little analysis or discussion is possible. It would appear that the tradition is responding to changes in the environment and that the narrative element is gaining importance; but the basis of the poetry remains closely comparable to less narrative genres such as the Yoruba *oriki.*

These royal and civic materials are found in regions adjacent to, or overlapping, those that provide the epic traditions of Central Africa. But one last body of literature should be mentioned here, if only briefly. Swahili, the coastal language of East Africa, has a tradition of epic recitation (the *utenzi*) in which at least one established narrative *(Liyongo Fumo)* is comparable to other African hero narratives.[53] The majority of the stories, however, are translations or adaptations from Arabic epic, which includes heroic and religious figures. The performance, moreover, seems heavily dependent upon manuscript transmission: reciters rely upon memorized texts that are circulated in written form.

Conclusion

This regional survey provides illustrations of a basic character type, perhaps to be considered a configuration of heroes, as a central ingredient of the African epic traditions. The heroes involved are clearly related to mythical culture heroes: they contribute to a self-definition of their cultures, and through their narratives the parameters of the cultures may be constructed. It is difficult to detect history in the epics. Rather, they concentrate on social concerns and entertainment. The epic traditions clearly merge with the world of the folktale and the actions of other typical folkloric characters such as tricksters. In this respect, these traditions seem more popular and folkloric than many of the examples from the Sahel. However, they can be matched with one broad—and again, multi-ethnic—body of stories from the Sahel, the literature of the hunters.

HUNTERS' TRADITIONS AND EPICS

HUNTERS ARE UBIQUITOUS in African folklore and culture. Whether they appear as mythical ancestors, providers of food, slayers of monstrous beasts, popular heroes standing against a corrupt aristocracy, or as modern adventurers and explorers, images of hunters and echoes of their practices and beliefs take various forms. The cultural importance of the hunter derives from the historical economic importance of hunting as a food source, as a supplement or substitute for irregular agricultural yields. It also acknowledges the hunter's role in exploring new territories that may be colonized as communities grow or as their soils deteriorate.

The Khoi-San people of Southern Africa are probably the best-known African hunters, but many other groups maintained a hunting lifestyle. The BaNyanga and the Mongo in Central Africa were essentially foragers, living in close association with pygmy groups that were considered specialists at hunting. In West Africa a variety of groups depended on a nonagricultural food supply until very recent times: the Nemadi of Mauritania, who lived as nomads with hunting dogs;[1] and the Sorko of the Niger river area, who combined fishing with hunting and who are still considered water-masters by their neighbors. The growth of sedentarized populations has now made a hunting lifestyle virtually impossible.

Throughout the more populous regions of West Africa, hunters are often organized in associations.[2] The purposes of the associations vary. The training of new hunters clearly has been one important task, and associations may have had regulatory functions as well, for instance, in helping to avoid the depletion of game. Another important task would have been to organize the hunting of large and dangerous animals such as elephants. Equally important in the modern era are the mystical aspects of hunting: hunters deal in death, and the forces released in the course of their dangerous activities must be channeled and controlled. Hunters work outside settled and ordered human communities, in the realm of nature where chaos and disruption are constant threats. The effects of these destructive forces must be averted for the community.

In modern times, hunting itself has lost almost all its economic importance, but the social dimensions of hunters' associations have become more central. The major organized events now seem to be the funerals of hunters at which the dirges and laments sung by the master singers are not only expressions of emotion but also apotropaic utterances meant to dispel the destructive energies that accumulated in the course of the deceased hunter's career and that have been released by his death.

Within the sphere of the verbal arts, a close and organic relationship links the hunters' prayers and addresses to game with the praise names or *devises* that capture the essence of an entity, from the lineage to its individual members to animals and things (see chapter 1). Some hunters' groups in West Africa practice the singing of narratives, and these are termed hunters' epics. Some scholars, particularly in Mande studies, are inclined to derive the entire epic tradition from hunters' songs. Such a view tacitly rejects the notion that epic-singing is an aristocratic entertainment that has filtered through society, or that two socially distinct traditions may be interacting. The explicit support for this view stems from the omnipresence of hunters' motifs in the epic of Sunjata, which in the Manden is considered the most prestigious of epics. Sunjata is identified as a hunter through his praise names ("Simbong"), his food-gathering activities, and the utterances of others who call him a hunter, although in insult.

A further element underlying this assumption is the acceptance among historians of the notion that hunters' associations served as organizational nuclei for the formation of states in the region. Examples would include Sunjata (see chapter 5) and Biton Koulibaly of Segou (see chapter 6). Hunters constitute organized groups of armed men and thus a potential military unit. If the kings were hunter-leaders, it stands to reason that they brought hunting traditions into the court with them; kings may have relied upon the mystique of the hunter for legitimation.[3]

Such a view, however, focuses on the Manden and tends to disregard the wider evidence. A broad set of apparently related narratives is found among specialized hunting groups from the Sorko of the Niger bend through the Manden and into the Gambia, and on to the Subalbe fishermen of the Senegal River. Many of these narratives are also reported as folktales among neighboring peoples, and the inclusion of this data would enlarge the region to all of West Africa. The evidence for epic performance, however, varies considerably from group to group, and epics are not found throughout this wider region. It seems likely that the primary genre of hunters' poetry is the dirge or lament, which in some areas and under some conditions develops into narrative song or epic.

The hunters' epics presented in this chapter share with the epics of Central

Africa a dissociation from political history. The narratives may move from folktale to epic and back (as with "Siramori," below), but they do not involve lineage traditions or notions of political history. Kings may appear in the stories, but only as stock figures. The material is thus seemingly more popular in origin and focus. A second feature that links these first two groups, in contrast to the historical traditions, is the nonhereditary status of the performer. The Mande hunters' bard need not be a griot by birth. One of the most famous, Seydou Camara, was a blacksmith, and others appear to be Fula in origin. Finally, the style of performance serves as a potential bond. A hunter's bard has accompanists and moves about somewhat more during his delivery, sometimes leading dances.[4]

This chapter introduces the major hunting groups and their principal narratives. Where a story recurs across ethnic or linguistic lines, a representative example is selected for reference. Hunters' traditions, then, will be presented as lore that cuts across most social divisions in the service of a greater craft-oriented unity. This notion is, in fact, an essential element of the ideology of the hunters' associations in the Manden and parallels the category of "occupational" or "corporatist" epics presented by Lilyan Kesteloot and Bassirou Dieng.

Peoples of the Niger: Sorko, Bozo, Gow, and Others

Along the Niger River, and particularly in the region of the inland delta lying between Djenne and Timbuctoo, groups devoted exclusively to fishing and hunting have survived as distinct entities through various changes of rule. Their distinctiveness derives principally from their way of life and from the identification made by other groups rather than from linguistic or other criteria. Ethnic identities are particularly slippery in this riverine region. While often considered to be of Soninke origin and granted a certain respect as the oldest inhabitants of the region, the groups have adopted the dominant local language, and so the common lifestyle is found along the river in graduated zones of Bamana speakers (the Bozo, found around Djenne) and Songhay speakers (the Sorko). The term *Gow* used in 1912 by A. Dupuis-Yakouba as the name of one "ethnic" group appears in modern usage to designate a profession and even ritual function. The French ethnographer Jean-Marie Gibbal refers to the officiating priest of spirit cults as *gow*, without ethnic reference.[5] This need not represent a transformation of the hunter's function; rather, it might suggest a refinement of interpretation and at most a different aspect of the same cultural complex. Among the Bamana and Malinke, the hunter, master of natural forces, is also the master of occult forces and so is esteemed a diviner or healer.

The collection of hunters' narratives dates back to the colonial era, beginning about 1900, and there is also relatively modern material.[6] The stories share a cosmography involving the relations of humans and spirits, a culture hero (Faran Maka, Moussa Gname, Fanta Maa) who is the offspring of a human woman and a spirit, and an essentially mythical world. The Songhay Faran Maka appears to be the most widely known figure, reported early by Dupuis-Yakouba in a cycle of stories involving conflicts with spirits. Later accounts concentrate on his conflict with a rival, Fono. In the earliest account, Faran Maka is born to battle a gigantic woman and her equally gigantic sons, who have killed his father.[7] Leo Frobenius tells of a male giant, Auadia, who is forced to leave Mecca and settles along the Niger, where he fathers two sons, Fara Maka [sic] and Fono.[8] The principal narrative associated with Fara Maka deals with the conflict between them.

Fara Maka and Fono

Fono wished to marry Nana Miriam, the daughter of Fara Maka; Fara Maka refused to give her away because she knew all the secrets of his hunting magic. After she swore never to reveal those secrets, he finally relented. Thereafter he would go fishing with his son-in-law; he was always successful, while Fono always returned home empty-handed. Nana Miriam eventually went to a Muslim holy man and asked to whom she owed a greater duty, her father or her husband. The holy man answered that the bond with her husband was stronger, and so she revealed to Fono enough magic that on his next expedition with Fara Maka, Fono was the successful hunter. Fara Maka realized his daughter had revealed his secrets and rushed back ahead of Fono; he killed his daughter and left a slave-girl to impersonate her. But Fono quickly discovered the imposture. The next day, he and Fara Maka went out in their boats to fight a duel; they unleashed all their magical powers. Finally, Fono ran away; his flight involved transformations into a variety of things, and Fara Maka followed him through all of them. Fono was finally transformed into a monkey, following Fara Maka as he traveled over the waters. Neither returned alive from this pursuit, although accounts differ as to which died first.[9]

The context into which the struggle fits may vary. The ethnographer Jean Rouch and an administrator and linguist, A. Prost, have both published variants in which Fono is first inspired to seek out Faran Maka by the taunts of a wife; on his travels he incurs the enmity of a serpent because he steals its eggs, and he later causes Faran Maka to kill a sacred hippopotamus that is the source of Faran Maka's power.[10] Rouch also offers a number of variants in which Faran Maka is a member of the pantheon of spirits that rule Songhay cosmology: Faran Maka is the sixth son of the water goddess Harikoy[11] as well as the ancestral culture hero of the Sorko fishermen.

In this regard, Faran Maka's function overlaps with that of Moussa Gname, who is the principal character of Dupuis-Yakouba's narratives of the Gow hunters; and the two bodies of narratives share concerns with social organization and structure at the expense of detailed hunting or fishing lore. The conflict of Fono and Faran Maka, for instance, may be couched in terms of rivalry of skills, but it is ultimately sparked and brought to its climax by questions involving men and women. The tensions derived from shifting social relations (daughter/wife, and in one case, at least, sister and wife, when the wife who leads Fono to challenge Faran Maka describes Faran Maka as her brother) and the changes of loyalty seem a stronger theme in the narrative than the actual venue of the conflict.

The same ambiguities and tensions are expressed in the Gow narratives of Dupuis-Yakouba and, indeed, throughout much of the hunting corpus. Moussa Gname, the Gow culture hero, has a daughter or wife or sister (the relations vary through the stories) named Meynsata who is his rival or pupil in occult power; the story of their relations thus becomes in some sense a source of accepted gender relations, as the following narrative shows.

Moussa and the Hira

A beast called a hira was ravaging the bush. Various leaders of the Gow went to hunt it, but they were all defeated. Moussa Gname refused to take part in this effort.

The Gow women, led by Meynsata, dressed up as men and went to hunt the hira, leaving the men in the village spinning. But as soon as they saw the hira they were afraid and wet their pants and ran away. Meynsata was left alone, and she fought the hira. Each threw the other.

The Gow women returned to the village and reported that Meynsata had been killed. Moussa, who had asked to marry her, then armed himself and went out. He overthrew the hira, and then, although Meynsata asked him not to kill the beast, he slashed its throat so hard his blade sank into the ground and he could not pull it free. She then transformed the hira into an elephant and broke its neck. He answered with another transformation, and they competed in magics for a time. Moussa placed a chain about Meynsata's neck; she removed it with a spell. Finally, he used a slender chain. None of her mother's spells worked on that one. He shook her; all her clothes fell off. She then apologized to him and dressed, and the two of them went back to the village. They encountered a herd of elephants on the way and killed all but one, which they rode back. When they got to the village, there was some question about who had killed the hira, but Meynsata confirmed that it was Moussa.[12]

Here, as in the other stories where she appears, Meynsata is a far stronger figure than Nana Miriam, daughter of Fara Makan, and might be compared with Nsongo, sister to Lianja. As a spouse, however, she will be subordinated to her husband as a consequence of their magical conflict. The relationship is not necessarily one of dominance, however; it also involves a division of labor between the husband and the wife. This theme is echoed through many of the Maninka hunters' tales, as will be seen below; the hunter frequently requires his wife's assistance to overcome the occult power of some wild foe.

The early narratives collected by Dupuis-Yakouba in *Les Gow* form a loose cycle, moving from the birth of Moussa Gname, child of a jinn and a human, to an image of the Gow as specialized hunters hired by the city of Djenne to rid them of a monstrous hyena. Four of the eight stories deal with the defeat of a monstrous animal, and this familiar pattern is encountered widely in the region. Some of the stories echo well-established mythic patterns: "Kelikelimabe et Kelimabe" recalls the Egyptian folktale/myth of "Anupis and Bata" (also known as the "Two Brothers") with its story of a false accusation of rape and a brother's subsequent flight. "Sanu-Mandigne et Djegere Mandigne" tells of two brothers in conflict over their inheritance and juxtaposes the worlds of the bush and of the dead.

These old stories have been updated with the epic of Fanta Maa, a culture hero of the Bamana-speaking Bozo. Shekh Tijaan Hayidara has edited and published two bilingual accounts of this legend. Like Moussa Gname and Fara Makan, Fanta Maa is the offspring of a human-jinn union. The first of the two accounts, by Myeru Ba, combines two stories: first, the "Siramori" pattern discussed below, in which the animals of the bush send one of their number to seduce the hunter; and second, a basic monster-slayer pattern in which Fanta Maa rids the land of an oppressive tyrant (or sorcerer), who takes the shape of a crocodile in order to devour people, especially young brides. The second account gives only the story of the crocodile.

Frobenius, following his account of the story of Fara Maka, also provides a number of narratives that he attributes to the Bozo and the Sorko. These include stories of the origin of Djenne and of a variety of hero figures (Paemuru, Mussenjeni, Sallo, and others) who are descended from Faran or Fono and who seem to form a bridge to other traditions: Paemuru, for instance, is the son of a king of Mali named Konko Musa, and in many regards his childhood echoes that of Sunjata (he uproots trees and breaks the bones of small children).[13] Another tale gives a lengthy account of the relations between the Sorko and the Tommo, who are now identified as the Dogon; yet another poignantly tells of a woman who learned to fly and to sing but was eventually brought down by a male Bozo singer who could not stand the competition.[14] These stories and legends need to be explored and perhaps confirmed by modern fieldwork. But at the very least, Frobenius has attempted to convey a sense of the cultural background underlying his translations/retellings in German. Even as they stand, without modern counterparts, they deserve to be more widely known and used.

Mande Hunters' Traditions

The hunters' associations of the Manden are among the most thoroughly and most recently studied of any such group, with a rich corpus of published texts.[15] The geographic area involved runs from the north of the Côte d'Ivoire through Mali and Guinea into the Gambia; and while there are local dialectal differences (Dyula, Maninka, Bamana, Mandinka), there is also a recognized stratum of continuity. All belong to the Manden.

It is within the Manden that hunters' associations seem to have acquired the greatest popular appreciation. In part, the hunters' tradition is seen as a core element of Mande culture, enduring through time and political or religious change. Membership in the association thus becomes an affirmation of Mande identity in a time of cultural flux and discontinuity. Representations of Sunjata, Biton Koulibaly, Dama Ngille, and other founding fathers of the region as hunters reinforce this sense of identity. The occult lore of the hunter is seen as an indigenous form of knowledge, distinct from the imported traditions of Islam and the West[16] (although it is evident that the epics contain at least a veneer of Islamic piety). As a weapons-bearing activity, hunting links the modern Malinke with a lost aristocratic tradition of warfare and becomes a vehicle for asserting masculine prestige. Finally, and to some extent undercutting some of the previous notions, there is the democratic structure of the hunters' associations. In a culture divided by social ranking and genealogical alliances, the hunters' associations are open to all regardless of rank; the hunter's status is established by seniority within the association and not by outside factors.

Thus, the association unifies society by transecting the lines of authority that divide it. A less well recognized feature of this openness is that it also serves as a mechanism for ethnic integration. The hunters' verbal art accords a place to the Fula and other groups within the polity (one of the best-known modern hunters' singers, Bala Jimbe Diakhite, has a Fula patronym). Within Mande historical studies, it is assumed that hunters' associations formed or contributed to the nucleus of the various states that have arisen; this idea, first propounded by the Malian scholar Youssouf Cissé in 1964, has been generally accepted, and so hunters' associations have become part of the Mande "national" tradition. But the function of ethnic integration also explains the historical importance of the associations. The evidence from the narratives—widely shared among the peoples of the region—supports the latter emphasis. It is on the basis of this assumption that Mande hunters' traditions are presented here in juxtaposition to those of other hunters' groups rather than with the Mande historical traditions.

The associations do not recognize external status markers, and so the performers of songs are not jeliw by birth;[17] rather, they have become singers by avocation and practice, stepping outside what might be their normal social roles. The best-documented artist is probably the late Seydou Camara, who served as informant and singer for Charles Bird and a generation of Indiana University fieldworkers; he left one of the largest individual repertoires of pieces available in a variety of published sources (a larger amount of unpublished material remains in the hands of collectors). Camara was by birth a *numu*, a blacksmith; he served with the French armed forces and then with the civil guard until 1950, when his health broke down while he was stationed in Timbuctoo.[18] He then became a hunters' bard, a gifted performer on the large harp-lute resembling a kora; he also developed a considerable reputation for occult expertise and power. Some of this may have been due to the association of blacksmiths with the secret Komo initiation society, which is reflected in his songs.[19] He died in 1983.

Performances are centered on hunters' ceremonies and on the funerals of noted hunters.[20] Laments are thus a staple element of the singer's repertoire and carry over into the epic narration, where the story is frequently interrupted with musical and lyric interludes that recall the fame of now-deceased hunters. Performances are a group activity involving an ensemble: the master singer, the *ngara*, plays the hunters' *ngoni* (the large harp-lute), accompanied by apprentices serving as *naamu*-sayers or respondents, who also play the *nyaringa* (a metal rasp, which also appears in the epic of Sunjata).[21] When the element of ritual costume is added to the large roster of performers (Seydou Camara, for instance, is portrayed in photographs as bedecked with amulets and charms),[22] the contrast between this performance mode and that of the historical traditions is striking, and so is the parallel with that of Central African traditions.

There is a sizeable corpus of transcribed Mande hunters' epics that vary both in length and in complexity of plot and performance style. Charles Bird and his students have identified three modes of delivery within a performance: narrative, song, and praise proverb. The shifts between modes serve to intensify emotions and respond to audience interest. The praise proverb mode permits a digressive commentary, often on social and self-reflexive concerns about the situation of the hunter. The commentary also creates a more relaxed rapport with the audience than is found, for instance, in the epic of Sunjata. The digressions may correspond to the stock of genealogical praises that are so essential to the historical epics. No study so far has collected and analyzed the praise lines used by different performers. Some stock phrases do seem to recur (e.g., "Look to the salt for the flavor of the sauce," or the frequent formula, "X and Y are not the same," or apostrophes such as "Kunbacibaa ni dabafarabagha" [Breaker of big heads, breaker of big mouths]),[23] and they include, curiously, the listing of the four Fula clans of the Manden, "Sidibe ni Sangare, Diallo ni Diakite."

Despite the relatively large number of transcribed texts available, it seems fair to ask how essential the narrative may be to the hunters' tradition. At a conference in 1992, the Malian scholar Karim Traore described his frustration after he had followed Bala Jimbe, the greatest living hunters' singer, on a two-week tour. Traore found that not once did he get a complete story in the course of an evening's performance.[24] This may have been intentional on the performer's part; still, it seems equally likely that in an ordinary evening, the story line is subordinate to other dimensions of the performance such as the solidarity-building digressions of the performer and, of course, the songs and dancing. Dosseh Coulibaly, who did record an extensive, if not absolutely complete, performance by Bala Jimbe, reports that the singer claims to have a repertoire covering forty-five master hunters, but so far no comparative enumeration has been made of the stories.

The patron divinities of the Mande hunters' associations are Sanin and Kontron (spelling may vary). Cissé reports a version of the story in which the virgin Sanin gives birth to Kontron, who then magically becomes the father of men after a sibling/spouse is born from his leg.[25] Another version reported by a student in Dakar, Fodé Moussa Balla Sidibe, says that Sanin and Kontron were married and that Sanin had never seen her husband by day. When she looked on him and saw that he was one-eyed, he vanished into an anthill. She also later disappeared, and so they have become the tutelary deities of hunters.[26] Seydou Camara tells a tale in which a hunter, Sunjata's brother Manding Bokari, marries an antelope who has taken the form of a woman. Their children's names include a Sanin and a Kontron.[27] These names are included in lists of the *boliw* (objects or beings of magical power) that are essential parts of the hunter's equipment. The variation and flexibility in the attribution of the patron deities suggest that hunters' lore is not fixed across regions but depends very much on the formulations of the individual informant or performer.

A preliminary analysis of the available narratives indicates that the actual corpus of story types may be relatively limited, although they may include extensive variation on a range of themes, such as the defeat of great monsters, as in the Gow narratives. Much of the action involves the domestic scene, perhaps reflecting the need for balance between the inner and outer communities, or a change in venue and audience from gatherings composed exclusively of hunters to ones with broader demographic representation.

The dividing line between the matter of hunters' epic and folktale is virtually nonexistent. Stories that are sung may be told elsewhere and in other forms. For instance, the narrative pattern in the episode of "The Buffalo-Woman of Du," from the epic of Sunjata,[28] shades in hunters' epics into a number of variants; here the "monster" is an alienated member of the human community whose secret is revealed after the protagonist has engaged in altruistic behavior, thus remedying whatever social violation triggered the initial disruption.[29]

Many of the stories do posit a greater opposition between the spheres of the human community and the natural world. One of the most widespread, found as a folktale, an epic, and as part of a ritual narration, and which does not involve an initial breach of order within the human world, tells how the animals respond to an overly successful hunter. In the Manden, this story frequently goes under the title "Siramori."

Siramori

Siramori was a hunter, a prodigious hunter. He was so successful that he brought home a full game bag every day, and after some time his success worried the animals of the forest. They saw that if he was not stopped, they would all be killed, and so they thought of a means to save themselves. They decided that one of their number should go to Siramori, disguised as a woman, and learn the secrets of his power. A number of candidates were proposed. [Frequently, the one selected is a buffalo, although an antelope may also figure. The animals laugh when the hyena or the warthog volunteers.]

Transformed into an extraordinarily beautiful woman, the chosen animal goes into town, refusing all advances until she meets with Siramori. He is entranced and invites her home, and there they spend their time in dalliance. At a moment of suitable intimacy, the animal-woman asks him the secrets of his power, and he begins to tell her. His mother, his sister, sometimes a daughter or even a co-wife all warn him not to reveal his secrets to a "one-night woman," but he does not listen: he begins to tell her how he can transform himself into a lizard, a stump, a whirlwind. . . . But the sequence is interrupted.

The next day, Siramori accompanies the woman back to her home. They leave town and go into the bush, further and further. Siramori does not have his weapons because the woman has laughed at him, saying he would not need them. Finally, they come to the place where the animals have laid their trap. The animals attack Siramori, and he escapes by transforming himself through the series of forms he had begun to reveal the night before. He escapes because he had not completed the list and the animals cannot identify the last form he has taken.[30]

In some versions of the story, Siramori's power comes from his hunting dogs, and the animal-woman tricks him into leaving them behind (or even killing them) when they go into the bush; the dogs are released (or, if dead, revived) by the suspicious female relative.[31] And sometimes the hunter then retaliates by leading a band of apprentices to the city of the animals during the night and massacring them.[32] This action then establishes the balance of nature, in which men may kill animals but animals succeed only by exception in killing men.

Wide distribution as a folktale is not the only notable feature of this story; it is found (or echoed) in other significant contexts. It is part of the initiatory narrative of the "Myth of the Black Bagre," collected in 1951 by Jack Goody among the Lo-Dagaa of northern Ghana. It appears, somewhat displaced and transformed, in the epic of Sunjata in the motif of seduction and the revealing of secrets. When Sunjata's sister Kulunkan goes to Sumanguru to learn the secret of his power, she arouses the suspicions of Sumanguru's mother. The mother warns her son not to trust a "one-night woman," but he disregards her advice. In some versions the secret revealed by the lustful king is that of his transformations, as with the hunter. This unusual configuration would make Sumanguru the hero/

hunter and would place Sunjata among the chaotic forces of nature; it represents a challenging inversion of their expected roles.

The story does not necessarily equate sexual femininity with wild nature, although the perspective is clearly androcentric. The husband-wife relations portrayed in hunters' epics cover a spectrum of possibilities.[33] In many of them the wife is an active helper. In at least one story, a wife saves her husband's life. Seydou Camara's rich version goes by the title "Famori."

Famori

At the start of his career as a hunter, Famori strikes a bargain with a jinn who is served by a crocodile: seven years of success in exchange for his life. And so Famori becomes an extraordinarily successful hunter, supplying the village with so much meat that they export their jerky; eventually he marries four wives. But he neglects the sacrifices that were due to the jinn.

After a time the jinn and the crocodile prepare magic to remind Famori of his obligations. They send a gazelle into town; Famori kills it. Another animal is sent. Famori decides to stop hunting and take up some other livelihood.

Famori becomes a merchant and loads a vast number of donkeys with dried meat, which he trades in the south for kola nuts. But all the kola nuts have worms or are spoiled. Famori becomes a farmer and clears his fields; the fields are planted, the rains fall, and all looks very promising. But nothing grows: the jinn has exacted its payment. Famori becomes a beekeeper, but the jinn places fish in his hives.

Finally, Famori is about to bed his voluptuous youngest wife when the jinn turns him into an even more voluptuous woman. Famori determines to pay the jinn its due. He goes off the next day, followed in secret by one of the other wives, who is in the role of the "despised wife." As the crocodile is about to kill him, Nuntenen, the despised wife, shoots it with Famori's gun. The hunter then trades clothing with her and marches into town singing her praises.[34]

The story of Kambili also ends with praises sung to the wife in two versions. But here the wife's role is somewhat more ambiguous. The man-beast who has terrorized the town turns out to be her rejected suitor, and she helps her husband learn the secrets of the beast's power by seducing him, although she does not carry the seduction all the way. This "espionage-by-femme-fatale" motif is widespread in the Mande traditions. The role of Sunjata's sister in discovering the secrets of Sumanguru has already been mentioned, and the motif also occurs as a staple device in the cycle of Segou, most particularly in the more entertainment-oriented pieces (see chapters 5 and 6).

So far, the stories that have been examined end happily for the hunter; but not all do so. Ndugace Samake, for instance, provides a short, grim piece in which a jackal, a vulture, and a bush-pig argue over the corpse of a hunter—each disclaiming interest in order to discourage the others, and each racing for the fresh meat as soon as the others turn their backs (the pig wins).[35] But one of the most tragic stories returns again to the sphere of marital relations.

Maghan Jan

Maghan Jan was a Fula who never spoke Fula, and he was a hunter. One day, an antelope changed into a woman and came to town. She and Maghan Jan loved each other and married. They had several children. But she had warned him early on that he should never threaten her with fire. One day, in a fit of blind anger, he did so: she left him and returned to the bush. [In another version, she leaves after gossip in the town exposes the secret of her origin.]

Maghan Jan was crazed and hunted through the bush. He caught and killed an antelope; he brought it home, but his children refused to eat the meat, knowing it to be their mother. Maghan Jan did eat, and died.

The version told by Seydou Camara complicates this story somewhat by making the hunter Manding Bokari, Sunjata's younger brother, and naming the children Sanin, Kontron, and Simbong. The first two names are those of the hunters' divinities, and the third is a hunter's honorific title (and a form of whistle) that occurs frequently in the epic of Sunjata. These added possibilities open up two perspectives on the story. The "Maghan Jan" version plays on identities affirmed and denied since the hunter himself denies his own genealogy by refusing to speak Fula, his mother tongue. The "Manding Bokari" version makes the story an aetiological myth with an almost allegorical structure in which hunters stem from the union of the human and animal worlds and must try to reconcile the conflicting imperatives of both.

While the corpus of Mande hunters' epics available for study is substantial, it is still not large enough for solid generalizations about themes, trends, individual particularities (the stamp of Seydou Camara, for instance, marks much of the material available in English), and performance variation. Still, this description of selected plot lines does show an emphasis on the social dimension of the hunter's experience—the human angle, rather than the world of tracking and killing. There is very little real hunting (as documented by ethnographic observation and historical records) in the epics. They appear, instead, to be vehicles for the exploration of cultural and social identities.

A slight exception might be made for the two texts from the Gambia, published by Gordon Innes and Bakari Sidibe. The Gambia is the western edge of the Mande world and participates strongly in the historical epic tradition as well (see chapter 8). The plots of these two texts clearly belong to the hunters' corpus; the second text, "Mamadou and the Great Beast," is a variant of the "Famori" pattern discussed above. The first, "Mambi and the Crocodile," might qualify as a hunters' version of the "Buffalo-Woman" episode from Sunjata (mentioned above) and also has parallels in the Gow and Sorko narratives of Dupuis-Yakouba and Frobenius. It is a nicely developed version of the story, and worth retelling.

Mambi and the Crocodile

A huge crocodile lived in the river and terrorized the region, eating people. It had a preference for young brides-to-be. A korte-master [korte is a traditional poison/harmful magic] tried to kill it, and then a Fula holy man from the Senegal River, but they failed: after a time, the crocodile reappeared to eat a bride. A young man, Booto, crossed the river to negotiate a marriage with his uncle; he was assisted by village figures such as Great Liar and Great Gossip. The uncle was reluctant to send his daughter over the water, exposing her to the crocodile, but Booto commissioned an escort of 1,444 hunters to cross the river and fetch the bride. The crocodile attacked, and despite the escort of hunters, the bride was lost. Wandering in grief, Booto encountered an old woman; wordlessly, he gathered her firewood and carried it to her house. She thanked him and asked his problem; he told her of his lost bride and the crocodile. She told him that only the hunter Mambi could settle the problem of the crocodile. So Booto went to Mambi and laid the problem before him.

Mambi performed a divination using roots and learned that an old woman was the solution to the problem. He prepared kola nuts and took them to her village; she was asleep, and he had to force himself on her in the rudest manner (he urinated on her while she slept) before she would talk to him. But after receiving gifts of snuff and other delicacies, she was mollified and eventually revealed her secret: she was the crocodile. Mambi then stalked the crocodile; he found the spot where it normally came to land and lay in wait, transforming himself successively into an anthill, a log, tall grass, and a vulture; but each time, the crocodile (who now regretted having revealed her secret) recognized him and escaped his trap. Finally he set a trap using the carcass of an antelope on the far side of the river, and there the old woman-crocodile was caught and killed.

Bakari Camara, the performer of this detailed narration, was an older and experienced hunters' bard at the time of the recording; he had taken to traveling extensively on tour in an adjustment to the new market conditions for his art. His story offers a wealth of detail for examination and analysis, from problematic gender relations (why does a grandmother prey on young brides?); to the humorous rendition of the marriage negotiations involving the parodic figures of Great Liar, Great Talker, and Great Gossip; and finally to the very personal drama of Mambi and the crocodile, which is marked by their intense awareness of each other. Mambi the hunter is set up as a clearly redemptive figure; he is praised as one who parted from his teacher on good terms, without dispute, unlike other apprentices or hunters (such as the 1,444 who fail to preserve Booto's bride but instead fill the canoes with urine) who have apparently violated this pact. Indeed, at one significant moment, Mambi compares his conduct with that of a dutiful wife:

I, Mambi Siriyang, never stole from my teacher,
I never lied to my teacher,
I fetched my teacher's water,
I filled his water pot,
I fetched water,
I filled the water pot in the women's quarters,
I gathered firewood for my teacher,
I was married to my teacher like a wedded wife.
I swear by God,
I swear by my mother, my gun will not fail against you, bastard Limbankuru
   crocodile.[36]

Mambi at this point has come between the crocodile, who is drawn to the antelope carcass he planted, and the crocodile's escape route in the water. The oath is intended to insure that his rifle will fire (as those of the 1,444 hunters did not).

The question is not entirely idle since the locally made flintlocks, the hunter's weapon of traditional choice, are not completely reliable. They may misfire; they may explode (as happened to the Dogon hunter Ogotemmeli). The logic of the oath asserts that Mambi's proven respect for social order should lead to the desired outcome; the same logic is evident in the epic of Sunjata at different points, for instance, when Sunjata's mother Sogolon swears an oath that her son may rise to his feet, or that he may become king of Mali.

A significant difference between heroes such as Mambi and Sunjata (although the latter is seen as a hunter) lies in their relations to political power and authority. Where Sunjata, although in many regards an exemplar, is associated with the claims to legitimacy of established clans and lineages, Mambi represents a moral order independent of actual lineage-based authority and thus may appeal to a wider audience, especially in a time of social transformation. From this perspective, the hunters' traditions in the Manden can be seen as an emergent medium for the exploration of social dynamics. It seems relevant that the "hero" of a recent Malian film such as *Guimba le tyran* is a hunter. But this function need not be a recent development. In fact, it is a rather attractive notion to suggest that Mande society has undergone numerous transformations over the centuries and that this mechanism has served to buffer the changes.

The Subalbe of the Senegal River

Among the Tukolor or Haal-Pulaaren (speakers of Pulaar/Fula) along the Senegal River, there is also an epic tradition associated with a specialized group of fishermen, the Subalbe (sing., *cuballo*), who correspond in a sense to the Sorko discussed above. This region, the Futa Tooro, is rich in historical epic traditions (see chapter 7). Other professional status groups also offer traditions of verbal art; weavers *(mabuube)*, for instance, have an extensive song repertoire.[37]

The Subalbe are somewhat distinct from the other status groups of the area. They are considered free, although professionally specialized.[38] The *pekane*, or epic songs, appear to be associated with the festival of the crocodile and may be a relatively recent development; the collector Amadou Abel Sy provides a chain of transmission for the masters of the genre (i.e., a list of teachers) that may not go very far back in time.[39] His two published pieces are relatively short (367 and 221 lines) but complete stories. While many of the elements come from the same worldview as other hunters' stories (or indeed, regional folklore), the tone of these pieces seems slightly dark.

The first story, "Segou-Bali," tells of a fisherman who had postponed marriage at his mother's request until he found himself working the fields with the sons of his own age-mates; he then married, but his wife demanded that he kill a powerful water spirit to compensate for the low (family-rate) dowry involved in the marriage. He does so at the cost of his life. The second, "Balla Dierel," tells of a "dry-lander" (someone who farms the lands beyond the riverbanks), who courted a woman cuballo. She helps him catch fish and perform properly, thus displacing his rivals until finally he attempts something too great and is washed up, naked and humiliated, on the riverbank. He abandons his pretensions to marrying a fisher-woman.

Conclusion

This cursory description of hunters' traditions collects comparable and related materials and presents them both for their own sake (the cultural complexity and wealth underlying these traditions is tremendous) and for their value in enhancing an appreciation of the other forms of epic tradition in the region. The question of the relationship between hunters' epics and political epics is important. Kesteloot and Dieng formulate the distinction in terms of royal as opposed to *corporatiste* epics (occupational epics? epics of specialized groups?); they view each as the preserve of an exclusive group.[40] Bird, John W. Johnson, and others would seem to view the hunters' traditions as more of a popular, folkloric form springing from the cultural dynamics of the people and thus (implicitly) as more "authentic" than the elitist royal traditions.

Judging by the exoteric aspects of the texts that have been examined, the Mande hunters' traditions reflect a greater concern for the social aspects of everyday life. Virtually every story turns on questions of domestic relations among co-wives, or on a husband's relations with a single wife. It is an interesting feature of the hunters' traditions that the gender roles appear to offer greater scope for gynocracy, or at least a greater balance between the genders: the frequency with which the male is rescued by the female (whether or not he returns to town in her clothes, as in "Famori" and "Kambili") and the importance of the woman's role suggest that this theme is somehow a central concern of the genre, beyond the technicalities of stalking game or other such hunting minutiae. Whether this focus represents the residuum of older cultural patterns (as suggested by an examination of the Gow material),[41] or whether it reflects the modern evolution of the form (the conclusion reached by viewing the hunters' epics as the dynamic products of contemporary communities) is a fascinating, but so far unanswerable, question.

In comparison with the more historically based materials to be examined later, the hunters' stories do appear to grow out of folktale types and motifs, and they respect the sort of narrative structuring that inspires systematizers such as Vladimir Propp and other devotees of morphology. But the caution gained from Karim Traore's experience should be recalled here: the story line is clearly not the central dimension of the performance in hunters' epics.

TRADITIONS OF THE SONINKE

THE SONINKE EMPIRE of Ghana is the first sub-Saharan state for which there are reliable contemporary records in the form of Arabic writings from Morocco and other parts of North Africa from the ninth century on.[1] But while these records reveal a functioning political state that regulated one end of the trans-Saharan trade in gold and other commodities, they are isolated beams of light in the dark. They leave areas of blindness: the origin of the state, its internal history and organization, and its relations with its southern neighbors. Archeology supplements the record, but much remains to be done.

Some writers have made imaginative attempts to relate known or inferred elements of African history to classical or biblical sources. The reports of Herodotus and the wanderings of the lost tribes of Israel are adduced to fill in the historical blanks. Such attempts are, and should be, suspect. Our relative ignorance of West African history prior to the most recent millenium may be difficult to accept, but it should be seen as a challenge to be met. It should not lead to acceptance of spurious and specious connections.[2] The durable solution is careful research.

Soninke history offers a number of open questions. The equation of the past empire of Ghana, centered on the site of Koumbi-Saleh (in present-day Mauritania), with the Soninke Wagadu of oral tradition is an assumption that seems confirmed by all available evidence.[3] Less certain are the early days and the foundation of the kingdom. Was trans-Saharan trade the catalyst, or were more local forces involved? The growing archaeological evidence suggests internal dynamics rather than foreign influences,[4] but certainly gold contributed to the power and the abiding image of the state. The causes of the decline of Ghana are a topic of current scholarly debate. The longstanding assumption that conflicts with the Almoravids, or even a conquest, destroyed the empire has been strongly challenged.[5] Local tradition recognizes a dispersal of the Soninke southwards to better-watered regions such as the Niger River valley and the Guidimakha of Mauritania. Concentrations of Soninke speakers are now found across the Sahel, from the Guidimakha and Gadiaga areas along the upper Senegal River into Mali, in the region of Nioro du Sahel, and then along the Niger River into the Republic of Niger. An isolated community exists in Borgu, in northern Benin. The distribution of Soninke speakers supports the hypothesis of a period of unity in the north followed by fragmentation and southerly migration. The cause of such a movement was far more probably the changes in the Saharan climate than particular political conditions.

Soninke is part of the Mande language family (the "northern Mande"), and while Soninke is not intelligible to a Bamana or Maninka speaker, there is a recognized similarity and kinship among the groups. Throughout much of their territory, which seems to circle the Manden, the Soninke are recognized as "senior" inhabitants, although they may not be politically dominant. There is some evidence that their cultural patterns influenced their successors. Some of the praise names of the Sunjata tradition may be of Soninke origin, and the language is used as well in Songhay praise songs.[6] In local historiography, the Soninke come first (after the jinns), and are succeeded by the states of Mali, Segou, and the Islamic rule of the Tukolor in the nineteenth century. In the Gambia, partly as a consequence of nineteenth-century wars, the term *Soninke* came to be used as a general reference for non-Muslim unbelievers, although in fact there is a significant Soninke presence as a southward extension of the Guidimakha and Gadiaga groups.

This chapter will consider a selection of Soninke historical traditions—those that are best known and seem to have exercised most influence in the region. Several of these narratives incorporate elements from biblical tradition. The vehicle was certainly popular Islamic accounts, the genre of *qisas al-anbiya* or "Tales of the Prophets," which constitute a legendary history of the world from the time of creation. The adoptions provide evidence for the Islamization of the Soninke, but they must also be examined as local constructions of history, corresponding in some way to the pre-Islamic historical or legendary tradition. The reader will also notice that Soninke tradition exists more as history than as epic.

Performance

The brief Arabic descriptions tell us little about the royal court of Ghana. In fact, there is very little information on the performance tradition of epic or other forms of song among the Soninke. Charles Monteil's description of the training and placement of the young gesere was quoted in chapter 1, but there is no guarantee that recruitment, training, patronage, and performance follow the same dynamics in the other stretches of Soninke territory.

The Soninke observe the hereditary distinction that sets the performer, here called the *gesere*, apart from other elements of society. The general term for these hereditary groups is very close to that used in the Manden (*nyaxamala* instead of *nyamakala*), and they are clearly part of the same broader cultural complex. In this pattern, the gesere are dependent upon noble patrons, although the alliance may well be individual rather than hereditary, and the substance of their performance may depend more on praise singing than on extended narrations of clan histories. Certainly, the evidence for the praises is stronger than evidence for narration.

Other than the highly romanticized images presented by Leo Frobenius (to be discussed at the end of this chapter), there is at this time virtually no reliable information on performance contexts and occasions among the Soninke.

Sources

The present-day sense of Soninke history and historiography depends largely on early colonial documents. A number of travelers and administrators working from Nioro du Sahel collected and published accounts drawn from manuscripts prepared by notables in that town, which lies close to the site of Koumbi-Sahel and was the capital of the kingdom of Jara.[7] A central figure in this process was the interpreter Mamadi Aissa Diakhite, who later became a *qadi* (Muslim judge) and who is mentioned by some as an informant. These local accounts list the series of kingdoms that rose and fell—Wagadu, Mali, Jara, Segou, and Kaarta—and they end with the Islamic rule of al-Hajj Umar Tall and his sons in the period from 1850 to the time of writing. They include local conflicts (the Sagone and Dabora), and represent a remarkably detailed synthesis of different ethnic-linguistic historical traditions. So far, no detailed comparative study has been made of these sources except for that portion dealing with Wagadu, but the larger project seems worthwhile. It is worth remembering as part of the historical context of these manuscripts that the town of Nioro was the fief of Muntaga Tall, a younger son of al-Hajj Umar, and Muntaga blew himself up in a conflict with his older brother Ahmed, who was established in Segou.[8] These events were recent history at the time the manuscripts were assembled. What emerges, then, is the image of French victors, newly come to Nioro around 1890, inquiring into local history; their informants were the survivors of a civil war fought by the Tukolor invaders who had conquered the region a generation before. The Diakhités, former followers of al-Hajj Umar, were appointed to their posts by the French. The complexities en-coded in the narratives are easy to imagine.

There are other collections of narratives, including rich material assembled by Leo Frobenius and some less accessible accounts published by Oudiary Makan Dantioko. A number of the later texts have been published in bilingual form but cannot be assumed to represent real "performances": the occasion was rather a collector's inquiry and a gesere's response. The principal narratives include the legend of Wagadu, the story of Dama Ngile and the foundation of Jara, and the legend of the dispersal of the Kusa.

The Legend of Wagadu

The legend of Wagadu divides naturally into two parts: its foundation and its fall. The story has remained quite stable over the years. While certain elements may be developed to a greater or lesser extent in any given narrative, there is little introduction of absolutely new material.

Dinga and the Founding of Wagadu

Dinga traveled around the east in the lands of Islam and then moved west to Koumbi [the archaeological site of Wagadu]. There, at a well, he asked for water and was refused. This led to a battle of magics with the mistress of the well, a spirit. Dinga won the battle, subdued the spirit-woman, and mar-ried her three daughters. Each bore a child, one of which was half-human, half-serpent and immediately took refuge under the earth. Dinga then trav-eled away, leaving word with a vulture that his heirs should come to this land.

Dinga's other two sons were of opposite character. The elder was incon-siderate and mistreated his father's old servant. He even wiped his hands on the man's head after a meal. The younger was kind and gave him the left-overs. So when Dinga, aged and now blind, felt death was near and told the servant to summon his eldest son, the servant instead warned the younger, Djabe Cisse. Djabe Cisse disguised himself as his brother and went to his father; he was given the secret of Dinga's magic power. He washed himself from seven jars of water and then rolled in the sand. His subjects would be as numerous as the grains of sand that stuck to him.

The deception was discovered. The older brother received what would have been the share of the younger brother: the power of rainmaking. Djabe Cisse, nevertheless, left his home and wandered, earning his living as a herdsman. One day he heard an ancient vulture addressing him, and after some conversation the vulture told him of his father's message: that he should go west to Koumbi. Djabe Cisse provided the vulture and his associate, the hyena, with forty colts so the two elders might regain their strength and lead him to the land.

There he found his half-brother, the Bida Serpent, living in a well. He reached an agreement with the Bida: every year, the Bida would receive a maiden and a horse, and in exchange the Bida would rain gold upon the land. It is sometimes added that the Bida gave them four drums, of different metals (copper, iron, silver, gold); only Djabe Cisse could lift the gold drum, and he therefore became king. And so Wagadu was established.

The Fall of Wagadu

After some time, a maiden named Sia Yatabere was chosen for the sacrifice. She had an admirer named Mamadi Sefa Dekhote, which means Mamadi the Taciturn, and he was unwilling to see her sacrificed. One possible amplification of the story tells how Mamadi's cousin (or uncle) Wagana Sakho was extremely jealous of his wife and kept her in a gateless compound whose walls only his own extraordinary stallion could leap. Mamadi had a mare bred in secret by the stallion, and so he too had an unparalleled horse. With it, he visited Wagana Sakho's wife. While they were talking, Wagana Sakho returned home and listened outside the door. He heard Mamadi compare himself and the wife to mice (which they had just seen), scurrying about in fear of the cat—who would be Wagana Sakho. Knowing they feared him, Wagana Sakho could not take vengeance.

When the day came for Sia Yatabere to be sacrificed, Mamadi Sefa Dekhote interfered. He cut off the seven heads of the Bida Serpent as they swung over the maiden; the last head flew into the sky and uttered a curse on Wagadu: for seven years, there would be no rain of gold, and the people would disperse. Mamadi Sefa Dekhote took Sia Yatabere (against her will, some say) on his horse and raced out of town. They were pursued, but only Wagana Sakho could come close—and he was constrained not to harm them. They reached the river where Mamadi Sefa Dekhote's mother lived, and she stopped the pursuit by announcing that she could feed Wagadu for the seven years.

The love intrigue ends unhappily. Sia Yatabere tricks Mamadi into giving a knuckle from a little finger, or a toe, to cure her headache and then tells him she could not love an incomplete man. He retaliates with a love potion that controls her completely and then in the dark sends his groom to sleep with her. She does not survive the humiliation when it is revealed in the morning.

The biblical, and more immediately Islamic, elements of the story are evident; the story of Djabe Cisse is that of Jacob and Esau transferred to a Soninke context. These echoes are reinforced by the geography of Dinga's travels: Yemen, "Lot," Hind (India), and other places—all lands of Islamic reference. But these recognizable elements are superimposed on an equally strong African pattern of migration and foundation legends. In his travels, Dinga (and his son) must reach an agreement with the local powers to justify and legitimate his future rule; this agreement is expressed through the exchange of women. Germaine Dieterlen reads the vulture and the hyena through her deep knowledge of regional arcana and connects them with initiatory symbolism that may go back to Egyptian times; the same might be done with the Bida Serpent, connecting it with chthonic deities and immortalized ancestors in regional creation myths. A widely reported regional practice of using a serpent to choose the king should also be recalled.[9]

Water is involved in the conflicts, hidden perhaps by other issues. Dinga's first struggle at the well, the elder brother's inheritance of rainmaking, and the Bida's curse of a drought all include water among other themes. These elements suggest connections with other mythological systems of West Africa in which the primary creative act, establishing the possibility of life, is not the creation of the earth but the regulation of the waters.[10] This is more than a literary echo; it reflects a pattern encountered widely in the Sahel in which the newer political rulers must share some measure of power with the original inhabitants, who are vested with the ritual power over the land.[11] The motif of a younger brother displacing his elder from the inheritance is one that also occurs repeatedly in the Sunjata epic and that reflects the social tensions that lead to both schism (Djabe Cisse leads his people away to a new land) and imbalance of power.[12]

The name "Wagadu" is generally interpreted to mean the land of the Wage; the Wage were the four noble clans who served the king and divided the land among themselves, and it is virtually certain that the listing of those clans reflects contemporary prominence rather than a deep historical record, although the gesere Diarra Sylla presents them as the four quarters of the kingdom.[13]

The fall of Wagadu is inseparable from its founding, and the story mixes narrative patterns and emotions in unexpected ways. The Perseus story is recognizable, but here Andromeda does not wish to be saved; the act itself causes a calamity. Mamadi Sefa Dekhote is portrayed as a selfish and headstrong young man. His speech defect ("the Taciturn") may easily represent some further moral disability.

It is obvious that the stasis of plenty that Wagadu enjoyed under the regime of the Bida could not last. It was a golden age lost through human action, but that golden age was possible only at an unnatural and unacceptable price—human sacrifice. The loss of plenty is also a purification, a step toward a better human order. Thus, the present less-than-ideal state of affairs is made more acceptable. The story also clearly encodes other possibilities through the device of the flight toward the river: one would be the movement of peoples caused by the desiccation of the savanas, with the causes and consequences clearly identified—drought and famine. One proposed, but less plausible, reading makes the story a historical allegory of the regional gold trade, in which the movement of the flying serpent's head represents a shift of gold mining from the Bambuk fields at the headwaters of the Senegal River south to the gold fields of Bure.[14]

The fall of Wagadu also involves subtle questions of kinship and gender relations. Often, Wagane Sakho is Mamadi's maternal uncle, and when he ends his pursuit at the home of Mamadi's mother (who lives by the river), he has come to his sister. This relationship may serve to explain his forbearance in the pursuit of his nephew (the incident in which he overhears Mamadi admit his fear is not widely reported). It may also be connected with historical theories that would make succession in ancient Ghana matrilineal.[15]

The story of Wagadu is, finally, one with no entirely positive heroes. Each character is presented with some ambivalence. Each situation is in some sense a compromise. The world of the story reflects the present world of the Soninke, who have seen their day of power come and go. This story is the myth of their unity, but it also tells of the fragmentation of that unity and thus of a coming to terms with the real effects of history. The next stories are far more local. The story of Wagadu is known from the Gambia to Niger (and Frobenius collected his version in northern Togo); the same is not true of the later traditions.

Dama Ngile and the Kingdom of Jara

The manuscript tradition of Nioro makes a smooth transition from Wagadu to Mali and Sunjata, and then back to the Soninke through the figure of Dama Ngile (or Daman Gille—spellings vary) who is the ancestor of the Diawara dynasty of the kingdom of Jara; there are also several versions that treat the story in isolation.[16] However smooth the transition, the scale is reduced from a widely known common myth of origin to what is essentially a dynastic legend.

Dama Ngile and Jara

Dama Ngile was a hunter of elephants who lived in the bush. His only contact in the human community was a leather worker. He once met a Muslim holy man who was traveling to Mecca and entertained him in the bush. The holy man forgot his purse of gold when he left. Dama Ngile followed him and returned it; the holy man asked what he might bring him from Mecca as a reward. Dama Ngile asked for a blade that would allow him to cut straight through the neck of elephants or buffaloes.

The holy man proceeded to Mecca and was about to return when a yet greater holy man asked him if he hadn't forgotten some errand. He remembered his promise to Dama Ngile and asked for a sword. The sword gave off light when drawn from the sheath and was a sign of royal power. He brought the blade back to the Manden and left it in the keeping of Sunjata, the ruler of Mali, to be given to Dama Ngile. But because the sword was a token of royal power, Sunjata wished to keep it.

Dama Ngile eventually came to ask for his blade. The ruler sent a servant (or his wife) to fetch a blade from the storeroom, and the magic blade was brought. Sunjata sent it back and ordered that another be produced. Each time, the marvelous blade found its way to the messenger's hand. Finally the emperor accepted the inevitable and gave Dama Ngile the blade but also ordered him to leave the kingdom.

Dama Ngile wandered for a while and fathered a son, Fie Mamadou. Fie Mamadou came to Jara, which was then ruled by the Niakhate dynasty. The ruler, Bemba, was notoriously cruel and the people were dissatisfied with him. Through magic, Fie Mamadou overthrew Bemba and established the Diawara dynasty of Jara. These last elements of the story are complicated by confusion with the migrations of the Deniyanke Fulbe (led by Koli Tengela, whose father had been given a woman by Sunjata . . .).

This story works with established regional building blocks of foundation legends:[17] hunters, delegation of authority, tokens of kingship. The future line of Dama Ngile is legitimated in at least three ways by the hero's actions: he is recognized by Sunjata, he is blessed by Islam, and his son is morally superior to the king he overthrows. The story thus appeals to a variety of local sources of power.

The story of the sword has a sequel. It appears in the myth of origin of Bondu, the story of Malick Sy, when Malick Sy stops in Jara on his way back from Mecca and cures a queen of childlessness. The sword is said to have vanished when al-Hajj Umar captured Jara. Whether this occurred because the mission of Islamization was now complete or should be seen as a veiled critique of the Tukolor leader is unclear.

The Dispersal of the Kusa

The Kusa or Kusantage are a Soninke-speaking group in the region of Nioro and Jara; they distinguish themselves from the Wago clans who trace their origin to Wagadu. Claude Meillassoux and Lansana Doucoure have published one text (from fifteen collected) of the Kusa tradition of origin, choosing the version of the gesere Diaowe Simagha because of his knowledge and reputation.[18] This published text is so far the best available example of a Soninke epic performance in reliable transcription. It is an excerpt from a longer narration, and digresses in some places to cover specific points requested by the host Amadou Doucoure.

Mareñ Jagu and the Dispersal of the Kusa

Garaghe Makhan ruled the Kusa. He was cruel and ungenerous, in contrast to Toumba Damba, a neighboring leader whose gifts to his griots were in units of hundreds. Garaghe Makhan killed a leader of the Kusa, Bincigi. After Bincigi's death, his son Mareñ Jagu was born and then disguised as a girl. The son was a precocious and troublesome child who even came into conflict with the ruler.

Mareñ Jagu went off to learn occult skills; he met and killed teacher after teacher until he came to Dinga. Dinga was able to teach him and to avoid being killed. On his return home, Mareñ Jagu encountered his sister, Haintainkourabe: he had sworn to sacrifice the first thing he met on his return. But he could not kill her until she took an awl and pierced her wrap-around cloth. He sacrificed her, but found her alive when he reached his home. Together they overthrew Garaghe Makhan, but Mareñ Jagu also proved a tyrannical leader, and after some time the Kusa left him and dispersed.

Mareñ Jagu echoes the Central African epics: the preternatural child assisted by a magical sister avenges their father by overthrowing a tyrant. This basic plot serves as a skeleton for a variety of other connections and concerns of which the principal is perhaps the contrast between past abundance and present impoverishment. The hero's progression at the end is not a gladsome romp assembling the elements of a civilization, as in the case of Lianja. It is a journey toward oppression in which Mareñ Jagu too easily becomes that which he overthrew. As such, it is probably a more realistic picture of the recent ecological and political history of the region.

This pessimism is brought out by sets of lines repeated in the performance. A first set is uttered by the generous lord Touma Damba as he enumerates the hundreds of gifts he will bestow. He punctuates the list with the prediction that:

> This world will come, it will pass.
> Other worlds will come after,
> Worlds of confusion and strife.[19]

A second set comes from the tyrant Garaghe Makhan as he predicts the troubles that Mareñ Jagu will cause. The occasion is the naming ceremony at which the heads of the newborns must be shaved. Through his magical power, Mareñ Jagu interferes with the process. Garaghe predicts:

> What you hear today will bring trouble tomorrow
> For tomorrow, when trouble appears,
> The sons of the Kusa will prefer death to life.[20]

He also asks, with an undertone of humor, whether this allegedly female baby really is a girl.

The use of repeated lines in this manner does suggest practice in the delivery of the piece and so seems to justify consideration of this text as the best available representative of the performance tradition. The content of the lines underscores the pessimism of the worldview espoused.

This story contains direct or indirect links with almost every other major legend of the region. A frustrating note by Meillassoux at the end of the published text indicates that Simagha continued for another half hour with the story of Sunjata, but he gives no further details. But the story offers other connections with the epic of Sunjata. At the start, as Diaowa Simagha is setting the scene, he tells how a Kusa ancestor in the form of a cat spied on Garaghe and learned the secret of music. This echoes the famous story of Jankuma Doka/Bala Faseke Kouyate, Sunjata's griot, and his encounter with Sumanguru, who then possessed the secret of the balafon (see chapter 1), and the echo is linguistic as well: in Maninka, *jankuma* means cat. The relations of the hero and the sister that come later in the story also recall the relations of Sunjata and his sister in two incidents: the sister brings Sunjata the secret of Sumanguru's power, and earlier she had almost lost her *pagne* (a wrap-around skirt) (see chapter 5).

The knife of Dama Ngile is mentioned—the Kusa specify that it was from them, and not from the Manden, that Dama Ngile obtained this knife—and in this story it is used to shave Mareñ Jagu. Dinga, the patriarch of the legend of Wagadu, also appears, here cast as a wise man who can train the young and violent hero. The magical preparation, bathing in pots of water, is the same as in the legend of Wagadu; and Dinga's wife is identifiable as the spirit of the well whom he defeats at the start.

It is not clear whether such parallels should be considered independent and autonomous variants of the other narratives, or whether they are partial appropriations from known traditions intended to buttress Kusa claims of autonomy and cultural identity. The parallels serve as indicators of the cultural horizons reflected by the epic, and they may illustrate the process of identity-formation in a very fluid region of the Sahel.

Dantioko and others provide other traditions, such as those of the Kagoro and the story of Mariheri of Dionkoloni. These stories also reflect a biblical appropriation. In this case, it is the story of Joseph, who was thrown into a well by his brothers. The same motif is used in the story of Sonsan, which comes out of the adjacent Bamana traditions of the Kaarta.[21] But again, there is not enough evidence on the performance tradition or a sufficient number of collected texts for conclusive analysis.

The extent and nature of the Soninke contribution to Sahelian epic traditions remains to be determined, but is probably great. Soninke gesere may have become praise singers at the courts of kings. Soninke praises persist in Songhay epics (and possibly in Sunjata), and the Soninke hegemony predates that of the other states in the region. Nevertheless, translation of these suggestions of influence into broader patterns does not seem possible at present.

In one external case, however, a view of Soninke epic art has become sufficiently influential to require separate discussion, and that is the legacy of Leo Frobenius.

Frobenius and "Gassire's Lute"

Leo Frobenius was a German Africanist and collector of stories and objects. His twelve-volume collection, *Atlantis,* remains the largest single-handedly collected of African oral traditions from a continent-wide variety of peoples. He wrote on African cultural history, attempting to establish trans-Saharan links with the classical past; and in the early years of the Negritude movement, his ideas were particularly influential. He has been criticized because he published no texts in their original languages, and questions have been raised, particularly by French scholars such as Charles Monteil,[22] about his qualifications and field methods. Some of his travel notebooks have been published; unfortunately, those dealing with his visits to West Africa and the material under discussion here have not.

Volume 5 of *Atlantis, Dichten und Denken im Sudan,* offers treatments of Sunjata, the Bamana, and the Mossi. Volume 6, *Spielmannsgeschichten der Sahel* (loosely translated, Minstrelsy of the Sahel), is of more immediate concern. In a lengthy introduction, Frobenius first describes the peoples of the Sahel, their instruments, and their musical traditions, and his discussion remains an interesting early witness today. His explicit purpose was to relate the ideology and culture of the Sahel to those of courtly medieval Europe, particularly as expressed through heroic song. Frobenius then presents stories from the Soninke and the Fulbe; according to his information, the Soninke had two "Books of Heroes"—a greater, the *Dausi,* and a lesser, the *Pui.* These, he believed, were the remains of a lost complete epic history of the people extending back twenty-five hundred years.

Unfortunately, no one else has confirmed the existence of these "books." *Poyi ni Payi* is a Bamana phrase used in some epics (such as *La prise de Dionkoloni*)[23] to indicate the intensity of conflict within the epic; it may imply a notion of battle poetry that is comparable to a book of heroes. But the exact reference has been lost. A further flaw in Frobenius's wonderful vision of the African epic tradition is that his Soninke material, for instance, was collected not in the Sahel but from a Djerma (or Zarma) informant from a Soninke community in Borgu, in what is now northern Benin.

The value of Frobenius's collection thus depends upon confirmation from independent sources—upon modern recordings to match his stories. Where such confirmation is possible, as with the legend of Wagadu and a number of other narratives, he does in fact offer valuable early versions. He may not give the original language in his published text, but he does provide phrases here and there, and his transcription was careful enough that one may occasionally recognize idioms and turns of phrase used in the transcriptions of modern recordings.

These phrases and words, however, also weaken his theories about Soninke books of heroes, for in fact the discernible language is more often than not Bamana, and the cultural horizon involved belongs to no single group but to a sort of generic heroic world that in modern and reliable transcriptions is best represented among the Fula.

These cautions seem necessary because of the wide influence of one particular narrative from Frobenius's collection, "Gassire's Lute." It is a lovely and evocative story.

> Gassire, son of a king, grew tired of waiting for his father to die. He consulted an old man who said he would never be king but would instead become the first griot. Gassire heard a guinea fowl singing in triumph at his victory over a snake and thus understood the power of song. Gassire went to a smith who made him a lute; the lute would not sing. Gassire went into battle; each day one of his sons died and he bore the body home on his back, the blood running over the lute. Finally, Gassire was exiled, and there in the wilderness the lute began to sing.

The collection then continues with a very poetic and detailed rendition of the legend of Wagadu. This heartwrenching song balances human ambition and desire against the power and immortality of song—an old and well-established equation. It is also a myth of origin of the griot. Gassire the hero is also the gesere, the Soninke griot: not an individual, but a social category. Frobenius notes that, having collected this story from Borgu, he tried to find it in the Sahel as well and could not. He found only the story of the guinea fowl (or partridge) singing.[24]

This raises the question of how to treat such unique phenomena. Literary appreciation does seem the appropriate response. But their singularity should also be acknowledged, and this has not been done. Alta Jablow has erected a vision of Soninke epic art on the basis of this one narrative, perpetuating the romantic vision that inebriated Frobenius himself; but she has done so without consideration of the related historical and ethnographic material provided by other scholars that would have provided a more accurate picture of the tradition she describes.

❖ 5 ❖

SUNJATA AND THE TRADITIONS OF THE MANDEN

THE MANDEN (sometimes Manding) is a space, in some way perhaps a time, and for many, an idea. The space is roughly defined by the headwaters of the Niger and its affluents and lies in western Mali and eastern Guinea; it is occupied by the Malinke, for whom it is a symbolic heartland from which the more widespread branches of their people have departed at various times to take on different names (Mandinka, Dyula, Konyaka, and others). As a time, the Manden looks back to its period of unification and glory under the emperor Sunjata. In his time (generally dated to the early thirteenth century), the separate kingdoms (or territories) of Do, Kri, and Tabon and Sibi became one; he ended the oppression of Sumanguru Kante and the Sosso around 1235 and made the Malinka the rulers of their world. To speak of the Manden is, of necessity, to evoke the time and space of Sunjata's rule: thus, the Manden is also an idea spread across West Africa.

The association is symbolic in many ways. Sunjata was the first in a line of rulers. A successor, Mansa Musa (r. 1312–1337), was far better known to the out-side world of his day. Mansa Musa made a celebrated pilgrimage to Mecca in 1324–1325, leaving enough gold in Cairo to depress its price for some time. His immediate predecessor, Abu Bekri II (r. 1310–1312), has inspired would-be Thor Heyerdahls who hope to show that Africans might have sailed to the Americas. Abu Bekri set sail in a fleet of war canoes in 1312, and nothing more was heard of him. Quite possibly his trip was a convenient way for Mansa Musa to take power. Virtually none of these successors has survived in the more popular oral traditions.[1]

Within sub-Saharan West Africa, the empire of Mali seems to have left a more durable impression. The wider territory of the empire, extending well beyond the Manden, is marked by a certain homogeneity of social institutions, such as the division of society into free-born, slaves, and artisanal status groups (the *nyamakala*), and a system of interethnic clan correspondences (e.g., Fula and

Malinka clans have recognized counterparts) lubricated by the tension-releasing *senankuya* or joking relationships and particularly by a wide network of commercial and trading relations. These forms of social organization quite probably spread during the *pax maliana* by diffusion and imitation, encouraged by an era of peaceful contacts.[2]

The oral traditions of the region do not really record these elements of social and economic history. Within the Manden, Sunjata serves as a focal point, a magnet to which many unrelated traditions attach in a very loose organization. Moreover, Sunjata is known outside the Manden: he serves as a reference point for non-Malinke states such as Jara (Soninke), Bondu (Khassonke), and the Deniyanke dynasty of the Futa Toro. The various pasts of the entire Sahel look back through local oral traditions to some point of origin. Very often, that point of origin is Mali, and the only real ruler of Mali who is recalled beyond the immediate territory of his descendants is Sunjata. His successors have been eclipsed. To some extent, they are irrelevant. Mali declined in the fifteenth century, during which time the Songhay gained power to the east. When the empire actually dissolved is unclear. The French historian Yves Person associates this event with the era of Nyani Mansa Mamadou in the sixteenth century,[3] but certainly Mali had been battered before then.

The political sway of the empire seems to have been replaced by the economic domination of Malinka traders, known as *julaw* [merchants], who moved south into the forest regions to establish commercial networks. They also appear to have disseminated Islam, although the world of the Manden is not so explicitly identified with Islam as polities such as the Futa Jallon or the Songhay empire.

The Manden thus represents a principle of cultural unity independent of geography or local historical traditions, and the figure of Sunjata is the key element for this cohesion. It is hardly surprising that the epic of Sunjata may be the best-known example of African oral literature. The epic had already gained wide diffusion within West Africa before it made the jump into print. Since the beginning of the colonial era (ca. 1895), historians, travelers, folklorists, and administrators have been researching and presenting the rich oral traditions of the Manden. As a result, an impressive number of versions of the epic of Sunjata now exist, along with copious historical analysis.

This chapter examines the story of Sunjata by sections; that analysis is followed by a description of some of the major categories of sources (colonial-era accounts, transcriptions from oral performance, literary treatments). The chapter concludes with some examination of later historical figures of the Manden, such as Samory Toure and el-Hajj Umar Tall, whose lives are the subject of epic performances now being collected by David Conrad and others. The survey includes the Gambian Mandinka versions of the Sunjata[4] but does not discuss those Gambian epics dealing with more recent figures (see chapter 8). More popular traditions of hunters' epics have been discussed in chapter 3. This chapter, then, concentrates on the historical and aristocratically oriented epics.

Performers and Performances

Central to the social organization of the Manden are the *nyamakala,* a much-discussed term that refers to the professional-status descent groups: smiths, griots (jeliw or jelilu), and others. The griot—the jeli—is central to the verbal and musical arts and has been widely studied.[5] As described in chapter 1, the popular vision of the jeli varies, from venerable lore-master to parasitic extortionist, depending on the context and the perspective of the viewer.

The epic traditions of the Manden are tightly interwoven with the corpus of clan praises in a variety of forms: *majamu, burudyu, faasa.*[6] These praises appear to be the true staple of the jeli's repertoire and are delivered on the numerous occasions enlivened by the music of jelilu: naming-ceremonies, marriages, or virtually any other festive or important occasion. Jelilu tour the villages, singing the praises of local notables and thus reaping rewards. The praises have an ennobling and coercive power over their hearers; vocalization of the praise is a public articulation of the stature of the lineage and the individual.

Praises are performed by men and women alike, perhaps most often by women, whose lyric abilities are widely recognized and appreciated. Epics are known as *kuma koro* [old speech] or *maana* (Arabic, lit., "meaning") or more recently perhaps, *tariku* (Arabic, "history"), and are associated more with male performance. The question of women's performance of epic is the subject of lively current debate. So far, no record or transcription has been found of a woman's performance of the epic of Sunjata. As John Johnson has noted, however, epic performance in the Manden is multigeneric.[7] It combines narrative, lyrics, and instrumental solos. While the established model for epic singing privileges the notion of a single male performer, the African data provide ample evidence of performance by teams that include women in featured roles who supply the lyric element.

Instrumentation varies. The most established instrument of the Sunjata tradition is probably the balafon, or wooden xylophone, whose origin is incorporated into the epic of Sunjata; but the kora and the ngoni, stringed instruments of varying sizes, are also well attested. Outside the Manden the kora may in fact be the first instrument associated with griot music. Some performers now use guitars.

Historians' interest in the epic of Sunjata has predictably influenced the nature of versions available in print. They have sought complete stories where complete performances seem rare, and they have combined information collected from different sources. The literary or printed artifact is therefore not an accurate reflection of actual performance practice, in which the story line may be adjusted to recognize a potential wealthy patron in the audience and in which complete narration is probably secondary to emotional effect. Episodes, rather than the complete epic, are probably the usual performance product. Many of the complete narratives by a single performer are the result of a direct request by the collector.[8]

The "complete" epic is said to be performed on at least one recurrent occasion, every seven years at the re-roofing ceremonies of the *Kama Bloñ* (House of Speech) in Kangaba. The ceremonies and the mythic account associated with the occasion were described by Germaine Dieterlen in 1954–1955 but have not been documented since then, and no recording has yet been made of the event.[9] Nevertheless, the occasion has acquired a good deal of symbolic historiographic importance for Malians. Oral tradition may be seen as mobile and changing unless anchored through some authoritative repetition. The ceremonies of the Kama Bloñ provide the necessary mechanism to explain a stable (and thus historically reliable) transmission of the tradition.[10] As a consequence, the jelilu of the Diabate (or Jebate and variants) clan from Kela, who perform in the ritual, have acquired a mantle of authority for their version of the tradition. A comparison of available versions for narrative content does suggest, in the present state of documentation, that theirs is the "standard" history of Sunjata, or at least the most stable narrative core discernible.[11]

It has certainly become the "standard" history since independence and the partition of the Manden into Mali and Guinea, and Malian intellectuals and scholars have adopted it. But there is room for skepticism. Kathryn Greene has questioned the antiquity of Kangaba's claim to authority.[12] Other lineages and centers might claim authority: the Kouyate lineage of jelilu is affiliated with the noble Keitas, descendants of Sunjata. But their centers of tradition are principally on the Guinean side of the border and are relatively undocumented save for what is perhaps the most influential single version of the story, that published by Niane in 1960. This isolation is coming to an end, however; David Conrad, Tim Geysbeek, and others have been collecting and documenting the traditions available in Guinea. Where the Kama Bloñ may claim authority as the center of the Manden, the traditionalists of Guinea claim theirs through direct connections with the epic: one Kouyate family preserves the balafon used by Sumanguru, Sunjata's opponent.

At this point, a study of the broader Sunjata tradition cannot be limited to oral performances only. The influence of written versions and the historical weight of the tradition have made it a multifaceted artifact subject to scholarly disputes, cultural agendas, and literary interpretation and revision. Table 5.1 offers a schematic presentation of the contents of the principal variant sources, listed chronologically by date of recording. No attempt will be made to analyze the table; it is presented here as a convenience and ready reference for the reader.[13]

The Story of Sunjata

Origins

Most complete narrative performances begin with events considerably before the time of Sunjata—they tell of creation and then bring the story down to the settlement of the Manden. Some versions speak of God and Adam; many look back to the time of the Prophet Muhammad and his black servant, Bilal, who is claimed by many lineages across the Sahel as an ancestor. Some versions show traces of pre-Islamic traditions and describe the migrations of three or four brothers named Simbong (the hunter's title) as well as the tests by which each acquires his attributes. The selection of a starting point does seem to depend on the performer.

The Buffalo-Woman of Du

[The first core episode describes the origin of Sunjata's mother and how she was taken from Du (or Do) to Narena, home of Sunjata's father, about whom relatively little is told.]

Du Kamisa was the sister of Du-Mogo-nya-mogo, ruler of Du and Kri, but at a family gathering she was excluded and not given her share of the meal. She became furious at this and began to transform herself into a buffalo that would ravage the fields and kill farmers and hunters so that the people of Du could not farm in peace. Word went out that Du was afflicted with this beast, and so two hunters, Dan Mansa Wulandin and Dan Mansa Wulanba of the Traore lineage, set off to attempt the task. They usually perform divination before they leave; often they stop in the Manden on their way.

At the edge of the town of Du, they encounter an irascible and solitary old woman. Warned by the divination, or out of their own kindness, they

Table 5.1. Episodes and Versions of the Epic of Sunjata

EPISODES	1	2	3	4	5	6	7	8	9	10	11	12
1. Origins of the Manden												
A. Mecca			x		x	x	x		x	x		x
B. The Manden	x	x	x	x	x		x		x	x		
2. Buffalo-Woman of Du		*					x	x				x
3. Birth of Sunjata	x						x	x				
4. Sunjata Rises	x		x		x	x	x	x	x	x	x	x
5. Witches of Manden	x		?	?	?	?	x	x	x		x	
6. Travels	x	x	x	?	x		x	x	x			
7. Sumanguru's Balafon		*	?				?	?		x	?	
8. Sunjata Is Summoned	x	x	x				x	x	?	x	x	x
9. Death of Sogolon	x	x		x			x	x	x	x	x	x
10. Seduction / Sumanguru	x	x	x	x	x	x	x	x		x	x	
11. Defeat of Sumanguru	x	x	x	x	x	x	x	x		x	x	x
12. Conquest of the Jolof	x							x	?			

Notes: A question mark (?) in the table means an episode has been transformed, an asterisk (*) that it includes information from a second short version.

Episode 1, Origins, includes mention of Jon Bilal in Mecca or the Simbong brothers in the Manden. Episode 3, Birth of Sunjata, includes the story of the double-birth with Dankaran Touman—other extraordinary births are not included; sorcery often follows this birth. Episodes 5 and 6, Witches of Manden and Travels, are often reversed in order; the episode Travels includes attempts by the brother to have Sunjata assassinated.

For information on the versions of the epic, see below:

Sigla	*Date*	*Informant*	*Source*	*Language*
1	1892	Anonymous	Quiquandon	French
2	1898	Anonymous	Monteil 1966	French
	1895–1900	Nioro Manuscripts	Adam, Arnaud,	
		(Other named	Delafosse, Labouret	French
		informants include		
		Hadi Ba and		
		Mamadou Sallama)		
3		Anonymous	Adam 1904, pp. 39–47	French
4		Anonymous	Arnaud 1912, pp. 144–85	French
5		Mamadi Aissa	Delafosse 1913	French
			(Arabic MS)	
6		Mamadi Aissa Kaba	Labouret 1929, pp. 209–10	French
7	pre-1909	Kieba Koate,	Frobenius 1913, 1921	German
		aka Korongo		
8	ca. 1910	Kande Kanote	De Zeltner 1913, pp. 1–36	French

Table 5.1. *continued*

13	14	15	16	17	18	19	20	21	22	23	24	25	26	27
	x	x		x	x			x	x		x		x	x
x	x			x	x			x	x	x	x		x	x
x	x	x	x	x			?		x	x	x		x	x
				x	x		x			x	?		x	x
x	x	x		x	x		x	x		x	x	x	x	x
x	x			x	x		x			x	x		x	x
x	?	x		x	x	x	x			x	x	x	x	x
x	?	x		x	x	x		?		x	x		x	x
x	x	x		x	x	x	x			x	x		x	x
x	x	x		x	x	x	x			x	x	x	x	x
x		x		x	x	x	x	x		x			x	?
x	x	x		x	x	x	x	x		x	x		x	x
	x			x	x		?						x	x

9	ca. 1910	Habibou Sissoko	De Zeltner 1913, pp. 37–45	French
10	1924	Anonymous	Vidal	French
11	1937	Mamby Sidibe	Sidibe 1959	French
12	ca. 1950	Anonymous	Humblot	French
13	1957	Mamadou Kouyate	Niane 1960	French
14	ca. 1963	Ibrahima Kante	I. Kante n.d.	French
15	ca. 1965	Babu Conde	Camara Laye	French
16	1967	Tiemoko Kone	Doucoure and Martal 1970	Bilingual/French
17	1967	Fa-Digi Sisókó	Johnson 1978, 1986	Bilingual/English
18	1968	Kele Monson Diabaté	Moser 1974 (See also Massa Makan Diabaté 1970a, 1970b, 1975, 1986)	Bilingual/English
19	1968	Dembo Kanute	Innes 1974, pp. 260–323	Bilingual/English
20	1969	Bamba Suso	Innes 1974, pp. 34–135	Bilingual/English
21	1969	Banna Kanute	Innes 1974, pp. 136–259	Bilingual/English
22	ca. 1970	Mahan Djebahate	Sory Camara 1992	Bilingual/French
23	1974	Magan Sisókó	Johnson 1978, 1979	Bilingual/French
24	1975–1976	Wa Kamissoko	Cissé and Kamissoko 1988, 1991	Bilingual/French
25	ca. 1975	Amadu Jebaate	*Recueil de littérature manding*	Bilingual/French
26	1979	Kanku Mady Jabaté	Jabaté 1987	Bilingual/French
27	1987	Lansina Diabate	Jansen, Duintjer, and Tamboura 1995	Bilingual/French

assist by bringing water and firewood and by helping her cook. Touched by their attentions, the old woman reveals her secret: she is the buffalo, and they can kill her by shooting a spindle at her.

They go to hunt her and shoot her with a spindle (there is usually an exchange between the brothers about following her instructions). The buffalo then pursues them in a magical flight pattern: they drop objects that become obstacles until they are almost cornered—and then the buffalo dies. One of the brothers often sings the praises of the other: this becomes the origin of the Traore and Diabate clan alliance.

They are eventually identified as the slayers of the buffalo and rewarded with their choice of a woman. Following the instructions of Du Kamisa, they choose the ugliest woman in the village, Sogolon Kuduma, who is hunchbacked and covered with warts. They take her away and try to sleep with her on their way back to the Manden; she foils them by sprouting porcupine quills from her groin or in some other monstrous way. When they reach the Manden, they are happy to give her to Nare Faman Cenyi, who will become Sunjata's father. He does succeed in overcoming Sogolon's active resistance and marries her. In some versions the touch of his knife causes the warts to fall away, and Sogolon is revealed to be an attractive woman.

Much of this episode is recognizable as folkloric motif. The pattern is familiar from the hunters' narratives (see chapter 3). The episode reproduces the theme of the monster-killer, presenting the monster as an alienated member of the community. It endows Sunjata's mother with a pedigree of considerable occult power, which will later serve her son well. Sogolon is widely seen as the heir to Du Kamisa's powers. She manifests her magic in her resistance to her husband, and she will eventually pass these powers on to her son.

This episode is also one of two moments in the epic in which the Traore lineage takes center stage, displacing the Keitas. The second is the conquest of the Gambia by Tira Magan, which follows Sunjata's victory over Sumanguru. Tira Magan is sometimes presented as the child of one of the two hunters. This point is of some significance in light of the politics of Mali since independence; the first president was a Keita who was overthrown by a Traore.[14] This episode also presents a myth of origin for the association of the Diabate clan of jelilu with the Traore line; in the story, one brother defers to the other because of his valiance against the buffalo. The theme of fraternal relations and precedence recurs throughout the epic and has some importance for Mande culture.[15]

The episode also has a clear association with hunting. The story type is widely distributed as a hunters' epic and as a folktale. Stephen Bulman analyzes it from this perspective and connects it with available information on hunters' practices and beliefs.[16] He also discusses the way in which the story articulates questions of political legitimacy within Mande culture, and he therefore provides a more focused and updated discussion of an issue raised by Leo Frobenius, who connected this narrative with monster-slaying stories used across West Africa as a myth of legitimation by relatively recent dynasties.[17]

Sunjata's Childhood

A number of stories are associated with Sunjata's birth. In many of them, he and a brother, Dankaran Touman, are born at the same time, but because of a negligent messenger, the actual order of their birth is reversed when the announcement is made to their father. This confusion leads to tensions and rivalry between the brothers. It is also said that Sunjata was covered with hair at his birth, so that he resembled a lion, or that he was in some other way extraordinary.

More important is the fact that as a child Sunjata is a cripple and walks on all fours. This is because of sorcery commissioned by his stepmother. His condition lasts until he is almost grown (and in some cases, ready for circumcision), when finally he is moved to rise. The occasion is almost always an insult to his mother. She asks a co-wife for baobab leaves to flavor a sauce, and the co-wife mocks her, saying she should have her son get her some. Sogolon weeps. Sunjata overhears her and determines to rise.

The manner of his rising exists in significant variants. In many versions, he raises himself on a staff cut by his mother (who swears an oath as she does so), or he leans on her shoulder, or even on the walls of her hut. This success follows attempts to rise using multiply-forged iron bars that bend and break beneath his weight. But sometimes he does rise using the iron bars or some token from his father—and the jelilu sing him the "Song of the Bow,"[18] inspired by the bent iron. His rising is the subject of great rejoicing, and his mother sings a variety of songs expressing her pride and delight.

Sunjata then marches to the baobab tree, whose leaves are needed for the sauce, uproots it, shakes out the little boys who are in its branches, and carries it home. "There," he tells his mother. "Now they will have to come to you for the leaves for their sauces."

The story of the simultaneous births does not occur everywhere. As Gordon Innes has noted, the motif of the tardy messenger appears frequently in myths of

the origin of death, but that is not the effect here.[19] Sunjata does not seem to be associated with the coming of death. A larger narrative purpose seems to be served
by this incident when it does appear. Sunjata must later go into exile, and therefore, retroactively, there must be tension between Sunjata and his brother to cause
that departure. A dispute over birth order is a convenient mechanism for establishing such tension and appears elsewhere in regional historical traditions. The
motif also raises the contemporary issue of co-wife rivalry that is a current staple
in almost any sort of performance and narrative.

The story of the rising is a far more central and essential moment and serves
as a criterion for distinguishing strands of the tradition: What does Sunjata use
for a support, and who sings the songs? A group of texts recorded in Kita in the
1960s fills this moment with lyric material, piling song upon song, many of of
them recognizable even in the earliest versions recorded before 1920: "Bi wo bi,
bi ka di de," sings Sogolon (Today, today, today is very good), and her delight is
the delight of the entire Manden, which sees Sunjata rising to fulfill his destiny
that will be their glory. Sogolon sings with other women after Sunjata has drawn
upon her power to rise: the metal bars were not enough. The theme stresses the
mother-son bond that is a crucial element in Mande social philosophy: a son becomes great because of his mother; she, more than the father, is responsible for
making him. This is a slightly different aspect of the well-established principles
of *badenya* and *fadenya* identified by Charles Bird and others: the two words,
"mother-childness" and "father-childness" evoke different principles of social behavior.[20] Children of the same mother are expected to cooperate, to stick together.
Children of the same father (i.e., step-siblings in a polygamous household) are rivals, in competition for the family's resources. The rivalry includes the father, who
is seen as the ultimate competitor. In this case, Sunjata's reliance on his mother's
power in order to rise is a reflection of badenya.

Food is involved in the underlying associations. The contention and insults
arise over a condiment. And the closest equivalent in everyday life to the staff that
Sogolon provides her son is probably the pestle that almost every woman in traditional West Africa used in past times on a daily basis (and that works as an
effective weapon).[21] This association opens a contrast with Sunjata's antagonist,
Sumanguru, whose birth is tied to the use of a mortar. The pairing of pestle
and mortar evokes the preparation of food, a gendered activity associated with
women, and the complementarity of the sexes.[22] These themes pervade the epic
and establish a contrast in the behavior of the protagonists.

Some versions of the story thus make this a festive women's moment; this point
has implications for an understanding of the performance mode as well. The lyric

material (some of Sunjata's forty praise songs) seems particularly designed for delivery by women. Whether this might imply an intended audience of women as well is impossible to determine, but the notion seems plausible.

The other narrative possibility expressed at the moment of rising comes in the written historical tradition, which includes indigenous African sources such as the Nioro manuscripts mentioned in chapter 5. The French administrator and Africanist Maurice Delafosse relied heavily on an Arabic-language manuscript from Nioro in his account of Sunjata. In these versions, Sunjata is the last of twelve brothers (like Joseph, perhaps) who are successively killed by Sumanguru when he conquers the Manden. Sunjata then rises using his father's scepter. These manuscript versions are noticeably Islamicized in tone, and this point should be considered when noting the shift to a paternal object of power. Niane's 1960 written version also excludes the women; it is the version in which Sunjata rises on the bent iron bars and onlookers sing the "Song of the Bow."

The two versions of the episode provide fairly clear interpretive choices that are not limited to the question of father or mother. First, there is the choice between two nyamakala groups, the griots and the blacksmiths. Iron bars come from blacksmiths, who represent specific forms of power and knowledge in the Manden. If Sunjata rises on iron bars, then the smiths have succeeded—a thematically curious point since in the epic, smiths are represented by Sunjata's enemy Sumanguru, who is a blacksmith. The "Song of the Bow," which is perhaps the best-known song associated with Sunjata, has thus been appropriated by one group. By contrast, versions in which Sunjata rises using wood attribute the "Song of the Bow" to a woman, a jelimuso named Tumu Maniyan who will accompany Sunjata into exile playing a hunter's instrument (an iron rasp) and singing.[23]

A second choice involves old and new forms of knowledge. Where Sunjata rises using iron or a token from his father, there is a connection with Islam and the written tradition—the new forms of knowledge. This formulation displaces the earlier importance accorded to Sunjata's mother (and associated women). The social importance of women is another theme that resonates throughout the epic, providing a criterion by which to differentiate versions of the epic.

Whatever the means, it is clear that Sunjata's success in overcoming his handicap is an augury for his (and the Manden's) future greatness. The contrast between this moment and his future victory over Sumanguru Kante lies in the nature of the obstacle. His later victory necessarily establishes social divisions since a smith should not be a king. Sunjata's first success marks a triumph of the will—and filial propriety—over the body.

Sunjata Goes into Exile

Having risen, Sunjata is now a rival to his brother Dankaran Touman. Sunjata becomes a successful hunter, providing his family with ample food. He is also the ideally deferential younger brother. Nevertheless, Dankaran Touman perceives him as a threat and enlists the Nine Witches of Manden to kill Sunjata. He offers them an ox in payment. Sunjata gives them nine buffaloes, and they spare his life. But it is clear he must leave the Manden. He departs, accompanied by his family (mother, sister, and a younger brother, Manding Bokary).

Along the way, he makes various stops; this portion of the narrative is quite flexible and subject to regional variation. Sometimes he moves on because his host has been paid to kill him, sometimes because of hostility. Sometimes he passes tests. He comes eventually to Mema, where the ruler Mema Farin Tunkara takes him in.

This section of the epic is a necessary transition but is never so polished as to command great attention for its literary value. It is of greater interest to historians and ethnographers. The travels link Sunjata with local traditions and families, depending upon the route selected. The Nine Witches of the Manden certainly merit examination (one of them, incidentally, is the woman often given to the Traore brothers in exchange for Sogolon Conde), although information on this group may be disappearing.

The travels are sometimes dramatized by incidents in which Sunjata's sister, also named Sogolon, restrains him from anger at various moments, warning him about prophecies that had been made. The presence of the sister, the mother, the brothers, and sometimes the jelimuso Tumu Maniya singing before them on the path might recall the motif of the marvelous march encountered in Central Africa and in the Kusa story of Mareñ Jagu.

Sumanguru Conquers the Manden

Many stories attach to Sumanguru Kante. He is said to have been born of three mothers. The unborn child passed from womb to womb, frolicking during the night and protracting the triple pregnancy. Finally, the women tricked him by placing a mortar in the room, which he mistook for the womb to which he was returning in the dark. When dawn came, he was found outside the womb and declared "born."

Later he is said to have exchanged his sister for the balafon that he got from the jinns. This was a voluntary act on her part; knowing her brother's need, she abandoned her child Fakoli and gave herself to the jinns.

Dankaran Touman sent a sister in marriage to Sumanguru, accompanied by a jeli, Jankuma Doka (Doka the cat). Jankuma Doka found Sumanguru's secret chamber, which contained the balafon, and could not resist the temptation to play it. Sumanguru caught him, and the jeli began to sing his praises. Sumanguru found this so sweet that he refused to let Jankuma Doka go. Sumanguru cut the tendons of the singer's legs so he could not flee and renamed him Bala Faseke Kouyate.

Sumanguru then betrayed Dankaran Touman and invaded the Manden. Dankaran Touman fled into the highlands of Guinea, and Sumanguru established his rule over the land. His oppression is most frequently described through the metaphor of putting gourds over people's mouths.

He also alienated members of his own family. His nephew Fakoli had a wife whose one pot could prepare as much food as the pots of Sumanguru's 333 wives. Sumanguru took the wife away. Fakoli abandoned him and went over to the side of Sunjata.

In many ways, Sumanguru is the antithesis of Sunjata: they contrast in birth, in behavior, in outlook.[24] But he was, and remains, a figure of power in his own right. One praise name widely accorded him makes him the "First and Native King" (mansa folo-folo ni mansa duguren), which is a curious title for a ruler often portrayed as a usurper.

He is not a simple usurper. He is also a blacksmith and in theory is thus barred from political authority—which he nevertheless seizes, disrupting the accepted social order. In some ways he is monstrous—not, perhaps, in his treatment of the sister married to the jinns (such exchanges are frequent), but in the image presented of him when Jankuma Doka penetrates his secret chamber. The griot's song says that Sumanguru enters the Manden wearing garments of human skin. The chamber is the site of sorcery and hostile magic. As a hunter, Sunjata also traffics in occult power, but his is used for beneficial ends (e.g., supplying each of the nine witches with her own buffalo to eat). Sumanguru's purposes seem darker.[25] In mythological terms, the contrast is between chaos and social order; and the actions of the two rulers constitute a checklist of themes and narrative details by which to differentiate the poles represented by the two figures.

But the opposition thus developed would of necessity be somewhat limited if the reality of Sumanguru's power were not recognized. Sumanguru taps into sources of power and is commemorated in lines of tradition somewhat different from those of Sunjata. He recalls the creative power of blacksmiths. He appeals to those not subject to Keita authority. Some griots note that the Bamana still worship Sumanguru, and the distinction between Sunjata and Sumanguru might reflect some symbolic dividing line between the closely related Malinka and Bamana groups.

Sunjata Is Summoned

The oppression of Sumanguru is such that the people of the Manden decide to seek a savior. Divination tells them they must find Sunjata, and so a delegation sets forth carrying Mande foodstuffs (spices and vegetables).

They come eventually to Mema, and Sunjata's sister Sogolon Kulunkan discovers them in the market, where they are selling their Mande foods. Delighted, she brings them home. To honor them, she prepares a meal but discovers she has no meat. She uses her occult power to remove by magic the inner organs of the animals that Sunjata and his brother, Manding Bokary, have just killed while hunting in the bush. When the brothers butcher their kills, they are somewhat surprised at the absence of organs, but Sunjata recognizes that this is his sister's doing. When they return home, however, Manding Bokary expresses his anger at Sogolon. In the altercation that follows, her wrap-around cloth falls off. Sunjata or the sister then curses Manding Bokary: his line will never gain kingship.

The messengers present their case, and Sunjata is willing to return home. But he will not go without his mother, and she is too old and ill to travel. He goes into the bush and prays: if he is truly to unite and lead the Manden, he asks that his mother die that night, and she does.

He then asks the ruler of Mema for land in which to bury his mother, and Mema Farin Tunkara demands gold. Sunjata instead sends him old potsherds with dust, arrowheads, gunpowder, and guinea fowl feathers. The prince's advisers interpret this riddle: if they do not give Sunjata the land, he will destroy the town like an old pot, with arrows and bullets, and guinea fowl will be left to play in the dust. The prince gives him the land, and Sunjata sets off for home.

Curiously, the death of Sunjata's mother and the riddle of the potsherds is perhaps the most constant element of the epic, present in almost every version with a minimum of change. This moment balances that earlier moment when his mother was at center stage, when Sunjata was inspired by her humiliation to overcome his limitations and rise. Here again the mother serves as a springboard, or perhaps as an offering to Sunjata's future power. The trade-off is almost explicit. Following her death, Sunjata begins to assert his power through the riddling response (with its implied threat) to Mema Farin Tunkara's demand for gold. The threat is taken seriously: this is a measure either of Sunjata's actual powers or of the king's assessment of his future capability.

The story of the messengers with their Mande foodstuffs (a device to find Sunjata) and the incidents involving the sister can be linked with many other details. The themes of food and social relations (respect for kinship and women) recur. Sogolon Kulunkan, the sister, now takes over from her mother as the female figure of power in the story, and her introduction at this point establishes her as an independent character. Later she returns as a seductress who helps Sunjata gain the secret of Sumanguru's power.[26] In her association with magic and her devotion to her brother's (the *good* brother's) good fortune, she recalls Nsongo of the Lianja tradition and Haintainkourabe of the Kusa. But she is far more individualized: her delight in the market, her concern for her guests (with her exceptional solution to a hostess's dilemma), and her anger at her brother make her a somewhat more firmly grounded character.

Sunjata Defeats Sumanguru

A wealth of different incidents may mark Sunjata's return to the Manden and his confrontation with Sumanguru: he crosses the river thanks to a bargain struck years before by his mother with the leader of the Somono boatmen; he is joined by generals who may or may not have a foregrounded role in the coming action; he sends a partridge with a message to Sumanguru. The details of these incidents vary with the individual version.

Sunjata is at first unable to defeat Sumanguru and is defeated in a series of battles. Things look very bad for the hero. Clearly Sumanguru's control of *nyama,* occult power, is greater than his own, and unless he can learn Sumanguru's secret, he will never succeed.

His sister, Sogolon Kulunkan, comes to his rescue. She goes to Sumanguru and offers herself to him, and as their intimacy progresses she lures him into revealing his secret. Sometimes his mother warns him against telling too much to a one-night woman. Sumanguru disregards his mother, or may even do violence to her in his passion. He reveals his secret to Sogolon Kulunkan: he can be killed only by an arrow tipped with the spur of a white cock.

She steals out at night—it is not always clear whether the relationship is consummated—and escapes. Sometimes she is helped by a hero who fights a rearguard action against Sumanguru's pursuing troops. She comes to her brother with the information, and the battle is won.

In the next battle, Sumanguru's army is defeated. The king himself is forced to flee, riding away with his wife before him on the saddle. He is pursued by Sunjata and his companions. Sometimes he vanishes into the caves at Koulikoro, a set of rapids on the Niger downstream from Bamako. Sometimes he leaps the river, and is struck by the arrow on the other side, and there he turns to stone. He remains venerated by the Bamana even today, it is said.

The social value of this opportunity to narrate the valorous exploits of the ancestors of noble (and rich) clans at critical moments in the story of Sunjata is clear: the performer can include audience members in the triumph of Sunjata himself, and this inclusion leads to material rewards.[27]

The action of Sunjata's sister seems more problematic. It is a Delilah-motif, widespread throughout the epic traditions of the Sahel. It occurs with variations in the hunters' traditions (e.g., in the stories of Siramori or Kambili) and in the cycle of the conquests of Segou (see chapter 6). The gesture marks the selflessness of Sunjata's sister and her devotion to her brother's welfare (hence, perhaps, the need for the previous incidents in Mema to explain the relationship). It is not clear whether it casts Sumanguru as a fool or as a victim, but it is proof that Sumanguru cannot control his appetites, as was already clear in the case of Fakoli's wife.

The erotic element, which was nonexistent in the case of Sunjata's conception, is problematic. Many versions deny that the couple actually slept together, either through some measure of prudishness or because of the social transgression involved. Sumanguru was a smith, a *numu,* and thus barred from union with the nobles, the *horon.* This aspect can easily compound Sogolon's appeal in his eyes— a forbidden fruit offering itself. It also explains some reticence in describing the fulfillment of the relationship. Of the available versions, that of Camara Laye (a literary version) carries the sex furthest, but it is unclear whether this was his embellishment or whether he got it from his jeli informant, Babu Conde. The topic raises the much broader issue of erotica in oral performance.

The importance of the magical element in the conflict can hardly be overstated; this runs counter to the battle orientation of much European epic. As Charles Bird and Martha Kendall note, the real conflict takes place on the level of occult power; once that is settled, the battle is something of a foregone conclusion and can be rapidly dismissed, as with the phrase "The laughter went to the Mande, the tears to the Sosso."[28] The magic involved is not simply a cheap form of sorcery. Rather, it expresses a world obeying hidden and not always positive forces, and the hero's creative relation with, and control of, those forces. It is thus attached to the notion of a deeper order in life.

Further, for the culture the fighting is not really that important, nor what makes the story central. Rather, the series of tests passed and choices made by Sunjata or Sumanguru in the course of the story define what the proper outcome should be: Sunjata wins because he is in the right.

Later Conquests

Following his victory, Sunjata holds an assembly of his generals at Dakajalan and allots lands to them all.[29] Thereafter, a number of incidents may conclude a given performance or be given separately. The most frequent is the conquest of the Jolof by Tira Magan. Sunjata sent a messenger to buy horses in the Tekrour. Returning through the Jolof, the messenger was summoned by the Jolof-fin Mansa. The king took away the horses and gave the messenger some dogs instead, saying that as Sunjata was only a hunter-king, he had no use for horses. The insult is compounded with the gift of buffalo hides to make sandals.

When the messenger returns to the Manden, there is some dismay and discussion about how to break this unpleasant news to Sunjata. A jeli does so. Sunjata is furious and swears revenge; his generals vie for the honor of completing the mission. The task is finally given to Tira Magan Traore, who has shown his determination by wrapping himself in a shroud and lying in a tomb (hence a Traore praise name, "Slave of the Tomb"). Tira Magan conquers a series of kings, saying that he is "walking the dogs."

A second possible sequel tells how Fakoli defeats the king of Nyani, who had refused to submit to Sunjata and who was known for wearing clothing of iron that made him invulnerable. Fakoli succeeds when the king's wife betrays her husband and lures him into a bath where he is naked and vulnerable. She is later killed.

The death of Sunjata is not recounted in performance. Rather, the moment of his victory carries over into stories of the establishment of empire, or the movement of peoples, and thus down into the present. Of these, the most important is that of Tira Magan and the conquest of the Jolof (or the Gambia). Where his story often closes the epic on the Mande side, it serves as a starting point for the traditions of Kaabu (or Gabou) in the Gambia. It is also the sort of narrative that might receive additional prominence when the President of Mali's last name is Traore, as was the case through the 1970s and 1980s. The stories of Fakoli and the king of Nyani, by contrast, are not so well attested in the Sunjata tradition and seem to reflect the influence of the traditions of Segou in which the motif of betrayal-by-wife marks one of the best-known episodes, that of Douga of Kore (see chapter 6).

The conquest of the Jolof is considered strong evidence for the role of hunters' associations at the beginning of the empire of Mali, if not for the process of state-formation in general. The king's insult provides, at least in reflected form, some suggestion of outside assessment of the nature of the Mande state. The insult about walking, echoed elsewhere in Sahelian tradition, reflects the symbolic and economic importance of horses in their roles as luxury items, status symbols, and military resources. The tsetse fly, it must be remembered, ensures that horses survive only on the northern fringe of sub-Saharan Africa. It was during the Middle Ages, the time of Sunjata, that large-scale importation of horses apparently took place.[30]

Why the epic should move from Sunjata to his generals, from victory to victory, without covering the hero's death, is almost self-explanatory. The story is not that of the hero alone, however much the narrative may reflect the patterns of traditional heroic biography. It is the story of the Manden and its days of greatness.

Other problems underlie Sunjata's death. David Conrad has written about the need for obscurity on such a matter: even Sunjata's resting place is unknown (or hidden) because it is the repository of such great power.[31] On a more material level, discussion of Sunjata's death also entails the question of his succession and opens the door to scrutiny of the claims to legitimacy and power of a variety of local ruling families who claim the name of Keita. The testimony of Arab authors establishes that succession in the empire of Mali did not follow a smooth father-to-son pattern but moved through fraternal succession, interrupted at least once by a usurper, Sekura. The link between the common myth of origin and the genealogical claims of a given ruling family is often somewhat suspect, and thus the shift of attention away from the figure of Sunjata himself into his delegation of authority and conquest serves to discourage uncomfortable inquiries.

Versions of the Epic of Sunjata

The number of versions of the story now available, from the earliest (1892, if the fourteenth-century mention of Mari Diata by Ibn Khaldun is excluded) to the most recent, is sufficiently great that some description and categorization may be useful. Readers should consult the work of Stephen Bulman, who has, in a sense, become a Sunjata archivist.[32] The major versions are listed in table 5.1 and in the appendix.

Colonial-Era Versions

This time frame covers the period of initial contacts and reports (ca. 1890) until independence (1960). None of these is a real transcription of an oral performance, although the versions of Frobenius and Franz de Zeltner identify their informants, and Frobenius especially gives a full and detailed story supplemented with genealogical information. Oral traditions were considered interesting primarily for their historic value. Most European writers consider their reports to be history and edit them accordingly, omitting legendary and supernatural details.[33] The culmination of colonial-era historiography was the 1929 monograph by Charles Monteil, *Les empires du Mali,* which synthesized the information then available from written and oral sources. This work has been superseded by that of later writers,[34] but it represents a useful window on the perspectives and information available at that time.

This period also provides some indigenous accounts. Nioro manuscripts and traditions have been described in chapter 4.[35] All of them give the story of the Manden following that of Wagadu. However, they represent an external, Soninke-based and Islamicized tradition. A common feature of this Islamicized tradition is that when Sunjata rises, he does so using his father's cane rather than a token from his mother; they also omit the story of the death of Sogolon Conde in Mema. In other words, this local written element represents something of a minority and revisionist viewpoint, one that should be contrasted with the valuable account by Mamby Sidibe.[36]

The principal and most useful extended accounts from this period are probably those of F. Quiquandon, Frobenius, de Zeltner, and Mamby Sidibe. While their representation of the living oral tradition is of necessity distorted by their methods of collecting, they do provide valuable detail for the study of the narrative content of the tradition.

Transcribed Versions from Oral Performance

Since the years of independence, a growing number of recordings and transcriptions have illuminated the dimensions of the oral tradition. A cluster of texts represent the traditions of the Diabate jelilu of Kita/Kela, who are associated with the septennial re-roofing ceremony in Kangaba: Kele Monson Diabaté, Mahan

Djehabate, Fa-Digi and Magan Sisókó (a father-son pair), Kanku Mady Jabaté, and Lansina Diabate. Of these texts, the earliest are the richest in verbal texture and poetic detail. The version of Kanku Mady Jabaté was produced under almost official pressure, in response to the visit of a governmental delegation intended to obtain a "standardized" version of the tradition for pedagogic purposes from a source then recognized as authoritative. The versions of this group of jelilu can be described as a regional variant; they do agree closely in much of their narrative content and in fact provide the core of the tradition. So far, there is little evidence for a rival regional variant, although the material now being recorded in upper Guinea, the other half of the Manden, may well challenge this Malian dominance.

The best-known English versions are those of Gordon Innes, collected in the Gambia.[37] He provides three versions of the epic, representing different tendencies among performers: the first, that of Bamba Suso, is a dry narrative by a performer reputed for his historical knowledge. Indeed, the last five hundred lines (of a total of some fourteen hundred) are devoted to the details of the settlement of the Gambia. The second, that of Banna Kanute, is a flashy performance of great artistic appeal but represents a very unusual—indeed, unique—arrangement of the story that seems to reflect the traditions of Segou as well as of Sunjata. The third, by Dembo Kanute, is an ordinary version of a selected portion of the epic, dealing with the exploits of Fakoli. The first and third, then, are regular versions, comparable in many ways with the group of texts from Kita; the second is anomalous.

A third major source is represented by the published words of Wa Kamissoko, the jeli from Krina who served as informant at the SCOA-sponsored conferences on the history of Mali, held in Bamako in 1975 and 1976. His contributions, recorded and transcribed by Youssouf Tata Cissé, have been published in two volumes.[38] They consist largely of separate interviews on historical topics (perhaps roughly comparable to Bamba Suso's presentation of his knowledge for a school audience) that cover most of the history of the Manden. But Wa Kamissoko's slant on the record, especially as refracted through the prism of Youssouf Tata Cissé's ideological agenda, is unusual; and his contributions should be read in combination with the analysis of Paolo de Moraes Farias, which contextualizes and helps to interpret this unique collaborative venture.[39]

Niane's Version

Perhaps the chapter should have begun with Niane's version. For much of the world, this is now the canonical version of the epic of Sunjata. It appeared in 1960, the fruit of Niane's research in upper Guinea (the English translation appeared in

1965). Since then it has been dominant, influencing curricula around the world and feeding back into the oral tradition.

Niane's version lies halfway between literature and history; it is a valorization of the oral tradition as a historical source, and it marks the first salvo in Niane's effort to recoup African traditions. But it is not a simple transcription from an oral source; while Niane no doubt did spend hours listening to Mamadou Kouyaté, he has recast the material for publication. A historian's sense of the probable and the acceptable informs some of the choices he has made, but so also has a poet's. He is sensitive to the needs of French prose, which was his medium, and his narrative is filled out with flowery phrases because sentences must be continuous and diction varied. Causality acquires greater weight, and transitions are less elusive because he provides the necessary background detail. He goes beyond any single performance to present a master narrative.

Niane presents a single story and makes no attempt to document the variant traditions encountered in the versions of different jelilu. He also nuances his story; the fantastic episode of the Buffalo-Woman is presented as hearsay, as a traveler's tale told by an unreliable (and left-handed!) narrator. Various heroes who later join Sunjata in his wars are made his childhood companions. And above all, griots are woven into the story.

Here, Niane follows his own purposes. Griots are indeed woven into the story in the oral traditions. At least two or three "origin of griot" legends can be identified in the ordinary narration (two of them are examined in chapter 1). Niane concentrates these stories in one figure: Bala Faseke Kouyate, Sunjata's griot, who is present to sing the "Song of the Bow" when Sunjata rises (he succeeds with the iron rods), who organizes his travels, and who finally comes to serve him. Thus, Niane diminishes the role of women in the story. As noted, most of the oral versions say that the songs sung when Sunjata rises (and not with the iron bars) are sung by his mother and other women. Often, in available recorded versions, the griot who accompanies Sunjata early in his travels is not Bala Faseke, but a woman, Tumu Maniya, and it is she who composes and sings the "Song of the Bow."

These points do not suggest inaccuracy on Niane's part, but they do draw attention to the nature and tendency of his editing. His hero is not so much Sunjata the king of Mali as it is the griots (jelilu), beginning with Bala Faseke Kouyate, who have preserved Sunjata's story and can recall him from oblivion. Niane wishes to rescue griots from the low esteem into which they had fallen and to recall the power and the magic with which they were formerly endowed: the power of creation, of reanimation, of memory. James Olney's essay, "Of Griots and Heroes," very appropriately recognizes that the major figure in Niane's book is the griot and in fact accurately identifies the "myth of the griot" as Niane presents it: as the repository of historical lore, the epitome of traditional wisdom.[40]

Camara Laye and Others

While Niane's version represents the most influential textualization of the Sunjata epic, it is hardly the only one. There is one other major literary rendering of the epic and a number of lesser versions. The second major version is Camara Laye's *Le maître de la parole* (*Guardian of the Word,* in James Kirkup's translation). Like Niane's version, it is based on the traditions of Guinea from a named informant, Babu Conde of Fadama; and also like Niane's version, it is not a simple transcription.[41] In many ways, it is a richer account. Laye's poetic sensibility accepts the marvelous and the fantastic in the story, and so he does not censor the more lurid details. It is clear that he intended to exploit the market appeal of the oral tradition with this work. He was in bad health and in need of money at the time the book appeared. Still, as a version of Sunjata the book is a solid and valuable resource. It is still finding its place in the public eye in relation to Niane and to Laye's earlier works.[42]

The Malian writer Massa Makan Diabaté has tried in three publications to render a single recorded performance by Kele Monson Diabaté into print. (There is also a separate transcription of the same recording with the original Maninka text.)[43] Most other written versions (Gbagbo, Konare Ba, Konake, and others described by Bulman) depend on available published sources, particularly on Niane and Wa Kamissoko. They represent a transformation and appropriation of traditional material. Adame Konare Ba's historical account is perhaps the most interesting, for while she attempts a synthetic history of the life of Sunjata for a popular press (the book is one of a series on great leaders of Africa), she also claims to be offering a woman's insights into the story. But it appears to be a standard account of the story.

Approaches to the Sunjata

Most work on the Sunjata epic has been historical in intent, aimed at documenting the oral tradition or elucidating specific aspects.[44] Literary analysis has concentrated on a vision of the work as an example of oral tradition and thus foregrounds the text's performative aspects. This focus may be helpful since it avoids the problem of expressing skepticism about the accepted historical record.

But it also represents hesitancy and uncertainty about methods for dealing with such a multifarious and weighty tradition. Visions of the Sunjata epic based on the English translations alone (usually Niane and Innes's three Gambian texts) are of necessity incomplete. The task of identifying, obtaining, and analyzing other versions can be intimidating. Study of the tradition, and of specific instances, would be facilitated by reference tools: a listing of names, for instance, or of motifs; but these have not yet been developed.

Sunjata is in many ways a hero of tradition in the sense generally employed by folklorists and others: his life story conforms to a widespread pattern and has been shaped according to definable narrative rules. But agreement between Sunjata and the hero's paradigm as defined by Lord Raglan may not be central to an understanding of Sunjata. Raglan's categories are so general that the specific cultural values of individual heroes dissipate. There would be a risk of confusing Sunjata with Theseus or Krishna. The pattern is valuable as an interpretive tool because it points to those elements of the story that show most signs of narrative streamlining, that make the hero almost generic. An example might be those versions that present Sumanguru as the reigning king at the birth of Sunjata so that the opposition of hero and tyrant is clean and direct, uncluttered by the confusion of sibling rivalry and vanishing fathers.

But where Sunjata the man may agree with the model hero of tradition in many particulars, Sunjata the epic does not. Instead of a clean biography, a single story line, there is a multiplication of threads. The epic works in at least four time frames, including the present of the performance or recording: it unites the pre-Sunjata past, often anachronistically, with the time and figure of Sunjata and the events after his time that are the past to our present. Of these three periods, those before and after Sunjata probably preserve information of the greatest historical value. The epic may also offer tales of creation (Eden, for instance) before shifting to the later periods of the lands of Do and Kri.[45] These episodes provide the necessary prelude to the story of the Manden and possibly also a thematic cue. The result is that Sunjata's life is only a part of the story. After Sunjata goes into exile, the field of action divides to incorporate Sumanguru and his actions; after Sunjata is victorious, Tira Magan marches off. The epic would seem to violate certain canons of artistic unity, unless the association of Sunjata with the larger story of the Manden is kept in mind.

Any study of the tradition must come to terms with its idioms and methods. Physical prowess is not valorized in this narrative world; what matters is moral character, strength of will and purpose, mastery of self and other. Sunjata's heroes define themselves not by killing giants or hosts but by demonstrating their determination. Tira Magan lays himself in his grave, and thereafter his conquests are simply enumerated. Fakoli's head swells at one point to unimaginable proportions (an objective correlative?). Sunjata himself has already demonstrated his will by overcoming his deformity and uprooting the baobab.

The victory over Sumanguru occurs through seduction and betrayal. Is this an instance of moral turpitude? The contrast with the same motif in "Bassi of Samanyana" from the cycle of Segou may be instructive. In Segou, the enemy is a rebellious vassal, the emissary a slave girl, and the audience's sympathy remains with the enemy. In the epic of Sunjata, the emissary is not a slave but a sister who goes voluntarily; Sumanguru betrays himself against the warnings of his own family. The opposition is not one of strength, physical or occult, but of social bonds: Sumanguru is only as strong as the loyalties he commands (and observes). Sunjata has the strength of those who support him.

This does not mean that Sunjata goes unquestioned. He is repeatedly tested within the story, from his childhood to his ultimate victory. In the patterns of contrast between Sunjata and Sumanguru, Sunjata defines proper social behavior and loyalty to the Manden. In the versions of Fa-Digi Sisókó and Magan Sisókó, Sunjata swears oaths—echoing those sworn by his mother to make him rise—that catalogue the clans of the Manden and link his fate to that of the people of the Manden. Sunjata does not seek power but the fulfillment of destiny. After the Manden summons him for redress against Sumanguru, Sunjata becomes the vehicle of the collective will.

This aspect of the epic reflects its function in binding the various elements of the Manden and the people who trace some attachment to Sunjata across substantial geographic distances. Such a purpose is rare in European epic; the "national epics" of the curriculum are largely the constructs of nineteenth-century nationalisms rather than the consensual collective histories of peoples. One exception might be the matter of Britain and the tales of King Arthur in all their fractured complexity.

Here Sunjata is perhaps not to be seen as a "human" figure at all, meaning by "human" that he could be subject to doubts, weaknesses, and failings. Rather, he is an embodiment of power, and in proportion as his destiny is glorious, he is possessed by the power to bring it about. This is not a purely positive vision. Heroes, in the Mande conception, are trouble, for they represent disruption, change, and the drive for self-fulfillment along the fadenya axis. Sunjata compels respect because of his power; the same is true of Sumanguru, and their struggle is not a simplified moral allegory of right and wrong. But the multiplication of other elements in the story, such as the repeated testing, establishes Sunjata as the proper focal point for multiple interests.

It is rewarding to view the performances as an effort to conserve and reconcile (within defined parameters) a multiplicity of local traditions. A significant difference between the Sunjata tradition and the stories of origin recorded in Central Africa lies in the cultural heterogeneity of the cultures associated with Sunjata and the relative homogeneity of the Central African milieu. The Sunjata tradition is not only a myth of origin merging into a politically significant genealogy. It is an almost self-consciously artificial construct regrouping many different traditions and providing common ground for the interrelations of many different populations. Such a vision reads the epic of Sunjata in terms of local idioms and interests and also recognizes the need to extend beyond the historical into the ethnographic realm, to incorporate available information on social patterns, beliefs, lifestyles, and practices. But in many ways the tradition is in flux, as is the world of the Manden. For this reason the colonial-era versions are, despite their possible flaws, vital objects of study since they serve to ground the contemporary renditions.

Other Traditions

Beyond Sunjata, the Manden offers a variety of heroes and cycles, although they are incompletely documented. The hunters' songs that have already been discussed are an important component of Mande oral art. The more recent narratives of the Gambia (dealing with the fall of Kaabu) are treated separately in chapter 8. The Manden has more recent heroes. The nineteenth century offers two great and terrifying men whose stories are emerging as the process of collection extends beyond Sunjata alone.

Samory Toure established a centralized state in the southern Manden and then proceeded to fight the French for some decades before he was defeated. Yves Person has documented his career in great detail. David Conrad has recently collected some texts in Guinea dealing with Samory Toure, which foreground in particular his younger brother Keme Brema, who died in battle. Samory also appears incidentally in the *Kambili* of Seydou Camara, a hunters' epic; the figure is not historical but represents a type of powerful and merciless ruler.

The second figure actually precedes Samory and represents a foreign intrusion: al-Hajj Umar Tall, the Tukolor religious leader who marched through the Manden while en route to Segou and Massina. The growing epic tradition associated with this figure (for he is sung in Fula and Zarma, as discussed in chapters 7 and 8) reflects his importance within the local vision of Islam. He is effectively portrayed as a second Prophet, charged with bringing Islam to the Sahel. Some accounts reported in the 1970s[46] touch on the actual wars fought by the Tukolor forces of the religious leader and seem to criticize his actions. Recent texts seem far more hagiographic.

In addition to the epics of these heroes, a wealth of localized historical narrative lends itself easily to epic singing in the hands of jelilu. As recording, rather than textual publication, becomes more widespread, a great deal more material from this fertile homeland will become available.

❖ 6 ❖

SEGOU AND THE BAMANA

THE KINGDOM OF Segou arose around 1700, during the extended period of anarchy that followed the dissolution of the Songhay empire, in a region that lay between the two former spheres of royal authority, the Manden and the Gao-Timbuctoo stretch of the Niger. The peoples of the kingdom were almost certainly an ethnic mix ultimately unified by a common language known as Bamana (or formerly Bambara). Bamana is a language of the Mande family, extremely close to the Maninka (or Malinke) of the Sunjata tradition, although differences are stressed by native speakers for whom the nonlinguistic connotations of the labels (i.e., being called a Malinke or a Bamana) may matter more than technicalities of dialectology.[1]

The traditions of Segou offer extremely rich material for study from all points of view. The history, ethnography, religion, and art of the Bamana have all been comparatively well documented and studied, thus providing a base for close analysis available for few other groups. One explanation for this serendipitous wealth of material is simply the time frame: the kingdom arose during the eighteenth century and reached its apogee in the early years of the nineteenth, before the tides of Fulbe-led Islam eroded its power and circumscribed its hegemony and before the end of the Atlantic slave trade dissolved much of its economic foundation. The events involved are thus recent enough to have been preserved in some detail within family traditions and other sources of oral history. The number of repetitions needed to transmit the information over the generations is relatively small. Two other factors also enrich the documentation. First, there are the reports of European travelers (for instance, an eye-witness report by Mungo Park of the hostilities between Monzon, king of Segou, and Dessekoro Kaarta in 1796); these reports provide contemporary, although foreign, accounts of the conditions in the area. And second, the intervention of Islam, which has left an indigenous written record.[2]

The end of Segou's power began with the defeat of its forces by the Muslim converts of Cheikou Amadou of Massina at the battle of Noukouma in 1818. The subsequent decline was exacerbated by the passage of the Tukolor forces of al-Hajj Umar Tall some forty years later. In the religious eschatology of the region, which is now predominantly Muslim, the traditions of Segou become emblematic of the immediate pre-Islamic past and the autochthonous history of the region.

Thus, there are three intersecting bodies of information on the history of the kingdom: the traditional oral sources, European travelers' reports, and "local" Arabic-language histories written at the beginning of the colonial period, around 1900. Historians have done good work sifting and processing this wealth of material, and there is now a foundation of historical information on which to approach the epic traditions—which have not been included in the category of historical sources for solid reasons—and to interpret their presentations, representations, and ellipses.[3] Such an opportunity for multiple perspectives on the content of a performance tradition is, to my knowledge, virtually unknown and endows the traditions of Segou with particular significance and value for the study of the shifting interests of history, ideology, and entertainment.

There is also a wealth of modern writings on Bamana ethnography and thought from a strong tradition of French ethnography.[4] Some American scholars may question the methods of the "savoir-africain" [African knowledge] school represented in this case particularly by Germaine Dieterlen and Youssouf Tata Cissé, because of a troubling absence of reference to specific informants and a willingness to generalize without acknowledging the multiple perspectives that exist within any society. But it must be admitted that their documentation of Bamana belief has been welcomed in Francophone circles as evidence of the sophistication of traditional thought and that they do offer a good deal of primary information. On this point, as on so many in African studies, scholars are caught in a crossfire of motives. The work of Dieterlen, Cissé, Dominique Zahan (and the American Pascal Imperato) on Bamana initiation societies affords the outsider a unique window on the complexity and multiplicity of experience within a "traditional" and nonliterate culture. It also permits the student to face the challenge of integrating religious beliefs and literary production, a task familiar within the traditions of European literary scholarship but often made problematic in other contexts by a lack of material. Of course, a simple one-to-one matchup of religious traditions and texts would not be productive. The challenge is far more complex, since the influence of Islam and a move toward religious syncretism within the performance tradition must be accommodated. Contemporary statements about past religious practice, or about the world of that past, must be carefully filtered. Nevertheless, however problematic the use of these materials, their existence as resources by which to expand interpretation and understanding of epic traditions must be acknowledged.[5]

Besides religion, there is the realm of art. Bamana sculpture has attracted attention and study by specialists such as Patrick McNaughton and by non-regional-specialists such as Robert Farris Thompson.[6] There is common ground in the aesthetics of statuary as identified by Sarah Brett-Smith and certain aspects of the oral tradition. Not all these features are positive: in her starkest statement, "The Voice of the Bamana Is Hard," Brett-Smith depicts a world of conflicting forces, of treachery and poisonous betrayal.[7] Betrayal and fraternal strife are trademarks of the Diarra dynasty of Segou. In other essays Brett-Smith addresses questions of secrecy and power, of silence and completeness, poison, fertility, and death, and all these themes are relevant to the world of the old kings of Segou.

The background resources for the traditions of Segou are thus particularly rich. Literary study of the traditions, however, has been relatively restricted. Lilyan Kesteloot and Amadou Hampaté Bâ have offered a series of essays over the years.[8] Kesteloot's insights are perceptive but have not yet been integrated into a general study,[9] and her voice is often one of uncritical affirmation that sometimes privileges pre-existing literary definitions over original observation of the material. However, she has been the pioneer. She was the first to publish a significant corpus of texts in translation;[10] she has remained in the vanguard at the University of Dakar, training new generations of collectors and students. In particular, her collection of translated texts, *Da Monzon de Segou,* contains a valuable descriptive and historical introduction and establishes the necessary distinction between what she terms the "chronicle" (or the unperformed historical recollections and narrations of persons with an authority to speak) and the griot tradition, in which the performance element dominates. Further interpretive material can be found in the introductions to the various editions of texts: Dumestre's *La geste de Segou,* Kesteloot and Dumestre's *La prise de Dionkoloni,* and Conrad's *A State of Intrigue.*

The traditions of Segou may be virtually unknown to English-speaking scholars of epic. They are occulted, it seems, by the sun of the Manden and by the presumption of homogeneity in oral epic traditions, which devalues the careful search for differences. This ignorance seriously distorts the image of African epic, for it obscures the particularities and differences in regional histories and oral literature. The Sunjata of Kele Monson Diabaté and, for instance, Baba Cissoko's "Betrayal of Bakari Jan" are light-years apart in terms of their literary effect and intent;[11] an appreciation of the difference will elucidate the operations of literary production in oral traditions far better than any dissection of manuscript traditions.

What marks the traditions of Segou is the sense of texture, the artistic handling of the material. The relation of performer and tradition shifts with the move from Sunjata to Segou. With Segou, the performer is freer. The story of Sunjata is imbued at times with awe and majesty: grandiose brush strokes that create a world. The world of Segou is one of irony, consciously exploited by the performers. The kings of Segou are counterpoints to Sunjata: they may be powerful, but they do not seem noble in behavior and they are not good. The narratives of Segou typically recount the conquests of the kings, but an audience's sympathies may as often be with the victims as with the victors. Sometimes the hearer may be torn, as in the case of Saran, wife of Douga of Kore, who betrays her husband for love of Da Monzon and is executed by Da. Segou is a realm of ambivalence and mistrust, of arrogance and illegitimacy, and finally of cruelty and death. The performers' evocations of these traditions appear far more nuanced, particular, and skeptical than the texts examined so far. A consciously defined distance separates subject and performer, and the jeli's voice conveys far less passion and more control.[12]

Not only is the background material copious; there is also a wealth of different stories in the traditions of Segou (see table 6.1), and this leads to another distinction. John Johnson, in his schematic typology of African epics, has defined the Segou cycle as episodic;[13] the stories may involve individual heroes and protagonists, but they do not involve entire lives. Rather, the history provides a broad tapestry of incident, of which selected details may be isolated for artistic narration. It is perhaps helpful to view the cycle of Segou as an extended king-list that gives the names and the manner of accession or succession to power and that culminates in a series of patterned or conventionalized narratives recounting the victories of the kingdom. Within the cycle, the traditional biography of the hero is rarely encountered. Relatively few birth stories occur in the cycle of Segou, despite the fact that it explicitly covers the reigns of four kings, not counting historical rulers omitted from the performance tradition. This is a strong point of contrast, then, with the stories of Sunjata and other heroes whose births are exhaustively narrated and whose life tasks might seem to be an extension of their fathers' work. The only birth brought significantly into the stories of Segou may indeed echo the double-birth theme encountered with Sunjata, yet in its principal purpose it calls into question the succession of Da to his father Monzon: Da displaced the older brother who would have been the legitimate heir. The incident thus highlights a theme that marks earlier episodes of the cycle: the question of the legitimacy of royal power. This theme is indirectly continued in the later (by chrono-logical reference) sections of the cycle in which the conventional cause of conflict is an insult directed at the *faama* [king] of Segou and the vengeance wrought to erase it.

The cycle of Segou thus establishes an almost dialectic relationship with the tradition of Sunjata. Where the Mande epic serves to affirm authority, legitimacy, and cultural community, the very matter of Segou calls those values into ques-tion. Often, insults to the king spark the events, and the suggestion of illegitimate rule motivates the epics. The conquests of Segou are never clean victories. They always involve furtive and sorcerous measures. These are, of course, part of the idiom of the West African epic tradition. Sunjata was also obliged to discover the sources of Sumanguru's occult power. It is a given that the battle takes place outside the material plane, that it is the hero's spiritual (albeit *not* religious) pro-tection and powers that allow him to overcome his foe, and considerably more interest is shown in this aspect of the story than in the actual combat. These com-monalities aside, there remains a significant difference in tone and attitude of the performer toward Sunjata—treated positively in relationship to the bad king Sumanguru—and toward the faama of Segou, who is kept at something of a dis-tance. Segou remains the city of the "four thousand four hundred and forty-four *balanza* trees and the little hunch-backed *balanza*," and that last little tree repre-sents either or both the twisted club used to bludgeon a king being dethroned or, more commonly, treachery.

Behind the cycle of Segou lies a complex history covering two dynastic families and many kingdoms, major and minor. Mamari Biton Koulibaly is the accepted founder of the state of Segou; but a narrator may precede his story with the legend of the two Koulibaly brothers who came to the Niger River and were assisted in crossing by a *poyon*, a species of fish, which one of them ungratefully killed. The legend explains why one branch of the Koulibaly clan ruled in Kaarta on the north bank of the Niger and the other in Segou on the south bank. The founding of Segou by Biton Koulibaly is generally dated to 1710.[14] The strength of the state was the strength of the armed association or *ton* founded by Biton Koulibaly (whose name, Bi-ton, in fact refers to his position as head of the association); the ton became his tool to power. The ton presumably took its origin from hunting as-sociations (Biton is always described as a hunter), or from initiatory societies like those that still exist (descriptions of the early activities of the association involve beer-drinking feasts rather than hunting). The ton became an organized system for plundering and exploiting the neighboring regions, and the power of Segou spread rapidly. The principal commodity upon which this state was based was humans: the slave-trade made Segou's fortune, and a generalized memory of this source of wealth underlies much of the ambivalence that marks the epic cycle.

Jean Bazin has provided the accepted description of the roles of war and slavery in the economy of Segou,[15] and his essay, offering a perceptive and analytic picture of an inhumane system, opens a valuable window onto the particular conditions of the region. He distinguishes three levels of slave-taking: warfare on a general level, the raids of mounted men (*so-boli*, literally "horse-running"), and individualized efforts on the level of kidnapping. These three methods come together in a process of "transformation" of humans from individuals to commodity, an operation effected both on the social identity and the labor of the victims. All three forms of slave-taking are reflected in the epics of the cycle, although in various ways. The wars between Segou and the neighboring states are the subjects of individual episodes, although slave-taking is not explicitly mentioned.[16] The individualized level appears in the actions of characters such as Bilissi (a vari-colored man-jinn killed by Bakari Jan), who would routinely capture two or three people on the way to market and sell them to pay for his beer. The raids of mounted bands (the horse-running) are not really in evidence in the traditions attaching to the kings of Segou but are to be found in more generalized narratives such as those collected by Leo Frobenius or Harold Courlander and Ousmane Sako.[17]

Biton Koulibaly's dynasty did not long survive him in Segou. Two sons came to power but were rapidly deposed or slain by the leaders of the armed association in the early 1750s. A period of anarchy followed, in which various men rose and were deposed until Ngolo Diarra took power around 1767. Tradition says that he had been a slave of Biton Koulibaly before gaining power. He established a dynasty that remained in control of Segou until 1890 and the arrival of the French, although in 1862 they were defeated by the Tukolor of al-Hajj Umar Tall and there was a change of rulers.[18] Across the Niger River in the Kaarta, a second Koulibaly dynasty survived until the time of Umar Tall. A continuing theme within the epic cycle is the conflict between the older established Koulibaly clan of the Kaarta and their adherents and the upstarts of the Diarra line.

The power of Segou reached its peak around 1810, extending from the Manden almost to Timbuctoo, north to Jara and south to the Mossi states. Thereafter it began to crumble. The first blow was the rebellion of the new Islamic community of Massina led by Cheikou Amadou (in 1818); the erosion of power continued with the buffeting of al-Hajj Umar Tall during the period around 1860.

Within the epic tradition, the Diarra dynasty clearly suffers from its upstart origins; Diarra enemies repeatedly call them slaves and descendants of captives. The treatment is almost a literary topos, an accepted convention by which to launch a (verbal) war. It reflects a broader concern over status defined not as the opposition of noble and commoner but of the free and the formerly enslaved: between *horonya* (the state of being *horon* or free) and *jonya* (the state of being a slave). Bazin credibly derives the term *horon*, usually translated as "noble," from the Arabic *hurr* [free][19] and traces the complexities involved in serving a family descended from the slaves of the rulers. In Segou, everyone was a *jon* [slave] in one sense or another: the institution permeated the entire social fabric. Rulers were invested not with right but with power. Biton Koulibaly became king by creating an instrument of violence, the armed association. Da later assumed the seat of power, an ox-hide, after clubbing the elders of the clans to force them to acknowledge him. The nuances are reflected in the different royal titles. Bazin notes an opposition between the term *mansa* [king] used by the Maninka and in the traditions of Sunjata, and the Bamana title *faama*. For Bazin, the *mansa* "is endowed with a holy power of arbitration, and is not necessarily either rich or powerful."[20] The title *faama*, while translated as "king," is most probably derived from *fanga*, power, and implies forcefulness rather than authority. Bazin provides an anecdote about a noble, Seribajan Traore of the lineage of Tira Magan (general to Sunjata and conqueror of the Gambia), who was invited to become a local governor by Faama Da but refused in order to avoid becoming the jon of the faama.

The combination of slave-taking and egregious anti-Islamic paganism (which in the epics is translated euphemistically into the leitmotivs of beer-drinking with the occasional human sacrifice) colors the image of Segou with unpleasant tones for the contemporary listener. This is perhaps the greatest and most significant contrast with the traditions of Sunjata. The question of the relations of the two traditions is still open. In general they are treated separately, and to my knowledge, little attempt has been made to identify points of convergence and conscious contrast. But the traditions do meet, if only in the mouths of modern performers and on the middle ground of Bamako, which lies between the Manden and Segou. A full appreciation of the cycle of Segou probably requires some sense of the Sunjata tradition as a backdrop. The linguistic difference between Maninka and Bamana may not be as great as the cultural or social difference (griots in fact regularly use dialectal forms from either side of the divide), and the apparently dialectic relations of the two traditions are worth exploring.[21]

Performers and Performances

The table of epics (see table 6.1) presents an arrangement of the available published texts, organized according to the reigns of the kings. They derive principally from three books. The first is *Da Monzon de Ségou,* an anthology of twelve

Table 6.1. Episodes of the Cycle of Segou

Performer	Episode/Title	*Source*
	Biton Koulibaly	
Kefa Diabaté	Biton Koulibali et le génie Faro	Kesteloot 1972, vol. 2, pp. 5–13
Tayiru Banbera	Biton et les genies	Dumestre 1979, pp. 359–99
———	Histoire de Biton Koulibali	Banbera 1978, pp. 612–81
**———	———	Conrad 1990, pp. 65–97
Fabu Kuate?	Die Geschichte Bitons	Frobenius 1925, pp. 344–51
	Accession of Ngolo Diarra	
Sissoko Kabine	Ngolo Diarra et Biton Koulibali	Kesteloot 1972, vol. 2, pp. 14–23
**Tayiru Banbera	———	Conrad 1990, pp. 105–33
**Kefa Diabate	See "Biton Koulibali et le génie Faro," above	
**Sory Camara	See "Douga de Kore" in Dumestre 1979, below	
	Monzon Diarra and the Accession of Da	
Sissoko Kabine	Monzon et Dibi de Niamina	Kesteloot 1972, vol. 2, pp. 24–33
**Tayiru Banbera	L'avènement de Da	Dumestre 1979, pp. 265–357
**———	———	Conrad 1990, pp. 143–91
**Sory Camara	See "Douga de Kore" in Dumestre 1979, below	
	Conflicts of Da Monzon	
	Douga of Kore	
Sory Camara	Da Monzon et Douga de Kore	Kesteloot 1972, vol. 4, pp. 24–42
———	"Douga de Kore"	Dumestre 1979, pp. 183–263
Bakoroba Kone	The Vulture	Bird 1972, pp. 468–77
	Bassi of Samaniana	
Sissoko Kabine	Da Monzon et Bassi de Samaniana	Kesteloot 1972, vol. 1, pp. 32–60
Moulaye Kida	Da Monson and Samanyana Basi	Bird 1972, pp. 457–67
**Tayiru Banbera	———	Conrad 1990, pp. 197–264
	Karta Thiema	
Gorke	Da Monzon et Karta Thièma	Kesteloot 1972, vol. 4, pp. 43–63
	Dietekoro Kaarta	
Seydou Drame	Da Monzon et Dietékoro Kârta	Kesteloot 1972, vol. 2, pp. 34–62
**Tayiru Banbera	———	Conrad 1990, pp. 248–59
	Mariheri of Dionkoloni	
Sissoko Kabine	*La prise de Dionkoloni*	Dumestre and Kesteloot 1975
Kefa Diabate	Kumba Silamagan et Da Monzon	Kesteloot 1972, vol. 3, pp. 70–80
Demba Diabate	———	Meillassoux 1978, pp. 373–91
Anonymous	Der Held Gossi	Frobenius 1921, pp. 115–28
Anonymous	Kumba Sira Maga	Frobenius 1921, pp. 128–32
	Bakari Jan and Bilissi	
Baba Cissoko	Bakari Dian et Bilissi	Dumestre 1979, pp. 111–81
Sissoko Kabine	Bakari Dian et Bilissi	Kesteloot 1972, vol. 3, pp. 3–39

Table 6.1. *continued*

Performer	Episode/Title	Source
**Tayiru Banbera	——	Conrad 1990, pp. 268–318
Anonymous	Bacari Dyan I	C. Monteil 1977, pp. 370–75
	Betrayal of Bakari Jan	
Baba Cissoko	La trahison de Bakari Jan	Dumestre 1979, pp. 61–109
Sissoko Kabine	La trahison de Bakari Jan	Kesteloot 1972, vol. 3, pp. 40–58
**Tayiru Banbera	——	Conrad 1990, pp. 318–324
Anonymous	Bacari Dyan II	Monteil 1977, pp. 376–79
	Bakari and the Fulbe of Kounari	
Sissoko Kabine	Bakari et les Peul du Kounari	Kesteloot 1972, vol. 3, pp. 59–69
**Tayiru Banbera	——	Conrad 1990, pp. 324–27

Note: A double asterisk (**) in the table indicates a segment of a larger narrative.

pieces by six different performers, with some supporting material published by Lilyan Kesteloot in 1972; it contains six pieces by Sissoko Kabine that form a loose but complete version of the cycle. The second is Gerard Dumestre's book, *La geste de Ségou,* which presents five performances by three different jeliw. The third is David Conrad's book, *A State of Intrigue,* which presents a single narrative history of the kingdom, given over several days by the jeli Tayiru Banbera.[22] Other pieces from a variety of sources have been incorporated in the table, but no attempt has been made to correlate them with the more historical accounts provided by Cheikh Moussa Kamara, Gaoussou Diarra (in Serge Sauvageot), or Kore Tammoura (in Monteil), although there is some overlap.[23] Kamara's account, for instance, shows clear echoes of the performance tradition. David Conrad's excellent annotations to Banbera's narrative indicate cross-references and variant accounts, and every student of Segou should explore this supplementary material.

The difference between "historical" tradition and "performance" tradition (in Kesteloot's terms, *chronique* and *épopée*) is particularly vital for this material. Within the Sunjata tradition, there is a chronological distinction. The material pertaining to Sunjata himself is anterior to localized history, through which contemporary families trace their ancestry backwards (sometimes, indeed, to Sunjata). The life and career of Sunjata provide the basis for the performance tradition, and the later portions serve as the local "historical" tradition. Two cultural imperatives (origins and local legitimation) are fulfilled by different bodies of material. With the traditions of Segou, these two functions involve a coincidence in content but a distinction in source and purpose. In his valuable study of the

Niaré traditions of Bamako, Claude Meillassoux outlines the characteristics of the griot performance tradition:

> The griot's story is public, and it agrees with a certain version of the approved history of the clan to which he is attached. The principal purpose of this epic is to arouse admiration, fear, or devotion towards the clan or the sovereign whose deeds are recounted. To this purpose, the marvelous is often substituted for the actual, and praise for criticism. . . . The oral tradition of the griots is less historical than political in intention; it serves mainly to reinforce the power of great men.[24]

It might be observed that while in the Manden the towns of Kela and Kangaba serve, however problematically, as something of a center for Sunjata traditions, independent of the lineage (see chapter 5), no such center or public event exists for the traditions of Segou. Intimate knowledge of the traditions reposes in the Diarra lineage, but the performance tradition is spread throughout the Bamana-speaking territory from Massina to Bamako. Bamako, the capital of Mali, has naturally become something of a center for griots of all sorts, as the modern state substitutes for older patterns of patronage. Even prior to the modern era of Bamako, however, the traditions are presented from multiple perspectives because they are not those of a single family or lineage.[25]

The difference between history and performance is well worth exploring, for it also serves to differentiate some of the performances before us. Tayiru Banbera, for instance, is presented as a specialist in the history of Segou. Indeed, the depth and the detail of his knowledge, as presented in Conrad's translation, is impressive. His narrative is filled with illuminating digressions that add texture and a sense of temporal depth to his subject.[26]

> When the Bamana went to war, they would divide the warriors into three
> different battle arms.
> They would divide them into three sections. . . .
> Those three ranks stood up like men lined up to pray.
> The people in front would fire, *wuu!*
> And empty their muskets.
> Then they would glide to the rear.
> That would leave the other two ranks of marksmen in front. . . . [27]

This historical tone contrasts with the more usual contrast of present and past to be found across all performance traditions.

> In those days, to be a *nyamakala* was like precious gems.
> If one of us destroyed a noble's reputation, the noble lost his place in society.
> No one would give ten francs for him, much less five thousand.
> If we praise a noble beyond his rank, no one will keep up with him.
> If a *nyamakala* told his patron to get beans, he would buy butter.

In those days there was no wealth but nobility.
Oh, nowadays nobility is dead.[28]

Or there is the more humorous:

> That is why there are now three types of sauce.
> But when a slovenly woman is involved there are four types.[29]

Banbera enumerates and explains them over the next twenty lines. By contrast, Baba Cissoko offers discrete polished units whose composition is carefully controlled. As Dumestre notes, the griot allows only one digression placed at the moment of greatest tension in each of his two published narratives.[30] His embellishments are not so much informative (about history) as entertaining, for instance, when he describes how the secret of a plot against Bakari Jan moves down a line of twenty-four women washing laundry at the river.[31] Baba Cissoko's concern is clearly the pleasure of his audience while Tayiru Banbera's is to inform his immediate patron, David Conrad. But besides the immediate questions of patronage, there are also those of the performer's qualifications. Tayiru Banbera was a recognized specialist in the history of Segou, and his knowledge shows.[32]

Despite the wealth of supplementary material on the traditions of Segou, there is little hard "performance data" on the presentation of such epics in their "natural" setting. The performers come from the professional *nyamakala* group of *jeliw* known as griots; their training is a form of family apprenticeship that may or may not involve fostering with a relative and that includes musical as well as verbal training. Dumestre (a linguist) offers an analysis of word flow and characteristic linguistic embellishments for the different performers in the introduction to his book. Conrad's work follows the laudable example of Gordon Innes's *Sunjata* in providing a musicological analysis of Tayiru Banbera's performance. Heroes do have their own signature tunes, as they might be called. But otherwise the sources are scanty.

There may be a hereditary bond with some local noble family, but clearly under modern conditions that old-fashioned relationship is vanishing. By and large, the performers in this tradition are professionals drawn to the vocation by talent, ability, and opportunity. It is nevertheless increasingly true that they do not derive their income principally from their performances but from other activities, such as farming. The model presented in published materials shows single performers, accompanying themselves on their instrument (or occasionally assisted by an accompanist). The *naamu*-sayer of the Sunjata tradition does not appear as a fixture, but other participants do. Women may sing a lyric accompaniment or interlude, for instance. Such a production varies with the occasion, the means of the patron, and the resources of the principal performer. Here also performers probably face the same audience preference Babalola observed for Yoruba *ijala* chanters: nowadays, the patrons want dance music rather than extended verbal pieces. So far, however, documentation has focused on the production or text rather than on the performer or context.

The episodes of the cycle can be defined in terms of the chronology of reigns, beginning with the founder of the state, Mamari Biton Koulibaly.

Biton Koulibaly and the Origin of the Kingdom

The epic cycle, as defined by the continuous narratives of Tayiru Banbera and Sissoko Kabine, starts with Mamari Biton Koulibaly, who established the kingdom; the story of his rise to power can be told as a separate narrative.

Mamari was a hunter. He once wounded an animal; while tracking it, he came to the fields of a kinsman. He stopped to help the kinsman and was rewarded with hunter's knowledge. When he continued on the track of the wounded animal, he met the wood spirits; one of them was wounded, and he was able to cure it. After that, he sat one evening beneath a tree and heard an ancient vulture and an aged hyena conversing; he learned that if he wished to rule the land, he should move to the location of Segou.

He and his mother moved to the site of Segou. His mother began to grow tomatoes, but her garden was raided at night. Mamari sat up to guard it and caught a river spirit, the child of Faro, ruler of the waters. He accompanied it under the waters; and following its advice, he refused Faro's offer of gold and silver and other forms of wealth and asked only for some millet. And from the water spirit mother, all he asked was that she pour some of her milk from her breast into his ear.

He sowed the millet and cultivated the crop, but when it was ripe he did not harvest it. On the advice of Faro, he left it for the birds. The prophecy was that his rule would extend to wherever the birds that fed on his millet traveled.

Thereafter, he joined the local association, the *ton*, and was selected their leader *(bi-ton)* by lot. People at first objected to a stranger becoming their leader, but when his token kept appearing no matter how they tried the selection, he was accepted. The ton then grew in strength until it began subjugating neighboring villages, and this was the nucleus of the kingdom.

Other accounts of the ton say that Biton's mother used to brew honey-beer, and the association was formed as a dues-paying organization to pay for the beer; as it grew in scale, they began to impose the dues on neighbors as a form of tax. Finally they captured a village that had refused to pay the tax, and they sold the inhabitants; this was the start of the military activities of the kingdom.

Tayiru Banbera provides the fullest versions of this episode[33] and includes incidents such as that of the vulture and the hyena that are not found elsewhere. The narrative may stand on its own or serve as an element in a series. A version by Kefa Diabate links the story of Biton's rise with that of his succession by Ngolo Diarra.[34] Kesteloot offers an analysis of this episode with a focus upon Jungian and initiatory mythological elements and the way in which the story draws upon the Mande creation myth and the figure of Faro, who represents water and the river Niger.[35] She bases her argument upon a collection of ten accounts of the story from a variety of performers. Kesteloot thus provides a methodological model and a firm basis upon which to venture more fine-grained interpretations.

The story of Biton can be divided into two parts: the first involves his move to Segou and his encounter with the water spirits (or gods?), who give him the secret to royal power. This section is marked by Biton's interaction with supernatural forces and questions of prophecy and predestination. For Kesteloot, this denotes the selection of the hero by the gods, which is followed later by a selection by humans. The second part involves Biton's organization of an association and its rapid demonstration of power. The world here is more specifically human. The two parts clearly reflect different aspects of accession to power: the first displays idioms of legitimation from a vocabulary shared with other groups of the western Sudan. The second presents a selective record of the events and prefigures the tone of the state to come.

Kesteloot treats the narrative as an essentially straightforward and positive statement about the rise of Biton Koulibaly. I have elsewhere offered an interpretation that finds darker shadows in the story by connecting the movements of Biton and his mother and her crop of tomatoes (*ngoyo* in most versions) with elements of the Mande and Bamana creation myths recorded by Germaine Dieterlen.[36] Kesteloot saw similar connections, but with different parts of the myth. The elements that seem to be most clearly echoed from the creation myths are those connected with the origins of death; and the possibility of this connection is intensified by the inherent destructiveness in the means of prophecy of

Biton's future power: the field of millet destroyed by the birds. That the token of Biton's power should involve not the generation but the destruction of foodstuffs is a considerable anomaly. Most kings justify their rule with munificence and by presenting an aura of fertility. The birds here foreshadow the armies of horsemen and others who will sweep across the region and devastate it.

The story of the ton is underplayed in the performance tradition. Usually the performer goes from Biton's magical selection[37] to the magical selection of his successor Ngolo, without lingering over the uncomfortable details of Biton's rule or succession (such as the murder of his sons and the period of anarchy). The lengthy account given by Tayiru Banbera is an exception.[38] Monteil's informant, Kore Tammoura, describes the politicking behind Biton's rise, giving names, factions, wealth, and incidents of conflict.[39] Tayiru Banbera simply attributes Biton's success to the support of his mother[40] and to fate; in his account, Biton becomes the leader of the ton after selection by lot.

Implicit in the narratives is the notion that Biton recruited his followers by providing them with free food and ample drink (and drink especially remains a theme in the epic cycle) until he had won their loyalty. The *ton* is like a cross between a hunting group (as Kore Tammoura describes it) and a college fraternity on a Saturday night. The incremental processes by which their activities extended into warfare, slave-taking, and pillage are not explicitly covered. But Banbera introduces suggestive wordplay on the *di-sòngò*, or beer-price, which begins as the dues paid by the members of the ton and then becomes the name by which the tax or tribute paid to Segou is generally known. The amount paid is increased by a payment in cowries (the traditional currency) known as the *ni-sòngò* or "soul-price."[41] The extraction of this payment from a recalcitrant member of the ton is the first instance of organized violence and portends the violence and power to follow. It does not seem far-fetched to read Banbera's version as suggesting that the power of Segou was purchased at a cost in human souls.

Ngolo Diarra and Monzon Diarra

The next element in the sequence of the performance tradition is the change in dynasties that occurred in the middle years of the eighteenth century. Biton Koulibaly is believed by historians to have reigned some forty years, from 1710 to 1755, to be succeeded by two sons. The first son was assassinated by the leaders of the ton, the network of war leaders who served the faama, in some dispute. The second was deposed and killed because he had converted to Islam.[42] Then followed a ten-year period of anarchy, perhaps not unlike the year of the four

Caesars in Rome: three leaders of the ton came to power and fell during those ten years. Finally, Ngolo Diarra established himself in power firmly enough to be succeeded by his son Monzon, and Monzon was in turn succeeded by several of his sons.

Little of this political chaos and opportunism appears in the performance tradition, which portrays Ngolo Diarra and Monzon Diarra in highly specific functions within a larger narrative of succession. The story of Ngolo Diarra tells how he succeeded despite all of Biton Koulibaly's attempts to thwart the fates that had predicted Ngolo's reign. The story is couched as a conflict of destinies, or perhaps vital forces, between a jealous king and the predestined child.

Ngolo Diarra

The origin of the Diarra [lion] clan goes back to two brothers born in the forest and suckled by lions. At the time of Biton, the clan was short on their share of the *di-sòngò*, the tribute. Ngolo's brothers substituted their youngest brother for their share, promising to redeem him later. Ngolo came to the court of Biton, then an aging king. The king performed various divinations to discover who would succeed him; the omens repeatedly indicated the slave-boy Ngolo. Biton sought a pretext to get rid of the boy: he entrusted a ring to him, which he then had stolen and thrown into the river. Ngolo wandered by the river, wondering how he might get back the lost ring; he found or was given the fish that had swallowed the ring.

This narrative says nothing of the two sons of Biton who ruled briefly before being murdered, or of the warlords who then attempted to hold power and failed. Ngolo's rise to power is justified before the fact by the predictions, and the mechanics of the actual rise are effaced. The dirty details of history appear to be irrelevant; in fact, recounting them might be subversive, for they treat of regicide and anarchy, and they call into question the hierarchized social fabric upon which the jeli depends for a living; however, the details are continuously recalled in the poetic evocation of Segou, city of the 4,444 *balanza* trees and the little hunchbacked *balanza,* which means treachery. The set of events following the death of Biton Koulibaly probably brought the crooked little club into prominence.

The transparency of the device of legitimation, however, is recognized by all. Some of the modes of divination used by Biton also appear in the Sunjata tradition (e.g., naming two animals and setting them to fight against each other) and elsewhere in the traditions of Segou; the story of the fish and the ring, as Conrad notes, goes back to Herodotus.[43] Nobody should be deceived by the fiction that Ngolo Diarra was the predestined successor to Biton Koulibaly—but then, the story is not entirely a fiction either, for he did seat himself as king, and he must therefore have been predestined. The story gives us, in the terms of an academic historian, a distortion amounting to falsification, for it omits the chaos that permitted Ngolo Diarra to succeed his former master. Nevertheless, from another perspective, the record is a selective representation of the events and happenings leading to the present; and they are significant, necessary, creditable, and thus worthy of performance. The narrative of the succession thus affords opportunity for a much appreciated structural pattern of direct and repeated symbolic oppositions that are easy for the performer to generate and exciting for the audience to follow, and such a piece possesses a certain market appeal.

No one is fooled by the political message. The bulk of the other published episodes of the cycle of Segou (two thirds of the total) involve insults to the power of Segou or humiliations inflicted on the ruler. The weight of those insults and humiliations stems from this moment of improper succession from noble Koulibaly to servile or captive Diarra. When a Koulibaly of the Kaarta refuses to recognize a Diarra because the family was slave to his lineage, it is evident that the stain is one that cannot be erased, and certainly not disguised by the smell of a ring-containing fish.

The succession from Ngolo to Monzon is marked by unpleasantness. A diviner had told Ngolo that he must sacrifice a child to ensure the stability of his line, and so he asked his wives if any would give up a son. The mother of Monzon alone agreed, on condition that the yet-unborn Monzon would then be made king, no matter how young. She sacrifices her child by pounding him in a mortar. This moment is not the subject of a specific piece, although it appears as an element in longer narratives. The historiographic problem is again to explain the irregularities of succession.

Monzon's next narrative function is to die and make way for his son Da, who will carry most of the weight of the epic cycle. Da ruled out of the regular order, before his elder brother Tiefolo, and this irregularity is explained in several ways in the tradition.[44] As with Sunjata, there is the motif of the virtually simultaneous births and the tardy messenger, and as with Sunjata there is variation on the actual primogeniture. In another formulation of the story, Monzon bequeaths some feuds to his sons. One account of the succession says that Monzon went first to his eldest son Tiefolo to ask him to avenge an insult. When Tiefolo refused, Monzon had him killed. Da then accepted the task. In another, the dying Monzon simply tells Da that there are three towns he failed to reduce, and Da undertakes to conquer them; Tiefolo never appears. None of these accounts is strictly accurate, for Tiefolo was not killed: he succeeded his brother Da. Dessekoro Kaarta was not defeated by Da but by Da's father, Monzon. The changes of the record represent embellishments for dramatic interest, and the mechanisms of telescoping and reduction are at work here. There are also varying interests reflected in different strands of the oral tradition. Serge Sauvageot collected information from Gaoussou Diarra, a descendant of the line. In Gaoussou's version of the transition, the dying Monzon assembles his sons and relates to them the fable of the sticks and the bundle: individually they break, together they do not. Gaoussou Diarra possesses authority and competence as a descendant of the lineage, but this pious account, denying the competition for power, looks like whitewash and should be balanced with other, far less positive views of the transition.

The recurring tone of performers' narrations defines this dynasty as one of dubious legitimacy. Its power is based on blood and fear and hate. Even an attempt to redeem Da, to make him the heroic and valiant son who fulfills his father's request, falls somewhat short. Douga of Kore's wife Saran may love Da so much that she betrays her husband, but she is then summarily executed by the tonjons, Da's retainers.

Da Monzon: The Accession

King Da, son of Monzon, reigned for some twenty years (1808–1828) and was the last great king of the dynasty. During his reign Cheikou Amadou successfully established an Islamic dina in Massina and defeated Segou at Noukouma, but that point is omitted in the epic cycle. The performance tradition designates Da as the representative king of Segou, the focus of creative energies, and all Segou's conquests of worthy opponents are attributed to his reign.

As noted above, the transition from Monzon to Da was neither regular nor smooth. At least three versions of the story answer to different ends. The first is the version by Gaoussou Diarra, a descendant of the line: on his deathbed, Monzon unites his sons and exhorts them to work together. Da succeeds him. The second has already been touched upon briefly; again, it involves the dying words of Monzon, who informs his sons of his unfulfilled desires and unaccomplished tasks. This approach ostensibly presents a positive picture of Da by displaying him as the warlike heir of a noble father, a son whose determination makes him more worthy than his cowardly brother. Finally, there is attached to Da a rather unpleasant account according to which he desires to take power but the people of Segou are reluctant to accept him. He gathers his retainers, the *tonjonw*, lavishes beer upon them, and summons a council of elders. The elders who refuse his authority are then slaughtered by the drunken retainers.

The massacre of the elders is a curious and unsettling motif, and there are good grounds for doubting its authenticity, or at least its placement. Tayiru Banbera is the principal source for this story of Da in the modern oral tradition. It is not found, for instance, in Sory Kamara's "Douga of Kore," although that narrative also tells of the transition from Monzon to Da. Other early reports attribute the incident to Biton Koulibaly, as one of the last steps by which he ascends to power.[45] In Biton's case, it appears to follow on the incident in which the members of the *ton* draw lots to determine their leader and the token of Biton repeatedly presents itself. Faced with reluctant elders, he eliminates them.

In Banbera's account of Da's accession, the story of the massacre includes and excludes some other significant elements. For instance, in the free-standing version published by Dumestre, Monzon mentions to his sons the three towns he wishes to capture, but the story does not continue with Da's pursuit of his father's enemies. (Another griot, Sory Kamara, does develop the motif.)[46] In the continuous account published by Conrad, Banbera does introduce this motif, although without bringing in the other brother. Banbera's two accounts tell how Da visits the town by night after his father's death to hear what people are saying. The opinions are universally negative. In the two accounts by Banbera as well as in Sory Kamara's "Douga of Kore," Da is advised that his power rests with his tonjonw and that he must keep them well supplied with food, and especially drink, to maintain their courage. These recurring elements therefore seem to be essential parts of the package. They reiterate the theme of the illegitimacy of the line by reflecting (or alleging) popular discontent and emphasizing the role of the slave-soldiery as the actual power base of the Diarra line.

The night visit through the town probably should be seen as an intrusive and ornamental folkloric motif. It recalls the tradition of Harun al-Rashid of the *Arabian Nights* and of Persian kings before him who went in quest of nighttime adventures. Da is accompanied by his griot Tinyetigiba Dante as Harun was accompanied by his vizir, Jaafar. Da, however, encounters no adventures. He hears only complaints and disapproval of the prospect of his rule.

This is another device frequently used in the traditions of Segou: kings are forced to listen to insults addressed to their persons. This is the starting point for many of the "conquest" stories in which (as here) the insult is later wiped out in blood. The potential historical referent is outweighed in this case by the fictional and literary elements of the pattern, and the same might be said of the the advice to liquor up the tonjonw. This somewhat metonymic depiction of the force of Segou evokes a complex association of ideas. Drunkenness and violence are explicitly linked with the fidelity of the slaves of the crown. Drunkenness also leads, through the di-sòngò (the beer-price), to the tax imposed by Segou—visible evidence of its secular power—and further (through a complex religious association in which sober Islam is contrasted with intoxicated paganism) to the four great fetishes of Segou and the allegations of human sacrifice and cannibalism that mark the traditions of the kingdom.

This raises three questions: Did this massacre occur? Under whose reign? And is there any significance to the variation in agents? Tayiru Banbera alone attributes the event to the time of Da. The earlier sources associate it with Biton Koulibaly. Yet elements of Tayiru's account can be recognized in the words of Sory Kamara.[47] Still, questions of accuracy may be irrelevant, for the point is that in the popular perception, either Biton the founder or Da the representative king ascended to the throne through force and the elimination of the elders who were the traditional representatives of social authority and who in many African kingdoms served as the check upon the license of the king. The story of the massacre may thus serve as another statement of the illegitimacy of the power of Segou and of the ambivalence with which the traditions of the past are viewed by the present.

Da Monzon: Conquests and Adventures

Through a telescoping of time, the major conquests and conflicts of Segou are shifted to the reign of Da, son of Monzon. His court provides the static and durable image of the kingdom. The conquests are the topics of individual pieces, although some may be linked (as when the dying Monzon asks his son Da to conquer the three towns that had eluded him). The narratives are very highly patterned and almost interchangeable save for idiosyncratic details. One that plays on the question of lineage and succession can serve here as illustration.

Da Monzon and Dietekoro Kaarta

Word came to Da Monzon of the beauty of a daughter (never named) of Dietekoro Koulibaly, ruler of the Kaarta. Da sent his griots to ask her for hand, but Dietekoro refused because Da's grandfather Ngolo had been the slave of Dietekoro's (distant) relative Biton Koulibaly. Da Monzon sent his armies to get the woman; they were defeated and sneaked back into town individually. Only when he happened to see one of his warriors in the market did Da learn what had happened.

Segou sent a beautiful woman named Samana to the Kaarta. She easily captivated Dietekoro Kaarta and learned the secrets of his power while they were drinking the *dolo* (millet beer) she had brewed. Then, as he was incapable of anything else, he asked her to wash his clothes. She went down to the river, boarded the boat that had brought her, and departed, leaving his clothes burning on the riverbank. The king noticed the smell and realized his mistake.

Da Monzon then led an expedition against the Kaarta. His soldiers defeated Dietekoro and killed him when he continued to refuse the hand of his daughter. Other kings, whose names translate as "Great Goat" and "Guinea Fowl," were killed on the return trip for previous insults to Segou.[48]

The narrative follows the standard lines (insult-betrayal-defeat). The version by Seydou Drame, as summarized above, is somewhat more ornate than the rather terse account given by Tayiru Banbera,[49] which also omits the insults addressed to Da. The embellishment derives not from greater contextual detail but from the use of narrative devices (e.g., taking the laundry to the riverbank) which occur in other epics. The historical substrate to this epic is particularly interesting: first, the war is the one witnessed by Mungo Park on his voyage to the Niger in 1796,[50] and Park gives an outsider's eyewitness account of some of the action; and second, it plays off the underlying social relations of the ruling houses. The Koulibaly clan myth of origin identifies two branches: the rulers of the Kaarta and the first dynasty of Segou. After the Koulibaly dynasty of Segou was deposed, the line surviving in the Kaarta refused to recognize the status of the succeeding dynasty, the Diarra—hence, at least in oral tradition, the war. The artistry that transforms this historical record is evident, not only in the rich verbal detail of the piece but also in the narrative twists: the encounter of Da with warriors who have returned in secret, the elaborate seduction of Dietekoro, the lively gesture of the burning laundry (which is not only a domestic chore but a narrative trick to allow the woman to leave town and get back to her boat on the riverbank). The same delight in storytelling enlivens other portions of the cycle.

This group of conquest narratives most clearly demonstrates the episodic nature of the cycle of Segou and the way it moves perceptibly from a historical record to a world of entertainment and polished artistry. In the published sources, five rulers come into conflict with Segou—six including Silamaka, whose story is told principally in Fula. There may be more. The pattern that shapes the stories is easily recognized: a tributary king becomes arrogant and insults Segou (the details of the insult are lovingly recalled). Initial reprisals fail because of the rebel's occult power, and Segou resorts to treachery of some kind. Bassi of Samaniana and Dietekoro Kaarta are brought down by women sent by Segou. Douga of Kore is betrayed by two women: a spy from Segou and his own wife (the same is said of Bassi in Conrad's text). Mariheri of Dionkoloni is defeated after Da enlists Kumba Silamakan, a Fula hero who has been found dallying with Da's favorite concubine.[51] The wars are fought to erase the insults. But the epics are recounted to recall them, it would seem, and so they should perhaps be examined.

Dietekoro Kaarta's offense (and remember that he is a Koulibaly, related to the line of Biton) is to refuse his daughter in marriage to Da because Da is a captive, the descendant of a slave. Douga of Kore's offense is unintentional: the son of Monzon's griot visits him and is so overwhelmed by his nobility and generosity that he returns to Segou to renounce his allegiance to a family of captives. The insult, coming from the mouth of a jeli, a nyamakala, is all the more stinging. This is not simple variation in obloquy, however. Griots and singing are an essential thematic element of the Douga of Kore story. The name Douga means "vulture" in Bamana and is also the title of what may be the best-known war song of the Sahel.[52] After Douga has been captured, his griots commit suicide rather than perform their song for Da. Songs, as will be seen most clearly with the Fula tradition, represent the individual and confer immortal nobility; as the Sunjata tradition shows with Fakoli and Janjon, they are also transferable commodities.

Some insults involve the questionable family antecedents described here. A number of others (not all of which are avenged) play on the name of Da, a word with a variety of significations. Karta Thiema is perhaps the most comprehensive:

> "My master has asked,
> He wishes to know the exact meaning of your name 'Da.'
> Is it *da*, the earthen pot?
> Is it *da*, Guinea hemp?
> Is it *da*, smallpox?
> Is it *da*, the mouth?
> Is it *da*, the door?
> Is it *da*, 'lie down'?
> If you are a pot, Karta Thiema will smash you.
> If you are Guinea hemp he will harvest you
> And give you to his fishermen to make nets
> If you are smallpox, he will treat you with red-hot iron.
> If you are a mouth, he will open you to the ears.
> If you are a door, he will ban you,

And you will no longer open any ways.
If you are *Da*, 'lie down'
He will raise you as a post on the top of a hill."[53]

This sort of wordplay is repeated throughout the tradition. The performer Gorke is not alone in stringing puns. Many of the most visible instances of word-play involve the names of characters. Many slaves of Segou, for instance, have meaningful and sometimes ominous names: "It Is Not Time For Good Things" or "Today Is Hard For Me."[54] In Sory Kamara's "Douga of Kore," Da announces his intention of erasing his father's shame by demanding that Douga rename his son "My Father's Shame Is Gone." In Seydou Drame's account of the war with Dietekoro Kaarta, Da concludes his campaign by capturing local chiefs and mak-ing puns on their names ("Big goat" and "Guinea fowl").[55] He is echoed in this by Bakari Jan, a hero who serves (and saves) Segou. At the start of Sissoko Kabine's version of the "Betrayal of Bakari Jan," Bakari conquers a long list of punningly-named kings.

While this concentration on verbal insult, especially when directed at the power of Segou, might be seen as a manifestation of negative feelings about the kingdom, these latent emotions should not obscure another essential underlying mechanism: the role of the insults in the compositional technique of the artists. Plays on words are the defining characteristics of the various episodes, more so perhaps than even the details of the confrontation and eventual conquest.

The underlying equation, the dialectic of event and verbalization, is easily grasped. The insults addressed to Segou are a jeli equivalent for the actual past socioeconomic and military grounds for confrontation and conflict. A jeli does not speak of land rights, or trade, or duties perceived or denied, except in general or symbolic terms. The history behind the stories is transmuted into a general pat-tern of dramatic opposition and resolution in which sympathy is most often with the victim or transgressor. Allusive and almost allegorical editorializing takes the place of detailed reporting. In this alchemical process, the verbal nature of the insult foregrounds the verbal nature of the narration, which commemorates and recreates events whose outcome was perhaps their most important aspect.

This points to a contrast with the tradition of Sunjata. His deeds, at least in theory, are commemorated by praise names and songs intercalated into the per-formance. The cycle of Segou exhibits a dearth of actual praise material, of clan names interjected to heighten the tone or mood in the narratives. Even in the per-formances of Tayiru Banbera recorded by Conrad, despite an abundance of digressions and nonnarrative interludes (he was being paid by cassette-side of recording time) there is little in the way of actual praise. There are songs and evocative anecdotes (far more than can be illustrated here), there is general commentary on society and humans, but there is rarely the kind of exalting movement of music and words that transports the noble listeners in the Sunjata tradition. Bamana traditions are down-to-earth. The kings of Segou are not heroes. They are powerful, to be respected and feared, but they are not admirable. Even Da fails to win us over, although he may have won the love of Saran, wife of Douga of Kore. This partially positive image of Da is more than counterbalanced by the image that emerges from the tales of his encounters with Fula heroes and particularly with his general Bakari Jan. In the matter of love, the "Capture of Jonkoloni" and its analogue "Kumba Silamakan" offer a specific counterpoint to the passion of Saran.

These two linked stories involve a foreign hero, a Fula. Kumba Silamakan rides into town and makes his way into the chamber of the king's favorite woman, with whom he dallies while the king fumes: his henchmen dare not attack this paragon of Fula valor. Eventually, the hero emerges from the chamber and makes his peace with the king by agreeing to defeat a hitherto undefeated town, Jonkoloni. His story then fuses with that of a more typically Fula hero, Silamaka (see chapter 7), and he joins the ranks of the rebels against Segou who are laid low. This last tragic ending appears to be a modern expansion. Frobenius reports a happy ending to the story: Da is forced to hand over the woman and the hero withdraws.

Kumba Silamakan is not alone in serving Segou; other Fula also line up at least temporarily with the king. One of these heroes, who will be discussed in greater detail in chapter 7, is Hambodedio Paté, who appears under different aspects in two of the episodes collected by Kesteloot. In historical tradition, Hambodedio (also known as Hama the Red) was a son-in-law to Da Monzon; he was the "Fula of Segou, the Bambara of Kounari," as the praise name notes, and he had two wives, one from each ethnic group. In an episode narrated by Sissoko Kabine, Hambodedio appears as the "enemy." After a domestic altercation between his wives, he raids the cattle of Segou, and the king is forced to enlist the services of Bakari Jan to recover his livestock; the emphasis in this story, however, is on the reconciliation between the king and Bakari Jan. Hambodedio does not appear in Tayiru Banbera's account of this incident. In a second episode, "Da Monzon and Karta Thiema," Hambodedio avenges an insult against Segou and defeats the enemy, Karta Thiema, in a climactic single combat after others have failed. This episode by Gorke is virtually unique, and it is a wonderful performance by someone Kesteloot identifies as a highly talented performer. His skill in verbal play in the insult to Da Monzon has been demonstrated above, and the accent is clearly on the entertainment value of a good story, well told and satisfactorily resolved.

Bakari Jan

The principal hero associated with Segou is Bakari Jan Kone (Bakari Kone the tall); there are several versions each of the three episodes associated with his name. These episodes also serve to close the cycle of Segou; both Tayiru Banbera and Sissoko Kabine end their grand narratives with the confrontation between Da Monzon and Bakari. The confrontation is anachronistic, however, and represents the displacement of events further into the past. Monteil dates the era of Bakari Jan Kone to a period of anarchy in the early 1840s, after the death of Da, and says that he repelled a Fula invasion.[56] Bakari Jan was a *foroba fula,* a town cattle-herder, not ethnically Fula, from a town near Segou. His portrayal in the epic cycle makes him almost an ethnic Fula, however, and especially in the last episode he is certainly their equal in war. In the epic, the action no longer involves the external enemies of Segou; it has moved into the city and points to the weaknesses of the kingdom.

Bakari Jan and Bilissi

Segou was terrorized by Bilissi, who would come into town and demand his share of the market's meat. No one could stop him. Finally, Bakari decided that he must oppose Bilissi. He consulted diviners; they told him what steps to take and furnished him with the protections he would need. On the next market day, Bakari Jan met Bilissi outside of town. They exchanged amenities, snuff, and kola nuts, and then began to fight. Each shot at the other: the bullets had no effect. Each cut at the other with a sword, which buckled. Other sorceries may also be invoked. Finally, Bilissi pulled out his magical fetters (or sometimes a quirt—a humiliating weapon) and Bakari Jan gave way and rode back to town (where Da had bolted the gates). Bilissi chased him several times around the town, until Bakari led him over a ditch. Bakari's horse could leap over it, but Bilissi fell into the ditch. Bakari then killed Bilissi, but the magic released in the process made him blind for a time. He only got back into town when one of his sons, worried, forced the king to open the gates and allow him out to go look for his father.

This episode calls for further field research and analysis; the figure of Bilissi is an extraordinarily rich and polyvalent symbol. His name is the local version of Iblis, an Arabic name for Satan. His physique offers magical symbolism; he is partially albino (and Tayiru Banbera says his head had three corners).[57] His behavior is essentially that of Segou: "When he was on his way to a drinking house he would capture any child he happened to meet. / He would take him and give him to the brewmasters. / He would sell him."[58] The share of meat reserved for him, day in and day out, suggests not so much tribute as some ritual offering. The question inevitably arises whether in this current form Bilissi is to be considered human. For Sissoko Kabine and Tayiru Banbera, Bilissi was definitely so.[59] Monteil's informant for an abbreviated version of the story, collected before 1905, also identifies him as a human warrior of Massina.[60] Baba Cissoko does not consider him entirely human: his ancestors were jinns or spirits, and the marabout engaged by Bakari must negotiate with the grandfather jinn to gain the promise of victory for his client.

This last detail can be chalked up to the "special effects" budget of a performance, but the question still seems valid. What did Bilissi represent in the moral economy of Segou? Is he emblematic of fractious warlords whom the king was unable to discipline, or is his significance to be found more on the spiritual plane? Might the defeat of Bilissi be regarded as the reflection of an iconoclastic act directed against the pagan symbols of Segou (and given a positive twist since that time)? It is equally easy to see the story of Bilissi historically as an indication of the tensions between the kings and their highest-ranking tonjon (although this term is never used of Bilissi), and such tensions would explain why the kings turned to foreign (Fula) heroes for support. But even these relations were not smooth, as the story about Hambodedio (discussed above) can demonstrate. Loyalty was not a commodity in free supply around Segou, and this discovery is the subject of the next episode dealing with Bakari Jan, the "Betrayal."

The Betrayal of Bakari Jan

Bakari had conquered a number of kings for Segou; he was proud of his deeds and boasted that Segou was like a canoe with a hole in it: his foot covered the hole and preserved the boat, and were he to withdraw it the boat would sink. Da Monzon heard about this and became enraged. He resolved to kill Bakari.

Word of the plan got out (in one case, it traveled down a line of women washing laundry at the river) and reached Bakari's wastrel son Simbala. Messengers from Da summoned Bakari to the palace; Bakari made his way there deliberately, and his son, unbidden, followed him with a loaded rifle.

Bakari came to Da's private chambers, and they sat there drinking until Da asked Bakari about his boast. Da then seized Bakari and prepared to split his skull with an axe. Just then, Simbala burst in with the rifle. He made Bakari repeat the insults, and then forced Da to walk them home. As he released the king, he fired his gun and Da scurried shamefully away to hide in his chambers.

Here, the performers play with the stock pattern of insult-vengeance. Bakari Jan boasts; the king learns of the boast and plans vengeance. Bakari's son intervenes to save his father just as the king is preparing to smash the hero's head in. The boast is well developed and involves the techniques of wordplay discussed above. It is also a stable feature of the story; the version published by Charles Monteil in 1905 offers virtually the same boast as the versions collected in the 1960s and later. This episode serves to explain the later disaffection of Bakari Jan, which may or may not be a matter of historical record. (The third episode, "Bakari and the Fula of Kounari," revolves around the efforts Segou must make to enlist his help after he has left town.) As these episodes close, the world of Segou folds in on itself, and all that is left to consider is the fate of Da Monzon, whose attempt to kill his own hero has failed. This image seems the fitting finale for the kingdom of Segou: a king cloistered in his palace, mocked by the household slaves, mistrusted by his heroes, and a line whose son will apparently die without issue. The image is one of sterility.

Poetic images, though, are illusions. The final images of Segou can also be seen through the prism of its later history. Segou fell eventually to the Muslim Fula and the Tukolor. The year 1818 marks the battle of Noukouma in which Cheikou Amadou Barry established the independence of the dina of Massina; it is entirely possible that the kingdom of Segou was "enriched" by a flow of Islam-resisting Fulbe from the region (there are traditions of such resistance and fugitive migrations such as that of Gueladio, son of Hambodedio Paté, south into Burkina Faso). Segou did eventually fall to the Tukolor of al-Hajj Umar and was then under the dominion of the Tukolor; this may reflect a market for a new variety of songs.

There is, in fact, an interaction of Fula and Bamana materials, encountered in the specific case of Kumba Silamakan, whose story is confounded with that of Silamaka of Massina. This world of hybridization, however, heads away from more historically centered narratives into the general world of conventionalized storytelling. Such performances, oriented toward entertainment, probably constitute the bulk of the actual oral tradition available in the field. The historical pieces are part of a specialized repertoire for a defined audience. The information needed for an accurate assessment is lacking: there are no repertoire studies and there is no reliable catalogue of the "standard" performance pieces. Materials of this sort are found in the collections of Frobenius or Courlander and Sako. Frobenius in particular offers a rich mine of stories that can be corroborated in the oral tradition. As they are given in German translation, their source languages are difficult to identify, but they partake fully of a regional culture in which Soninke, Bamana, and Fulbe share equally. The venue here appears to be the region lying north of the Niger—Beledougou, the Kaarta, Massina; the enemy comes more often from the desert for cattle-raids than from the city on slave-hunts (although Courlander and Sako offer examples to the contrary). It is in this region, to which the published record is blind, that the details of the historical record are disassembled and retooled to become the polished motifs of stories in which the complex pre-Islamic past is reshaped into an evocative world of courage, violence, pride, and arrogance. Echoes of this transformation are to be found not only in these Bamana stories dissociated from Segou (and even in some of those told of Segou), but also in the traditions of the Fula.

❖ 7 ❖

TRADITIONS OF THE FULA

THE FULA ARE A linguistically related group of peoples spread across West Africa from the Futa Tooro in Senegal to northern Nigeria and beyond into the Cameroon and Chad.[1] In English-speaking areas, especially Nigeria, they are known as Fulani, in French as Peul. The language is generally termed Fulfulde and the people Fulbe in the plural, Pullo in the singular. They are known by other local names, of which the most important is Tukolor, which applies to sedentarized Fula of the Futa Tooro in Senegal who speak a dialect of Fula known as Pulaar. The general term Fula will be used in this discussion.

Language and cattle are central features that define the Fula in their many divisions. Fulfulde is a richly articulated tongue, comprehensible across the peoples' geographical range despite dialectal variations and everywhere connected with poetry. Whatever their current activities, the Fula consider themselves pastoralists by origin, their lives intimately entwined with their cattle in a tradition that some scholars have connected with neolithic Saharan rock paintings. Traditionally they were nomads, and their concentrations of population are still to be found in the savanna grazing lands.

Another unifying element comes from their more recent history: Islam. Across West Africa, the period from 1780 to 1870 was marked by a series of violent Islamic conversions and movements in which the Fula were leaders, beginning in northern Nigeria with the Caliphate of Uthman Dan Fodio, continuing with Cheikou Amadou Barry in Massina (Mali), and ending most spectacularly with al-Hajj Umar Tall and the Tukolor of the Futa Tooro, who were forced to move east by the French and who then conquered Segou and Massina.[2] One legacy of these movements is a large class of Fula religious leaders, especially in the Tijiani sect of Islam.

This chapter does not deal with the Fula of Nigeria, Cameroon, or Chad. The documented literature of these eastern regions is poetic but does not include traditions of oral epic.[3] Instead, the discussion will concentrate on the Fula of Massina, along the Niger, and of the Futa Tooro along the Senegal River, among whom a lively epic tradition has been observed and transcribed. A third western region of Fula concentration, the Futa Jallon of Guinea, exhibits poetic and narrative literature but no tradition of epic performance.[4]

These three western regions are linked by common traditions of origin and subsequent historical migrations. The Fula enter the history of the Sahel in the fifteenth century, on the western borders of the Songhay empire, and their arrival is recorded in the *Tarikh es-Soudan* of Abd al-Rahman al-Sa'di (Abder-rahman es-Sa'di). One group settled in Massina, a rich grassland on the northern bank of the Niger. Their rulers were subject to the Songhay empire (the chronicler al-Sa'di reports that the Askia Mohammed despised the Fula) but gained independence after the Moroccan conquest of Timbuctoo in 1591. Other Fula groups moved through the Manden to the savannas of upper Guinea, the region now known as the Futa Jallon, probably in the fifteenth century. A third wave eventually moved north from the Futa Jallon under the leadership of Koli Tengela around 1500, fought the Soninke kingdom of Jara (near present-day Nioro) but was defeated, and so turned west into the Senegal River valley and the kingdom of Jolof.[5] Koli's descendants established the Deniyanke dynasty of the Futa Tooro.

The most probable explanation for the "emergence" of the Fula is climatic: as the Sahara expanded, the pastoral Fula moved south to find new grazing grounds. Another factor may well have been the weakening of political authority in the fifteenth century: as the empire of Mali declined, that of Songhay grew, and between these poles a door opened for southward migration. In many regions, the southward movement led to an integration of Fula pastoralists and Mande agricultural communities. Some Fula settled down and became village herdsmen. Transient nomads were allowed to graze the harvested fields in exchange for the fertilizing manure left by the herds. The people of the Wasulu region of Mali claim Fula origin but have lost their language and changed their lifestyle completely.[6]

The epic traditions presented here come from Massina and the Futa Tooro. There appears to have been some exchange between the regions (the same stories told, similar heroes), but this may be a recent occurrence, and it is simplest to discuss each region separately, after a general description of performance styles. The Futa Jallon offers no epic material at this time but possesses instead a wealth of devotional poetry and historical writing. However, the region has contributed to a Gambian Mandinka epic tradition based on Fula heroes such as Musa Molo and the explosive capture of Kansala during the Islamic Fula invasion from Timbo in the nineteenth century.

Although individual heroes of the Fula traditions are in some sense regional figures and have a historical basis, the epics themselves seem to have lost all connection with history. They have become almost purely fictive, shaped by the imagination and creativity of the performers. Christiane Seydou, the greatest student of the subject, defines the epics as a sort of collective praise for the culture and the perfect expression of *pulaaku,* the ineffable quality of being a Pullo: the shift is clearly into the realms of ideals and ideology.

Performance Conditions

Among the nomadic Fula there is a substantial body of lyric poetry, and anyone may sing regardless of social status.[7] There is also a body of allegorical and initiatory poetry dealing with the mystique of pastoralism (the best known is *Kaidara*) and associated particularly with the name of Amadou Hampaté Bâ.[8] But the epic performances appear to be centered among the sedentary populations, which have also adopted the social divisions encountered in the Mande world: a distinction between free and captive, and professionalized status groups.

Musicians are given a variety of names across the range: *gawlo, bambaado, jeeli, maabo.*[9] Some of these names *(gawlo, jeeli)* are clearly taken from neighboring populations such as the Wolof and the Bamana. Others represent a shift in occupations. The "court musicians," most involved in the production of epics, call themselves *maabo;* the term originally refers to the weavers' group. Boûbacar Tinguidji (see chapter 1) makes the distinction between a *maabo,* who performs only for the nobles, and a *gawlo,* who performs for anyone.

It seems certain that the epic performance tradition is an importation to Fula culture. The source, however, is less easy to define. Since many of the traditions of Massina attach themselves to the history of Segou, Bamana culture is a probable partner. However, in deeper layers the Fula epics also show connections with the Soninke and the Songhay, and the issue may therefore be more complex.[10]

The performance style of the maabo closely resembles that of some Bamana or Maninka jeliw: a solitary performer accompanies himself on a stringed instrument while delivering his story at high speed, stopping occasionally for instrumental breaks. The usual instrument is the *hoddu;* it is a small four-stringed instrument with a rectangular sound box, virtually identical to the Bamana ngoni. There are so far no reports of team performances; the maabo has no *naamu-namina,* as among the Maninka, nor do women or assistants provide lyric interludes.

Narrative predominates in the performance. While clan and individual praises are important among the Fula, they are relatively rare in the epics. One reason is probably that the connection of history and lineage has been broken. Intrusions and digressions serve as distractors and intensifiers in the published texts. They are placed as markers for the high points of the stories. They also indicate the fame and importance of the heroes. One piece discussed here revolves around the hero Hambodedio's dissatisfaction with his given praise names and his quest to establish a new reputation.

A novel feature, which distinguishes the texture of Fula narrative from that of neighboring groups, is the occasional use of set poetic passages to describe repeated actions. Here, for example, Hambodedio mounts his horse, Mad Mane:

> [Hambodedio] trod on the smith; the harness-maker stretched.
> He settled himself on the saddle-maker.
> He rested his hand on a harness-maker.
> He seized a woman leather-worker; the smith said he was there
> In the mouth of Mad Mane.[11]

The various craftspeople mentioned and maltreated by Hambodedio serve here as metonymy for their products: the stirrups and straps, the saddle, the reins, the bit. This feature does not appear to be very widespread (only a few performers, in the published sources, make use of it), but students of literary form will find it significant. It suggests the development of a specific poetic diction and a repertoire of images upon which the poet may draw at will, and thus an incipient formulaic system.

Music also plays a significant role in performances. Tunes "belong" to heroes. The story of the acquisition of a tune is a staple theme in the narrative repertoire, and a hero may be wordlessly evoked through his music. In principle, a gifted performer with a musically informed audience could almost do without the words, letting the interplay of proprietary melodies tell the story.

The Traditions of Massina

The Background

Massina is a broad, flat, and grassy land lying on the north bank of the Niger as the river turns north into the Sahara toward Timbuctoo and forms an inland delta. In the fifteenth century, when the Fula first entered the region, they came under the dominion of the Songhay empire. After the Songhay fell in 1591, there was a period of anarchy during which the Fula enjoyed some autonomy but also came into conflict with the Moroccan pashas of Timbuctoo who attempted to restore the empire. In the eighteenth century, the Fula of Massina came under the

power of Segou, although exactly when, how, and to what extent is not pre-
cisely known. Early in the nineteenth century, a religious leader named Cheikou
Amadou Barry arose and established a Muslim *dina,* an ideal state, in Massina.
In 1818, the forces of Massina and Segou met at the battle of Noukouma. The
Muslims won and Massina became independent. Despite the common faith, the
dina was attacked and conquered by al-Hajj Umar Tall in the 1860s; after his
death, another period of anarchy followed until the French established control.
The epic traditions to be examined look to a period before 1818, to a time when
Bamana and Fula interacted in a number of ways. One hero, Silamaka, fought
Segou; another, Hambodedio, is said to have served Segou and won a bride before
returning home to become the quintessential Fula hero.

Following the battle of Noukouma and the victory of Cheikou Amadou there
was a falling-out between Gelaajo, son of Hambodedio, and the Muslim leader.
Gelaajo withdrew with his people across the Niger bend, to a region downstream
from Gao, rather than submit to Cheikou Amadou. This exile community (which
includes artists such as Tinguidji) has preserved its traditions in some isolation
from the development of the stories found in the original heartland, and some
attention to the sources and lines of tradition therefore seems necessary.

Hambodedio, or Hama the Red

Hammadi Paté (or Pathé) was a historical figure who lived in Kounari (a region
adjoining Massina and Segou) around 1800. The German traveler Heinrich Barth
met Hammadi Paté's son Gelaajo in 1853 and reported some of the deeds of the
father: Hambodedio was remembered particularly for destroying four villages in
a single day.[12] He was apparently an ally, if not a tributary, of Segou. An established praise name calls him the "Fula of Segou, the Bamana of Kounari," and
thus points to his double loyalty. He appears in the cycle of Segou at the end of
the story and thus is sung in two languages.

Among the Fula, he is the protagonist of a variety of stories, few of which have
any historical validity. He has become a legendary hero, the symbol of a bygone
era of Fula greatness, valor, and violence. He expresses the Fula fascination with
their pre-Islamic past and an exploration of the core values of the culture. His
nickname, "the Red," reflects the way in which the Fula distinguish their skin
color from that of the neighboring peoples, and it thus reinforces his function as
a collective symbol. Three stories associated with Hambodedio are discussed below, the first about his rise to power. This story has undergone noticeable changes

in tone since it was first reported by Frobenius and Vieillard at the beginning of the twentieth century, and so two separate versions are given here:

Hambodedio and Besma Sougui (Version One)

Hambodedio's father ruled Kounari and died when the prince was still young. Besma Sougui became regent and usurped power. The young prince went into exile and came to Segou. In one version of the story he killed a water-monster that prevented the people from drinking and to which they had sacrificed a maiden each year. Hambodedio arrived right before the sacrifice, just in time to save the maiden. In another version, he assisted the king of Segou in conquering a town that had long resisted him.

His reward was an army, with which he returned home and defeated the usurper. The king of Segou also gave him his daughter, Tenen, as a bride.

This story follows a recognizable standard "hero pattern"; the same story is told of Samba Gueladio in the Futa Tooro, and of Perseus and Bellerophon in antiquity. The story of usurpation need not be accepted as truth. Such a construction is usually erected after the fact to justify a seizure of power. It is quite possible that Hambodedio became king with the support of Segou, and this story puts a conventional face upon the event. The modern version of the story, as told by Sambourou Parita, is more interesting:

Besma Sougui (Version Two)

Hambodedio needed to have his hair braided. He heard of a very skilled woman in Sougui and went to her. He arrived shortly before Besma Sougui's [the title indicates that Besma is the master of Sougui] regular appointment. The woman did not know Hambodedio, so upon the arrival of Besma Sougui, who was in her eyes the greater man, she stopped work on Hambodedio, leaving one-half of his head still unkempt. Hambodedio went home into hiding. His regular hairdresser was able to match the work and finish the job.

After some time, Hambodedio sent his men against Sougui to defeat Besma and avenge his shame. Two attacks failed before Hambodedio swore

he would die rather than fail and led the third attack himself. They captured
Besma Sougui but were unable to kill him until they undid his braids and
removed the magical protection hidden in his coiffure.[13]

This second piece is far more lighthearted and the scale much reduced. The
central theme is no longer an inheritance won or lost but the establishment and
recognition of reputation. The arena is no longer a kingdom but the courtyard
of a hairdresser. Sambourou Parita exploits a number of the conventions used
in more warlike pieces (e.g., the "Capture of Saa," discussed below) such as the
hero's resolution expressed in his willingness to die, and the manner in which
Hambodedio batters the walls of Sougui. Still, it is impossible to believe that he
is entirely serious.

Another story of Hambodedio is widely attributed to other heroes as well,
among them his son Gelaajo. It tells how Hambodedio avenged a beautiful
woman, possibly at the cost of his life.

The Capture of Saa

The ruler of Saa had dogs whom he loved dearly and whom he allowed
all sorts of liberties. No one could touch them. Fatimata Ham-Sire was a
beautiful young woman, and every day her door was crowded with young
nobles playing checkers and boasting of the deeds they could perform. Her
mother went to the market one day to sell her milk. One of the ruler's dogs
came and lapped at her milk. She hit it with a switch and it ran off yelping.
The ruler's men fetched her. She was taken to the king, and there her head
was shaved with a dull razor and pepper and ashes rubbed into the wounds.
She was sent home weeping.

Fatimata called for vengeance, but none of the nobles stepped forth.
She sent out word that she needed help. No one came. Finally she heard of
Hambodedio. She took her boat and her most beautiful attendants, and they
sailed down the river to the home of Hambodedio. He came to greet her,
marveling at her beauty and the display, and she entertained him lavishly.
Finally, he asked what he might do for her, and she told him of the insult to
her mother. He swore vengeance and promised he would come—not immediately, perhaps, but in the proper season.

Time went by, the season of the year arrived, and Fatimata realized that

Hambodedio's army was on the move when wild animals began to rush through villages to escape the oncoming mass of men. They came to Saa and besieged the town. In one variant, Hambodedio makes his way into the town in disguise and then chains himself to the ruler by a trick. They sit playing checkers while waiting for the fighting to be settled. In another, Hambodedio throws a golden axe into the town, and this spurs his men to break through the walls.

Hambodedio wins, of course, although in some versions there is a price: when performing divination to discover the outcome of the battle, he is told he will die if he undertakes it; he refuses to turn back.[14]

On one level, this story is a gallant adventure, contrasting false and true heroism and featuring the indomitable spirit of Fatimata Ham-Sire, who does indeed display the female side of pulaaku in her quest for vengeance. From this perspective, historical accuracy does not matter. It is also possible to view the story against a backdrop of cultural conflicts and tensions associated with the era of the historical Hambodedio and the advent of Islam. The issues become clearer if parallel material is considered. In their history of the dina of Massina, Bâ and Daget report an incident that helped precipitate the battle of Noukouma: Ali, son of the Fula *ardo* [leader] Guidado, took a blanket from a follower of Cheikou Amadou and was later murdered in the marketplace in retaliation.[15] Frobenius reports a story about Boubou Ardo Gallo, a Fula hero considered contemporary with Hambodedio: Boubou fights Cheikou Amadou after the Muslim leader had a Fula woman punished publicly.[16] Boubou loses and dies.

These incidents embody the themes of arrogant rulers and victimized women seeking champions that are relevant to the story of the "Capture of Saa." Since Hambodedio and his son Gelaajo (who also appears as the hero in some versions of the story) appear in history as Fula who resisted Islam to the point of emigration, it is tempting to see the story as a critique of the social changes brought about by Islam. But in fact the terms seem to have been inverted in the modern narration. The dogs are most probably not lapdogs but hunting dogs, and they probably recall the hunting kings of the Manden, Sunjata and perhaps also Biton Koulibaly. The implication is that the ruler is a pagan, an opponent of Islam, as well as an oppressor of Fula women. The ideology of the piece seems somewhat revisionist. It does not reflect an actual record of events except in the most distorted fashion. It does reflect a modern vision of past Fula identity in which the victorious Muslim Fula have carried the day.

The Quest for "Saïgalare"

["Saïgalare" is the tune associated with the name of Hambodedio. This
tale, narrated by Hamma Diam Bouraima of Konza in 1970, weaves together
a number of strands that not only explain how Hambodedio came to "possess" the tune but also what that possession means. While parts of the narrative (particularly the "three fears") are encountered elsewhere and may be
considered traditional, this particular combination seems to be unique and
provides a wonderful example of the creative potential of the tradition.]

Voices offer Hambodedio praise names; he refuses them and asks for more
individual names. He then narrates the three times he has felt fear. Once
when he was visiting a young woman, a huge snake crawled over him in the
dark. He controlled himself until the snake had passed and then killed it.
A second time, he was accompanying his wife Fadia along the river when a
herdsman on the other side insulted him. He crossed the river in spite of the
crocodiles and other dangers and punished the herdsman by tearing out his
tongue. A third time, he was returning in the dark from an unsuccessful cattle raid—Fadia had said she wanted the tawny cows of Bongowel, a former
suitor—when he came upon a woodchopper perched high in a tree. Although he was sure he was dealing with a spirit, Hambodedio took the man
upon his saddle.

Hambodedio awoke one night: a spirit was playing a tune before his doors,
and the tune haunted him. He summoned all the musicians and told them
he had heard a tune and they must find it for him or die. On the last day of
the time allotted, the griot Ko Biraima Ko was passing an anthill when he
encountered a spirit; the spirit took him into an underground chamber and
taught him the tune, "Saïgalare." It took several tries. Ko returned to town
and played the tune for Hambodedio, who claimed it and dispersed the unsuccessful musicians with gunfire.

Ko played "Saïgalare" for Hambodedio in front of the quarters of Tenen,
Hambodedio's second wife and a princess of Segou. His first wife, Fadia, became jealous. She bribed Ko with gold to stay behind one day and play
"Saïgalare" for her. But after riding out, Hambodedio decided he could not
continue without his music, so he returned home and found his wife and the
musician together. He raised his spear, unsure which to strike. Fadia taunted
him—he could not kill his musician, he must kill her. She bared a thigh;
Hambodedio pierced it. She bared the other thigh; he pierced that one too.

Then he summoned all the holy men to heal her, threatening death if they failed. One particularly wise man succeeded. The others were dispersed with gunfire.

Fadia then taunted Hambodedio. His courage was only good for spearing women. A real man, she said, would go drink beer in Kouna at the market, where other Fula heroes of reputation went. Among them was Bongowel, her former suitor.

Hambodedio first sent Ko to Kouna, and Ko encountered Gnamoy, the woman who sold beer. She refused to sell him any because she did not know him or his master. Ko asked the different heroes who visited Kouna on market day to get him some beer. Gnamoy refused their intercession and they declined to act as go-betweens for griots. Ko returned home and reported his failure to Hambodedio. So Hambodedio rode into Kouna on market day. As he entered the town, he killed a pair of lovers, caught in the dawn, to mark the day. Hearing he was in town, several of the heroes left. Only Bongowel remained, and after some interaction and an exchange of provocations, he and Hambodedio came to a duel. Hambodedio won and marked his victory by changing Kouna's market day and by marrying Gnamoy to Ko.[17]

This story is entirely concerned with the question of reputation and fame through the songs of the poet. Many of the elements are highly conventional. The throngs of musicians and marabouts who attempt to find "Saïgalare" and to heal Fadia might recall the requisite unsuccessful suitors in fairy-tales. The showdown between Hambodedio and Bongowel is presented in almost ritualized reciprocity and can be matched with any number of other such combats elsewhere in the tradition.[18] The three fears that start the series are highly suggestive in their folk-loric and cultural connections (and so deserve further research). They also expand upon a device frequently encountered in Fula and Bamana epic narratives by which a hero is identified by a threesome in his behavior: e.g., three things he would never do (such as listen to someone behind him, answer the first time when called, etc.). Where this device normally requires perhaps twenty lines, here it is expanded to some three hundred.[19]

While the initial incidents, the three fears, set the stage for what is to come (it becomes clear, for instance, that Bongowel had courted Fadia), the body of the narrative is concerned with the tune "Saïgalare" and a demonstration of its meaning. Christiane Seydou reads the quest for "Saïgalare" in terms of initiatiatory lore, and the behavior of the spirit or jinn is consistent with current information on spirit cults in the region.[20] The notion that music is a gift of the spirits is widespread in the region. In the Sunjata tradition, for instance, it is said that Sumanguru acquired his balafon from a jinn in exchange for his sister.

The reader should also observe the doubling of quests and characters. Hambodedio acts (and is insulted) through Ko. Fadia and Gnamoy, each in her own way, compel Hambodedio to action. These linkages and oppositions reflect the basic social divisions of Fula society between nobles and status groups (the *nyeenyo*, which may correspond to the Mande *nyamakala*: the general term covers all crafts-related groups), and between men and women. The dynamic tensions between these categories, as represented by these individuals ("Brrrr!" cries Fadia to Hambodedio, as he stands irresolute, with his spear poised over the woman and the musician), provokes each to surpass him—or herself. Pride of self is a central feature of this ideology, in contrast perhaps to the family-centered *badenya* and *fadenya* (mother-childness and father-childness) of Mande society; lineage clearly counts for less than individual achievement within the accepted functions of society.

The social vision presented is both radical and conservative. Hambodedio is violent. He attempts to kill the unsuccessful musicians and marabouts. He marks his entry to Kouna with a gratuitous killing. Most dramatically, he twice stabs his wife. The respect paid to him is clearly tinged with fear and apprehension. But his behavior is sanctioned by wife and musician. Neither challenges the rightfulness of Hambodedio's anger at the clandestine performance of the tune, which arouses his anger on two counts: the "theft" of his music and the potentially compromising situation in which he finds his wife. A strong element of sexual tension runs throughout the story, beginning with the mention of Fadia's former suitor Bongowel and continuing through the co-wife rivalry that incites Fadia to bribe Ko, the intimacy of the stolen performance, the erotic connotations of Fadia baring her thighs, the violent symbolism of the spear. This tension is in part resolved by the marriage of Ko to Gnamoy at the end.

But this vicarious resolution highlights another feature, in which social conservatism is at work. The story does not challenge the class division between Hambodedio and his servant Ko. Instead, it falls back (to justify it?) upon a vision of mutual dependency. Hambodedio depends upon Ko for the magical and exalting power of music; Ko requires the deeds of a Hambodedio to make the music. Each has a function to perform—and this system may be expanded to include the women. A degree or mode of pulaaku could be identified for each class or category; all participate in the exalting collective vision that "Saïgalare" makes possible.

A revolutionary interpretation might identify not Hambodedio but Ko as the hero of the piece; the story can support such a single focus. It would also be possible to adopt a metaperformance stance and consider the relation of Ko and Hambodedio to that of the performer and his material. Mutual dependence is the key phrase. Similar issues, couched in different terms, are also at the heart of the story of the next heroes, Silamaka and Poullori.

Silamaka and Poullori

Where almost no two stories of Hambodedio are the same, the stories about Silamaka and his retainer Poullori do show stability through the many versions collected and published in the last seventy years, although Frobenius offers evidence for significant variants.[21] The basic story is that of an unsuccessful uprising, of the death of the master Silamaka and the grief of the surviving Poullori.

At a time when Massina paid tribute to Segou, the *Ardo* [ruler] and his retainer both conceived children by their wives on the same night. The two sons were born at the same time. The noble was Silamaka, the retainer, Poullori. When the tribute-takers from Segou came to Massina, they knew the young prince would eventually cause trouble: even when a horsefly bit the baby so that blood flowed, the child did not utter a sound. When Silamaka and Poullori grew up, they determined to revolt against Segou. They consulted a diviner who told them they must capture the huge snake that lived outside of the town and make amulets from its skin. They did this. They took the skin to a leather worker who made them cases and sheaths. They got weapons from a blacksmith. Finally, they had the protective amulets made by a marabout and sewn up in the snakeskin pockets. They then killed all their helpers so they could not perform equal work for anyone else.

They rebelled against Segou, stopping the tribute-takers and sending them maimed back to their king. Segou sent armies against them. They easily repelled all the attacks. The king of Segou became more and more furious and finally resorted to divination and sorcery.

[At this point, the story of the cattle raid, discussed below, sometimes occurs.]

Several stories tell how the secret of Silamaka's protection was discovered: by simple divination, betrayal by a woman, betrayal by a dissatisfied maabo or other underling. The king had the appropriate magic prepared: a bull was hoisted to the top of a tree and sacrificed, its blood was used to bathe objects, and an albino boy was given a bow and a treated arrow and placed at the top of the tree where Silamaka usually rested after driving off the troops of Segou.

Silamaka somehow guessed that his end was coming and sent Poullori off on an errand so that he would not be present at the death. Then Silamaka rode out to battle as usual, drove off the troops of Segou, and rested under the tree. The albino boy was so frightened he could hardly shoot the arrow, but as it fell, the point grazed Silamaka and that was enough: the magic worked and the warrior knew he had a mortal wound.

His family tried to hide his death from Poullori when he returned. They dressed another man in Silamaka's clothes and tried other substitutions. Poullori saw through them all: nothing matched the nobility of the true Silamaka. Poullori guessed that Silamaka had been killed. Poullori then lamented Silamaka, recalling the only times when the master had shown him he was of lower status. Once when they were bathing, some women came up; Silamaka sent Poullori to fetch their clothes. Outside a mosque, Poullori once almost put on Silamaka's sandals. Silamaka gently reminded him that they would not fit. The servant's feet were not as fine as the noble's. The list of anecdotes varies slightly from performance to performance but concludes with the point that by not allowing Poullori to join him in death, Silamaka has insulted him and treated him as a servant.

The next day, Poullori takes Silamaka's son on his saddlebow and rides out against the horsemen of Segou. He puts them to flight and continues to chase them. He chases them still, and when it thunders, the Bamana say, "Poullori be nana" [Poullori is coming].[22]

Most scholars consider the story of Silamaka to be in some way historical and connect it to the period of expansion of the kingdom of Segou between 1780 and 1810.[23] However, there is no certainty which king of Segou faced this revolt of the Fula and there is sufficient uncertainty about Silamaka's lineage to justify doubts about the historicity of the episode. The region offers a number of heroes named Silamaka or Sira Maga. The story is vague enough in its details of time and place that the connection with Segou might be a rationalized link between a floating legend and a recognized period of history. Further back in time, in the seventeenth century, Massina struggled with Timbuctoo for its independence. An ardo named Sira Maga who reigned for only two years (1625–1627) is reported in the Arabic chronicles of Timbuctoo and in local written tradition.

Silamaka is not as popular a hero as Hambodedio. He does appear in a few other stories as an incidental character (in the story of Hambodedio and "Saïgalare" given above, Silamaka is one of the regulars at the market of Kouna), but he is rarely a protagonist and he has relatively few distinguishing features. Incidents that serve to illustrate his character (the horsefly, the quest for the talismans) are told of other heroes as well. He is fearless, proud, valiant, dangerous, self-restrained, impervious to pain—but all this is typical of any number of Fula heroes.

What does distinguish Silamaka is his companion Poullori. They are an insepa-rable pair, and the core of the story would appear to lie not in the account of Silamaka's revolt and battles with Segou but in Poullori's reaction to his master's death. Grief and loyalty combine to push Poullori toward a form of apotheosis in which he transcends himself. (It may be a literal apotheosis; among the spirit cults documented along the Niger, there is a thunder cult, and further investigation might well connect Poullori with the central figure of that cult.)

It is tempting to draw a parallel between Poullori, lamenting and exalting his dead master, and the maabo who performs the piece for his living patron, espe-cially in the case of Tinguidji, who has painted such an intimate picture of his re-lationship with his patron.[24] That social dynamic matches the self-reflexive artis-tic dynamic of the "song within the song" that concludes the story. Hambodedio's story of the "Quest for 'Saïgalare'" offers the same sort of meta-narrative in which the hero's need for a story generates the action. In this case, the story's central purpose seems to establish a context for Poullori's "performance" of his lament. Such an interpretation receives some support from two variants. In one, the per-former gives only the story of Poullori's lament.[25] The other is a Bamana version of the story in which Silamaka, before his death, asks his jeli and his two wives (this suggests a confusion with the figure of Hambodedio) to show him how they will mourn him after he is gone.[26] This Bamana version is quite different from the Fulfulde accounts of Silamaka and Poullori. Nevertheless, it seems significant that the motif retained (besides the heroic figure of Silamaka himself) is the notion of visible mourning for the dead hero.

The curious point, however, is the way in which the lament is phrased. Poullori does not praise Silamaka directly for his heroism, his nobility, or his valor, as might be expected if Silamaka were indeed the focus of the story and the function of the lament were to shape and articulate an intended audience reaction to the hero's death. Instead, he recalls the occasions on which Silamaka showed him the difference between their social levels. It is a very curious and ambivalent formu-lation: Does he recall insults, or does he justify the hierarchical social system by his acceptance of the disparities involved?

In giving voice to this social distinction, Poullori transfigures himself. It is presumably the process of voicing the lament that exalts him so that he may ride out against the horsemen of Segou the next day, and that exaltation may well evoke the power of epic singing that Seydou has described for the Fula. Poullori also expands the notion of pulaaku, at least implicitly; for while highlighting the inequalities of the social system, he also reaffirms its fundamental values, as illustrated by Silamaka. In this way, as with "Saïgalare," the different segments of Fula society (or at least the upper and lower divisions) find themselves represented and so share in the grand finale of the piece. The story's message is one of social integration.

Cattle Raids

A theme encountered frequently in the Fula epics is cattle-raiding (Hambodedio set out to capture Bongowel's cattle, for instance), and it occurs in Massina and in the traditions of the Futa Tooro, independently and as part of the larger story of Samba Gueladio. The genre can be illustrated with a well-attested story in which Silamaka and Poullori take cattle from Hambodedio to prove a point. The story is incorporated into the longer version of the life of Silamaka by one or two performers; Boûbacar Tinguidji performed it separately after the full story.

Foreseeing war, Silamaka wishes to provide a refuge for his aging father. He and Poullori ride to the home of the ruler of Goundaka (Hambodedio, usually) to request his assistance. When they arrive, the ruler's slaves insult them through a play on the usual Fulfulde greeting, "peace." Essentially, the slaves say that Silamaka and Poullori are powerless to disturb their master's peace. The ruler of Goundaka does not rebuke his slaves for this implied insult, and the two visitors take offense.

They leave and find the king's herdsmen, quickly defeating them and capturing the cattle. They drive off the cattle, and Silamaka stops and waits closer to town while Poullori goes on with the livestock. It is understood that no one will get past Silamaka as long as he is alive.

The king learns of the raid and sends out warriors; Silamaka easily defeats them. There is a stand-off, broken by an intrigue involving the ruler's wife, whom Silamaka had courted before she married. Silamaka has taken her cattle; without their butter she cannot treat her hair. A go-between brings

Silamaka a token from the woman, learns his grievance, and then goes to the ruler to show him how to make peace.

The ruler of Goundaka rides out with his prize warriors. They come upon Silamaka and talk; apologies are offered. Goundaka sends his men to get the cattle from Poullori, although Silamaka has warned him that he, Silamaka, should go in person: the ruler's warriors will not succeed. Poullori sees the warriors coming, infers that Silamaka has died, and attacks them savagely. They flee, and a remainder are saved only because they reach Silamaka before Poullori reaches them. When Poullori finds Silamaka alive, he reproaches Silamaka strongly for having broken his word and leading him, Poullori, to think his master was dead.[27]

Appreciation of this particular story is complicated by Poullori's outrage over Silamaka's supposed death. The emotion creates a resonance with the larger story of Silamaka and Poullori and to some extent duplicates its themes, showing that the "underling" is fully as worthy as the noble. In other regards, however, it is a typical cattle-raid story in which cows are less important than reputation; it revolves around a conflict between two heroes, and it ends relatively harmoniously. No one of consequence is killed and Silamaka and Poullori have together erased the insult to their worth, proving that heroes are trouble.

The same features mark the available cattle-raid stories from the Futa Tooro.[28] The focus there may be more upon the cattle; profit rather than pique may motivate the theft. But the stories resolve into a conflict of two well-matched men, and the outcome can be peaceful once an understanding has been reached and their worth has been mutually recognized.

Traditions of the Futa Tooro

The region known as the Futa Tooro lies along the Senegal River, surrounded by lands of the Wolof, the Soninke, and the Moors. The Fula, known locally as Tukolor (from Tekrour, the name of an old kingdom in the area) or Haal-Pulaaren [speakers of Fulfulde], are relatively recent arrivals. The Deniyanke dynasty ruled the area from the arrival of Koli Tengela in the sixteenth century (legend says he came into the country following a parrot with a stalk of millet in its beak) until 1776, when a form of Islamic rule known as the Imamate was established. The Almamy (from the Arabic *imam*) was elected for a year from the cadre of Islamic scholars. This system lasted (not always peacefully) until the 1830s, when al-Hajj

Umar Tall began to establish his power on the basis of his appointment in Mecca as Caliph of the Tijiani brotherhood for West Africa. Al-Hajj Umar was eventually driven off by the French and withdrew inland, through Nioro and the Kaarta. He conquered Segou and then Massina. This last action involved warfare against Muslims and led to popular resistance. He was finally driven out of Hamdallaye, the capital of the Islamic dina, and died in an explosion near Bandiagara in 1862.

The strong Islamic past of the Futa Tooro has left a large body of written material that has somewhat eclipsed the oral traditions of the region.[29] Collection of oral traditions there is of relatively recent date. Besides the historical material, there are cattle-raiding stories of the kind already discussed, which deal with local and somewhat ahistorical protagonists, and the *pekane* epics of the Subalbe, the fishermen of the Senegal River (see chapter 3). At present, the documented historical epic traditions of the Futa Tooro center on two figures: Samba Gueladio and al-Hajj Umar Tall. Of the two, Samba Gueladio has the better-established record; the epics dealing with the Tukolor leader appear recent and the tradition is still developing.

Samba Gueladio

Samba Gueladio was a Deniyanke prince of the early eighteenth century, according to the latest evidence. Displaced from the succession, he fought his uncle Konko Bou Moussa and did gain power for a time before being defeated. His principal supporters were the French, who were seeking to penetrate upriver. The epic disregards much of this history to make the story of Samba Gueladio a somewhat typical hero's story of exile and return, although with significant nuances of character.

Samba was the posthumous son of the king. Samba's uncle Konko Bou Moussa took power at the king's death. Some versions say that he sought to have Samba slain at birth, and Samba escaped only by being disguised as a girl, or by being passed off as the child of a servant. Reaching adolescence, Samba asked the king for his inheritance. Some versions say the king offered a string of false gifts, attempting to defraud the callow young man. One of the gifts was sleep, but the fraud backfired. Samba then created a tremendous noise in the village to prevent anyone from sleeping until they had paid him his due. Samba proved himself equally troublesome in other ways.

Other versions present Samba as something of a simpleton: he asked the king for his inheritance and the king gave him a horse. Only when prompted did Samba ask for more. The question of the inheritance, and other incidents, led to friction. One of them involved a European trader on a boat and the payment of trade duties. Others involved attempts on Samba's life in the course of circumcision ceremonies or other activities. Samba ended up fighting a son of Bou Moussa and decided to go into exile. He took with him his griot and his horse Umm Latouma; sometimes their two mothers accompany them.

He first met a spirit in a pool. The spirit provided him with magical protection and weapons. He used the weapons to kill the spirit. He also acquired his musical theme, a tune called "Laguiya," from a bird singing in a tree above his head. He and his griot left their mothers in the care of the *tunka* [Soninke ruler] of Tiyabu and went into the land of the Moors.

He came to the city of the king of the Moors and found lodging with an old woman. She had no water to give him—the city's water supply was controlled by a monstrous serpent to whom the town sacrificed a maiden each year or month, in exchange for which the serpent allowed them to take water. Coincidentally, the sacrifice was to take place the next day. Since it was the end of the month, the old woman had run out of water. However, there was the serpent's river running next to them. Samba took his horse down to the river to water it. The serpent attacked him and he killed it with his magical rifle. Then he cut out its tongue and left one or both of his sandals on the bank and returned to the old woman. The next day they brought the sacrificial maiden to the serpent. There was some dismay when the serpent failed to respond: Was the maiden not a virgin? Was the sacrifice deficient? The maiden jumped on the carcass, protesting her virtue, and then realized it was dead. In due course Samba was recognized and took service with the king of the Moors.

He was sent on missions, some of which were intended to kill him. He defeated a rebel Fula, Ngourori, and brought his herd of milk-white cattle to the king of the Moors (courteously, though, he left some cattle for Ngourori). He defeated other kings and monsters. He also escaped palace intrigues. Finally, he was promised an army to restore him to his throne. A log was laid across the path and the horsemen rode over it until the log was cut through by the hooves. That is how many soldiers were sent with Samba.

On the way back, he and his griot found that their mothers had been mistreated by the king to whom they had given gold for their care. They punished him and exacted a great price in cloth, piled higher than a rider's head, for his misbehavior.

Having returned home, Samba sneaked into town the night before the battle and encountered his uncle (or participated in a dance). Then, the next day, at the battle of Bilbassi, he defeated Konko Bou Moussa and took power. He died alone, perhaps poisoned by his wife. But he remained deadly even in death: his head killed a man who touched it.

Samba may be the earliest West African hero to have had his story recorded as a performance narrative rather than as a historical tradition. The French soldier and explorer Anne Raffenel (a man, despite the name) provides a version in an appendix to his *Nouveau voyage au pays des nègres* in 1856. There are also early versions (ca. 1910) of the story in Equilbecq, Frobenius, and de Zeltner.[30] Reliable transcriptions of oral performance versions are relatively recent; fortunately, there are now two.[31]

Although in many details the epic does preserve a recollection of the pre-Islamic period, the actual historical record has clearly been lost in this classical pattern of the monster-slayer. It is pointless to treat the story as history. Rather, it is a construct appropriating incidents from other traditions to establish a local hero. For instance, the episode of the mothers and the tunka of Tiyabu clearly evokes the death of Sunjata's mother, although the ransom of trade goods that embellishes this particular story may actually recall one of the underlying causes of the historical rivalries of Samba Gueladio, his uncle, and the Moors.

The temporal span of versions of this story is greater than for any other (140 years). Its basic lines have remained stable throughout that time. The centerpiece of Samba's adventure is the slaying of the water-monster. This action defines him as a hero, though it is the least credible of his adventures, recalling as it does a three-thousand-year-old tradition of monster-slayers. But the story has local resonance within the West African context. The reader may recall the Soninke legend of Wagadu, in which the killing of the Bida Serpent represents a breach of agreements and kinship and thus ends a true golden age for the Soninke. The contrasts are evident: where the Soninke serpent is protective (at the price of an occasional maiden), this monster is tyrannical and withholds the water supply of the town. The common ground is perhaps curiously focused: both of the heroes are fundamentally antisocial. The Soninke hero acts against the will of the maiden, out of selfish passion. Samba Gueladio acts out of an arrogant concern for his horse and never even sees the maiden.

It may be more relevant that the monster-slaying story is found elsewhere within the sphere of Fula Islam as a justification for the taking of power by a Muslim and Fula ruling family.[32] This association would add a religious dimension to the understanding of the legend. The serpent-slayer could be seen as the iconoclastic convert who attacks the central symbol of the old earth-centered cult: Muslims and Christians alike share an antipathy for the residual religions and view serpents as the symbol of the devil. But such an interpretation would require seeing Samba as a Muslim. He has become one in modern tradition; in the historical record, however, he showed no signs of religious fervor. It seems simplest to view the monster-story as a thrilling tale attached to a local hero. This point could be carried even further: the story serves as a sort of catch-all excuse for the assistance provided by the Moorish king. It is not essential to the appreciation of the local characteristics of this hero.

Samba represents the *ceddo* (or *thiedo*) of the Deniyanke period: a member of a "caste" of warriors that engaged in no productive work but lived only to fight (this function probably developed in response to the slave trade). A similar group, the *nyancho,* is found in the Gambia some time later (see chapter 8). They are marked by an aristocratic warrior's ethos. Arrogance and violence are their fundamental traits. Samba shares these traits to some extent with figures such as Hambodedio and Silamaka. The heroes may inspire admiration for their strength of character, for the force of their will, for their courage; those same features set them against the ordinary norms of the society in which they live. They are, as Birago Diop termed them, "turbulent princes," and the days of their turbulence were days of glory but also days of trouble. The passing of those days is not regretted, especially since Islam has now intervened and changed many of the fundamentals of the cultural ethos. Samba Gueladio represents the pre-Islamic period of ignorance and troubles—and perhaps provides an explanation of why the new way became better. Since he is recalled only for his battles and the trouble he caused, he cannot be seen as a heroic figure who rose to greatness during his rule.

Al-Hajj Umar

Al-Hajj Umar Tall was probably the most influential individual in the Sahel in the nineteenth century. The religious organization he established, the Tijiani brotherhood, still thrives, and the effect of his conquests is felt from Senegal to the Dogon country. It is hardly surprising that an epic tradition has begun to develop around him, nor are performances limited to Fulfulde. Stories of al-Hajj Umar have been recorded in Maninka, Bamana, and Zerma. So far, however, few

performance pieces of significant weight have appeared. Instead, there are hagiographic legends: the infant Umar was so devout that even as a suckling babe he
observed the fast of Ramadan. Through divine grace he knew the hours of the
beginning and end of the fast, so people could use his suckling as a guide.[33] There
is a parallel development in upper Guinea, where David Conrad has recorded one
version of the life of al-Hajj Umar, of which more than half is devoted to the trials
of his mother before his birth; the accent in this story is apparently on the notion
of submission inherent in Islam.[34]

The tradition has one feature of some interest for comparative scholarship: it
is rooted in Islam and so is bound up with literacy. There is an early poetic life of
Umar by Mohammadou Aliou Tyam, a *qacida* (an Arabic poetic form) in Pulaar/
Fulfulde of some twelve hundred lines.[35] This text is apparently memorized and
recited by performers, as are others on similar topics. Presumably the content of
the poem will have some influence on the shape of later oral narrations. But these
developments are so far virtually unstudied and far too new for serious analysis
or assessment.

Conclusion

The Fula epic traditions considered here are only a small portion of the wealth
of material available in published form; that material can be expected to increase
with time. The performance tradition, adapted in places to new techniques of
recording and distribution via cassette, is lively. In some regards the Fula epics are
the most accessible of the various traditions considered. Each story appears to be
a self-contained unit featuring distinct and dynamic heroes engaged in great
deeds, occasionally embellished with graceful passages that do not intrude into
the narrative. The themes involve easily presented notions such as self-worth
and pride, and the self-reflexive artistry of the performers will delight students of
meta-narrative. The contrast is with the grander, but more hermetic, Sunjata tradition, in which episodes are part of a larger whole, praise songs may distract the
unfamiliar reader, and the motivation for action is occasionally obscure.

Some explanation for this openness seems possible. The Fula epic traditions
have cut the tie to lineage and history, and even to place. This genre was apparently adopted as entertainment, as fiction rather than history. The consequence
has been to clarify the artistic endeavor considerably, for the accent is now on the
qualities of wholeness and comprehensibility. The audience is no longer a select
aristocratic clique but, potentially at least, the general public, and this populari-
zation would also reinforce those qualities.

Massina appears to be the cradle of the Fula epic tradition, despite the well-established tradition behind Samba Gueladio in the Futa Tooro. This locus may explain the general appeal of the epics, for in Massina the Fula are surrounded by the Soninke (in various factions), the Bamana, and the Songhay, and the contacts go back for centuries. Excluding the recent period of Islam and colonial domination, the region has existed largely a borderland between states: Songhay and Jara and Kaarta and Segou. It can be assumed that political fluctuations have led to shifts in allegiance and encouraged cultural borrowings: the less historical epics are set in a curious kind of no-man's land. In a collection of general material such as Frobenius's *Atlantis,* in which the original languages are somewhat obscured by the translation, it is difficult to attribute stories to any group with certainty: the stories share characteristics and suggest a common fund of heroes and adventures set in a common era.

One local measure of the effectiveness of the Fula transformation of the epic tradition is the way in which Fula stories influence Bamana epic pieces. The most sympathetic heroes of the cycle of Segou are presented as Fula. Fula heroes are sung in Bamana and in Zarma. The interaction of material from strong historical traditions with the liberty, and obligation, to shape the material for the purposes of entertainment and art has created a particularly rich vein, one whose worth—designed locally to appeal to a variety of communities—can easily be appreciated by outsiders.

EMERGENT TRADITIONS

THE TERRITORY IN which the traditions of the Soninke, the Maninka, the Bamana, and the Fula of Massina are found constitutes a geographic region that corresponds roughly to the old empire of Mali. This chapter describes groups that lie on the periphery or the marches of that core, from a Mande-centric perspective. To the east, a variety of peoples along the Niger River—the Sorko, the Songhay, the Zarma—look back beyond the Songhay empire (ca. 1400–1600) to some connection with Mali in their traditions of origin. They too were caught up in the nineteenth-century wave of Fula expansion, and their oral traditions show the influence of these invaders. The second region lies to the west, in Senegal and the Gambia. Chapter 5 described the Gambian versions of Sunjata; this chapter will discuss the more recent historical traditions of the polities of Kaabu and Fuladu and the period down to the arrival of the English, as well as the traditions of the Wolof, which have only recently made their appearance in print. This area was affected by Fula-led Islam, although mostly from the Futa Jallon in Guinea.

A common feature of the epics from these two regions is the importance of relatively recent history. The epics center on figures from the nineteenth century who fought local wars, such as Issa Korombe among the Zarma, or Janke Wali of Kansala and Kelefa Sane in the Gambia; or figures who fought the Europeans, such as Fode Kaba of the Gambia, and in particular the Wolof *damel* [king], Lat Dior, who died fighting the French in 1886. Another common feature, more subjectively defined, is the absence of a recognizable local performance tradition, meaning in part that the epics do not have the polish of some of the more brilliant examples from the Bamana or Fula traditions. Nor are they marked by the evocative intrusion of songs like those in the Sunjata tradition (e.g., "Take up your bow, Simbon . . . "). These two traits suggest the strong possibility that in some of these areas the adoption of epic-singing (noble historical narratives performed to music) may be relatively recent, owing much either to the Fula domination of part of the region (since in style they resemble the Fula epics), or perhaps simply to the free movement of peoples during seventy years of colonial rule and thirty years of independence. The premise behind this hypothesis is that while praise singing and the institution of the griot are deep-rooted features of West African culture, the transition to the singing of narrative is less widespread and may owe much to cross-cultural imitation.

One practical feature that influences the assemblage of texts in this chapter is that of volume. There are fewer published texts for these groups than for those discussed earlier, although this may reflect only the vagaries of the collecting process. It seems very likely that in the coming years the quantity of available material will increase, bringing about a change in the understanding of these traditions.

The Peoples of the River: Songhay, Zarma, and Others

Down the stream of the Niger, north and east of Segou and Massina, there are a number of groups that are united to some extent by language but distinguished by nomenclature and historical identity. Another common feature is their association with the river, either as a source of food (as with the Sorko) or as the transportation artery of the empire (from Gao to Djenne and beyond for the Songhay). Questions of identity become slippery, as indicated in the discussion of the hunters' traditions of the region (see chapter 3). Nor should these groups be considered "merely" the eastern fringe of the Mande world; the Songhay empire was not purely a successor state but defined its own identity, particularly through Islam. The region provides its own rich mix of cultures, with elements shared along the Niger, through Hausaland, and into the Yoruba kingdoms.

The Songhay empire began its expansion from Gao and Timbuctoo in the fifteenth century; by 1500 it was sending expeditions as far west as the Futa Tooro; at one point, around 1545, Songhay soldiers sacked the palace of the king of Mali and filled his house with excrement.[1] The empire was based on trade along the Niger, and its backbone ran along the northern loop of the river from Djenne to Timbuctoo to Gao. The northern trade across the Sahara is the most visible in the historical record, but it should not overshadow the possibly larger southbound trade to the land of kola nuts, ivory, and other commodities. The empire fell abruptly after the Moroccans launched a trans-Saharan expedition during the winter of 1590–1591. The force was equipped with firearms and arrived at a time of internal dissension (the empire was prone to weakness at times of succession because of the rivalries between competing brothers). The Moroccans defeated the Songhay armies but failed to conquer the empire. They established pashas in Timbuctoo and tributaries to the Caliph in Morocco, and these surrogates attempted to restore the old hegemony but in fact failed to extend it much beyond the city (their descendants are known as the Arma). Thereafter the empire dissolved into two great divisions: the Moroccan-controlled area between Timbuctoo and Gao, and the independent regions downstream from them, including smaller principalities such as Dendi, on the borders of Hausa land. But even these smaller states collapsed in the nineteenth century during the invasions of the Fula and the Tuareg, which reduced many inhabitants to the status of "captives."[2] In the modern era, although Songhay elements are still present in the republic of Mali, the principal center of study is in the republic of Niger, where Songhay-speakers (successors to those who resisted the Moroccans) are generally identified as Zarma (Zerma, Diarma, Dierma).

The region's history is well documented, thanks largely to the *Tarikhs* (histories) written in Timbuctoo in the seventeenth century by Abd al-Rahman al-Sa'di and Mahmoud Kati. The work of al-Sa'di in particular, the *Tarikh es-Soudan,* offers a wealth of information on the early history of the Songhay and their neighbors.[3] The *Tarikh el-Fettach* of Kati was rewritten in the nineteenth century to incorporate prophecies foretelling nineteenth-century religious leaders, and scholars have raised questions about the accuracy of the manuscript tradition of Kati's work. These two locally produced windows on the past are virtually unique resources in West African historiography. Despite the weaknesses now identified in the French translations by Houdas and Delafosse, the books are widely studied as the best internal evidence for their period. They are supported by other documents such as the *Tedzkiret el-Nissian*[4] (a rather dry set of biographies of the pashas of Timbuctoo) and the histories of Ahmed Baba, all stemming from the Islamic tradition.

These works have been extended by modern historiographers, working with local traditions collected under colonial rule and more recently. The best general synthesis is still the 1953 study by Jean Rouch, *Contribution à l'histoire des Songhay.* He incorporates both the local traditions he encountered and the unpublished records collected by early colonial administrators in his examination of the written sources. The Nigerien Boubou Hama, in a series of works, has established the national historical tradition for a variety of groups (the Zarma, the Fula, the Tuareg), as well as the cultural tradition for the modern republic of Niger.[5] He is in some ways comparable to the Malian Amadou Hampaté Bâ in his presentation and defense of local tradition against the foreign intellectual hegemony. As a historian, he is more concerned with establishing a record than with the analysis and critique of sources, and this absence of distance from his material is considered a weakness by some.[6] Thomas Hale has published a version of the epic of Askia Mohammed performed by Nouhou Malio, along with an analysis that matches the narrative traditions of the griot and the writers of the *Tarikhs*.[7] This text remains the best example of Songhay historical epic available in English.

Over the past twenty-five years, the Centre d'Etudes Linguistique et Historique par Tradition Orale (CELHTO) in Niamey has done yeoman service in collecting and publishing a wide variety of transcribed oral traditions from across West Africa (often in stencil or mimeograph form, a concession to low budgets). Mahmoud Zouber and Julde Laya have edited several volumes of local traditions from the Anzuru and Dosso regions of Niger; they were collected from village elders and vary in length, but all are presented in bilingual format.[8] Concentrating on Zabarkane, a mythical ancestor, Fatimata Mounkaila provides a number of versions of the legend from a variety of sources.[9] And various narratives have been collected by Jean-Pierre Olivier de Sardan from levels of society not often recognized: from the peasantry, the former captives/slaves of the society.[10] In this regard, Olivier de Sardan's effort parallels (and precedes) that of Mamadou Diawara for the Soninke, and it recognizes the need to incorporate the full social spectrum in order to achieve the most reliable history. It also acknowledges a particularity of the more recent history of the region: that it was subjected to Tuareg and Fula domination and fragmented into a disunited mosaic of struggling communities.

The nineteenth century, the period of subjection and dislocation, is the period of texts most comparable and closest in style to those examined so far. Ousmane Mahamane Tandina collected four texts in bilingual format for his thesis; three of these deal with Issa Korombe, a nineteenth-century Zarma warlord who fought the Fula in the period immediately before the arrival of the French, and the fourth with the arrival of the Fula.[11] Oumarou Watta has published two epic texts. One of them, "Donda Garba Dikko,"[12] is an ahistorical hero-tale virtually identical to Frobenius's "Der Held Gossi" and the Fula tale of the three fears of Hambodedio (see chapter 7). The second tells of a conflict between al-Hajj Umar (in his image as religious leader and bringer of Islam) and the Fula warrior Boubou Ardo Gallo.[13] The traditions of the Gow hunters and the Sorko, the fishermen and their heroes Moussa Gname, Faran Maka, and Fono, were discussed in chapter 3. It seems inappropriate to view these as historical materials, although they were treated as such in their first analysis by Louis Desplagnes (or A. Dupuis-Yakouba) and Maurice Delafosse. But reading the struggles with various beasts that occur in the hunters' songs as an allegorical presentation of wars between clans of different animal totems suggests a regression to a long discredited methodology and view of "primitive" societies.

The variety of texts available presents a challenge: the various traditions do not necessarily fit together. Traditions of Mali Bero and Zabarkane do not intersect with those of Faran Maka. Faran Maka has nothing to do with Mamar Kassay. Moussa Gname, offspring of a jinn and leader of hunters, does not really invite historical analysis. Jean Rouch provides one legend from the Kakoro (a Soninke subgroup) that links them genealogically. According to this legend, King Si had three sisters.[14] Kassay gave birth to Mamar Kassay, the Askia Mohammed of Islamic and imperial tradition; another sister married a blacksmith; and the third married Faran Maka Bote and became the ancestor of the river people. Beyond this tenuous connection, little unites the traditions.

From a comparative perspective, the Songhay-Zarma traditions offer a wealth of possibilities. The multiplicity of their formulations constitutes almost a repertoire of the idioms through which political power is constructed in Sahelian historical traditions. The parallels with the traditions of Sunjata and of Segou, in particular, provide a useful filter for sifting out regional commonplaces from particular inventions; they also raise questions about the movement and influence of traditions. When Faran Maka calls for a harpoon with which to fish and the smiths forge him a tremendous iron weapon that he keeps breaking, there may be a parallel with the iron bars forged to help Sunjata rise. When Mamar Kassay (the Askia Mohammed) seeks help from his father, the jinn of the waters, there is a certain similarity with the accession of Mamari Biton Koulibali, who visited the underwater realm of Faro.

The parallels also point to differences, and the reference to Sunjata allows the clearest illustration of the principal difference. Whereas Maninka traditions are in large part articulated around the central figure of Sunjata, and whereas the Soninke look back to the lost unity of Wagadu, there is no single core to Songhay and Zarma traditions. Perhaps surprisingly, even the tradition of empire recorded in the chronicles of al-Sa'di and Kati fails to provide a common cultural ground. The Zarma traditions presented by Mounkaila and Laya look more often to some vague "Mali" as their starting point than to the old empire based in Gao, although this Malian origin is also often doubled with some reference to Mecca and the Prophet Muhammad. This orientation is presumably a very old pattern. The *Tarikh es-Soudan* dates the origin of the Songhay empire to the flight of two brothers from the court of Mali, and the motif of the flight of brothers on horseback is widely echoed through all sorts of oral traditions, from the legend of Wagadu to stories of the origins of griots.

The perception that there is no single core to the traditions may well be due to the incomplete state of the collections. There is only one extensive publication of the tradition of Mamar Kassay, the Askia Mohammed, although Mamar appears

frequently in other localized narratives.[15] Quite possibly the existence of the written record of the *Tarikhs* has distracted attention from the existence of a more
generally accepted and central oral tradition. Thomas Hale, who published the
text of Nouhou Malio's performance, reports having recorded at least a dozen versions by different performers throughout western Niger. It seems possible that the
specific focus in the research interests of Mounkaila, Laya, and others has created
a fragmented sense of history.

Outside study of Songhay and Zarma traditions has not been limited to
their historiography; in fact, the region may well be better known for its magico-
religious cultural dimension than for its history. The works of Jean Rouch, Jean-
Marie Gibbal, and Paul Stoller provide an extensive corpus of information on beliefs, practices, and myths of local possession cults, all of which offer pertinent
background material for the study of not only Songhay epic but all the regional
traditions. Nor is print the only medium in which information is delivered; Jean
Rouch pioneered a branch of ethnographic cinematography to which Jean-Pierre
Olivier de Sardan has made contributions; and Thomas Hale has added a short
videotape on *griottes,* one of the few treatments of female performers available.[16]

The Performance Tradition

In many regards, Songhay-Zarma epic performance traditions are hybridized
or derivative. Within the sphere of courtly panegyric (the classic griot genre), performers are endowed with a status parallel to that of the jeliw of the Mande world
and are termed *gesere:* a Soninke term that reflects the origin claimed for the
group and that is further justified by the use of Soninke as a performance language in parallel with Zarma-Songhay. Several of Mounkaila's texts on Mali Bero
were performed bilingually, sung first in Soninke by the senior performer and se-
quentially translated into Zarma by an assistant (at least once by a woman). Hale's
transcription of the epic of Askia Mohammed is marked by untranslatable
passages, particularly of praise singing, which are apparently in Soninke. This
Soninke praise-singing complex extends as far down the river as Borgu in northern Benin, where Paolo de Moraes Farias has documented the survival of the tradition in an isolated enclave.[17] The probability of Fula influence has also been
noted. In a brief discussion of performance conditions, Mounkaila refers grate-
fully to the descriptions given by Seydou of Fula performers as applying also to
her own. Watta's texts appear to be Zarma versions of Fula stories, and Tandina's
thesis shows a heavy Fula presence. Even Nouhou Malio's account of the Songhay
empire, in Hale's edition, brings in nineteenth-century Fula figures.

A more popular praise-singing tradition is found among the many possession cults for which the Songhay are known; the cults may link them with such institutions as the Yoruba *ijala* (cult praises) tradition found further to the south. Typically, the music for these sessions is provided by the *jinbe,* the "possession" drum, which has a tight metallic sound. The singing involves praise chanting to the various entities of the different pantheons or families; Rouch describes the various families of spirit beings known to him in the 1950s, and Gibbal provides evidence for more modern forms of the cults as they have spread west into Mali.[18] But these instruments and this style of singing have nothing in common with the performance modes of the epic tradition. The narratives associated with these cults may strongly resemble those of the hunters' societies in the Manden, judging by the collection of Dupuis-Yakouba and the elements provided by Rouch; but there is virtually no information available on the performance context and modes of those hunters' narratives.

In their present state of documentation, then, the Songhay and Zarma traditions seem useful mainly for the purposes of narrative analysis and comparative work. Clearly, they are products of the cultural complex associated with the former Great States, and whether the discernible parallels derive from a Songhay contribution to the complex (dating presumably to the era of the empire) or from Songhay adoption of borrowed material is moot. It does seem probable that in this region the pre-Islamic elements have been better preserved than in the former realm of Kankan Musa the pilgrim and king of Mali, despite the presence in Songhay oral and written tradition of the pilgrimage of the Askia Mohammed.

The Heroes and Their Stories

The appendix presents a selective list of the most substantial narratives available, grouped by principal character. They show little developed unity. Each group defines itself by a distinctive set of traditions of origin, and for the most part these are couched in mythical rather than historical terms. At times, some traditions appear to centralize the figure of Mamar; but such integration has certainly not proceeded as far as it has within the Sunjata tradition, where Tira Magan, Fakoli, and other ancestral figures are subordinated to their king. Nor does it appear that the stories have been made to mesh, as they do with Sunjata.

Traditions of the Empire

As noted above, the epic of Askia Mohammed as sung by Nouhou Malio[19] is really the only available published example of a "performance" version of this material. The seemingly continuous narrative is actually the product of two performance sessions, of which the first (to line 609) deals with the accession to power of Askia Mohammed (r. 1493–1528), known in oral tradition as Mamar Kassay (Kassay is the name of his mother), and the second with the fall of the empire. The story of Mamar will seem familiar in parts.

Mamar Kassay

King Si had heard a prophecy that a son of his sister Kassay would overthrow him, and so he killed her first seven children. Her eighth is the product of a union with a water spirit who comes to her at night. At the birth, she exchanges her male child with that of her captive. Mamar is raised as a servant but hardly fits the mold. Eventually, after a confrontation with his mother, he goes into the river with a token, finds his father, and receives weapons. He then kills Si as the king sits on a prayer mat, after repeated (and dramatically described) false charges on horseback. He scares off the sons of Si, takes power, and eventually makes the pilgrimage to Mecca to atone for the kin-killing. In Mecca, miracles demonstate the worthiness of Mamar, and on his return he begins to convert people.

At this point the story can lead into local traditions such as those collected by Zouber and Laya, where Mamar rides through villages bringing Islam.[20] The underlying narrative is almost a generic hero-pattern story and echoes or reiterates idioms and details encountered before. There is little distinctive material here. The second portion of the performance (approximately one thousand lines, many of which appear to be cryptic praises in Soninke or genealogical material) tells of the fall of the empire; but it conflates this event with the acute troubles of the mid-nineteenth century. In fact, as Hale suggests,[21] the historical record gives way to a picture of Songhay society that turns on the central distinction between slave (or captive) and free, translated into a family dynamic of tragic proportions.

Amar Zoumbani and the Fall of Songhay

Soumayla had usurped power and then married Sagouma, daughter of the ruler he had displaced. Her brother was thus dispossessed. This marriage, however, was Soumayla's second. He had slept with a slave-woman belonging to Sagouma's family, but never bothered to buy her freedom. From this union came a son, Amar Zoumbani. Soumayla's neglect of the mother meant that Amar was of servile status, and this led to great problems.

At a festival, Amar (the wealthy son of the ruler) won praise by distributing horses to the griots. Sagouma's brother complained to his sister that he could not match Amar's gifts, and she told him to give the griots Amar, the son of their captive. The brother did so, which of course humiliated Amar. Another incident involving a horse again underlined Amar's captive status. Soumayla then had the brother killed. Sagouma swore revenge and traversed the land seeking a hero who would offer the dowry she asked: the deaths of Soumayla and Amar. She met a hero, the Fula Bayero, who brought war to the land. Gao was destroyed, but the continuation of the war was ultimately unsuccessful. At one dramatic moment, while Sagouma and Bayero were traveling down the river in a boat and discussing Soumayla's worth, Sagouma claimed that Bayero was no match for Soumayla. She seized her attendant's *godye* (a musical instrument) to sing Soumayla's praises, so that Soumayla was magically drawn to the water. Soumayla speared Bayero and rode off.[22]

The version of Nouhou Malio is distinctive in its presentation and its referential time frame. For instance, he gives the victory to Soumayla (thus proving the truth of Sagouma's words), where other versions have the two men fight to the death, perhaps like Faran and Fono. While in some regards he preserves the record of the Moroccan expedition,[23] he also brings in other material. The name "Bayero" was that of a nineteenth-century Fula warlord who accompanied Ahmadou Cheikhou, son and heir of al-Hajj Umar in Segou, when the French displaced him; he most clearly illustrates the anachronisms of this image of the past. The versions that Prost and Rouch both obtained from the Mayga family in Tera are slightly different. The figure of Amar Zoumbani is not so central, although he still appears under a different name. The hero enlisted by Sagouma is here a Moroccan (Sidi Moulay), and Soumayla drowns when Sagouma calls him to the river. Rouch also dates this war to 1639–1640.[24]

This more complex half of the epic revolves around questions of social status, subordination, and the legitimacy of power. Amar Zoumbani, seeking repeatedly to prove he is not a captive but failing each time, and Sagouma, seeking vengeance for the death of her brother but nevertheless filled with such admiration for her former husband that she sacrifices her new lover Bayero to him, are parallel figures in an artistic sense and poles of tension in a sociological sense. The personal drama of their situations might be contrasted with the conventional heroism of Yefarma Issaka, a minor figure who joins the wars of Bayero knowing he will die.[25]

The conflicts that they embody and cause between Zarma and outsider (Fula or Tuareg) resonate throughout nineteenth-century Songhay and Zarma history; the best evocation of that era is through the work of Olivier de Sardan.

The figure of Bayero points to a mixing of traditions. Sagouma's quest for vengeance might well recall the quest of Fatimata Ham-Sire in the Fula story of the "Capture of Sa," just as Amar Zoumbani's struggle with his status might recall the laments of Poullori (see chapter 7). These parallels strengthen the suggestion that the present performance tradition owes something to Fula models and may help to explain some of the particularities of Malio's performance. Nevertheless, there are too few examples to make a firm judgment.

The Askia Mohammed also occurs in a semiliterary narrative in Zouber's collection, although only tangentially: his horse has been stolen and various heroes attempt to retrieve it. A hero named Djouma succeeds in finding it after a visit to the jinns; later there is a dispute over his quality as a warrior. The tradition of empire in this case is no longer historical but fabulous.

Mali Bero and the Origin of the Zarma

This narrative, which Mounkaila terms the *geste* of Zabarkane[26] in a reference to an ancestor of the hero Mali Bero, is more properly a myth of origin that derives the Zarma from Mali through migration. The Zarma at first were oppressed in Mali: the actual form of oppression, repeated throughout the six versions presented by Mounkaila, involves a situation in which "noble" Fula and Tuareg youths would use the clothes of the Zarma to dry themselves after bathing. The issues of servility and submission (and of the oppressors), central in nineteenth-century Songhay-Zarma history, resurface here. Mali Bero decides to end the oppression and kills the youths. He then constructs a granary floor of woven straw and flies away with it down the river, taking his people with him. Other details of presumably symbolic importance link the versions: a bull leads them, a leather worker betrays the slaughter of the princes to the Fula or the Tuareg but is nevertheless brought on board. The story continues in some cases with the stories of the four sons of Taguru who tried to kill their father. Essentially it is a series of linked legends of origin whose resonance in some cases may evoke Judeo-Islamic traditions (servitude in Mali as a parallel to the captivity in Egypt, the sons of Taguru as a parallel with the sons of Noah) but in other regards have local connections: the historical and regional reference to Mali, the Fula, and the Tuareg, or the mythical detail of the flying granary floor that might evoke the descent of the Celestial Granary in Dogon mythology.[27]

The legend of Zwa from the Anzuru, as narrated by Alfa Suley Yuusuru, is also relevant here.[28] Zwa is a hunter who settles in the empty land and becomes the ruler after acquiring a wife. He is originally from Mali. He is recognized by Mali Bero as the granary flies through, and he also welcomes the sons of Si after their father has been killed by Mamar. His story connects with all the possible local sources of legitimation.

The form of some of Mounkaila's transcribed texts is particularly noteworthy. She provides an example of bilingual performance, an utterance in Soninke translated consecutively into Zarma, and in the song "Tilwâti," a polished poetic structure. But one cannot say that from a narrative perspective the texts offer the same complexity and wealth as one finds with the fall of the empire or outside the Zarma tradition.

Issa Korombe and Other Nineteenth-Century Heroes

A smattering of other texts deals with heroes of the nineteenth century: Issa Korombe, considered the liberator of the Zarma because he made war against the invading Fula and drove them off during the wars of 1856–1866 (although he died in battle against the real Bayero and Ahmadou Cheikhou around 1896, after forty years of rule).[29] In style and performance characteristics, the texts share a great deal with the Fula traditions already examined, and the fourth text presented by Tandina is in fact a history of the Fula migrations into the region. As a hero, Issa Korombe is cut from a general pattern (childhood adventures, quests for power, battles, and a final glorious death) in which some of the details are quite striking: for instance, he learns the magical secrets of warfare from a woman with one breast. His death (he is shot with an arrow from a tree) recalls that of Silamaka.

Oumarou Watta presents two texts, the first in his dissertation ("Donda Garba Dikko") and the second in a recently published book, *Rosary, Mat and Molo*. "Donda Garba Dikko" is a Zarma version of the story of Gossi/Hambodedio/Kumba Sira Maga, telling the story of the three fears and the invasion of the king's women's quarters encountered in Fula epics.[30] His second text also reflects the Fula tradition. It narrates a confrontation between al-Hajj Umar and the pagan hero Boubou Ardo Gallo that revolves around Boubou's refusal to convert. It is not a historical piece, although the names are historical. It offers an interesting example of the homeostasizing operations of oral tradition,[31] through which the very problematic aspects of the wars of al-Hajj Umar are transformed into a currently acceptable issue of conversion. The image of al-Hajj Umar in this case partakes of that of Mamar Kassay in the nonepic narratives collected by Laya and Zouber, where the king is a pioneer of Islam remembered for his forcible conversions (and thus perhaps comparable with the Scandinavian kings who brought Christianity to their lands).

A wonderful counterpoint to all the aristocratic traditions is the collection made by Jean-Pierre Olivier de Sardan, *Quand nos pères étaient captifs,* which presents narratives from peasants centered on the town of Sassalé. This is not exactly epic material, although the informants discuss Issa Korombe and a Tuareg hero, Anawar; but it is a valuable and unusual source that sets off, to some extent, the style and the content of the more formal and polished performances by griots. The works of Olivier de Sardan are marked by his concern for the common people, for the underlings of a hierarchized society; and his perspective is convincing, although it paints a bleak picture (for the precolonial period) of a lawless land in which men and women farmed, weapons close to hand and ever attentive to the lookout guarding against slave-raiders and looters.

It should be added in conclusion that the printed record of Zarma epic performance is an inadequate reflection of a vigorous and growing tradition. The principal medium of diffusion at the local level is the cassette tape recording, which (as in the Futa Tooro) has transformed the marketplace. Any observations about the traditions, then, are to some extent premature and of necessity incomplete. Still, it seems probable that the mode of narrative, rather than panegyric, performance is either a newcomer to the region, brought by the Fula, or at least has been heavily colored by the Fula domination of the area in the last century. From the stylistic and performative aspects, the Songhay-Zarma traditions throw little light on their neighbors, although the polyglot mixture of Soninke and Zarma is unique. They belong to a general pattern of narrative accompanied by music. On the question of narrative material, however, their contribution is quite valuable because of the way in which they echo and reshape the traditions of Sunjata and the Manden. It seems highly probable that there is a common cultural core, buried deep in time (Roderick McIntosh's "deep symbolic reservoirs"), which unites the groups and which invites further analysis and study.

Senegambia

Gambian Mandinka

In one sense, the epic traditions of the Gambian Mandinka are a subset of the wider traditions of the Mande diaspora. The hunters' epics and the Gambian versions of the epic of Sunjata are evidence for these wider cultural horizons, but at this point a claim for the autonomy of at least parts of the Gambian epic tradition must be asserted. While the epics owe something to their participation in the wider Mande world, they are also a particular and unique fusion of elements, and they have developed the Mande inheritance in their own way.

Gambian oral traditions are likely to be more familiar to a contemporary American public than many other African histories. It was in the Gambia that Alex Haley found the connection he sought for his family history and its African origins. That the Gambia was colonized by England rather than France, and so is essentially English-speaking, also helps to explain this greater awareness. Few outsiders are likely to have grasped the complexities in the history of this relatively small region, however: the successive Mandinka kingdoms, the Fula invasions, or the "Marabout-Soninke" wars of the nineteenth century. Works such as Charlotte Quinn's *Mandingo Kingdoms of the Senegambia* or the numerous works of Donald Wright[32] on the history of Niumi provide accessible sources for those complexities. Neither of these historians shares in the popular idealization of the griot as a historical repository, even though Wright started with some optimism in this regard; each of them can therefore be considered an accessible corrective to those who overestimate the powers of the griot. Wright's two volumes of interviews with Mandinka griots and with elders[33] are valuable examples of the challenges and problems of fieldwork in oral history, and they offer nice parallels and background for the epics. Other materials, perhaps less easily obtained, come from the Gambia, including the writings of Patience Sonko-Godwin and the dated but still useful history by W. T. Hamlyn.[34]

The specific epics considered in this section are a reflection of this localized history and the distinct Gambian fusion of cultures and traditions. They stand apart from the Sunjata tradition of the Gambia both because they come after it and because they form a separate tradition. Though there is one case[35] in which the story of Sunjata leads into a five-hundred-line description of the movement of the Mandinka into the Gambia, even that continuation fails to link the era of Suntaja and the more recent times now being considered. Sunjata, and more specifically Tira Magan, who is said to have conquered the Gambia, are associated with traditions of origin: with the arrival of families, the invention (or importation) of royalty *(mansaya)* from the Mali, and the establishment of Kaabu (or Gabou, in French transcription). More recent history (of the eighteenth and nineteenth centuries) looks to a tumultuous period of warring states associated with the princely group of the *nyancho* (an aristocratic class said to be the offspring of a woman and spirits and considered either divine or non-human), who may be compared with the Deniyanke dynasty in the Futa Toro or the warlords of Segou and the Zarmatarey. The modern epic period begins with the fall of the kingdom of Kaabu and the city of Kansala through the excesses of the nyanchos. The problematic Kelefa Sane may embody the martial spirit of the era. Two other elements also play a considerable role: Islam, imposed by the Fula of Timbo in Guinea (central to the story of Janke Wali and the fall of Kansala), and the period of European intervention.

Performance practices and standards for this region are unusually well documented. Roderick Knight's dissertation, "Mandinka Jeliya," is highly informative on musicology and performance. The texts edited by Gordon Innes include valuable notes on musical modes and tunes (by Anthony King and Lucy Duran, respectively) as well as information on the performer and the circumstances of the recording. To these one might add Seni Darbo's *Self-Portrait of a Griot* for an inside look at a performer's life and perspective. Other resources are available: films and recordings, for example. At least one active Gambian griot, Papa Bunka Suso, now resides in Washington, D.C.

Relatively few texts are available from this more purely Gambian repertoire: seven published by Innes in bilingual versions in two books, to which might be added, as supplementary material, some of the interviews conducted by Wright, and (if accessible) a number of texts distributed in 1980 on the occasion of a conference on the history of Kaabu.[36] The Oral History and Antiquities Division of the Ministry of Culture of the Gambia, formerly under the direction of Bakari Sidibe, has been very active in collecting, and a valuable repository of material is therefore likely to exist in Banjul.

The performance tradition in the region is very strong and deep-rooted, and its effects are noticeable in the modern material. The point can be illustrated by contrasting Nouhou Malio's story of Soumayla and Sagouma with Bamba Suso's (or another's) account of Janke Wali and Kansala:

The Fall of Kansala

When Janke Wali was installed in power, they asked him to make three predictions. His three words foretold the end of Kansala in varying ways. In one interesting variant the king removed his trousers to put on a woman's cloth: the message was that what they would see would be as unheard-of as such an action on a king's part. Some time later, the Fula invaded under the leadership of the Almami of Timbo. Janke Wali sent one son to the Almami. On his return, the son said the Fula were as numerous as grains of sand and advised flight. Janke Wali disowned him (or had him executed). A second son went, returned, and described the Fula the same way, but he said it was time to die. His father praised him.

The Fula approached and attacked. Some warriors buried themselves to the waist so they could not run. Princesses threw themselves in a well rather than yield to the Fula. And Janke Wali, when he was told that the fighting was hand to hand and the town was so packed with men that the dead could not fall, fired a pistol into the stacked powder kegs of his arsenal and destroyed the whole town.

The conflict with Timbo and the invasion of the Fula may be developed in varying ways in different versions. Sometimes there is an intimation of injustice and high-handedness on the part of the nyanchos who dominated Kaabu, and an appeal is made to Timbo for redress. This last king's grand gesture is certainly sufficient inspiration for the story. Other elements are worth explicating, if only tentatively: the fall of Kansala and the kingdom of Kaabu explicitly mark the end of the old Mande-connected world and the transition to a new combination of forces. The irruption of the Fula changes the ethnic composition of the region. Whereas the Mandinka and the Soninke[37] had clearly managed to co-exist, the Fula throw all arrangements into question. They overturn the nyancho power structure, and they bring in a new religion. And shortly after their arrival, the region becomes a colony of England: the Fula install Alfa Molo as king in Kansala and Alfa Molo's son Musa dies in 1931. The story of Janke Wali thus resonates with a sense of the history of contemporary Gambia: it unites movements of history, ethnic groups, and faiths in a way that the more specific traditions of Sunjata and Tira Magan do not.

What this Gambian story offers is the sense of a shaped and discrete unit: movement is from the prophecy of Janke Wali, made at his accession, to the destruction of the town and a sense of fulfillment since the terms have been made explicit. Jumps in the story seem attributable to ellipsis rather than ignorance. By contrast, this story lacks the passion that animates Sagouma or Amar Zoumbani. While Janke Wali's self-destruction at the fall of the town is a grand gesture, it does not always demand empathy, as do the painful situations of the two Songhay figures.

The stories of the two warlords Musa Molo and Fode Kaba[38] do not seem to be well-established narratives that have been polished in performance. Innes's published texts present episodic biographies from the end of the last century and so cover a period of great interest for historians and nationalists. But the stories themselves lack an overriding narrative coherence for anyone not well acquainted with the careers and contexts of the two individuals. A feature of some interest in the performance of Ba Ansu Jebate[39] is the enrichment of the narrative with praise songs and digressions that clearly evoke the performance mode of the Sunjata and that ennoble the piece considerably.

Finally, there is the story of Kelefa Sane, an archetypal nyancho who, says Innes, had no effect on the history of his times but nevertheless evokes for the modern listener the panache and arrogant nobility of the period and an idealization of the courage of the man of war.[40] Innes has published two versions of the story, one by Bamba Suso and another (partial) by Shirif Jebate, and Wright offers an "interview" with Jebate in which the jeli first explains the origin of the conflict between the Sonko of Niumi and the Samakes of Jokadu and then brings in the story of Kelefa Sane.[41]

Kelefa Sane

As a child, Kelefa and his mother were enslaved by a prince; when Kelefa grew up, he was given his father's gun. One day, his jeli asked him what he had accomplished, and Kelefa promised him a deed: as the prince's women came in a line down to the well for water, he shot off the head-pads underneath the water pots, and no one drank from the well that day. The prince had Kelefa bound and sold him into slavery. Kelefa rapidly bought his freedom by raiding cattle for his master. And then he became a warrior, a nyancho.

The kingdoms of Niumi and Jokadu came into conflict. Kelefa went to join the war. There was a prophecy that he would not return from the war, and so the king of Niumi sent Kelefa off to collect tribute in an out-of-the-way town to keep him out of the battle. While he was there an old woman asked him for tobacco and promised him news. She told him why he had been sent away from Niumi. Kelefa immediately returned and joined in the battle. He put the forces of Jokadu to flight until he was killed by an albino hiding in a tree, using a magical projectile. The vultures spared his body because he had fed them so well while alive, and he was buried at the foot of a bitter tree.

It is pointless to view this story as history; almost every element of it can be matched to heroic traits found throughout the Sahel, and the common thread lies in the Fula epic tradition. The death of Kelefa Sane echoes that of Silamaka of Massina, down to the albino in a tree who kills him. The mission by which the ruler of Niumi hopes to avoid the hero's death (for ambiguous reasons involving divination) and the old woman who reveal the truth may both be found in Zarma-Fula tradition in the story of Yefarma Issaka (and they invert, curiously, the story of Poullori, who was sent away so that he would not witness the death of Silamaka). The juvenile turbulence of the hero is matched by that of Samba Gueladio.

Clearly, the more modern Gambian epic traditions involve a fusion of worlds, the accommodation of a variety of origins. When the eminent griot Bamba Suso starts his song of Musa Molo with praise of Koli Tengela (appropriate, since Musa Molo is of Fula origin),[42] or when the elder Unus Jata narrates at some length a regional version of the story of Koli Tengela as the origin of the kingdom of Niumi,[43] when Kelefa Sane can be fairly described as a Fula hero appropriated into the Mandinka idiom, the hybrid nature of the modern Gambian Mandinka epic tradition becomes clear. Nor do the Fula provide the only influence. There is also an echo of the Wolof story of Njaajaan Njay (also written Djadjane Ndiaye), who went into the water and emerged speechless far downstream;[44] and of the tradition of Bondu in which Malik Sy acquired territory by agreeing to fix the boundary between two kingdoms at the place where he met the neighboring king.[45] The protagonists here are al-Hajj Umar and Alfa Molo, and the point of the story is the modesty of the hunter rather than the trickery of the holy man; but this is, nevertheless, familiar ground.

Two points emerge from these considerations. First, the history of the Gambia is one of interpenetrating groups and influences. The content of oral traditions gains in clarity when points of origin are assigned to recognizable elements and when they are read as a symbolic construct rather than as *prima facie* evidence. Islamic and Koranic intrusions in local histories are readily acknowledged; borrowings from regional traditions should also be recognized as such.

The second point may somewhat undercut the first. It looks to the time frame and the qualities of the heroes under consideration. The heroes of recent history are very conventional rather than effectively individualized, and the same might be said of the image of the era in which they lived, the cultural and temporal divisions projected into the past. What emerges are the features of the generic warlord, a type character rather than a distinct person, who may be used to evoke a past of ambiguous value. Whether this similarity is due to cultural influences (particularly the Islamic Fula) or to some particularity of the operations of oral tradition in recent (rather than mythical) times is the question, one worth examining given the ample evidence available in West African traditions.

The Wolof and Other Peoples of Senegal

The kingdom of Jolof is the land to which Sunjata sent for horses and which returned the insult that he was only a hunter king (in a curious echo of this term, a later figure in the history of Kajoor refused the kingship of Saloum, saying he preferred to be a hunter in Kajoor). For the Wolof, the Jolof kingdom represents the period of unity to which the various states look back: Waalo, Kajoor, Baol, and the Serer principalities of Sine and Saloum. Around 1500, after being repulsed by the kingdom of Jara, the Fula leader Koli Tengela moved into the area and came to terms with the *Buurba* of Jolof (king of Jolof), then still the preeminent power. In the years of European contact, the Wolof turned to trade, and in the region from the Gambia north to the Senegal River, where the Wolof set the dominant tone, they are considered to be quintessential intermediaries.

Senegalese history is very well documented, thanks to long-established literacy. Besides the extensive work done on local traditions, there is rich documentation, much of it in Portuguese, from traders in the region from the fifteenth century on. Jean Boulègue provides a valuable synthesis for the early period of Jolof unity. Boubacar Barry covers the kingdom of the Waalo, and Abdoulaye Bathily has written on Galam and the Soninke of Gajaga. Many valuable studies have also been published in two of the organs of the Institut Fondamental d'Afrique Noire (IFAN), the *Bulletin* and *Notes Africaines*.[46]

Senegalese literary and cultural life is so massive in volume as to defy quick description: some of the more important figures are Léopold Sédar Senghor, former president of Senegal and man of letters; Birago Diop, the veterinarian and storyteller (*The Tales of Amadou Koumba* and others that have not been translated); Ousmane Sembène, the novelist and filmmaker; and Mariama Bâ, the novelist. The list could be extended. One aspect of Senegalese literary and cultural life that affects some of the scholarship on epic and historical traditions and that should be mentioned here is the tradition of nationalism and pan-Africanism that is deeply engrained in Senegalese intellectual culture. In the 1950s, Senghor and others established the Negritude movement in the face of colonialism. The later work of Cheikh Anta Diop marked the period of independence and established the foundations of Afrocentrism. The political, and often polemic, nature of these enterprises must be recognized; but sympathy with the mission should not preclude some caution about the methods. Affirmation, rather than critique, is the principal tool used by the followers of these movements; and at times there seems little leeway for honest skepticism.

In Wolof the griot is known as *gewel,* a word most frequently connected with Arabic (Hassaniya Arabic, *iggiw,* griot, or Standard Arabic, *qawal,* speaker),[47] and probably the source of the Fulfulde term *gawlo.* The performers are known particularly for their praise singing (and, negatively, for their rapaciousness: they may have established the stereotype).[48]

The praise singing of Wolof griots is well documented, and so is the genealogical aspect of their performances.[49] Less well documented is the narrative element. Lilyan Kesteloot included a selection from the history of Kajoor in her 1972 anthology, *L'épopée traditionelle,* but the anticipated collection of Pathé Diagne has yet to materialize. Bassirou Dieng's *Epopée du Kajoor* is the first substantial documentation of the tradition for one of the Wolof kingdoms, although several theses written at the Cheikh Anta Diop University in Dakar also present texts and are available on microfilm.[50]

Lineages, genealogy, and king-lists are the staple performance ingredients of the gewel, and it seems likely that interesting comparative work might be done with Yoruba praise-singing traditions. Wolof history narrates the conflicts and unions of a series of territories and cities ruled by connected lineages, and the historical parallel evoked is not so much the series of conquests of Mali or Segou as the pattern of occasionally subjected and unified city-states of the Yoruba world.

The praise-singing tradition is supported by a body of historical information preserved largely by the gewel. Judith Irvine offers one of the few close examinations of the value of such traditions, and her findings contrast with the established (and skeptical) view of oral genealogies. She believes the gewel does manage to preserve information with some accuracy. Her examples come from the village-level performer. Until relatively recently, there was also a royal level, and that is the tradition collected in Bassirou Dieng's work. It is possible to identify a number of mnemonic devices that are evidently at work in the reported texts: phrases and oaths that determine events, such as the striking moment in the story of Maka (a town) in which, while Bigue Ngone and her sons wander in exile, she places a single bone in the common dish served to her sons and so reminds them that they are fleeing a single man: the sons resolve to return and overthrow their cousin. These narrative techniques have been encountered before, for instance, in traditions of Segou, where the remembered boast of Bakari Jan about preserving Segou anchors and motivates the story of Da's treachery (see chapter 6).

Some elements have also been borrowed, most probably from the Futa Tooro but also from Mande traditions. A famous Pulaar war song is echoed at places in the performances,[51] and the characterization of heroes occasionally echoes the problematic description of Samba Gueladio and the Gambian nyancho class. Such borrowings (if indeed they are such) need not be entirely passive and imitative. In the epic of Sunjata, Sogolon, Sunjata's mother, swears an oath on her purity and her respect for her husband, either to make Sunjata rise or to bring him power. In Lamine Diouf's account of the battle of Guy Njulli, which opposes a father and a son, the wife and mother is induced to swear a very similar oath: if she has been a good wife, let her husband win—and if not, let her son win. . . . The conflict of loyalties underlying this second oath is entirely foreign to the unified perspective of the Sunjata.[52]

Dieng's collection contains thirteen pieces in two loose sequences, each by a different performer, covering the history of the kingdom of Kajoor from the time of its "liberation" from the rule of Jolof by the hero Amari Ngone to the death of Lat Dior at Thiès, fighting the French. While on points of fact their narratives intersect and agree, the styles and treatments of the two performers are quite different. One is more conservative and less elaborate, the second perhaps somewhat more concerned with the storytelling. Dieng had some trouble finding performers of the royal tradition of Kajoor; it is fortunate that he succeeded so well.

The various episodes deal particularly with accessions and struggles for power, and in this regard their connection with the information base of a king-list is evident. In some cases, the genealogical complications that determine alliances and partisanship can be daunting. In others, the conflicts are relatively straightforward. Although no attempt will be made to give a complete summary of the dynastic sweep, a few highlights can be identified. Amari Ngone, who liberated Kajoor and established the dynasty, echoes Silamaka in withholding tribute from the overlord—but his rebellion succeeds and he survives, thanks to a trick by which he cached weapons along a line of retreat.[53] The epic of Maka, which tells of the exile and return of the sons of Bigue Ngoni, and in particular of Massiri Issa, is also given independently by Dioum.[54] Mention has already been made of the mother's taunt, expressed through the single bone in the stew, which galvanizes her sons to war; that episode also features her son Massiri and his warlike prowess (most comparable, in many regards, to that of Samba Gueladio).

Lat Dior, the last damel of Kajoor, is a national hero of resistance to colonialism. In some regards he embodies the trouble-making and destructive qualities of the aristocracy, recognizable also among the nyancho and in the warriors of Massina. But he also embodies a determination and an expression of will that earns him his narrator's respect. His story tells of conflicts over succession (a familiar theme), complicated here by a French preference for his rival. While initially Kajoor chose a juvenile Lat Dior, he was eventually deposed from rule over his two kingdoms, Kajoor and Bawol, and he was forced to wander. The French cornered him at the railway station in Thiès.

A discussion of Wolof traditions would be incomplete without at least an acknowledgment of the major tradition of origin of the Jolof: the story of Njaajaan Njay, for which a number of versions go back two hundred years, from one collected by Le Brasseur ca. 1775, to a recent one collected by Samba Diop.[55] In a very interesting analysis, Victoria Bomba connects Wolof traditions with those of the neighboring Moors and Soninke, and she makes a convincing case for some genealogical connection of Njaajaan Njay with the Moors.[56] The story itself is not so much genealogical as mythological, however, and this aspect has been analyzed by Lilyan Kesteloot, Bassirou Dieng, and Lampsar Sall.[57]

The story says that Njaajaan Njay's father died; when the mother wished to remarry a social inferior, the son dove into the river and did not emerge. He did not drown, however; he lived there for a number of years until he came ashore to stop fishermen fighting over the division of their catch; he is credited with the invention of a string to run through the gills. The people of the village were impressed by his judgment and so trapped him, preventing him from returning to the river. He did not speak until a woman tricked him: the stories vary on the motivation, but essentially the woman attempted to balance her cooking pot on two stones until he spoke up and told her to use three (either in Pulaar or in Wolof). Once he had begun to talk again, he was integrated into society and chosen king.

The documentation of Wolof narrative or epic performance by a gewel is sparse, and the evidence suggests that epics were not a common pastime at any level of society. The study of epic performance also turns on perception: anything a griot sings may be considered epic (in a polemical sort of interpretation), or alternately the need for a degree of explicit narrative may vary according to the sophistication of the audience. Another hypothesis suggests that it is the changes in patronage and the presence of other models (the Sunjata and Fula-Pulaar traditions) in written or recorded form that has opened the door to new ways of presenting the material. A third, more critical, view suggests that it is the need to establish a Wolof epic tradition that has led to the presentation of relatively ordinary dynastic history in epic form. Pathé Diagne, who began the epic-collecting enterprise in the 1960s, is a cultural nationalist.

The simplest assumption is that the mode of narrative singing is something of a recent development, owing much to the contact of cultures either in the movements of the nineteenth century or as a result of the mobility of the colonial era.

The assumption is strengthened by the number of recent historical figures commemorated in this manner and the absence of earlier figures. This distribution suggests that there is no established performance tradition for earlier figures and narratives. But as this perception is in some sense shaped by a comparison with Malinke and Bamana material, the bias in the collection of those materials to the older stories should be recognized. Nevertheless, comparison of the available materials from two widely separated traditions—the Songhay-Zarma and the Wolof—reveals enough common features to support the hypothesis of a relatively recent importation of the performance mode into these two cultures. One difference, of course, is that organized clan histories in the Wolof material can be fused with the new mode, whereas in the politically disunited and subjected region of the Songhay and Zarma, no such organized core of information is recognizable in the disparate strands of the tradition. It cannot be stressed too strongly that, from the perspective of the outsider, these traditions are still emergent.

CONCLUSION

THIS EXAMINATION OF African epic has treated separate traditions as individual and discrete entities. While parallels and possible connections have been outlined, the emphasis has been on the autonomous cultural importance of the epics for the various language and ethnic groups involved. Insofar as the epics reflect historical tradition, they define peoples and communities. But readers may finally wonder if, as a genre, African epics share anything beyond their geographic origin. Is there a common ground for Lianja and the Fang mvet, for Sunjata and Lat Dior, for Mareñ Jagu and al-Hajj Umar? Are there qualities or traits that might help with classification and with interpretive approaches to specific texts? That question raises the corollary question, what is the best general approach for African epics, and further, will that approach align study of African epic traditions with the scholarship applied elsewhere in the world?

Regional unities are readily apparent. In Central Africa, the epics evoke a world more mythical than historical. Heroes controlling extraordinary magical powers embark on world-defining journeys to other planes. Their antagonists and their adventures echo from region to region. Ozidi, Jeki, and Lianja are all triumphant and perhaps over-proud battlers who are called to a quest and are then free to seek out or await other antagonists. Male protagonists are balanced by female relatives; and each hero derives his fundamental power from that woman's abilities. The overall structure of the narratives is linear and highly episodic, although on occasion the talent of the artist complicates the plot (as seen in the *Ozidi Saga* and the mvet tradition). The identifiable historical content of the stories is limited at best, consisting of fragments of migration legends and a residuum of bygone practice. Instead of history, the reader grapples with complex details of lifestyle and social organization.

In the Sahel, the seat of bygone empires and kingdoms, there is a similar regional unity. Over the centuries, the various cultures of the region have shared elements ranging from trade goods and social institutions to the panoply of state. Verbal art is perhaps the most fluid commodity of all, traveling easily through the polyglot world of trading networks and over the widespread system of alliances established among the clans and lineages of different but neighboring peoples. While this fluidity does not make the different historical traditions underpinning the oral epics equally mobile, it does suggest the possibility of intertradition awareness and imitation. Over the centuries a common repertoire of motifs and idioms has developed; through them the history and legitimation of political power are expressed and cultural identity and values are affirmed. There is a mix of rooted traditions, expressed in the individual heroes, and of common themes. There are also distinctions. Sunjata is a hero of the Manden, the world of old Mali, and he is associated with the beginnings of Mande culture and its days of glory (other Mande heroes such as Tira Magan or Fajigi or Fakoli have different associations). Samba Gueladio is a hero of the Futa Tooro and recalls the region's anarchic pre-Islamic past. Hama the Red is the quintessential Fula of the regions of Kounari and Massina near the middle Niger bend; less closely linked to history than Sunjata or Samba, he inhabits the realm of cultural values. Yet despite the differences, Sunjata and Hambodedio, for instance, are loosely linked by common regional idioms of heroism. They share a praise name, "Stranger of the Morning, Master of the Town at Night." They are united not only by the conventions of poetic and heroic language but by an organic, historic bond. Sunjata is a child of the Conde-Diarra line, to whom the praise name belonged, and Hambodedio marries into that line when he becomes the son-in-law of Da Diarra, king of Segou. This network of relations extends to include other heroes and epics.

The principles of unity underlying each tradition are slightly different. In Central Africa, a kind of master narrative emerges from the many variants; in the Sahel, on the other hand, the connections derive rather from historical contacts, imitation, and appropriation. The distinctions do not render general questions impossible. Instead, they accentuate the need for careful selection and precise definition in making comparisons and for the articulation of realistic expectations. The concept of an underlying unity does not imply uniformity or homogeneity. Differences in social context and function, in performance mode, in content, and in tone must be respected. But the question is whether these differences indicate radical disjunctions between unrelated corpuses of narrative, or whether the differences can be understood through a series of minimal shifts and changes. This applies not only to evident similarities among the epics (e.g., in plot or diction), but also to their visible participation in a network of possibilities and relationships expressed through internal and external factors.

One example of such a network of connections is performance modes. Christiane Seydou distinguishes between the austere and solitary performance of a

Fula maabo such as Boûbacar Tinguidji, sitting motionless as his words flow to the accompaniment of his hoddu for the private entertainment of his patron, and the more exuberant and collective events described in Central Africa, where the lead singer, accompanied by a retinue of musicans and a chorus, dances through the public space as he narrates, sings, and mimes the action. These two modes mark the extremes in a spectrum of styles whose intermediary points can be documented in other traditions. The Manden furnishes perhaps the clearest middle ground, offering the combination of historical and hunters' epics. All Mande epic involves, besides the principal performer, the naamu-sayer who serves as respondent to the narrator and whose exclamations provide a rhythmic regularity to the narration.[1] Historical epics may also introduce female soloists for lyric passages and praise songs. The performance of hunters' epics adds musicians, instruments such as the *nyaringa* [iron rasp], and sometimes apprentice singers. The hunters' bard not only sings, he dances. In other words, this third case provides the necessary elements for moving from the Central African model to that represented by Tinguidji. It is simply a question of subtracting elements, of refining (or economizing) the performance. Tinguidji also conforms to the regional social pattern of relations of griot and patron, which link his function with that of the Malinke jeli.

The question of unity thus looks toward fundamental elements that may be elaborated in different ways. Two such elements are the historiographic function of the epics, their role as representations of a cultural past—and the central hero or protagonist through whom this function is articulated.

With few exceptions, African epics remain socially functional images of the past. They define the origins and norms of their respective cultures in ways that epics elsewhere in the world seem to have lost. Admittedly, they do so within varying frameworks and conceptions of history. Lianja may define his people, but he offers no retrievable political history; the same may be said of Mwindo, Jeki, Ozidi, and others. Still, Lianja establishes the origin of the Mongo, just as Sunjata establishes the origins and glory of the Manden. Sunjata in turn shares the regional idioms of epic expression, so to speak, with more recent, non-Mande heroes such as Lat Dior or Musa Molo. Their stories come from a past just slightly beyond the limits of living memory, but since the tradition in which they now live reaches well beyond the immediate past, they are placed in a glorious continuity. Epics do not offer a detailed record of events as their primary function. They conflate the events of the past into a mirror for the present. The individual will find models for conduct and inspiration for undertakings. The community finds the bond that unites it.

This historical function has undoubtedly been eroded in recent decades. Modernization, with its transformations in social structure and economic patterns, has altered the communities that produced the epics. Older master griots are dying without leaving behind accepted and worthy replacements.[2] The lore they carry is being lost, except where by happy accident it has been recorded. But despite these changes, epics survive and continue to be performed. Their content may be changing somewhat—there is less history and more storytelling in many of Meyer's Tukolor epics from the Futa Tooro or Ousmane Bâ's Bamana versions of Silamaka. New protagonists are emerging, such as al-Hajj Umar Tall, bringing with them a new vision of the past in which Islam plays a greater role. These changes might be seen as denaturing the older function of the epics, or as the natural adaptation of the form to new circumstances—or both. But audiences still care for and about epics.

With regard to the hero, the challenge involves not only delineating the typical traits of African heroes but also differentiating African idioms of heroism and their expression in narrative from those of worldwide patterns. Heroes are found everywhere, and their stories often echo each other—so much so that the "hero-pattern" is a standard analytic tool for folklorists.[3] It is not surprising to find African heroes sharing traits and actions with characters from other traditions—after all, in many regards they reflect essential elements of the human experience.

One weakness of these "global" models is their reliance upon figures from the Eurasian traditions for definition of narrative content. Lord Raglan, in constructing his comparative hero pattern, may have included some figures from southern Sudan (from the Shilluk and the Nuer), but he omitted the protagonists of most African epic traditions. The same is true of Joseph Campbell's influential *Hero with a Thousand Faces*. African and other non-Western figures have not contributed as they might to these models, and the inclusion of African and other materials would inevitably strengthen (and change) them. Still, these models are useful in identifying general narrative elements: the extraordinary birth of the hero, the conflict with the father-figure, the exile-and-return pattern, and general techniques of monster-slaying.

Is it possible to look beyond these conventional elements to identify the significant and differentiating traits of the African epic hero? Sunjata does seem to share more with Lianja than he does with the Germanic Siegfried the dragon-slayer, or with Native American figures such as the Hero Twins, whose task is to cleanse the earth of monsters and prepare the way for humans. Sunjata kills no dragons—others characters do that before his birth in the story. Instead, Sunjata shares with Lianja an emphasis on a preternatural childhood expressed in a variety of distinct ways,[4] as well as reliance upon the assistance of a sister. Both men assemble and lead their peoples through conflict toward a greater destiny. Lianja has been presented here as an exemplary type of a regional hero also embodied in varying ways by Mwindo, Jeki, and Ozidi. The features common to Lianja and Sunjata link the latter with a number of his neighbors as well, for example, the Soninke Mareñ Jagu, the Fula Samba Gueladio, and the hunter Kambili.

It thus seems possible to sketch out a fundamental hero-type common to many African cultures, and perhaps also reflected outside the epic traditions in other forms of narrative and cultural expression.[5] Such a hero-type might be used to explore deep-lying patterns in African epics and myths and could serve as a bridge between the two principal regions identified here. However, these heroes should not be seen as reflections of a monomyth but, once again, as individual expressions within a range of possibilities. It is important to respect the texture and nuances of the different traditions. While a comparison of Sunjata with the faama Da of Segou, for instance, might easily be drawn up and would be quite illuminating, such a comparison should not obscure the equally illuminating differences between the two: a biographical rather than an episodic narrative; reliance on, and association with, mother or father; enthronement by victory and acclaim rather than by treachery and deceit. The list might continue. The differences must be observed because they constitute the great appeal of the study of African epic traditions within the larger community of the humanities. The range of visible variation on the basic idea of a lengthy, performed narrative of "historical" content is unique.[6] The traditions of African epic in all their variety offer a wealth of material for the analytic and theoretical exploration of general notions of epic.

Another, perhaps better, reason to stress the variety of the traditions lies in the artistic differences among them. A basic or generic type—such as Lianja, in the versions now available, or perhaps a composite of Lianja and Sunjata—is not necessarily the most interesting or the most polished. The function of such a basic type is rather to throw into relief the particular features of other traditions. For instance, in Central Africa, the mvet tradition of the Fang shares the performance style of Lianja, Jeki, and the rest, but eschews the central hero as protagonist. Instead, the mvet tradition offers a fictional world, an assortment of established characters, and freedom of narrative development. The world of the clans of Oku and Engong resembles in many ways the worlds of Lianja and Mwindo, and the mvet stands in close relation to their performance tradition. But the freedom given the narrator makes a critical difference. These stories are no longer interpreted as reflections, in some sense, of a larger tradition established in the community. Each performance must be engaged on an individual level in order to appreciate the artistic intention of the performer. The artistic, rather than ethnographic, challenges of the mvet will seem somewhat more familiar to the reader. The same dichotomy exists within the traditions of the Sahel. Sunjata stands as a grand and somewhat hermetic monument. The epic of Sunjata may seem perplexing because of the weight of potentially significant detail, the intrusion of obscure language, or the genealogical references, all of which are important components of the cultural tradition behind any given oral performance of this epic. It is difficult to treat the epic of Sunjata as art for art's sake—although this statement should not be construed as a dismissal of the artistry involved in the performances of a great jeli—because of the cultural investment (continuing into the written forms) in the content of the tradition.

By contrast, the epics of Bamana Segou and of the Fula are far more accessible to the outsider. Narrative devices and plot lines play a far greater organizational role in these traditions: each epic is a self-contained unit. Admittedly, a jeli such as Tayiru Banbera controls and may interject a wealth of corroborative and illustrative detail, nor should the potential historical content of the epics be underestimated. Nevertheless, the artistic intent and control of the performer are more easily perceived in these pieces—in Sissoko Kabine's *La prise de Dionkoloni*, for instance, or Hamma Diam Bouraima's "Hambodedio and Saïgalare"—and they invite literary analysis and appreciation. Next to the Sunjata, they might be seen as "entertainment." Next to them, the epic of Sunjata seems at times unwieldy, perhaps too serious, and almost certainly too sprawling.

Appreciation of the nuances that exist among heroes and worlds requires some knowledge of the actual range of epic traditions in Africa. At the beginning of this study, an argument was made for an African-centered approach, not because cross-cultural comparisons are undesirable but because of the risk that in any such comparison the particularities of the African member would be lost. Western readers might distinguish between Gilgamesh and Charlemagne as they would not between Sunjata and Samory Toure because they have the materials with which to approach and classify the first pair. Scholarship on Western epic traditions may be limiting in some ways (and hence the old cry, "Make it new!"), but it provides background information and a variety of perspectives from which to approach the material, information that is less readily available for the African epic. At this point, it is up to the reader to judge whether an aproach to epics grounded in African idioms of history and narrative convention is justified.

Epics evoke a sense of wonder and delight as literature, as cultural keys, as windows to past worlds. And epics, with their details of place and people, are perhaps the best way to approach the local traditions of Africa; for epics represent a concentrated (and still valid) statement of cultural identity. To study the world of African epic is to enter into the African sphere in ways that no novel or play demands. African epics portray an African past that is too little known, and even in translation, they can evoke the poetry of African languages. Reading African epics may seem a challenge, but it is immensely rewarding.

APPENDIX:
PUBLISHED EPIC TEXTS

The following list is designed to allow quick reference to the epics discussed in this volume and to provide a sense of the available corpus for each grouping. It also recognizes the performer's role and groups the different published pieces performed by the same artist. The material follows the order of the chapters, and each entry provides the name of the performer, the title of the piece, the language and date of the performance (when available), and a short bibliographic citation that includes information on the language of publication.

Epics of Central Africa

The Mongo or Nkundo: Lianja

(Boelaert collected all these versions between 1920 and 1960; de Rop edited and published them somewhat later. Many of the versions are identified principally by clan of origin [given in parentheses under the performer's name] but the narrator is occasionally listed.)

Performer	Title	Language of Performance	Date Recorded
Anonymous (Bamala Louis?)	Nsong'a Lianja	Mongo	pre-1940
	(Boelaert 1949, composite; bilingual with French)		
Anonymous (Bokala)	Lianja chez les Bokala	Mongo	(written?) 1920–1960
	(De Rop 1978, pp. 120–75, bilingual with French)		
Anonymous (Bokote)	Lianja chez les Bokote	Mongo	(written?) 1920–1960
	(De Rop 1978, pp. 310–31, bilingual with French)		
Anonymous (Bolenge)	Lianja chez les Ntoma-Bolenge	Mongo	(written?) 1920–1960
	(De Rop 1978, pp. 12–119, bilingual with French)		
Anonymous (Lingoi)	Lianja chez les Lingoi	Mongo	(written?) 1920–1960
	(De Rop 1978, pp. 240–67, bilingual with French)		
Andre Ekamba (Elanga and Imomo)	Lianja chez les Elanga et les Imomo	Mongo	(written?) 1920–1960
	(De Rop 1978, pp. 268–309, bilingual with French)		
Daniel Ilofo (Lilangi)	Lianja chez les Lilangi	Mongo	(written?) 1920–1960
	(De Rop 1978, pp. 176–239, bilingual with French)		

Performer	Title	Language of Performance	Date Recorded
Victor Lokamba (Ekota)	Lianja chez les Ekota *(De Rop and Boelaert 1983, pp. 82–95, bilingual with French)*	Mongo	1920–1960
Pierre Mbanja (Ntomba)	Lianja chez les Ntomba *(De Rop and Boelaert 1983, pp. 96–119, bilingual with French)*	Mongo	(written?) 1920–1960
Joseph Njoli (Bakaala)	Lianja chez les Bakaala *(*De Rop and Boelaert 1983, pp. 6–55, bilingual with French)*	Mongo	1920–1960

*De Rop and Boelaert 1983 includes some thirty other shorter and anonymous versions for a total of over fifty.

BaNyanga

Candi Rureke	Mwindo Epic *(Biebuyck and Mateene 1969, bilingual with English)*	Banyanga	1956
Nkuba Shekarisi	Mwindo Epic *(Biebuyck 1978, pp. 184–232, English translation)*	Banyanga	ca. 1952
Shekwabo	Mwindo Epic *(Biebuyck 1978, pp. 134–73, English translation)*	Banyanga	1952
Muteresi Shempunge	Kahindo Ngarya *(Biebuyck and Mateene 1970, pp. 28–47, bilingual with French)*	Banyanga	1952
Sherungu	Mwindo Epic *(Biebuyck 1978, pp. 240–71, English translation)*	Banyanga	ca. 1952
Sherungu	Wanowa's Epic *(Biebuyck 1978, pp. 273–78, English summary)*	Banyanga	ca. 1955

Jeki La Njambe of the Duala

Anonymous	Jeki and His Ozazi *(Nassau 1969, pp. 378–86, English translation)*	Duala?	ca. 1880
Anonymous	Jeki Episodes *(Kesteloot 1970, pp. 41–46, French translation)*	Duala?	1966
Anonymous	Jeki (episodes) *(Epanya-Yondo 1976, pp. 48–64, French translation)*	Duala	1966
Jo Diboko'a Kollo	Jeki la Njambe *(Bekombo-Priso 1993, bilingual with French)*	Duala	1969
Tiki a Koulle a Penda	Jeki la Njambe *(Tiki a Koulle a Penda 1987, bilingual with French)*	Duala	pre-1986

[See also Austen 1996, which provides a collection of translated excerpts.]

Ozidi of the Ijo (Nigeria)

Okabou Ojobolo	Ozidi Saga *(Clark-Bekederemo 1991, bilingual with English)*	Ijo	1963

Performer	Title	Language of Performance	Date Recorded

Mvet Traditions (Cameroon and Gabon)

Performer	Title	Language of Performance	Date Recorded
Philipe Essogo	La Guerre d'Akoma Mba *(Awona 1965 [and 1966], bilingual with French)*	Fang	ca. 1964
Daniel Osomo	Mvet Moneblum *(Eno-Belinga 1978b, bilingual with French)*	Bulu	ca. 1975
Tsira Ndong Ndoutoume	Le Mvett *(Ndoutoume 1970, French)*	French prose	
Tsira Ndong Ndoutoume	Mvett II *(Ndoutoume 1970–1975, French)*	French prose	
Tsira Ndong Ndoutoume	Le Mvett: L'homme, la mort, et l'immortalité *(Ndoutoume 1993, French)*	French	
Zwe Nguema	Mvett *(Pepper 1972, bilingual with French)*	Fang	1960

Related Texts

Performer	Title	Language of Performance	Date Recorded
Esangolongo	Lofokefoke *(Jacobs 1961, pp. 81–92, French translation)*	Mbole	1957
Ambroisine Mawiri	Epopée Mulombi *(Mawiri and Mbumba [1985?], French translation)*	Fang	ca. 1985
Anonymous	Les fils de Hitong *(Ngijol 1980, bilingual with French)*	Basa	ca. 1975
Akilimali kya Kabamba	Kiguma kya Kansindi *(Wamenka 1992, vol. 1, bilingual with French)*	Lega	1968
Gerard Amisi Ngoma	Museme W'Idali *(Wamenka 1992, vol. 2, pp. 1–129, bilingual with French)*	Lega	1976
Fidele Mundende	Wabugila Ntonde *(Wamenka 1992, vol. 2, pp. 131–252, bilingual with French)*	Lega	1982

Hunters' Traditions and Epics

(The following listing is selective for the older collections without identified performers.)

Niger River Peoples: Gow and Sorko (Faran Maka and Fono)

Performer	Title	Language of Performance	Date Recorded
Anonymous	Farang and Lovely Fatimata *(Desplagnes 1907, pp. 386–412, French translation)*	Zarma	pre-1907

Performer	Title	Language of Performance	Date Recorded
Anonymous	Farang and Korarou *(Desplagnes 1907, pp. 425–33, French translation)*	Zarma	pre-1907
Anonymous	Farang et le Gondo *(Desplagnes 1907, pp. 441–50, French translation)*	Zarma	pre-1907
Anonymous	Mousa-Gname *(Dupuis-Yakouba 1911, pp. 1–19, bilingual with French)*	Zarma/ Songhay	pre-1910
Anonymous	Mousa et le Hira *(Dupuis-Yakouba 1911, pp. 20–39, bilingual with French)*	Zarma/ Songhay	pre-1910
Anonymous	Fono et Faran *(Prost 1956, pp. 189–99, French translation)*	Zarma	1950s
Talata Nabo Kantabo	Faran et Fono *(Rouch 1989, pp. 41–67, French translation of extracts)*	Zarma (Sorko)	ca. 1955
Nuhu	Fara Makan *(Rouch 1978, French translation)*	Zarma	1947

[Dupuis-Yakouba 1911 offers many other narratives, as does Frobenius 1924.]

Mande Hunting Traditions (includes Maninka, Bamana, Gambian Mandinka, Jula)

Performer	Title	Language of Performance	Date Recorded
Mieru Baa	Fanta Maa *(Hayidara 1987, pp. 14–111, bilingual with French)*	Bamana/Bozo	1977
Seydou Camara	Nyakhalen la forgeronne *(Thoyer-Rozat 1986, bilingual with French)*	Maninka	ca. 1980
Seydou Camara	Manden Mori *(Cashion 1984, vol. 2, appendix 2, pp. 1–166, bilingual with English)*	Maninka	1976
Seydou Camara	Kambili *(Camara 1974 [English translation], 1976 [Maninka text])*	Maninka	ca. 1970
Seydou Camara	Famori *(Cashion 1984, vol. 2, pp. 1–332, bilingual with English)*	Maninka	1977
Seydou Camara	Bilali of Faransekila *(Conrad 1989, pp. 47–59, English translation)*	Maninka	October 16, 1975
Seydou Camara	Fajigi *(Conrad 1981, pp. 730–65, English translation)*	Maninka	September 1975
Seydou Camara	Sumoso Yiraba *(McNaughton 1979, pp. 40–41, English summary)*	Maninka	1976
*Seydou Camara	Neri Koro *(McNaughton 1979, p. 13, English summary)*	Maninka	1976

*See also Other Mande Traditions, below.

Performer	Title	Language of Performance	Date Recorded
Bougoba Djiré	Boli Nyanan *(Cissé 1994, pp. 180–299, bilingual with French)*	Maninka	1970–1980?

❖ Appendix ❖

Performer	Title	Language of Performance	Date Recorded
Djogo	Flani Boyi	Maninka	1970–1980?
	(Cissé 1994, pp. 162–76, bilingual with French)		
Amara Fofana	Bamori and Kowulen	Dyula	March 4, 1975
	(Dérive 1982, bilingual with French)		
Bala Jinba Jakite	Dingo Kanbili	Bamana	1979
	(D. Coulibaly n.d., French translation)		
Mamadu Jara	Sirankomi	Bamana	ca. 1975
	(Thoyer-Rozat 1978 [reprinted 1995], pp. 27–98, bilingual with French)		
Mamadu Jara	Kambili	Bamana	ca. 1978
	(Thoyer-Rozat 1978 [reprinted 1995], pp. 177–255, bilingual with French)		
Mamadu Jara	Manding Mori	Bamana	ca. 1978
	(Thoyer-Rozat 1978 [reprinted 1995], pp. 131–75, bilingual with French)		
Mamadu Jara	Banjugu	Bamana	ca. 1978
	(Thoyer-Rozat 1978 [reprinted 1995], pp. 99–129, bilingual with French)		
Bakari Kamara	Mambi and the Crocodile	Mandinka	1969
	(Innes and Sidibe 1990, English translation)		
Bakari Kamara	Mammadu and the Great Beast	Mandinka	1969
	(Innes and Sidibe 1990, English translation)		
Ndugace Samake	Birisi Ngoni	Bamana	ca. 1978
	(Thoyer-Rozat 1978, vol. 3, pp. 138–81, bilingual with French)		
Ndugace Samake	Misiba	Bamana	ca. 1978
	(Thoyer-Rozat 1978, vol. 3, pp. 90–137, bilingual with French)		
Ndugace Samake	Bolinyana	Bamana	ca. 1978
	(Thoyer-Rozat 1978, vol. 3, pp. 182–265, bilingual with French)		
Ndugace Samake	Maghan Jan	Bamana	ca. 1978
	(Thoyer-Rozat 1978, vol. 3, pp. 8–90, bilingual with French)		
Batoma Sanogo	Bani-Nyenema	Bamana	ca. 1975
	(Fodé Sidibe 1984, bilingual with French)		
Batoma Sanogo	Ndoronkelen	Bamana	ca. 1975
	(Fodé Sidibe 1984, bilingual with French)		
Mahamadu Lamini Sunbunu	Fanta Maa	Bamana/Bozo	ca. 1980
	(Hayidara 1987, pp. 113–201, bilingual with French)		

[Additional narrative material from the Mande and Zarma narrative traditions is to be found in Frobenius 1924.]

Performer	Title	Language of Performance	Date Recorded

Traditions of the Soninke

Legend of Wagadu

Anonymous	Serpent de Bambouk *(Bérenger-Féraud 1885, pp. 185–90, French)*	French	1885
Anonymous	Legend of Wagadu *(Tautain 1895, French)*	Soninke	1897
Anonymous	Legend of Wagadu *(Arnaud 1912, pp. 145–52, 155–58, French)*	Soninke?	ca. 1905
Anonymous	Legend of Wagadu *(Frobenius 1921, pp. 60–72, German retelling)*	Soninke	pre-1910
Anonymous	Legend of Wagadu *(Dantioko 1987b, pp. 117ff., bilingual with French)*	Soninke	ca. 1980
Mamadi Aissa Diakite	Legend of Wagadu *(Adam 1904, pp. 5–20, French translation)*	Arabic	ca. 1900
Mamadi Aissa Diakite	Legend of Wagadu *(Delafosse 1913, pp. 6–18, French translation)*	Arabic MS	ca. 1900
Bugari Kanaji	Wagadu-Bida *(Soumare 1987, pp. 37–189, bilingual with German)*	Soninke	1982
Mamadu Talibe Sisoxo	Legend of Wagadu *(A. Bathily 1975, pp. 71–94, bilingual with French)*	Soninke	1966
Diara Sylla	Legend of Wagadu: Dinga *(Dieterlen and Sylla 1992, pp. 163–82, bilingual with French)*	Soninke	ca. 1978
Tudo Yaresi	Legend of Wagadu *(C. Monteil 1953, pp. 383–96, bilingual with French)*	Soninke	1898?

Dama Ngila, Jara, and the Nyakhate

Anonymous	Sword of Dama Ngile *(Frobenius 1921, pp. 76–79, German retelling)*	Soninke?	pre-1910
Anonymous	Knife of Dama Ngile *(Frobenius 1921, pp. 89–90, German retelling)*	Soninke?	pre-1910
Mamadi Aissa Diakite	The Diawara *(Adam 1904, pp. 25–38, French translation)*	Arabic (MS?)	ca. 1900
Mamadi Aissa Diakite	The Niakhate *(Delafosse 1913, pp. 30–51, French translation)*	Arabic MS	ca. 1900

Performer	Title	Language of Performance	Date Recorded
Dogo Jawara	Legend of Daman Gille *(A. Bathily 1975, bilingual with French)*	Soninke	1966
Jaayi Maadi Nyakhate	Dispersal of the Nyakhate *(Dantioko 1985, pp. 220–37, bilingual with French)*	Soninke	1979
Sanba Jabate	Legend of the Nyakhate *(Dantioko 1985, pp. 238–59, bilingual with French)*	Soninke	1979

The Kagoro, the Kusa and other Traditions

Anonymous	Badiara Wage *(Dantioko 1987a, pp. 136–53, bilingual with French)*	Soninke	ca. 1980
Mamadi Aissa Diakite	The Doucoure Clan *(Delafosse 1913, pp. 99–104, French translation)*	Arabic MS	ca. 1900
Samba Drame	Legend of the Bathily *(I. Bathily 1969, pp. 100–105, bilingual with French)*	Soninke	ca. 1968
Bugary Kanaji	Legend of the Kagoro *(Soumare 1987, pp. 228–345, bilingual with German)*	Soninke	1982
Daaman Simagha	Legend of the Kagoro *(Dantioko 1985, pp. 9–101, bilingual with French)*	Soninke	1976
Diaowe Simagha	Dispersal of the Kusa *(Meillassoux, Doucoure, and Simagha 1967, bilingual with French)*	Soninke	1964–1965
Janme Tunkara	Kaka Balli of Gunbu *(Dantioko 1985, pp. 260–96, bilingual with French)*	Soninke	1979

[Many additional narratives attributed to the Soninke are to be found in Frobenius 1921 and are also available in English translation, e.g., in Courlander 1972.]

Sunjata and the Traditions of the Manden

Anonymous	Sunjata and Simanguru *(C. Monteil 1966, pp. 166–70, French)*	Maninka?	ca. 1898
Anonymous	The Mande and Sunjata *(Arnaud 1912, pp. 166–72, French)*	Soninke?	ca. 1905

Performer	Title	Language of Performance	Date Recorded
Anonymous (griots of Kela)	Legend of Sunjata	French	1920s
	(Vidal 1924, pp. 317–28, French)		
Anonymous	Sunjata (The Magic Arrow) *(Guillot 1950, pp. 54–73, French)*	French	1950
Anonymous	Episodes of Sunjata *(Humblot 1951, pp. 111–13, French)*	Bamana	ca. 1950
Babu Conde	Kuma lafolo kuma *(Laye 1978, French)*	Maninka	ca. 1970
*Kele Monson Diabaté	Sunjata Faasa	Maninka	1968?
	(Diabaté 1970a, pp. 29–36, French translation)		
*Kele Monson Diabaté	Epic of Sunjata	Maninka	March 1968
	(Moser 1974, pp. 205–328, bilingual with English)		
*Kele Monson Diabaté	Coming of Sunjata's Ancestors *(Bird 1972c, pp. 443–48, English translation)*	Maninka	1968
*Kele Monson Diabaté	Sunjata (Kala Jata)	Maninka	1968
	(Diabaté 1970b, French translation)		
*Kele Monson Diabaté	L'aigle et l'épervier *(Diabaté 1975, French translation)*	Maninka	1968
*Kele Monson Diabaté	Le Lion à l'arc	Maninka	1968
	(Diabaté 1986, French translation)		

*All of these versions appear to be based on the same performance recorded in 1968. See also Other Mande Traditions, below.

Performer	Title	Language of Performance	Date Recorded
Lansine Diabaté	Epic of Sunjata *(Jansen, Duintjer, and Tamboura 1995, bilingual with French)*	Maninka	1992
Mamadi Aissa Diakite	Sunjata and the Mande *(Adam 1904, pp. 39–47, French translation)*	Arabic MS	ca. 1900
Mamadi Aissa Diakite	Histoire de la lutte *(Delafosse 1913, pp. 19–30, French translation)*	Arabic MS	ca. 1900
Yeli Fode Gibate	Mande Sunjata *(Jackson 1979, pp. 101–103, English retelling)*	Kuranko	1970
Amadu Jebaate	Sunjata's Childhood *(Recueil de littérature mandingue, pp. 108–125, bilingual with French)*	Mandinka	ca. 1980

Performer	Title	Language of Performance	Date Recorded
Kanku Mady Jabaté	L'histoire du Mandé *(Jabaté 1987, pp. 76–289, bilingual with French)*	Maninka	ca. 1985
Mahan Jebate	Histoire du Mandé *(Sory Camara 1992, pp. 265–78, 307–20, bilingual with French)*	Maninka	1970
Wa Kamissoko	Sunjata (various episodes) *(Cissé and Kamissoko 1988, 1991, French)*	Bamana/Maninka	1975
Kande Kanote	Sunjata *(De Zeltner 1913, pp. 1–36, French translation)*	Khassonke	ca. 1910
*Banna Kanute	Sunjata *(Innes 1974, pp. 136–259, bilingual with English)*	Mandinka	1969
*Dembo Kanute	Faa Koli *(Innes 1974, pp. 260–323, bilingual with English)*	Mandinka	1968

*Also listed under Gambian Mandinka.

| Ibrahima Kante | Epopée du Manding
(Kante, Kaba, Conde, typescript, French) | Malinke | ca. 1975? |
| *Mamadou Kante | Makan Sunjata
and Simangourou
(Meyer 1991, pp. 141–146, French) | Pulaar | 1976–1979 |

*Also listed under Fulbe, Futa Tooro.

Kieba Koate Korongo	Die Sunjattalegende *(Frobenius 1925, pp. 303–31, German)*	Maninka	ca. 1910
Tiemoko Kone	Soundiata *(Doucoure and Martal, 1970, bilingual with French)*	Maninka	ca. 1970
Mamadou Kouyaté	Soundiata *(Niane 1960, French)*	Maninka	1957?
Mamary Kouyate	Sunjata *(Conrad 1981, pp. 711–18, English translation)*	Maninka	August 16, 1975
Noah Bokari Marah	Rivalry of Half-brothers *(Jackson 1979, pp. 97–98, English)*	English	1970
Ali Sawse	Lion of Manding *(Courlander 1972, pp. 71–78, English translation)*	Wolof	1950
Mamby Sidibe	Sunjata *(Sidibe 1959, pp. 41–50, French)*	French	1937
Fa-Digi Sisókó	Sunjata *(Johnson 1978, vol. 2; Johnson 1986, bilingual with English)*	Maninka	1967
Magan Sisókó	Sunjata *(Johnson 1978, vol. 3, bilingual with English)*	Maninka	1974
Jeli Baba Sissoko	Wagadu and Sunjata *(Conrad 1981, pp. 649–710, English translation)*	Bamana	July 24, 1975

Performer	Title	Language of Performance	Date Recorded
Habibou Sissoko	Sunjata *(De Zeltner, pp. 37–45, French translation)*	Khassonke	ca. 1910
*Bamba Suso	Sunjata *(Innes 1974, pp. 34–135, bilingual with English)*	Mandinka	1969

*Also listed under Gambian Mandinka.

Other Mande Traditions

Anonymous	Conquests of al-Hajj Umar *(Tradition historique peul 1974, bilingual with French)*	Maninka/Bamana	pre-1974
Seydou Camara	Fajigi *(Conrad 1981, pp. 730–65, English translation)*	Bamana	1975
Kele Monson Diabaté	Dispersion des Mandeka *(Cisse and Diabaté 1970, bilingual with French)*	Maninka	1967
Wa Kamissoko	Fila Kali Sidibe *(Tradition historique peul 1974, bilingual with French)*	Maninka/Bamana	pre-1974

Bamana of Segou and Kaarta

Anonymous	The Koulibaly Family *(Arnaud 1912, pp. 176–85, French)*	Soninke?	ca. 1905
Anonymous	Dawning of Segou *(Courlander and Sako 1982, pp. 11–23, English)*	Bamana	1970s
Anonymous	Ngolo Diarra *(Courlander and Sako 1982, pp. 25–43, English)*	Bamana?	ca. 1970
Anonymous	Samaniana Bassi *(Courlander and Sako 1982, pp. 69–83, English)*	Bamana?	1970s
Anonymous	Da Monzon and Chiaro *(Courlander and Sako 1982, pp. 85–93, English)*	Mamari Bamana?	1970s
Anonymous	Sekuruna Toto and Da Monzon *(Courlander and Sako 1982, pp. 95–98, English)*	Bamana?	1970s
Anonymous	Bakaridjan Kone *(Courlander and Sako 1982, pp. 99–149, English)*	Bamana?	1970s
Anonymous	Kumba Sira Maga *(Frobenius 1921, pp. 128–32, German)*	Bamana?	pre-1910
Anonymous	Bakari Jan *(C. Monteil 1977, pp. 370–75, bilingual with French)*	Bamana	pre-1905

Performer	Title	Language of Performance	Date Recorded
Anonymous	La trahison de Bakari Jan *(C. Monteil 1977, pp. 376–79, bilingual with French)*	Bamana	pre-1905
Anonymous	Mariheri of Dionkoloni *(Dantioko 1987a, pp. 156–69, bilingual with French)*	Soninke	ca. 1980?
Tayiru Banbera	Election of Biton Koulibaly *(Dumestre 1979, Recueil de littérature Manding, pp. 34–47, bilingual with French)*	Bamana	1971
Tayiru Banbera	Accession of Da *(Dumestre 1979, pp. 265–357, bilingual with French)*	Bamana	ca. 1970
Tayiru Banbera	Biton et les génies *(Dumestre 1979, pp. 359–99, bilingual with French)*	Bamana	ca. 1975
Tayiru Banbera	Biton Koulibaly *(Banbera 1978, pp. 612–81, bilingual with French)*	Bamana	ca. 1970
Tayiru Banbera	Epic of Bamana Segu *(Conrad 1990, English translation)*	Bamana	1975
A. Bime	Segou Koro and Mamari Biton *(Bime 1957, French)*	French	1957
Sory Camara	Da Monzon and Douga of Kore *(Dumestre 1979, pp. 183–263, bilingual with French)*	Bamana	ca. 1970
Sory Camara	Da Monzon and Douga of Kore *(Kesteloot 1993, vol. 2, pp. 104–122, French translation)*	Bamana	ca. 1969
Baba Cissoko	Bakari Jan et Bilissi *(Dumestre 1979, pp. 111–81, bilingual with French)*	Bamana	ca. 1970
Baba Cissoko	Trahison de Bakari Jan *(Dumestre 1979, pp. 61–109, bilingual with French)*	Bamana	ca. 1970
Kefa Diabate	Biton Coulibaly et Faro *(Kesteloot 1993, vol. 1, pp. 65–73, French translation)*	Bamana	ca. 1970
Kefa Diabate	Kumba Silamakan and Da Monzon *(Kesteloot 1993, vol. 2, pp. 72–82, French translation)*	Bamana	ca. 1968
Mamadi Aissa Diakite	Massassi du Karta *(Adam 1904, pp. 56–69, French)*	Arabic MS	ca. 1900

Performer	Title	Language of Performance	Date Recorded
Mamadi Aissa Diakite	Les Massassi *(Delafosse 1913, pp. 52–61, French translation)*	Arabic MS	ca. 1900
Gaoussou Diarra	Testament de Da Monzon *(Sauvageot 1981, pp. 289–95, bilingual with French)*	Bamana	1955
Seydou Drame	Da Monzon and Dietekoro Kaarta *(Kesteloot 1993, vol. 1, pp. 95–123, French translation)*	Bamana	ca. 1970
Laaji Sumayla Fane	Accession de Da *(Bazin 1979, pp. 438–45, bilingual with French)*	Bamana	August 14, 1970
Gorke	Da Monzon and Kaarta Thiema *(Kesteloot 1993, vol. 2, pp. 123–44, French translation)*	Bamana?	ca. 1970
Sissoko Kabine	Ngolo Diarra and Biton Koulibaly *(Kesteloot 1993, vol. 1, pp. 75–84, French translation)*	Bamana	ca. 1968
Sissoko Kabine	Monzon et Dibi of Niamina *(Kesteloot 1993, vol. 1, pp. 85–94, French translation)*	Bamana	ca. 1968
Sissoko Kabine	Da Monzon et Bassi de Samaniana *(Kesteloot 1993, vol. 1, pp. 33–62, French translation)*	Bamana	ca. 1968
Sissoko Kabine	Bakari Jan et Bilissi *(Kesteloot 1993, vol. 2, pp. 2–40, French translation)*	Bamana	ca. 1968
Sissoko Kabine	Trahison de Bakari Jan *(Kesteloot 1993, vol. 2, pp. 41–60, French translation)*	Bamana	ca. 1968
Sissoko Kabine	Bakari et les Peuls du Kounari *(Kesteloot 1993, vol. 2, pp. 61–71, French translation)*	Bamana	ca. 1968
Sissoko Kabine	La prise de Dionkoloni *(Dumestre and Kesteloot 1975, bilingual with French)*	Bamana	ca. 1970
Cheikh Moussa Kamara	Histoire de Segou *(Kamara 1978, French)*	Arabic MS	ca. 1920
Moulaye Kida	Da Monzon and Samanyana Basi *(Bird 1972c, pp. 457–67, English translation)*	Bamana	January 1967

Performer	Title	Language of Performance	Date Recorded
Mamadou Kida	Silamaka Fara Dikko	Bamana	Summer 1983
	(Ousmane Bâ 1988, pp. 20–163, bilingual with German)		
Bakoroba Kone	Douga, the Vulture	Bamana	April 1968
	(Bird 1972c, pp. 468–77, English translation)		
Mamary Kouyate	Sonsan	Bamana	1975
	(Conrad 1981, pp. 578–648, English translation)		
Fabu Kuate	Biton Koulibaly	Bamana	pre-1910
	(Frobenius 1925, pp. 344–51, German)		
Kore Tammoura	History de Segou	Bamana?	ca. 1900
	(C. Monteil 1977, French retelling)		
Dominique Traore	Samaniana Bassi	French	1947
	(D. Traore 1947, French)		

Traditions of the Fula

Massina and the East

Gouro Ahmadou	Hambodedio et Fatumata Ham-Sire	Fula	ca. 1927
	(Vieillard n.d., pp. 53ff., bilingual with French)		
Gouro Ahmadou	Hambodedio and Hamma Alla Seyni	Fula	ca. 1927
	(Vieillard n.d., pp. 65ff., bilingual with French)		
Gouro Ahmadou	Silamaka Yero and Pulloru	Fula	1927
	(Vieillard n.d., pp. 88ff.; Seydou 1972, pp. 242–61; bilingual with French)		
Beidari Allaye (de Ngouma)	Poullo Djom Ere et le Touareg	Fula	1984
	(Allaye 1984, bilingual with French)		
Anonymous	Maaju et le Peul du Toro	Fula	ca. 1928
	(Vieillard n.d., pp. 135–42, bilingual with French)		
Anonymous	Maaju le Torodo et Kumbo Budi	Fula	ca. 1927
	(Vieillard n.d., pp. 129–34, bilingual with French)		
Anonymous	Abu Lasan et le Futanke	Fula	ca. 1927
	(Vieillard n.d., pp. 121–28, bilingual with French)		
Anonymous	Hama Funa et Safalbe	Fula	1927
	(Vieillard n.d., pp. 114–19, bilingual with French)		

Performer	Title	Language of Performance	Date Recorded
Anonymous	Hamidou Hamarou Kulle *(Vieillard n.d., pp. 108–13, bilingual with French)*	Fula	1927
Anonymous	Samba Kullung the Coward *(Frobenius 1921, pp. 95–106, German)*	Fula/Bamana	pre-1910
Anonymous	Sirani Koro Samba und Samba ta Samba *(Frobenius 1921, pp. 106–11, German)*	Fula/Bamana	1910
Anonymous	Buge Korroba *(Frobenius 1921, pp. 111–15, German)*	Fula/Bamana	ca. 1910
Anonymous	Hammadi Fing and Bassala n'Sa *(Frobenius 1921, pp. 132–37, German)*	Fula/Bamana	pre-1910
Anonymous	Sagate Singo *(Frobenius 1921, pp. 142–45, German)*	Fula/Bamana	ca. 1910
Anonymous	Goroba Dike *(Frobenius 1921, pp. 171–79, German)*	Fula/Bamana	pre-1910
Anonymous	Hamidu Hama Nkulde *(Frobenius 1921, pp. 179–82, German)*	Fula/Bamana	ca. 1910
Anonymous	Hambodedjo *(Frobenius 1921, pp. 182–88, German)*	Fula/Bamana	pre-1910
Anonymous	Hamma Alseini Gakoy und Hambodedios Tod *(Frobenius 1921, pp. 188–90, German)*	Fula/Bamana	1910
Anonymous	King Djennewerre *(Frobenius 1921, pp. 190–92, German)*	Fula/Bamana	ca. 1910
Anonymous	Bongoe *(Frobenius 1921, pp. 192–94, German)*	Fula/Bamana	ca. 1910
Anonymous	Bubu Ardo Gallo *(Frobenius 1921, pp. 195–97, German)*	Fula/Bamana	ca. 1910
Anonymous	Siga Sanke *(Frobenius 1921, pp. 197–202, German)*	Fula/Bamana	ca. 1910
Anonymous	Besma Sougui *(Frobenius 1921, pp. 203–205, German)*	Fula/Bamana	ca. 1910
Anonymous	Duldibulukassu *(Frobenius 1921, pp. 205–208, German)*	Fula/Bamana	ca. 1910
Anonymous	Maliki Edugusega *(Frobenius 1921, pp. 208–10, German)*	Fula/Bamana	ca. 1910
Anonymous	Hassum Labo *(Frobenius 1921, pp. 210–12, German)*	Fula/Bamana	ca. 1910

Performer	Title	Language of Performance	Date Recorded
Anonymous	Legend der Bailu *(Frobenius 1921, pp. 212–13, German)*	Fula/Bamana	ca. 1910
Anonymous	Legend der Mabo *(Frobenius 1921, pp. 214–15, German)*	Fula/Bamana	ca. 1910
Anonymous	Kombe Alhassu *(Frobenius 1921, pp. 216–20, German)*	Fula/Bamana	ca. 1910
Anonymous	Sidi Baba *(Frobenius 1921, pp. 221–26, German)*	Fula/Bamana	ca. 1910
Anonymous	Origin of the Fula *(Frobenius 1921, pp. 226–28, German)*	Fula/Bamana	ca. 1910
Idrissa Batal	Hambodedio et Hamma Alasseyni Gakoy *(Seydou 1976, pp. 317–53, bilingual with French)*	Fula	1970
Yero Battare	Silamaka à l'étang Jibo *(Seydou 1972, pp. 268–71, bilingual with French)*	Fula	1928
Hamma Diam Bouraima	Hambodedio et Saïgalare *(Seydou 1976, pp. 41–131, bilingual with French)*	Fula	1970
Yero Camara	Da Monzon et le Peul *(Meyer 1991, pp. 173–80, French)*	Fula	ca. 1977
Kolado Cisse	Hambodedio et Besma Sougui *(Vieillard n.d., pp. 15–21, bilingual with French)*	Fula	ca. 1927
Kolado Cisse?	Hambodedio et Tene Monzon *(Vieillard n.d., pp. 23–29, bilingual with French)*	Fula	ca. 1927
Kolado Cisse	Hambodedio et Boubou Ardo *(Vieillard n.d., pp. 31–37, bilingual with French)*	Fula	ca. 1927
Kolado Cisse	Ousmane Hambodedio, Fadia et Durowel *(Vieillard n.d., pp. 39ff., bilingual with French)*	Fula	ca. 1927
Kolado Cisse	Gelaajo et Cheikou Amadou *(Vieillard n.d., pp. 72ff., bilingual with French)*	Fula	ca. 1927
Samba Gawlo Futanke	Silamaka I *(Seydou 1972, pp. 262–67, bilingual with French)*	Fula	1928

Performer	Title	Language of Performance	Date Recorded
Samba Gawlo Futanke	Silamaka II	Fula	1927
	(Vieillard n.d., p. 102, Fula)		
Mammadou Ham-Barke	Silamaka and Poullori	Fula	1967
	(Seydou 1972, pp. 218–41, bilingual with French)		
Amadou Mabo	Hambodedio et le Peul Dembere	Fula	1975
	(Seydou 1976, pp. 355–415, bilingual with French)		
Paate Ndiaw	Hambodedio et Fatimata Baaba Lobbo	Fula	ca. 1977
	(Meyer 1991, pp. 228–39, French)		
Sambourou Parita	Hambodedio et Besma Sougui	Fula	ca. 1970
	(Seydou 1976, pp. 201–205, bilingual with French)		
Sambourou Parita	Hambodedio et ses compagnons	Fula	1970
	(Seydou 1976, pp. 133–99, bilingual with French)		
Maabal Samburu	Silamaka et Poullori	Fula	1965?
	(Kesteloot 1993, vol. 2, pp. 83–103, French translation)		
Amadou Sangor	Origin des Mabo	Fula?	pre-1913
	(De Zeltner 1913, pp. 143–45, French)		
Ougoumala Sare (de Ngouma)	La guerre entre Ndje Fara Ndje et Hambodedio Hammadi	Fula	1974
	(Ougoumale Sare [1974?], bilingual with French)		
Ougoumala Sare	L'exploit de Mamadou Ndouldi	Fula	1974
	(Ougoumala Sare [1974?], bilingual with French)		
*Boûbacar Tinguidji	Silamaka and Poullori	Fula	1967, 1968
	(Seydou 1972, pp. 78–173, bilingual with French)		
*N.B. This text combines two performances.			
Boûbacar Tinguidji	Silamaka and Poullori	Fula	1964
	(Seydou 1972, bilingual with French)		
Boûbacar Tinguidji	La guerre contre Saa	Fula	1967
	(Seydou 1976, pp. 265–315, bilingual with French)		

Performer	Title	Language of Performance	Date Recorded
*Boûbacar Tinguidji	Silamaka et Amirou Goundaka *(Seydou 1972, pp. 174–213; bilingual with French)*	Fula	1968

*N.B. This text combines two performances.

*Fashir Abbakar Hassan	Baajankaro *(Abu-Manga 1985, Fula with English summary)*	Fula	1980

*From the Sudan.

The Futa Tooro

Performer	Title	Language of Performance	Date Recorded
Abdel Kader (son of Fama Mademba)	Samba Gueladio *(Equilbecq 1974, pp. 92–96, French)*	French	1914
Anonymous	Samba Gueladio *(Raffenel 1856, vol. 2, pp. 323–47, French)*	Fula	1846–1850
Anonymous	Ballade de Samba Foul *(Bérenger-Féraud 1885, pp. 39–49, French)*	French	1885
Anonymous	Samba Gueladio *(Steff in Equilbecq 1974, pp. 97–100, French)*	French	pre-1910
Anonymous	Koly Satigny *(Bérenger-Féraud 1885, pp. 211–18, French)*	French	1885
Anonymous	Naissance de Samba Gueladio *(Sar 1980b, pp. 94–98, bilingual with French)*	Pulaar	pre-1980
Anonymous	Samba Gueladio *(Gaden 1913, pp. 104–13, bilingual with French)*	Pulaar	pre-1913
Anonymous	Samba Gueladio *(Frobenius 1921, pp. 233–46, German)*	Pulaar	pre-1910
Anonymous	Samba Gueladio *(Sy 1980, bilingual with French)*	Pulaar	ca. 1975
Anonymous	Samba Gueladjie *(De Zeltner 1913, pp. 151–57, French)*	Pulaar?	pre-1913
Demba Mallal Ba	Ama Sam Poolel et Hammel Tyam *(Meyer 1991, pp. 13–29, French)*	Pulaar	1976–1979
Kalidou Ba	L'enfance et la jeunesse d'el-Hajj Umar *(Meyer 1991, pp. 99–118, French)*	Pulaar	1976

Performer	Title	Language of Performance	Date Recorded
Guelaye Fall	Segou Bali *(Sy 1978, pp. 16–39, bilingual with French)*	Pulaar	ca. 1975
Guelaye Fall	Balla Dierel *(Sy 1978, pp. 42–57, bilingual with French)*	Pulaar	ca. 1975
Baani Giise	Umar and the Jinns *(Kane and Robinson 1984, pp. 123–27, bilingual with English)*	Pulaar	1968
Amadou Kamara	Samba Gueladio *(Correra 1992, bilingual with French)*	Pulaar	1975–80?
Oumar Kane	Samba Gelajo-Jegi *(O. Kane 1970b, pp. 911–26, French retelling)*	French	1970
Mamadou Kante	Malik Sy and Bondou *(Meyer 1991, pp. 87–95, French)*	Pulaar	1976–1979
Mamadou Kante	Makan Sunjata et Simangourou *(Meyer 1991, pp. 141–46, French)*	Pulaar	1976–1979
Adama Koume	Ama Sam Poolel et Goumallo *(Meyer 1991, pp. 30–63, French)*	Pulaar	1976–1979
Yero Boubou Koume	Gueladio *(Meyer 1991, pp. 181–90, French)*	Pulaar	ca. 1977
Yero Boubou Koume	Gueladio et Fatimel Sire Bii Dane *(Meyer 1991, pp. 191–213, French)*	Pulaar	1977
Adama Koume	Guelel et Goumallo *(Meyer 1991, pp. 64–83, French)*	Pulaar	1976–1979
Yero Boubou Koume	Yero Maama et Saa *(Meyer 1991, pp. 228–39, French)*	Pulaar	ca. 1977
Boubakar Mamadou	Samba Gueladio I *(Equilbecq 1913–1916, vol. 2, pp. 3–40, French)*	French	ca. 1910
Boubakar Mamadou	Samba Gueladio II *(Equilbecq 1974, pp. 64–85, Pigeon French)*	Pigeon French	ca. 1910
Mammadu Njaari Mbeng	The Toorobbe and the Deeniyankoobe *(Kane and Robinson 1984, pp. 25–33, bilingual with English)*	Pulaar	1969
Sidi Mbothiel	Goumalel Samba Diam Diallo *(Ngaïde 1981, pp. 35–87, bilingual with French)*	Pulaar	1973
Sidi Mbothiel	Amadou Sam Polel et Hamme Thiamel *(Ngaïde 1981, pp. 91–161, bilingual with French)*	Pulaar	1973
Sidi Mbothiel	Silamaka et Poulori *(Meyer 1991, pp. 149–72, French)*	Pulaar	ca. 1977

Performer	Title	Language of Performance	Date Recorded
Sidi Mbothiel	Seykou Oumar et Tamba Boukari *(Meyer 1991, pp. 119–37, French)*	Pulaar	ca. 1977
Aamadu Weendu Noodi Njay	Umar, Faidherbe, and the Holy War *(Kane and Robinson 1984, pp. 107–13, bilingual with English)*	Pulaar	1968
Mamadou Pahel	Samba Gueladiegui *(Amadou Ly 1991, French)*	Pulaar	1974

Emergent Traditions

Zarma/Songhay

Traditions of the Empire

Anonymous	Moroccan Conquest of Gao *(Prost 1956, pp. 199–201, French translation)*	Zarma	1952
Nouhou Malio	Epic of Askia Mohammed *(Hale 1990, pp. 184–279, bilingual with English)*	Zarma	1980

Mali Bero/Zabarkane

Anonymous	Mali Bero *(Mounkaila 1989, pp. 128–37, bilingual with French)*	Zarma	1973
Anonymous	Sambo Zabarkane *(Mounkaila 1989, pp. 146–51, bilingual with French)*	Zarma (written)	n.d.
Anonymous	Zabarkane *(Mounkaila 1989, pp. 138–45, bilingual with French)*	Zarma (written)	n.d.
Anonymous	Mali Bero *(Mounkaila 1989, pp. 152–63, bilingual with French)*	Zarma (written)	n.d.
Badje Bangna	Zabarkane *(Mounkaila 1989, pp. 90–105, Soninke, Zarma with French)*	Soninke and Zarma	1968
Badje Bangna and Barba Gangna	Tilwati *(Mounkaila 1989, pp. 62–89, Soninke and Zarma with French)*	Soninke and Zarma	1968
Djeliba Badje	Zabarkane *(Mounkaila 1989, pp. 106–27, Soninke and Zarma, and French)*	Soninke and Zarma	1982?

Performer	Title	Language of Performance	Date Recorded

Other Heroes and Stories

Djeliba Bague	Jihad Epic of Alhadj Umaru Futa *(Watta 1993, English translation)*	Zarma	1975
Djibo Bague Djoliba	Donda Garba Dikko *(Watta 1985, English translation)*	Zarma	ca. 1980

The Gambia

Sherif Jabarteh	Kelefa Sanneh and Niumi/Jokadu *(Wright 1979, pp. 95–109, English translation)*	Mandinka	1975
Amadu Jebaate	Janke Waali *(Innes 1976, pp. 31–71, bilingual with English)*	Mandinka	1969
Ba Ansu Jebate	Musa Molo *(Innes 1976, pp. 181–254, bilingual with English)*	Mandinka	pre-1969
Shirif Jebate	Kelefa Sane *(Innes 1978, pp. 79–115, bilingual with English)*	Mandinka	pre-1968
Banna Kanute	Sunjata *(Innes 1974, pp. 136–259, bilingual with English)*	Mandinka	1969
Dembo Kanute	Faa Koli *(Innes 1974, pp. 260–323, bilingual with English)*	Mandinka	1968
Kemo Kuyate	Early History of Niumi *(Wright 1979, pp. 73–89, English translation)*	Mandinka	1974
Sana Kuyate	Battle of Kansala *(Sidibe 1980, English translation)*	Mandinka	pre-1980
Bamba Suso	Kaabu *(Innes 1976, pp. 72–126, bilingual with English)*	Mandinka	1969
Bamba Suso	Kelefa Sane *(Innes 1978, pp. 28–78, bilingual with English)*	Mandinka	pre-1968
Bamba Suso	Musa Molo *(Innes 1976, pp. 127–80, bilingual with English)*	Mandinka	1969
Bamba Suso	Fode Kaba *(Innes 1976, pp. 255–306, bilingual with English)*	Mandinka	1969
Bamba Suso	Sunjata *(Innes 1974, pp. 34–135, bilingual with English)*	Mandinka	1969

Wolof Traditions

Dieng 1993 is thus far the only substantial collection of Wolof historical epics; it presents the performances of two gewel in series, thus giving two parallel accounts of the history of Kajoor (Cayor).

GLOSSARY

Abomey. Capital city of the kingdom of Dahomey in the modern republic of Benin.

Almamy. Title used by various groups in West Africa, derived from the Arabic *imam,* a religious leader.

Anzuru. Region of the modern republic of Niger.

Ardo. Fula ruler, formerly a leader of the nomadic groups. See chapter 7.

Arma. Songhay/Zarma group in the modern republic of Niger who trace their ancestry to the Moroccan invaders of the late sixteenth century.

Ashante. Language and people of the modern republic of Ghana in West Africa.

Askia. Title used by the later Songhay rulers of Timbuktu and Gao. See chapter 8.

Badenya [**mother-childness**]. Mande term denoting a principle of social cohesiveness. See chapter 5.

Balafon. Wooden xylophone used by griots in the Manden, said to have been obtained by Sunjata's enemy Sumanguru from the jinns.

Balanza. Bamana name for the *acacia albida,* a tree associated with the city of Segou. See chapter 6.

Bamako. City on the Niger River, capital of the modern republic of Mali.

Bamana. Language and people of the middle Niger valley in West Africa, closely related to the Malinke/Maninka and associated with the states of Segou and Kaarta in the eighteenth century. See chapter 6.

Bambaado. Fula term for a special category of griot. See chapter 7.

Bantu. The family name for a number of closely related languages spread from Central through Southern Africa, derived from the Zulu word for humans.

BaNyanga. People of eastern Congo, creators of the Mwindo epic. See chapter 2.

Bebom-mvet. Performer of the *mvet* among the Fang and other peoples of Cameroon and Gabon.

Beledougou. Region of Mali in West Africa.

Bisogo. Poetic form in Rwandan court poetry. See chapter 1.

Boli, boliw. Bamana term for a magically powerful object.

Bozo. River people of the middle Niger, specialists in fishing, hunting, and boating; speakers of Bamana. See chapter 3.

Buurba. Wolof, title of the king of Jolof.

Ceddo (**or** *thiedo*). Warrior class of the Futa Tooro in the period of the Deniyanke dynasty. See chapter 7.

Conde. A lineage or clan of the Manden, equated with the Diarra/Jara clan; the clan of Sunjata's mother.

Da. A Bamana word of multiple significations. See chapter 6.

Dahomey. Old kingdom of West Africa centered in the modern republic of Benin.

Dakajalan. Town in the Manden, possibly the resting place of Sunjata. See chapter 5.

Damel. Wolof term from Senegal meaning "king."

Dausi. Hypothetical Soninke "book of heroes" reported by Frobenius but unconfirmed by later scholars.

Deniyanke. Fula dynasty of rulers of the Futa Tooro, established by Koli Tengela in the sixteenth century. See chapter 7.

Devise **(French).** Praise song or praise name of West Africa.

Diabaté. *See* Jebate.

Diame (also Jamme, Jammeh). Mandinka clan name in the Gambia.

Diarra (Jara). Maninka/Bamana clan and lineage name, associated with the Conde lineage. Name of the second dynasty in Segou. In Bamana, *jara* means "lion."

Diawara. Soninke lineage, rulers of the kingdom of Jara. See chapter 4.

Dina. An Islamic community established in the early nineteenth century by Cheikou Amadou in Massina.

Dionkoloni. *See* Jonkoloni.

Di-sòngò. Bamana, "beer-price." Euphemism used to designate the tribute paid to the kingdom of Segou, which paid for the honey-beer (mead?) drunk by the warriors. See chapter 6.

Dogon. People of the modern republic of Mali living along the escarpment of Bandiagara. Their mythology and oral traditions have been intensively studied and are used for comparative purposes with those of their neighbors of the Manden.

Dolo. West African millet beer.

Dosso. Region of the republic of Niger.

Dougha (also Douga, Duga). Title given to the chief griot in the medieval empire of Mali, according to Ibn Battuta. The word can also be associated with *Duga* (The vulture), the title of a famous West African war song. It is also the name of a king of Kore defeated by Segou (see chapter 6).

Du. Kingdom of the old Manden before the time of Sunjata, home to a monstrous buffalo and to Sunjata's mother Sogolon Kuduma Conde. See chapter 5.

Duala (or Douala). City and people of coastal Cameroon; home of the epic of Jeki la Nzambe. See chapter 2.

Duga. *See* Dougha.

Dyula (or Jula). Mande-language speaking groups settled in Côte d'Ivoire, traditionally associated with trade. In Bamana, a *jula* is a trader.

Engong. Clan of immortals in the *mvet* tradition of the Fang peoples of Cameroon and Gabon. See chapter 2.

Faasa. Mande praise song devoted especially to recalling the memory of great men and so closely associated with the content of epic performances.

Fadenya **[father-childness].** Mande term implying competition and rivalry. See chapter 5.

Fama. "King." Bamana title for the ruler of Segou, probably derived from *fanga*, power.

Fang (also Pahouin). General name for a group of peoples of southern Cameroon and northern Gabon, creators of the *mvet* epic tradition. See chapter 2.

Faro. Mande god of waters and the Niger. See especially chapter 6.

Fon. Language and people of the modern republic of Benin, associated with the old kingdom of Dahomey.

Fula (also Pullo/Fulbe, Peul, Tukolor, Pulaar). Language and formerly pastoral people widely spread over West Africa from Senegal to the Sudan and concentrated in various regions of Mali (Massina, Kounari), Guinea (the Futa Jallon), and Senegal/Mauritania (the Futa Tooro), where they have sedentarized.

Fuladu. Kingdom or region in Gambian epic traditions associated with the Fula. See chapter 8.

Futa Jallon (or Djallon). Region of upper Guinea inhabited especially by Fula and associated with early Islam in West Africa.

Futa Tooro. Region of Senegal and Mauritania along the Senegal River, associated with the Fula, who are known there as Tukolor (presumably derived from the old kingdom of the Tekrour) and whose language is called Pulaar.

Gambia. Modern state along the Gambia River in West Africa, inhabited by the Gambian Mandinka, a branch of the large Mande family, and conquered by a general of Sunjata, Tira Magan. See especially chapter 8.

Gawlo. Fula term for a special category of griot, probably derived from Wolof. See chapter 7.

Gesere, geseru. Soninke term for griot.

Gewel. Wolof term for griot.

Ghana. Former Soninke kingdom of the northern Sahel, identified with Wagadu. (N.B. Not the modern republic.) See chapter 4.

Godye. Stringed musical instrument used among the Songhay of Niger.

Gow. Hunters' group of the Songhay peoples; the term now designates specialized hunters and ritual priests. See chapter 3.

Griot. Musician, performer, singer of various West African peoples, often a member of a hereditary status group. See especially chapter 1.

Guidimakha. Region of southern Mauritania inhabited by Soninke groups. See chapter 4.

Al-Hajj. Muslim title for a person who has performed the pilgrimage to Mecca.

Hamdallaye ("Praise to God"). Capital of the Islamic *dina* of Massina, a Fula state established in Mali in the early nineteenth century. See chapter 7.

Hausa. People of northern Nigeria.

Hoddu. Fula term for a small stringed instrument. See also *ngoni* and *molo.*

Horon **[noble/free] and** *horonya* **[nobility].** Mande term designating a social class of the free, in opposition to the *jon,* or slaves. See chapters 5 and 6.

Ijala. Yoruba praise-singing genre.

Ijo (or Ijaw). People of Nigeria, creators of the *Ozidi Saga.* See chapter 2.

Ikyevugu. Praise-singing genre in Rwanda and among the Bahima of Uganda.

Ile-Ife. Mythical center of the world in Yoruba belief.

Impakanizi. "Refrain." Poetic term used in Rwandan court poetry. See chapter 1.

Jamu, zamu. West African praise-singing genre focused on clan and ancestral names. Probably from the Arabic *ismu,* "name."

Jara (or Diara). Late Soninke kingdom in the Sahel, north of the Manden. Also a dynastic name in the history of Segou.

Jebate (or Diabaté). Clan name of griots in the Manden.

Jeli (or *jali;* pl., *jeliw* or *jelilu;* feminine, *jelimuso*). Griots of the Mande peoples (the Maninka, Bamana, Gambian Mandinka).

Jinbe. Small drum used in possession-cult rituals of the Niger River.

Jolof. Wolof kingdom of central Senegal.

Jon [slave/captive]. Mande term indicating a social category. See chapters 5 and 6.

Jonkoloni (or Dionkoloni). Town in Mali, conquered by Segou in various epic stories. See chapter 6.

Kaabu (Gabou). Mandinka kingdom of the Gambia, established by Tira Magan. See chapters 5 and 8.

Kaarta. Bamana-speaking region and kingdom in the Sahel, lying north of the Niger, ruled by the Koulibaly family. See chapter 6.

Kagoro. Subgroup of the Soninke living north of the Niger River. See chapter 4.

Kaidara. Title of a Fula initiatory poem published by Amadou Hampate Ba. See chapter 7.

Kama Bloñ [**House of Speech**]. Shrine in the Mande town of Kangaba; it is the object of a septennial ritual for the replacement of the thatch roof and the recitation of the history of the Manden.

Kangaba. Town in western Mali (the Manden), site of the *Kama Bloñ* [House of Speech] which is considered by some the center of the Manden and which is the center of a ritual at which the epic of Sunjata is said to be recited. See chapter 5.

Kansala. Capital city of the Gambian kingdom of Kaabu, which fell to the Muslims in the nineteenth century. See chapter 8.

Karisi. Spirit cult among the BaNyanga of Congo to which epic performers belong. See chapter 2.

Kasala. Genre of praise poetry of the Luba people of Congo.

Kayor (or Kajoor). Wolof kingdom of Senegal. See chapter 8.

Keita. Clan name of the descendants of Sunjata, sometimes derived from the words for "taking the inheritance."

Kela (or Keyla). Town in western Mali associated principally with griots and linked with the town of Kangaba for a ritual event.

Komo. Initiatory society in the Mande/Bamana cultural area.

Kontron. Mande hunters' divinity. See chapter 3.

Kora. Large stringed instrument (a harp-lute) used by many griots in West Africa.

Koulibaly. Clan name of the Bamana rulers of the Kaarta and the first dynasty of Segou. See especially chapter 6.

Koulikoro. Rapids on the Niger River, said also to be the resting place of Sumanguru. See chapter 5.

Koumbi-Saleh. Site in Mauritania identified as Wagadu, capital of the Soninke empire of Ghana. See chapter 5.

Kouna. Town in the Fula epic tradition. See chapter 7.

Kounari. Region of Mali along the middle Niger River associated particularly with the Fula. See chapter 7.

Kouyate (Kuyate). Clan name of Malinke griots associated particularly with the Keita lineage, descendents of Sunjata's griots.

Kri. One of the kingdoms of the Manden in the time before Sunjata. See chapter 5.

Kuma koro [old speech]. Mande term to designate epic traditions. See chapter 5.

Kusa. Subgroup of the Soninke in the region north of the Niger River. See chapter 4.

Laguiya. Name of the tune dedicated to Samba Gueladio, Fula epic hero of the Futa Tooro. Probably from Arabic, "melody." See chapter 7.

Lamido. Fula term (from the Arabic, Imam?) for a ruler.

Lega. People of eastern Congo, creators of the Mubila and other epics. See chapter 2.

Luba. People of south-central Congo.

Maabo, mabo. Fula weaver and sometimes singer of epic songs.

Maana. Mande term (derived from Arabic?) often used to designate epics. See also *kuma koro* and *tariku*, and see chapter 5.

Majamu. Mande form of praise song.

Mali. Modern republic of West Africa, medieval empire of the Maninka or Malinke people, founded by Sunjata Keita ca. 1240.

Malinke. People of the Manden, a region of Mali and Guinea.

Manden (also Manding). Homeland of the Mande-family languages and peoples, associated with the empire of Mali. See especially chapter 5.

Maninka. Linguistic group and people of the Manden in West Africa. See especially chapter 5.

Mansa. "King." Maninka/Bamana term.

Mansaya. "Kingship." Maninka/Bamana term also used by the Gambian Mandinka.

Marabout. West African term for a Muslim scholar/leader. From the Arabic *Murabitun*, "people of the fortress [*ribat*]" (which also gives "Al-Moravid").

Massina. Region of the republic of Mali in the middle Niger valley inhabited especially by the Fula.

Molo. Songhay/Zarma term for a small stringed instrument used in epic-singing.

Mongo (also Nkundo). People of northeastern Congo, creators of Lianja. See chapter 2.

Mvet. An instrument, and also the epic recitations associated with that instrument among the Fang peoples of Cameroon and Gabon in Central Africa. See chapter 3.

Naamu-namina (or *Naamu*-sayer). Participant in epic performances in the Mande world; respondent who answers the lead performer. *Naamu* is probably Arabic, "Yes."

Ngara. Maninka/Bamana term to indicate a master-singer, the lead griot.

Ngoni. Small stringed instrument used by Bamana and other performers of West Africa. The *donso-ngoni*, or hunters' *ngoni*, is a larger version, closer to a kora. In Fula called the *hoddu*; among the Zarma termed the *molo*, for the Wolof the *xalam*.

Ngourori. Fula name of several kings: the father of Silamaka of Massina, the owner of cattle in the epic of Samba Gueladio. See chapter 7.

Niagassola. Town of Guinea, center of Sunjata tradition, place where the *balafon* of Sumanguru is kept.

Niani (also Nyani). Town of the Manden, proposed as a capital for the empire of Mali.

Nioro (or Nioro du Sahel). Town in northwest Mali, near the capital of the old Soninke kingdom of Jara, conquered by the Muslim Tukolor in the nineteenth century.

Niumi. City and kingdom in the western Gambia, associated with the Mandinka and the Fula. See chapter 8.

Noukouma. Historic battle in 1818 between the Muslims of the *dina* of Massina and the forces of Segou, won by the Muslims. See chapters 6 and 7.

Numu, numuw. Mande blacksmiths, members of the *nyamakala* groups.

Nyama. Mande term for occult energy or power. See chapter 5.

Nyamakala. General Mande name for the status groups, which include blacksmiths, griots, leather workers, and other specialized and hereditary groups of artisans.

Nyancho. Warrior class of the Gambia in the nineteenth century. See chapter 8.

Nyanga. *See* BaNyanga.

Nyaringa **(or** *ngaringa*). Iron rasp used in Mande hunters' performances.

Nyeenyo. Fula term, roughly equivalent to the Mande *nyamakala*. See chapter 7.

Oku. Human clan in the *mvet* traditions of Cameroon and Gabon. See chapter 2.

Oriki. Yoruba clan and lineage praise songs.

Pagne. Women's skirt, a wrap-around cloth.

Pekane. Epic songs of the Pulaar-speaking Subalbe fishermen of the Senegal River. See chapter 3.

Peul. *See* Fula.

Poyon. Bamana term for a fish that carries two brothers across the river in legend. See chapter 6.

Pulaaku. Fula term meaning the abstract quality of being a Fula, with the behavior, culture, and character associated with this identity. See chapter 7.

Qisas al-anbiya. Arabic, "Tales of the Prophets." A category of popular narrative religious histories of the world widespread in Islam.

Rara. Yoruba praise singing performed by new brides.

Rwanda. People, nation, and old kingdom of Central Africa.

Saa. Town in Fula epic tradition, home of a tyrannical king who is defeated by Hambodedio. See chapter 7.

Sagbata, Sakpata. Fon and Yoruba names for the god of smallpox.

Sahel. (Arabic, Shore). Savanna region of West Africa lying south of the Sahara desert and stretching from the Atlantic to the Nile.

Saïgalare. Musical air associated with the Fula hero Hambodedio. See chapter 7.

Saloum. Region of central Senegal, former kingdom.

Samaniana. Tributary town in the region of Segou whose king is defeated in the cycle of Segou. See chapter 6.

Sanin, Sanen. Mande hunters' divinity. See chapter 3.

Segou. City on the middle Niger River in the modern republic of Mali, former capital of the kingdom of Segou. See chapter 6.

Segou-Bali. Title of an epic song of the Subalbe of the Senegal River. See chapter 3.

Senankuya. "Joking relationship," which links paired clans among many peoples in the wider Mande world.

Senegal. Modern republic of West Africa.

Sibi. One of the kingdoms of the Manden in the time before Sunjata. See chapter 5.

Simbong. Hunters' whistle and praise name of the Mande peoples; also a title applied to Sunjata.

So-boli [**horse-running**]. Mode of slave-taking employed by the kingdom of Segou, described by Bazin. See chapter 6.

Somono. Boatmen of the Manden and the Niger. See chapter 5.

Songhay. Language and people associated with the fifteenth to seventeenth century empire of Gao and Timbuktu on the eastern bend of the Niger River, now principally in the Republic of Niger. See especially chapter 8.

Soninke. Language (of the Mande language family) and people of the Sahel, associated with the former empire of Ghana or Wagadu. See chapter 4.

Sorko. Hunting people of the Niger River, associated with the Songhay. See chapter 3.

Sosso. Region (and people?) ruled by Sumanguru, opponent of Sunjata. See chapter 5.

Subalbe (sing., Cuballo). Specialized Pulaar-speaking fishermen of the Senegal River. See chapter 3.

Tabon. One of the kingdoms of the Manden in the time before Sunjata. See chapter 5.

Tarikh el-Fettach. Late seventeenth-century Arabic chronicle of Timbuktu written by Mahmoud Kati.

Tarikh es-Soudan. Seventeenth-century Arabic chronicle of Timbuktu written by Abd al-Rahman al-Sa'di.

Tariku. Mande term derived from Arabic to designate epics. See chapter 5.

Tekrur. Early Muslim state along the Senegal River.

Tige. Dogon genre of praise singing and naming poetry.

Tiv. A people of northern Nigeria.

Ton. Bamana term for an association or brotherhood. See chapter 6.

Tonjon (tondyon). Bamana, "slave of the association." Designation of the members of the association which lay at the base of royal power in Segou. See chapter 6.

Toure. Lineage name of the Manden, associated with early conversion to Islam.

Traore. Malinke clan name associated in the epic of Sunjata with the brothers who slay the Buffalo-Woman of Du and the general, Tira Magan, who conquers the Jolof. See chapter 5.

Tukolor. Name given to Fula-speakers (the *Haal-Pulaaren*) of the Futa Tooro along the Senegal River.

Tunka. Soninke title for a ruler.

Tutsi (Wa-Tutsi). Cattle-herding aristocratic rulers of the old kingdom of Rwanda.

Twa. Indigenous peoples conquered by the Tutsi in the old kingdom of Rwanda; also associated with pygmies.

Umutwe w'Abasize. Institution of the old kingdom of Rwanda, the "army of poets" devoted to composing, singing, and preserving the praises of the king.

Wagadu. Legendary Soninke city, capital of the empire of Ghana, identified as Koumbi Saleh in modern Mauritania. See chapter 4.

Wage, Wago. Four noble clans of the Soninke, associated with the kingdom of Wagadu.

Wasulu. Region of the Manden in Mali inhabited by a Bamana/Maninka-speaking group of Fula origin.

Wolof. Language and people of northern Senegal who formed the kingdoms of Jolof, Kayor, Baol, and others. See chapter 8.

Xalam. Wolof term for a small stringed instrument used in epic singing. See also *ngoni,* and see chapter 8.

Yoruba. Language and people of southwestern Nigeria associated with a number of city-states and forms of verbal art.

Zarma (Zerma, Djerma). Language and people of modern Niger; closely related to Songhay. See chapter 8.

NOTES

Introduction

1. Niane 1960; translated into English as *Sundiata: An Epic of Old Mali* by G. D. Pickett (London: Longmans, 1965). C. Miller 1990 contains an assessment of Niane's work.

2. Biebuyck and Mateene 1969 and Biebuyck 1978 present the collected texts. The Mwindo epic has been anthologized without Biebuyck's valuable and extensive ethnographic annotation.

3. Alta Jablow's work (1984, 1991) with "Gassire's Lute" represents a special case and is discussed in chapter 4.

4. See Finnegan 1970, pp. 99–101, for initial skepticism, and responses in Johnson 1980 and Okpewho 1979.

5. There have been some specific studies on this topic; see Bird and Kendall 1980 on the Mande hero, and Seydou 1976 (introduction), and 1992 for Fula examples. See also Mbele 1982 for an interesting discussion.

6. See Goody 1987, pp. 78ff., for a discussion of this notion.

7. Orality is the focus of Isidore Okpewho's work (1979, 1990), which builds on the copious literature concerning notions of orality and oral performance; see Foley 1988 or Fine 1984 for bibliographic and theoretical discussions.

8. See Drewal 1991.

9. In Seydou 1976, pp. 41–131. An abridged English translation is given in Johnson, Hale, Belcher 1997. The story is described and discussed in chapter 7.

10. Dumestre and Kesteloot 1975. Meillassoux and Sylla 1978 provide an interesting discussion of the history of Jonkoloni and the version of Sissoko Kabine; see Belcher 1994b and Belcher 1998 for a discussion of the literary qualities of this text.

11. Fine 1984 provides a solid analysis of the ideals and constraints operating in this system. The literature on performance studies is copious.

12. Specifically, there is volume 5, *Dichten und Denken im Sudan,* which contains a lengthy version of the Sunjata epic along with Mossi and Bamana traditions; volume 6, *Spielmannsgeschichten der Sahel* (Minstrelsy of the Sahel), which, as the title indicates, is almost entirely given over to epic narrations; and volume 7, *Dämonen des Sudan,* which contains much valuable material on Mande and Sorko hunters (Frobenius 1925, 1921, and 1924, respectively).

13. These texts are discussed in greater detail in chapter 4; they provide the basis for the works of Adam 1904, Lanrezac 1907, Arnaud 1912, and for Delafosse's *Traditions historiques et légendaires.*

14. See Innes 1974, pp. 37–38.

15. Jabaté 1987.

16. His questions and answers were privately published in bilingual format by the Fondation Société Commerciale de l'ouest Africain (SCOA), and have since been reworked

and published by Youssouf Tata Cissé in two volumes (Cissé and Kamissoko 1988, 1991). The case of Wa Kamissoko is a special one, best described in de Moraes Farias 1993.

Chapter 1

1. For example, Vansina 1985; Diawara 1990; Bathily 1975, 1989.

2. See A. Bâ and Daget 1962; Coupez and Kamanzi 1962.

3. See Herskovits and Herskovits 1958, pp. 20–21. The first record of the work by Melville and Frances Herskovits in Dahomey appeared in 1938: Melville Herskovits, *Dahomey: A West African Kingdom.*

4. See Roberts and Roberts 1996 for a discussion of Luba *minkisi* and the "making of history" or Adandé 1962 for a catalogue of the royal staffs of the kings of Dahomey.

5. Henige 1974.

6. See Goody 1968, pp. 31–33; the original source is Bohannan 1952.

7. See Malinowski 1954.

8. See de Heusch 1982a; J. Miller 1980, and various essays by Vansina 1983.

9. See Mamadou Diawara in Austen forthcoming, or Mounkaila 1989, 1993.

10. Cissoko and Sambou 1974, pp. 33–37.

11. Koli Tengela (spellings vary) is generally associated with the establishment of the Deniyanke dynasty in the Fula/Tukolor state of the Futa Tooro; his movements are dated by the chronicles of Timbuctoo to a period around 1500. His presence in Gambian tradition is evidence for the interpolation of Fula tradition into local Mandinka history. See Wright 1978 for a discussion of this issue.

12. Diawara 1990 on Soninke oral traditions relating to the kingdom of Jara is exemplary in identifying the range of sources, from nobles to slave-women.

13. Niane 1960, p. 1 (trans. Pickett 1965).

14. Probably the most visible expression of this new perspective is the multivolume *UNESCO General History of Africa.* Readers of the first volume, on methodology, will find the contrast between the essays of Amadou Hampaté Bâ and Jan Vansina on the topic of oral history illuminating.

15. See Conrad and Frank 1995, pp. 3–4, for a discussion of etymologies. The most plausible suggestion is that of Eric Charry (1992), who would connect it with the Arabic *qawwal* [speaker], although Charles Bird prefers a local etymology (personal communication) and Thomas Hale is working on different possibilities.

16. Barber 1991 is essential for the study of Yoruba *oriki* and very valuable for a general understanding of African forms of oral tradition.

17. See the works of Pascal Boyer, especially Boyer 1988.

18. Much ink has flowed on the topic of nyamakalaw; see Camara 1992 for an early analysis of griots in Mande society. Conrad and Frank 1995 offer a more recent and wider survey of the institution; it is essential reading. Charry 1992 is an excellent survey of musicians in the Mande; Hoffman 1990 and Harris 1992 along with essays by Jansen (in Austen forthcoming) provide an ethnographic perspective. Tamari 1991 and 1995 argues for historical linkage of the institution across various ethnic groups in the Sahel through the empire of Mali.

19. See Tegnaeus 1951 or Herbert 1993 for insights into the mythic and cultural significance of blacksmiths throughout Africa; McNaughton 1988 deals with Mande blacksmiths.

20. See Camara 1992 for a Malian view of griots; Hoffman 1990 and Harris 1992 present a more sympathetic insider's view.

21. For discussion of the musical activities of griots, see the excellent work in Knight 1973 and Charry 1992. Knight describes the Gambian Mandinka; Charry's perspective is somewhat broader, but both are essential.

22. See Duran 1995 for a more detailed and informative discussion of women's musical roles; see also Jansen 1996 for a tribute to a great woman singer.

The fact that women have not been recorded singing should not imply that they cannot but simply reflects a past division of labor. It is certain that if a market develops, women will begin to sing epics.

23. See Coupez and Kamanzi 1970, and Kagame 1950, 1969, for discussions of Rwandan poetic practices and institutions; these practices constitute a valuable parallel case for the study of West African oral traditions.

24. Mamadou Diawara 1990, p. 79 (my translation).

25. Diabaté 1986, p. 31.

26. C. Monteil 1953, p. 363 (my translation). The piece was published posthumously by Monteil's son.

27. Germaine Dieterlen gives the major description of the event (1955, 1959); her account can now be supplemented with that of Solange de Ganay (1995). There are some questions about the reliability of Dieterlen's report, which clearly mixes a large number of sources.

28. He was, however, a native of Kela, and his version of the Sunjata is very close to that of his relative Kele Monson Diabaté. See Johnson 1986, pp. 91–92, for information on the griot; for a comparison of versions, see Belcher 1985, pp. 262ff., and Bulman 1990.

29. See Seydou 1972, pp. 10–11.

30. Seydou 1972, p. 13 (my translation).

31. A useful starting point is the chapter on the subject in Finnegan 1970; Gleason 1994 contains a good selection of praise poems.

32. See, for instance, Morris 1980, Schapera, Kunene 1991, and Opland 1983 for case studies on individual traditions. Of these, that of Opland is the most recent and takes into account non-African theories of oral literature. Works by Faïk-Nzuji 1974 and Mufuta 1968 document the Luba. Kagame, in numerous works, offers a wealth of Rwandan material (see, e.g., Kagame 1969), as do Coupez and Kamanzi 1970.

33. Vail and Landeg 1991 provide an interesting analysis of the political impact of praise poetry in modern Southern Africa.

34. Kagame 1950, 1969. His Christian poetry appeared in 1952. For other valuable studies, see Coupez and Kamanzi 1962, 1970.

35. Kagame 1950, pp. 67–68 (my translation from the French).

36. The refrain varies from poem to poem. Another poet chooses to stress the king's connection with cattle: "Through long days may you milk them, the Cattle, / For you have kept them from great misfortunes" (Kagame 1950, p. 101).

37. Kagame 1950, p. 89. The poet's name was Sekarama, and he actually gives eleven lines to Mukobanya. The other lines are an extended bovine metaphor that may relate to the "Reign-cow." This poet seems to suggest that the son displaced the father on the throne. Yet another poet, Karera, also reduces the story to two lines: "Then the Incomparable charged into battle / And stretched out the corpse of the Mushi" (Kagame 1950, p. 101).

38. De Ganay was a member of the team lead by Marcel Griaule that studied the Dogon and their neighbors; the impact of that team's work in African studies has been enormous.

39. De Ganay 1941, pp. 1, 164ff.

40. Hale 1990, p. 66.

41. De Ganay 1941, pp. 63–64 (my translation).

42. De Ganay 1941, p. 66 (my translation).

43. Dieterlen 1951, p. 76.

44. See Doucoure and Martal 1970. It seems relevant that this version of the epic, celebrating the Traore lineage, was published fairly soon after Moussa Traore overthrew Modibo Keita.

45. Doucoure and Martal 1970, pp. 147–51.

Chapter 2

1. Finnegan's objections, expressed in 1970, single out the Central African traditions as being prose rather than poetic in form.

2. See Coupez and Kamanzi 1962.

3. See Ikiddeh 1985 for a discussion of the multimedia aspects of Clark-Bekederemo's work on Ozidi. Ruth Stone (1988) attempts a more complex reproduction of the performance event. She deals with Sierra Leone, which is well outside Central Africa, but her protagonist is cut from the same cloth as those covered here. A sense of the disjunction between published text and original performance drives much of Okpewho's writing on the subject (1980b, 1990, 1992).

4. Biebuyck and Mateene 1969 (1971), p. 14; de Rop 1964, pp. 15ff.; Austen 1995, p. 14.

5. De Rop 1964, pp. 15ff.

6. Clark-Bekederemo 1991, p. lii.

7. Clark-Bekederemo 1991, p. lii.

8. Biebuyck and Mateene 1969 (1971), p. 13. See also Biebuyck 1972.

9. Seydou 1982.

10. For a general bibliography on the Mongo, see de Rop 1974; published versions of the texts include Boelaert 1949, de Rop 1978, de Rop and Boelaert 1983. Hulstaert 1978, 1984, offers background materials on history and poetic traditions. There are also Flemish publications I have not examined; see Biebuyck 1972 or 1978b for references. A term also applied to this group is Nkundo, which Hulstaert suggests may be an older form now being replaced.

11. Hulstaert 1984, pp. 32ff.

12. Boelaert 1949, de Rop 1978, de Rop and Hulstaert 1983.

13. Boelaert 1949, pp. 4–5. See also de Rop 1964, pp. 71ff.

14. De Rop 1974, p. 9.

15. Boelaert 1962 also documents a quasi-ritual reenactment of Lianja's procession, for the purpose of dispelling evil forces when misfortunes have occurred. I am indebted to Brunhilde Biebuyck for this reference.

16. The beginning is a different story: the father must succeed in climbing a tree in which women live; he then throws the women down and different animals take their mates. He and his spouse descend and travel on, visiting various animals, until they come to his friend the stinking rat *(rat puant)*. When the wife complains of the stench, the friend is offended and has the husband killed. He takes the widow; she becomes pregnant and spends the time lamenting her dead husband.

17. See Jacobs et al. 1961.

18. See Biebuyck and Mateene 1969, 1970; Biebuyck 1972, 1978b, 1992.

19. Biebuyck 1978b, p. 18.

20. Biebuyck and Mateene 1969, p. 79.

21. Biebuyck 1978b, pp. 117–18.

22. Biebuyck and Mateene 1969, p. 82; Biebuyck 1978b, p. 212.

23. See, for instance, de Heusch 1982a and 1982b; Smith 1970, 1979.

24. Biebuyck and Mateene 1969, pp. 24–47; an English translation is available in Johnson, Hale, Belcher 1997, pp. 294–301.

25. Wamenka 1992.

26. Biebuyck 1992. The edition will be trilingual.

27. Tiki a Koulle a Penda 1987 is a two-volume bilingual presentation of a "complete" version of the cycle. Bekombo-Priso 1993 offers a bilingual version of selected episodes taken from one night's recording.

28. Austen 1995.

29. Tiki a Koulle a Penda 1987, pp. 146–47, ll. 857–62.

30. Austen 1995, pp. 13–14.

31. Bekombo-Priso 1993, pp. 34–35.

32. See also Eloise Brière 1993, pp. 22–33.

33. Clark-Bekederemo 1991 (first published in 1977 in Ibadan).

34. See Okpewho's critical introduction in Clark-Bekederemo 1991 and the essays in Okpewho 1990c.

35. Agbogidi also appears in the traditions of Benin, as part of an epic recitation that is as yet unpublished (Ben Amos, personal communication).

36. Although in Native American traditions, the hero twins who shape the world are most commonly associated with a grandmother.

37. For an early critique of the methods of interpretation, see Herskovits and Herskovits 1958, pp. 81ff. See also Finnegan 1970, pp. 315ff., and Okpewho 1983.

38. Riesman 1986.

39. "Littérature orale et comportements sociaux en Afrique noire," in Paulme 1976, pp. 51–69.

40. See Austen 1995, pp. 20–21, and Austen 1986; Biebuyck 1978b, pp. 102–105.

41. See Görög et al. 1980. The story could also be seen as a parody or inversion of the

widespread folktale of the kind and unkind girls in which the good girl does things right and is rewarded while the bad girl ends up being punished or killed.

42. The Mande world exhibits the same ideology; see the classic essay, Bird and Kendall 1980, on the Mande Hero.

43. E.g, Pepper 1972, T. Ndoutoume 1970–1975, 1993.

44. Assoumou Ndoutoume has attempted to document these clan relations, relying in part on the work of Tsira Ndong Ndoutoume.

45. See Alexandre 1974 and Towo-Atatanga 1965 on the topic. Boyer 1988 is a stimulating exploration of the world of the mvet-performer.

46. Awona 1965, 1966; Eno-Belinga 1978. These are transcriptions of performances. The exact source of the *Epopée Mulombi* (Mawiri) is difficult to ascertain.

47. In Pepper 1972.

48. See Awona 1965, 1966.

49. See Eno-Belinga 1978. An excerpted translation of this text is available in Johnson, Hale, Belcher 1997.

50. Vansina 1966, p. 9.

51. Mufuta 1968, Faïk-Nzuji 1974.

52. Coupez and Kamanzi 1962, p. 8.

53. See Knappert 1967 and especially 1983 for a discussion of Swahili epic; see also Mbele 1986. We do not consider *Ibonia,* the Malagasy epic edited by Lee Haring, because of the distances (in space and culture) which separate it from the other African materials.

Chapter 3

1. See Chatwin 1987 for an evocation of the lost world of the Nemadi.

2. For information on hunters, see Cissé 1964; Cashion 1984; Mariko 1981; Bird 1971, 1972a, 1972b, 1976; and the introductions to the various texts cited below.

3. See on this topic, Tegnaeus 1950 or Pâques 1977.

4. See Cashion 1984, pp. 291ff. for a description.

5. The more usual term is *zima;* see Olivier de Sardan 1982b, pp. 166–68.

6. The best collections are probably those of the administrator A. Dupuis-Yakouba published in his own book (1911) and as an appendix to Lieutenant Louis Desplagnes' early and interesting description of the Niger bend (1907, pp. 383–450). He provides little information on the circumstances of collection but does give the texts in bilingual format. Frobenius 1924 also offers a valuable collection of Sorko stories. Jean Rouch and other specialists of the Songhay have added to the corpus.

7. See Desplagnes 1907, pp. 386–412.

8. See Frobenius 1924, pp. 135–47.

9. Retold from Frobenius 1924, pp. 135–47.

10. Rouch 1989, pp. 53ff.; Prost 1956.

11. Rouch 1989, pp. 52–74.

12. Retold from Dupuis-Yakouba 1911, pp. 20–39.

13. Frobenius 1924, pp. 147–52.

14. Frobenius 1924, pp. 162–73; the story of the woman is "Banna Bainde," pp. 201–204.

15. For background, see the references in note 2, above. For texts, see Cashion 1984, vol. 2; Thoyer-Rozat 1978, 3 vols.; Dérive 1978; D. Coulibaly 1993; Innes and Sidibe 1990.

16. This is particularly evident in Cissé 1994.

17. In fact, there seems to be some discomfort at calling the singers *donso-jeliw* [hunters' griot]; the preferred formulation is probably *donso-ngoni-fola* [player of the hunter's harp-lute]. See Cashion 1984, pp. 284ff. David Conrad also drew my attention to this nuance of usage (personal communication).

18. Conrad 1989, pp. 42–43, contains a biographic sketch.

19. See McNaughton 1979, pp. 13, 40–41, for Seydou Camara's Komo songs.

20. See Cashion 1984, pp. 290ff.; Dérive 1978; and Cissé 1994, pp. 118ff. For parallels among the the Yoruba, see the collection of hunters' songs in Ajuwon 1982.

21. See Cashion 1984, pp. 275ff., for a valuable discussion of the importance of the naamu-sayer in defining the poetic line.

22. See also McNaughton 1982 for a description of hunters' shirts.

23. Thoyer-Rozat 1978, vol. 2, pp. 45–46; Fodé Sidibe 1984.

24. Cashion 1984 reports similar experiences, although he was able to collect complete texts. From his discussion, it would appear that Coulibaly's published version of *Dingo Kanbili*, recorded from Bala Jimbe, is part of a thirteen-hour recorded performance.

25. Cissé 1964, pp. 176–77; Cissé 1994 offers quite different versions of the myth.

26. Fodé Sidibe 1984, pp. 164–69.

27. Cashion 1984, appendix 2.

28. For an excellent analysis of that episode in terms of hunters' lore, see Bulman 1989.

29. This is the premise of *Kambili* (Seydou Camara 1974) and of "Mamby and the Crocodile" (Innes and Sidibe 1990).

30. Retold from the version of Mamdou Jara in Thoyer-Rozat 1978, pp. 27–98 (see 1995 reprint).

31. So in Frobenius 1924, pp. 43ff.; Meyer 1987, pp. 25–29. See also Herskovits and Herskovits 1958, pp. 235–37.

32. Dupuis-Yakouba 1911, pp. 190–239.

33. See Belcher 1995 for a preliminary listing of possibilities.

34. Retold from Cashion 1984, appendix 1.

35. Thoyer-Rozat 1978, vol. 3, pp. 120–57.

36. Innes and Sidibe 1990, p. 68.

37. See Dilley 1989. Note a difference between the Futa Tooro and the Malian region of Massina. The *maabo* of the Futa Tooro is not a singer of epics, but in Massina he is. In both regions the word is primarily associated with weavers, however.

38. Ibrahima Sow 1982, p. 238. This essay is a valuable introduction to the subalbe.

39. Sy 1978, pp. 77–79. The notion of a chain of transmission for the teachings is clearly related to the Arabic and Islamic concept of the *isnad,* the chain of authorities used to measure the validity of traditions concerning Muhammad.

40. Kesteloot and Dieng 1997.

41. Cissé notes of his version of the myth of Sanen and Kontron, in which the son Kontron engenders his own wife from his leg, that he has thus been blessed with the power of motherhood, and this life-giving property carries over to his devotees. See Cissé 1964. We have already observed the importance of the female element in the Gow traditions.

Chapter 4

1. For historical background, see Levtzion 1973. The Arabic records are now most conveniently collected in Levtzion and Hopkins, *Corpus*. Dieterlen and Sylla 1992 is a recent study based on the oral traditions.

2. For instance, a General Frey wished to connect Ghana (or Ghanata, a local variant) with Canada, based on the similarity of the sounds. See Delafosse 1911–1912, vol. 1, p. 204.

3. See especially A. Bathily 1975.

4. See Munson 1980 and McIntosh and McIntosh 1981, 1984, 1993.

5. See Conrad and Fisher 1982, 1983; the rebuttal in Burkhalter 1992; and a reprise by Masonen and Fisher 1996.

6. See Hale 1990 and de Moraes Farias in Austen forthcoming for the Soninke-Songhay connection.

7. Adam 1904, Arnaud 1912, Delafosse 1913, Lanrezac 1907, and Labouret 1929 are the major published sources. Dieterlen and Sylla 1992 reproduces excerpts dealing with Wagadu from most of these sources but does not cover their very interesting later historiography. Soares 1997 provides a good deal of historical information on Nioro at the beginning of the colonial era. Bulman 1990 includes an analysis of the informants. The topic and the set of texts deserve fuller investigation.

8. His father also died in an explosion near Bandiagara, after his newly conquered subjects around Segou and Massina revolted in 1862.

9. For the esoteric interpretation, see Dieterlen and Sylla 1992, pp. 79–80, 114ff. On the choice of a king, see the narratives of Cissoko and Sambou 1974, or Wright 1979, 1980.

10. The importance of water in Mande mythology (Dieterlen 1955; Griaule 1965) is well-established. Herskovits and Herskovits 1958 presents a series of stories on the mythical regulation of the rains (pp. 126–34); the theme is also to be found in Yoruba mythology. See also the end of Amos Tutuola's *The Palm-Wine Drinkard*.

11. See Bazin 1988 for one unique configuration near Segou.

12. See Jansen and Zobel 1996 for essays on the topic of the younger brother.

13. See Dieterlen and Sylla 1992.

14. Another quasi-allegorical reading might make the killing of the snake a metaphor for conversion to Islam. Where both Islam and Christianity interface with traditional African religions, the snake seems to represent the original beliefs.

15. See Levtzion 1972.

16. See G. Boyer 1953 and Mamadou Diawara 1990 for historical analyses that also summarize the previous sources and documentation.

17. See the essays by Mamadou Diawara and Belcher in Austen forthcoming.

18. Meillassoux, Doucoure, and Simagha 1967.

19. Meillassoux, Doucoure, and Simagha 1967, pp. 47–49, ll. 299–301, repeated at ll. 304, 306, 315.

20. Meillassoux, Doucoure, and Simagha 1967, pp. 74, 78–79, ll. 587–89, repeated at ll. 629, 633, 699, and 738.

21. See Dantioko 1985, 1987a; Meillassoux and Sylla 1978; Conrad 1981; C. Monteil 1977 for the Soninke and Bamana versions of the stories.

22. See C. Monteil 1953.

23. See Kesteloot and Dumestre 1978.

24. Frobenius 1921, p. 38.

Chapter 5

1. David Conrad (1992) has explored the echoes of royal pilgrimages in oral tradition, concentrating on the figures of Fajigi and Sunjata's general Fakoli.

2. Tal Tamari (1991, 1995) has best documented the parallels among status groups in the region and has suggested that the patterns may have been imposed from above, but the idea has met resistance.

3. See Person 1981.

4. See Innes 1974; Bakari Sidibe 1980.

5. See Camara 1992, Knight 1973, Charry 1992, Duran 1995, Hoffman 1990, Harris 1992, and Jansen 1998 for discussion specifically of griots. Conrad and Frank 1995 offers the most accessible survey of the nyamakala groups of the Mande. McNaughton 1988 discusses the *numuw*, blacksmiths, as does N. Kante 1993.

6. See Zahan 1963 for a fuller discussion of the forms. *Majamu* and *burudyu* appear to be name-centered declamations, whereas *faasa* evokes a more complex and potentially narrative form.

7. See Johnson 1978, 1980, 1986.

8. In one case, the request had the weight of a governmental commission behind it. See Kanku Mady Jabaté 1987.

9. In fact, documentation of the ceremony is problematic. The basic source is a lengthy article, Dieterlen 1955, which has been updated by the account of the same ceremonies in de Ganay 1995. Meillassoux et al. 1968 includes an account of his relatively unsuccessful attempt to observe the ceremonies. The event was scheduled to occur in 1996 but for a variety of reasons occurred late.

10. See the essay by Seydou Camara (not the hunter's bard) in Austen forthcoming.

11. See Belcher 1985 for a first analysis; Bulman (1990) studied a larger number of versions and reached the same conclusions.

12. See Greene 1991. Solange de Ganay reminds us that the ceremonies at Kangaba were actually modeled on another nearby center (1995, pp. 62ff.), and M. P. Ferry documents a similar ritual in eastern Senegal (1968, pp. 183–85).

13. Tabulations of narrative motifs are to be found in Belcher 1985, pp. 226–68, and in Bulman 1990. Both works offer a master chart similar to this one, then break the story down further into detailed elements. Bulman's is the more recent and comprehensive tabulation.

14. The current president has no genealogical connection to Sunjata, but his wife might be said to have appropriated the king by writing a book on him; see Adame Konare Ba 1983.

15. See Jansen and Zobel 1996.

16. See Bulman 1989.

17. Frobenius 1913, vol. 2.

18. The "Song of the Bow" *(Bara kala ta . . .)* is perhaps the principal song associated with Sunjata and figures largely in the *Sunjata-Faasa,* which might be considered the established Keita praise song. See Belcher 1985, appendix 2, for a discussion of the songs in the Sunjata epics, and Knight 1973 for the repertoire of Gambian Mandinka griots.

19. Innes 1974, p. 104.

20. See Bird 1971, 1972b, and the introduction to Seydou Camara 1974; see also Bird and Kendall 1980.

21. See Conrad in Austen forthcoming.

22. Zahan 1963, p. 130, documents the sexual symbolism of this pair of implements.

23. Fa-Digi Sisókó, in Johnson 1986, interweaves this song exquisitely with Sunjata's travels in exile.

24. This theme deserves further exploration. See Belcher 1985, 1991.

25. The contrast might also be seen in the terms defined by de Heusch (1982a) for the Central African myths: between the drunken king and the virtuous hunter.

26. Different versions ascribe a different number of sisters to Sunjata. One widespread variant says that Bala Faseke Kouyate accompanied one of Sunjata's sisters, who was sent to marry Sumanguru.

27. Innes 1974 notes how the third of his three versions, performed by Dembo Kanute, was oriented to highlight the deeds of the Darbo ancestor of the host for the performance.

28. See Bird and Kendall 1980, p. 20. Frobenius (1925, p. 325) also notes a similar phrase.

29. This occurs in Niane 1960 but not in most of the oral versions.

30. See Law 1980 for a study of the horse in West African history.

31. See Conrad 1994.

32. See Bulman 1997.

33. See Quiquandon 1892, Humblot 1951, Pageard 1962, Vidal 1924, C. Monteil 1929, and Delafosse 1913.

34. E.g., Levztion 1973; Ly-Tall 1976, 1977; Niane 1972, 1974, 1975; and others. One virtue of Monteil's work is that he recognized very early the importance of working with oral traditions and did so carefully; a disadvantage is that he did not reproduce his informants' words exactly.

35. Represented by the publications of Adam 1904, Arnaud 1912, Lanrezac 1907, Delafosse 1913, and Labouret 1929.

36. The account was written in 1937 but published in *Notes Africaines* only in 1959.

37. See Innes 1974.

38. Cissé and Kamissoko 1988, 1991.

39. See de Moraes Farias 1993.

40. Olney 1975.

41. Lilyan Kesteloot has evidence that it is based on actual recordings. Personal communication, June 1994.

42. See Adele King 1980 and Hale 1982.

43. Diabaté 1970a, 1970b, 1975, 1986. The Maninka version is given with an interlinear translation in Moser 1974.

44. The essays of David Conrad (1984, 1985, 1992, 1994, 1995a, and 1998 [forthcoming]) provide valuable analyses of the Sunjata tradition. Conrad is also editing texts collected in Upper Guinea that will vastly expand the material available.

45. The mention of Eden, as in Johnson 1986, would be an Islamic intrusion. Do and Kri are two of the states that pre-existed the Manden. Do or Du is the site of the "Buffalo-Woman" episode.

46. For instance, in *Tradition historique peul.*

Chapter 6

1. C. Monteil 1977 and Tauxier 1942 offer early syntheses of Bamana history. Since that time, various works by Jean Bazin (1970, 1975, 1979, 1982), David Conrad (1990), Adame Konare Ba (1987), and others have filled in the picture in great detail. On questions of the "ethnicity" of the Bamana/Bambara, see Bazin 1985.

2. Travelers through the region after Mungo Park include René Caillié, Heinrich Barth, Anne Raffenel, Eugène Mage, and Captain Binger. Tauxier offers a review of their testimony. For the perspective of Islam, see Cheikh Moussa Kamara's history of Segou, the various reports in the Nioro manuscripts cited in chapter 4, and documents later in the century edited by Hanson and Robinson 1991.

3. See the references cited in note 1. Of particular interest is, for example, Bazin's essay on the "production of a historical narrative" (1979).

4. See the works of Germaine Dieterlen, including her later collaborations with Youssouf Tata Cissé, for explorations of religious life and institutions that might be considered the basic statements. The works of Dominique Zahan may not be so well known, but they are equally useful.

5. Lilyan Kesteloot's study of Biton Koulibaly (1978b), and my own follow-up essay on the topic (1995a) represent attempts to integrate belief and narrative.

6. The largest corpus of work is that of Sarah Brett-Smith, whose recent book, *The Making of Bamana Sculpture* (1994) is perhaps the most accessible statement of traditional beliefs as expressed in nonverbal media (see also her extended interview with Nyamaton Diarra, 1996). Patrick McNaughton offers well-informed writings focusing on the world of the blacksmiths. Robert Farris Thompson's view of the Manden is included in his *Flash of the Spirit.*

7. This essay evoked a fair amount of criticism when it first came out, although many of the voices were oversensitive in the protection of their research turf. In fact, in the epic traditions, the themes she raises recur again and again.

8. Bâ and Kesteloot 1966a; see also Kesteloot 1972, 1978, 1987a and 1987b, 1991; and Kesteloot, Dieng, and Sall 1983.

9. See Kesteloot and Dieng 1997.

10. A short anthology of epic pieces in 1971; and in 1972, a four-volume collection of the cycle of Segou, now reissued in two volumes by L'Harmattan (1993).

11. Kele Monson's version exists in multiple printed forms: Massa Makan Diabaté 1970b and 1976, and in the original with interlinear translation in Moser 1974. Baba Cissoko's text is in Dumestre 1979.

12. Both David Conrad and Lilyan Kesteloot have questioned my assertion of this darker side to the tradition, arguing that the kings are still seen as *horon* [nobles] and kings, figures of power and authority (personal communications). My description suggests that the picture of the kings of Segou presented in the epics has almost no counterpart in other traditions.

13. Johnson 1978, 1980.

14. Earlier authors such as Delafosse had dated it to 1660, and that date is still encountered. The legend of Biton Koulibaly says that Soninke were living in the territory before he arrived, but it does not speak of a town. It seems likely that there was already a settlement there, and the date of origin applies more specifically to the dynasty and its claim to power.

15. Bazin 1975; see also Bazin 1982 and Roberts 1980.

16. Except, perhaps, by Tayiru Banbera; see Conrad 1990.

17. See Courlander and Sako 1982; Frobenius 1925.

18. See C. Monteil 1977, pp. 99–101.

19. Bazin 1975, p. 174.

20. Bazin 1975, pp. 140–41, n. 10. "Not necessarily rich and powerful" may underline an opposition with the image of the Diarra, whose *devise* includes the line *Diarra banna ni khaya*, translated as "Rich and powerful Diarra." See the discussion of this *devise* in chapter 1.

21. I am thinking of the way in which some Maninka griots will associate Sumanguru with the Bamana as well as the way in which the Bamana epics echo and transform motifs and incidents from the Sunjata tradition.

22. Banbera's names are spelled variously: Tairu, Tahirou, Tayirou, Tayiru, Bambera, Bembera, Banbera. In this discussion I follow Conrad's usage.

23. Kamara wrote an Arabic history of Segou ca. 1900 (Kamara 1978); Gaoussou Diarra was a family member interviewed extensively by Serge Sauvageot, and Kore Tammoura was the principal informant behind Charles Monteil's account of the kingdom.

24. C. Meillassoux 1963, p. 220 (my translation).

25. The best illustration is the material in Frobenius 1921.

26. See Conrad 1990, p. 10.

27. Conrad 1990, p. 252, ll. 5611–12, 5616–20.

28. Conrad 1990, p. 136, ll. 2226–32.

29. Conrad 1990, p. 214, ll. 4285–86.

30. Dumestre 1979, p. 33.

31. Dumestre 1979, pp. 76–77, ll. 180ff.

32. Conrad 1990, pp. 9–11; Dumestre 1979, p. 41.

33. In Conrad 1990, Dumestre 1979, and Kesteloot 1978a, 1978b.

34. In Kesteloot 1993.

35. Kesteloot 1978b.

36. Belcher 1995. The creation myths are given in Dieterlen 1951 and 1955.

37. It shows strong echoes of the Aarne-Thompson tale-type 550.

38. Conrad 1990, pp. 80–99.

39. C. Monteil 1977, pp. 39–44.

40. This is the conventional Mande belief in badenya: behind every great man is a great mother; it also calls to mind Sunjata. See chapter 5.

41. Conrad 1990, p. 97; Kesteloot 1978b, p. 681.

42. Conrad 1990, pp. 13–20.

43. Conrad 1990, p. 117. The motif is known as the "Ring of Polycrates."

44. Bazin 1979 offers a complex analysis of this question.

45. See Frobenius 1925, pp. 344–51; C. Monteil 1977, pp. 39–40. Tauxier 1942, p. 72, repeats Monteil's story.

46. In "Douga of Kore," in Kesteloot 1993, vol. 1, pp. 104–22. See also Bazin 1979.

47. As noted above, Da offers a feast for the tonjonw and inebriates them before asking for their help. See Dumestre 1979, pp. 222ff; Kesteloot 1993, vol. 1, p. 106 (given in summary).

48. Retold from the version of Seydou Drame, in Kesteloot 1993, vol. 1, pp. 95–123.

49. Conrad 1990, pp. 248–55. Banbera calls the king Dese or Desse, which is the more usual form of the name.

50. Park 1907, pp. 79–81. See Conrad 1990, p. 248.

51. This story is given by Sissoko Kabine as *La prise de Dionkoloni* (Dumestre and Kesteloot 1975) and appears in Frobenius 1921 as two separate stories. Meillassoux and Sylla 1978 give a historical analysis of the original Soninke tradition.

52. Lanrezac (1907b) published a version of this song that for some reason is reproduced in the collected poetry of Léopold Sédar Senghor. Cissé 1994 (pp. 305–57) offers a small collection of more recent versions as well as a discussion connecting these West African war vultures with ancient Egypt.

53. Kesteloot 1993, vol. 2, p. 131; performed by Gorke.

54. Conrad 1990, p. 161; see Kesteloot 1993, vol. 2, p. 4, n. 3, for other examples.

55. Kesteloot 1993, vol. 1, pp. 121–23; see also the incidents involving Nwenyekoro in Conrad 1990, pp. 245–59.

56. C. Monteil 1977, p. 98.

57. Conrad 1990, pp. 268ff. Bilissi also appears as a figure in puppet masquerades (Robert Newton, personal communication; and Arnoldi 1995, p. 83).

58. Conrad 1990, p. 271, ll. 6137–39.

59. Kesteloot 1993, vol. 2, p. 6; Conrad 1990, p. 270.

60. C. Monteil 1905, pp. 82–83.

Chapter 7

1. Their origins, history, habits, and language are much discussed. See Adebayo 1991; Diallo 1972; Faliu 1980; Hama 1968; V. Monteil 1963; Sarr 1978; Tauxier 1937. For ethnography, see the works of Marguerite Dupire and references in Seydou 1973.

2. The basic source for the dina of Massina is Bâ and Daget 1962, reiterated by Sanankoua 1990. For al-Hajj Umar Tall, see Robinson 1985; Kane and Robinson 1984; Hanson and Robinson 1991.

3. See Arnott 1985 and Seydou 1973 and 1977a for general descriptions and bibliography of Fula literature.

4. See Sow 1966, 1968 for examples of poetry and prose going back to the eighteenth century from the Futa Jallon.

5. See Niane 1972 and Boulègue 1987 for discussions of these migrations.

6. See *Tradition historique peul* and the accounts given by Wa Kamissoko in Cissé and Kamissoko 1991, pp. 153–200.

7. See Seydou 1991 for a collection.

8. See Bâ and Dieterlen 1961; Bâ and Kesteloot 1969 (an English translation by Daniel Whitman is available); Bâ et al. 1974; Bâ 1984; Ndongo 1986. Le Pichon and Baldé (1990) provides an ethnographic context for this genre and lifestyle.

9. See Seydou 1972, pp. 18ff. for a discussion of terms and categories.

10. See Belcher in Austen forthcoming for an exploration of this topic.

11. Seydou 1976, pp. 51, 61, 124.

12. See Barth, *Travels*, vol. 2, pp. 182ff.

13. Retold from Sambourou Parita in Seydou 1976, pp. 201–25.

14. Retold from the version of Boûbacar Tinguidji in Seydou 1976, pp. 265–315.

15. Bâ and Daget 1962, pp. 29–31.

16. Frobenius 1921, pp. 195–97.

17. Retold from Hamma Diam Bouraima in Seydou 1976, pp. 41–131. An excerpted English translation is available in Johnson, Hale, Belcher 1997.

18. See Seydou 1992 for a detailed study.

19. See Belcher 1994b for a discussion of some of this material.

20. See the works of Jean-Marie Gibbal (1982, 1984, 1994) or Paul Stoller (1978, 1989; Stoller et al. 1987) for a description of the spirit cults of this region.

21. Seydou 1972 offers the best recent variants and reprints some of the older ones. For a listing, see the table of epics in the appendix.

22. Retold from the versions of Boûbacar Tinguidji in Seydou 1972 and Maabal Samburu in Bâ and Kesteloot 1969 (reprinted in Kesteloot 1993, vol. 2; a partial English translation is available in Johnson, Hale, Belcher 1997).

23. See Belcher in Austen forthcoming for a discussion of this problem.

24. A captive *(nyeenyo)* and a singer *(maabo* or *gawlo)* are of different social categories, however, and no Fula would consider them equivalent. I owe my sense of this distinction to Christiane Seydou (personal communication).

25. The version of Samba Gawlo Futanke, in Seydou 1972, pp. 262–67. This version was collected around 1928 by Gilbert Vieillard. The same performer gave Vieillard a second version as well. See Vieillard n.d.

26. See Ousmane Bâ 1988.

27. Retold from the version of Boûbacar Tinguidji in Seydou 1972, and Maabal Samburu. An English translation of Tinguidji's version is available in Johnson, Hale, Belcher 1997.

28. See Ngaïde 1981 and various narratives in Meyer 1991.

29. See Soh 1913 and the works of C. Kamara 1970, 1975, 1978.

30. See Raffenel 1856, vol. 2; Ecquilbeq 1913–1916, 1974; Frobenius 1921, pp. 233–46; de Zeltner 1913, pp. 151–57.

31. Ly 1991 and Correra 1992. See also the extracts published by Sar 1980a, 1980b.

32. See, for instance, Hassan and Shuaibu 1952. The story is treated in Frobenius 1913 and in Belcher 1994a.

33. Told by Kalidou Ba in Meyer 1991, pp. 99–118.

34. Conrad, unpublished ms. I am grateful that he has shared these materials with me.

35. See Tyam 1935. His name is occasionally spelled Cam in modern orthography, but it seems less confusing to use the published form.

Chapter 8

1. Rouch 1953, p. 200.

2. Olivier de Sardan's compilation of oral testimony, *Quand nos pères étaient captifs* (1976) recalls that era vividly.

3. Both have been published in bilingual editions edited by O. Houdas ca. 1913 and since reprinted by Maisonneuve (Houdas 1966). New editions are long overdue.

4. See Houdas 1966.

5. See Hama n.d., 1964.

6. For example, by Olivier de Sardan (1984, p. 16).

7. See Hale 1990, 1996.

8. See Laya n.d., 1969; Zouber 1983.

9. See Mounkaila 1989.

10. Olivier de Sardan 1976. This book unfortunately patches the testimony together, although sources are identified in notes.

11. Tandina 1983–1984. An excerpt from the epic of Issa Korombe is now available in Johnson, Hale, Belcher 1997.

12. Watta 1985, pp. 186–234, presented in bilingual format on facing pages.

13. Watta 1993.

14. Probably Sonni Ali, founder of the Songhay empire and the recognized ancestor of the Sohance sorcerers of modern Niger (Rouch 1953, p. 188). For the Sohance, see Rouch 1989 and the works of Paul Stoller.

15. See Zouber 1983, pp. 25ff.; Laya 1970, pp. 62–77; Laya [1970], pp. 33ff.; Rouch 1953.

16. Rouch's cinematography is the topic of Paul Stoller's study, *The Cinematic Griot*. Manthia Diawara has added a film "interrogating" the ethnographer, Rouch in reverse.

17. De Moraes Farias in Austen forthcoming.

18. Rouch 1989, pp. 45–93; Gibbal 1982, 1994.

19. Hale 1990, 1996.

20. Testimony of Hamadoune Morikoyra in Zouber 1983, pp. 27–30, 35–36; Laya 1970, pp. 62–77.

21. Hale 1990, pp. 123–24.

22. Retold from the version of Nouhou Malio.

23. For example, in the detail of the preparations for the trans-Saharan expedition, Hale 1990, pp. 253ff.

24. Rouch 1953, pp. 221–22; Prost 1956.

25. This incident matches a Gambian story about Kelefa Sane almost exactly, as will be seen below. The connection is most probably through the Fula.

26. Use of the term *geste* rather than *épopée* puts the accent on the historical rather than the poetic qualities of the texts.

27. The relations appear to have been close in an earlier time. Desplagnes links the Sorko and the Dogon, whom he calls by a Fula name, *Habbe* (sing., *Kado*), meaning "unbeliever." For the Dogon, see Marcel Griaule's *Conversations with Ogotemmeli* (see Griaule 1948b), a problematic book.

28. See Laya [1970], pp. 10–29.

29. See Tandina 1983–1984. Tandina's thesis should be available in microform through the O.C.L.C.

30. His version of the "Three Fears" incidents seems somewhat better organized than that of Hamma Diam Bouraima.

31. The term "homeostasizing" is from Goody and Watt 1968.

32. Wright 1972, 1977, 1978, 1979, 1980, 1987, 1991.

33. Wright 1979, 1980.

34. Hamlyn 1931; Sonko-Godwin 1986, 1988. Both her books have gone through successive editions.

35. The performance of Bamba Suso, in Innes 1974.

36. Innes 1976, 1978; Wright 1979, 1980. The proceedings of the conference on Gabou were reported in a special issue of *Éthiopiques* (no. 28, July 1981). I am indebted to Lilyan Kesteloot for sharing materials from the conference on Gabou with me.

37. By *Soninke*, I am referring to the language-group tracing its origin to Wagadu. In the Gambia the word has acquired the religious connotation of "pagan," independent of its linguistic or ethnic reference, in somewhat the same way the term Bambara was used in Mali.

38. Given in Innes 1976; see also Roche 1970.

39. See Innes 1976, pp. 181–254.

40. Innes 1978, p. 6. See also Wright 1979, pp. 95–96.

41. Innes 1978; Wright 1979, pp. 97–107.

42. Innes 1976, pp. 130–31.

43. See Wright 1979, pp. 30–37.

44. In the origin of the Kamara and Saabali, told by Bamba Suso in his version of Kelefa Sane, Innes 1978, pp. 52–53.

45. In Bamba Suso's account of Janke Wali and Ba Ansu Jebate's account of Musa Molo, Innes 1976, pp. 80–81, 184–85. For the story of Malik Sy, see Saki N'Diaye 1971 and Curtin 1975.

46. Boulègue 1987, Barry 1985, I. Bathily 1969, A. Bathily 1989, Becker 1985, Bomba 1977, Charles 1977, Suret-Canale 1988, V. Monteil 1966. All offer focused studies.

47. See Charry 1992, pp. 57ff.

48. Michael Coolen describes the music of their instrument, the *xalam.* Isabelle Leymarie has written on the sociology of the group. Emil Magel and Edris Makward provide case studies of individuals, and George Joseph has published the transcription and translation of a praise song. Given the male-oriented documentary record, it seems unusual that this song is by one woman in praise of another, a princess. It seems less atypical that when Joseph sought to interview the performer he was referred to her husband.

49. See, e.g., Irvine 1978.

50. Diakhaté 1987–1988, which tells of a Moor bandit; Dioum 1977–1978, which gives an episode from the cycle of Kajoor; Cheikh Ndiaye offers a rare example of Serer performance.

51. *Ngiwa gaynaako,* "The elephant has no shepherd": B. Dieng 1993, p. 139.

52. B. Dieng 1993, pp. 178–79, 180–81. Incidentally, the husband in this case is the man described above who "parodies" Sunjata by saying he would prefer to be a hunter in Kajoor than king in Saloum: two possible echoes of the Sunjata tradition in the same piece may be more than coincidence.

53. This motif is also encountered in a Gambian version of the epic of Sunjata (Dembo Kanute in Innes 1974).

54. Dieng 1993, pp. 80–127, 214–323; Dioum 1977–1978.

55. Le Brasseur is reproduced in Boulègue 1987, pp. 25–26; Diop 1993.

56. Bomba 1977.

57. Kesteloot, Dieng, and Sall 1983.

Chapter 9

1. See above, chapters 1, 3, and 5, for discussion of the various elements of the Mande performance style.

2. A skeptic might suggest that this has always been the case—that no successor ever completely controlled the information passed from the previous generation but instead transformed and added to it. This operation would correspond to the homeostatic function described in Goody and Watt 1968. The answer, I believe, is that in past years the position of master-griot, the *belen-tigi,* would have attracted more candidates as a position of desirable status. But now many younger griots would consider that course of training to be a path toward a dead end.

3. See Alan Dundes's bibliographic remarks in his introduction to Lord Raglan's essay on the hero in *The Study of Folklore* (Englewood Cliffs: Prentice Hall, 1965, pp. 142–44).

4. Examples might include the fetuses who leave the womb (in Lianja or Sunjata) or older children who paralyze their villages at critical moments (Mwindo, Sunjata, Samba Gueladio, Mareñ Jagu), particularly at circumcision.

5. A link with trickster figures in particular would seem promising. See, e.g., Austen 1986.

6. So also is the way in which the performance modes of some epics challenge the generic categories of the Western literary tradition; see the discussion of the *Ozidi Saga* in chapter 2.

REFERENCES

On the list of references, items marked with an asterisk (*) represent primary sources (i.e., they contain, in some form, material from the oral tradition), whether or not they appear in the tabulation given in the appendix.

Aarne, Antti, and Stith Thompson. 1987. *The Types of the Folktale.* Helsinki: Academia Scientiarum Fennica.

*Abu-Manga, Al-Amin. 1985. *Baajankaro: A Fulani Epic from Sudan.* Marburg/Lahn: D. Reimer. Africana Marburgensia Sonderheft 9.

*Adam, M. G. 1904. *Légendes historiques du pays de Nioro (Sahel).* Paris: Augustin Challamel.

Adandé, Alexandre. 1962. *Les récades des rois du Dahomey.* Dakar: IFAN.

Adebayo, A. G. 1991. "Of Man and Cattle: A Reconsideration of the Traditions of Origin of Pastoral Fulani of Nigeria." *History in Africa* 18:1–21.

Ajuwon, Bade. 1982. *Funeral Dirges of Yoruba Hunters.* New York: NOK.

Alexandre, Pierre. 1974. "Introduction to a Fang Oral Art Genre: Gabon and Cameroon Mvet." *Bulletin of the School of Oriental and African Studies* 37:1–7.

*Allaye, Beidari. 1984. *Poullo Djom Ere et le Touareg.* Ed. and trans. Bocar Cisse and Al-mamy Maliki Yattara. Niamey: CELHTO/OUA.

Amselle, Jean-Loup. 1985. "Qu'est-ce qu'un *kafo* ou *jamana*? Le cas du Gwanan ou les faux archaïsmes de l'histoire africaine." *Cahiers de l'ORSTOM,* Sciences Humaines series, 21:43–56.

———. 1987. "L'ethnicité comme volonté et comme représentation: A propos des Peul du Wasolon." *Annales ESC* (March–April):465–89.

———. 1988. "Un état contre l'état: Le Keleyadugu." *Cahiers d'Etudes Africaines* 28:463–83.

———. 1990. *Logiques métisses: Anthropologie de l'identité en Afrique et ailleurs.* Paris: Editions Payot.

*Amselle, Jean-Loup, Zumana Dunbya, Amadu Kuyate, and Mohamed Tabure. 1979. "Littérature orale et idéologie: La geste des Jakite Sabashi du Ganan." *Cahiers d'Etudes Africaines* 19:381–433.

Amselle, Jean-Loup, and Elikia M'Bokolo, eds. 1985. *Au coeur de l'ethnie: Ethnies, tribalisme et état en afrique.* Paris: La Découverte.

Andrzejewski, B. W., S. Pilaszewicz, and W. Tyloch, eds. 1985. *Literatures in African Languages: Theoretical Issues and Sample Surveys.* Warsaw: Wiedza Powszechna; Cambridge: Cambridge University Press.

Ardouin, Claude Daniel. 1988. "Une formation politique précoloniale du Sahel occidental malien: Le Baakhunu à l'époque des Kaagoro." *Cahiers d'Etudes Africaines* 28.3–4:443–61.

*Arnaud, Robert. 1912. "La singulière légendes des Soninkés: Traditions orales sur le royaume de Koumbi." In *L'Islam et la politique musulmane en Afrique occidentale française.* Paris: Comité de l'Afrique Française. Pp. 156–84.

Arnoldi, Mary Jo. 1986. "Puppet Theatre: Form and Ideology in Bamana Performances." *Empirical Studies of the Arts* 4.2:131–50.

——. 1995. *Playing with Time: Art and Performance in Central Mali.* Bloomington: Indiana University Press.

Arnott, D. W. 1985. "Literature in Fula." In Andrzejewski, Pilaszewicz, and Tyloch 1985. Pp. 49–96.

Austen, Ralph. 1986. "Social and Historical Analysis of African Trickster Tales: Some Preliminary Reflections." *Plantation Society* 2:135–48.

——. 1990. "Africans Speak, Colonialism Writes: The Transcription and Translation of Oral Literature before World War II." Boston: Boston University African Humanities Program Discussion Papers.

——. 1992. "Tradition, Invention, and History: The Case of the Ngongo (Cameroon)." *Cahiers d'Etudes Africaines* 32.2:285–309.

——. 1993. "'Africanist' Historiography and Its Critics: Can There Be an Autonomous African History?" In *African Historiography: Essays in Honor of Jacob Ajayi,* ed. Toyin Falola. Essex: Longman. Pp. 203–17.

——. 1995. *The Elusive Epic: Performance, Text and History in the Oral Narrative of Jeki La Njambé (Cameroon Coast).* African Studies Association Press.

——, ed. Forthcoming. *In Search of Sunjata: The Mande Oral Epic as History, Literature, and Performance.* Bloomington: Indiana University Press.

*Awona, Stanislas. 1965. "La guerre de Akoma Mba contre Abo Mama (épopée du mvet)." *Abbia* 9/10:180–213; 12/13:109–209 (1966).

Azuonye, Chukwuma. 1983. "Stability and Change in the Performances of Ohafia Igbo Singers of Tales." *Research in African Literatures* 14.3:332–80.

——. 1990. "The Performances of Kaalu Igirigiri, an Ohafia Igbo Singer of Tales." *Research in African Literatures* 21.3:17–50. Also in Okpewho 1990c. Pp. 42–79.

——. 1994. "Oral Literary Criticism and the Performance of the Igbo Epic." *Oral Tradition* 9:136–61.

Ba, Adame Konare. 1983. *Sunjata: Le fondateur de l'empire du Mali.* Libreville: Lion.

——. 1987. *L'épopée de Segu.* Paris: Pierre-Marcel Favre.

*Bâ, Amadou Hampaté. 1959. "Bambara Knights." *Black Orpheus* 6:5–12.

——. 1966. "Des Foulbé du Mali et de leur Culture." *Abbia* 14/15:23–54. English translation pp. 55–88.

*——. 1969. "Une épopée peule—Silamaka." *L'Homme* 8:1–36. Reprinted in Kesteloot 1972, vol. 4, and Kesteloot 1993, vol. 2.

——. [1970?]. *Koukamonzon.* Niamey: Centre National de Recherche en Sciences Humaines.

*——. 1984. *Njeddo Dewal, la mère de la calamité.* Dakar: Nouvelles Editions Africaines.

Bâ, Amadou Hampaté, and J. Daget. 1955. "Note sur les chasses rituelles Bozo." *Journal de la Société des Africanistes* 25:89–97.

——. 1962. *L'empire peul du Macina.* Paris and The Hague: Mouton.

*Bâ, Amadou Hampaté, and Germaine Dieterlen. 1961. *Koumen—Texte initiatique Peul.* Paris: Mouton.

Bâ, Amadou Hampaté, and Lilyan Kesteloot. 1966a. "Les épopées de l'ouest africain." *Abbia* 14/15:165–69.

*——. 1966b. "Da Monzon et Karta Thiema." *Abbia* 14/15:179–206.

*——. 1969. *Kaïdara, récit initiatique peul*. Paris: Julliard. English translation by Daniel Whitman. *Kaidara*. Washington, DC: Three Continents Press, 1988.

*Bâ, Amadou Hampaté, et al. 1974. *L'éclat de la grande étoile, suivi du Bain rituel*. Classiques Africains. Paris: Armand Colin.

Ba, Oumar. 1971. "Les Peuls Bouméyâbé et Rangâbé (Sénégal et Mauritanie)." *Bulletin de l'IFAN*, Series B, 33:747–65.

——. 1975. "Notice sur les Peuls du Tôro (Sénégal et Mauritanie)." *Bulletin de l'IFAN*, Series B, 37:457–62.

*Bâ, Ousmane. 1988. *Silamaka Fara Dikko: ein westafrikanisches Epos in den Bambara-Versionen von Mamadou Kida und Almami Bah (Mali)*. Berlin: Dietrich Reimer Verlag.

Babalola, S. A. 1966. *The Content and Form of Yoruba Ijala*. Oxford: Clarendon Press.

*Banbera, Tayiru [Tairou Bembera]. 1978. "L'histoire de Biton Koulibaly." Transcribed by Mamadou Boidié Diarra, translated by Lilyan Kesteloot. *Bulletin de l'IFAN*, Series B, 40:613–81.

Barber, Karin. 1984. "Yoruba *Oriki* and Deconstructive Criticism." *Research in African Literatures* 15:497–518.

——. 1991. *I Could Speak Until Tomorrow: Oriki, Women, and the Past in a Yoruba Town*. Washington, DC: Smithsonian Institution Press.

Barber, Karin, and Paolo F. de Moraes Farias. 1989. *Discourse and Its Disguises: The Interpretation of African Oral Texts*. Birmingham: Center of West African Studies.

Barry, Boubacar. 1985. *Le royaume du Waalo: Le Sénégal avant la conquête*. Paris: Karthala.

Barth, Heinrich. 1965. *Travels and Discoveries in North and Central Africa*. 3 vols. London: Frank Cass.

Bathily, Abdoulaye. 1975. "A Discussion of the Traditions of Wagadu with Some Reference to Ancient Ghana." *Bulletin de l'IFAN*, Series B, 37:1–94.

——. 1989. *Les portes de l'or: Le royaume de Galam (Sénégal) de l'ère musulmane au temps des négriers*. Paris: L'Harmattan.

Bathily, Ibrahima Diaman. 1969. "Notices socio-historiques sur l'ancien royaume Soninké de Gadiaga." Ed. Abdoulaye Bathily. *Bulletin de l'IFAN*, Series B, 31:31–105.

Bazin, Jean. 1970. "Recherches sur les formations socio-politiques anciennes en pays bambara." *Etudes Maliennes* 1:29–40.

——. 1975. "Guerre et servitude à Ségou." In Meillassoux 1975. Pp. 135–81.

——. 1979. "La production d'un recit historique." *Cahiers d'Etudes Africaines* 19:435–83.

——. 1982. "Etat guerrier et guerres d'Etat." In Bazin and Terray 1982. Pp. 321–74.

——. 1985. "A chacun son Bambara." In *Au coeur de l'ethnie*, ed. J.-L. Amselle and E. M'bokolo. Paris: La Découverte. Pp. 87–127.

——. 1988. "Princes désarmés, corps dangereux. Les 'rois-femmes' de la région de Segu." *Cahiers d'Etudes Africaines* 28:375–441.

Bazin, Jean, and Emmanuel Terray, eds. 1982. *Guerres de lignages et guerres d'Etats en Afrique*. Paris: Editions des Archives Contemporaines.

Becker, Charles. 1985. "Histoire de la Sénégambie du XVe. and XVIIIe. siècle: Un bilan." *Cahiers d'Etudes Africaines* 25.2:213–42.

*Bekombo-Priso, Manga, ed. 1993. *Défis et prodiges: La fantastique histoire de Djèki-la-Njambé*. Paris: Les Classiques Africains.

Belcher, Stephen. 1985. "Stability and Change: Praise-Poetry and Narrative Traditions in the Epics of Mali." Ph.D. diss., Brown University.

———. 1991. "Sunjata, Sumanguru, and Mothers." Paper presented at the African Studies Association Annual Meeting, St. Louis, Mo.

———. 1994a. "Constructed Heroes: Samba Gueladio Diegui." *Research in African Literatures* 25.1:75–92.

———. 1994b. "The Framed Tale and the Oral Tradition: A Reconsideration." *Fabula: Journal of Folktale Studies* 35:1–19.

———. 1995a. "Of Birds and Millet: Problems in African Mythology." *Yearbook of Comparative and General Literature* 43:52–66.

———. 1995b. "Cross-Dressing and Other Switches: Gender in Hunters' Epics." Paper presented at the African Studies Association Annual Meeting, Orlando, Fla.

———. 1988. "Heroes at the Borderline: Bamana and Fulbe Traditions in West Africa." *Research in African Literatures* 29(1995):43–65.

———. Forthcoming. "*Sinimogo*, the Man for Tomorrow." In Austen forthcoming.

Belvaude, Catherine. 1989. *Ouverture sur la littérature en Mauritaine*. Paris: L'Harmattan.

Bérenger-Féraud, L. J.-B. 1879. *Les peuplades de la Sénégambie*. Paris: Leroux. Kraus Reprint 1973.

*———. 1885. *Recueil de contes populaires de la Sénégambie*. Paris: E. Leroux. Kraus Reprint 1970.

Biebuyck, Daniel. 1972. "The Epic as a Genre in Congo Oral Literature." In Dorson 1972. Pp. 257–73.

———. 1978a. "The African Heroic Epic." In Oinas 1978. Pp. 336–67.

*———. 1978b. *Hero and Chief: Epic Literature from the Banyanga (Zaire Republic)*. Berkeley: University of California Press.

———. 1992. "Mwindo, a Nyanga Epic Hero, and Mubila, a Lega Epic Hero." *Cahiers de Littérature Orale* 32:39–62.

*Biebuyck, Daniel, and Kahombo C. Mateene. 1969. *The Mwindo Epic*. Berkeley: University of California Press. Paperback edition 1971.

*———. 1970. *Anthologie de la littérature orale Nyanga*. Brussels: Mémoires de l'Academie Royale des Sciences d'Outre-Mer. N. S. 36.1.

Biernaczky, Szilard. 1983. "The African Heroic Epic Exists!" *Folklore in Africa Today*. Budapest: African Research Project. Pp. 221–34. (Also in *Artes Popolares* 1 [1983].)

Bime, A. 1957. "Segou-Koro et le Biton Mamari." *Notes Africaines* 75 (July):92–95.

Bird, Charles. 1970. "The Development of Mandekan (Manding): A Study of the Role of Extra-Linguistic Factors in Linguistic Change." In *Language and History in Africa*, ed. D. Dalby. London: Africana. Pp. 146–59.

———. 1971. "Oral Art in the Mande." In Hodge 1971. Pp. 15–25.

———. 1972a. "Aspects of Prosody in West African Poetry." In *Current Trends in Stylistics,* ed. B. B. Kachru and H. Stahlke. Edmonton and Champaign: Linguistic Research Inc. Pp. 207–15.

———. 1972b. "Heroic Songs of the Mande Hunters." In Dorson 1972. Pp. 275–93.

———. 1976. "Poetry in the Mande: Its Form and Meaning." *Poetics* 5:89–100.

———. 1977. Review of Gordon Innes, *Sunjata: Three Mandinka Versions. Research in African Literatures* 8:353–69.

*———, ed. and trans. 1972c. "Bambara Oral Prose and Verse Narratives." In Dorson 1972. Pp. 441–77.

Bird, Charles, and Martha Kendall. 1980. "The Mande Hero: Text and Context." In *Explorations in African Systems of Thought,* ed. Ivan Karp and Charles Bird. Bloomington: Indiana University Press. Pp. 14–26.

Bird, Charles, and Kalilou Tera. 1995. "Etymologies of *Nyamakala.*" In Conrad and Frank 1995. Pp. 27–35.

*Boelaert, E. 1949. *Nsong'a Lianja: L'épopée nationale des Nkundo.* Antwerp: De Sikkel. Kraus Reprint 1973.

———. 1962. "La Procession de Lianja." *Aequatoria* 25:1–9.

Bohannan, Laura. 1952. "A Genealogical Charter." *Africa* 22:301–15.

Bomba, Victoria. 1977. "Traditions about Ndiadiane Ndiaye, First *Buurba* Djolof." *Bulletin de l'IFAN,* Series B, 39:1–35.

Boulègue, Jean. 1987. *Le grand Jolof (XIIIe–XVIe siècle).* Paris: Editions Façades/Diffusion Karthala.

Boyer, G. 1953. *Un peuple de l'ouest soudanais: Les Diawara.* Dakar: IFAN. Mémoires No. 29.

Boyer, Pascal. 1980. "Les figures du savoir initiatique." *Journal des Africanistes* 50.2:31–57.

———. 1982. "Récit épique et tradition." *L'Homme* 22.2:5–34.

———. 1988. *Barricades mystérieuses et pièges à pensée: Introduction à l'analyse des épopées fang.* Paris: Société d'Ethnologie.

———. 1990. *Tradition as Truth and Communication: A Cognitive Description of Traditional Discourse.* Cambridge: Cambridge University Press, 1990.

Brett-Smith, Sarah. 1982. "Symbolic Blood: Cloths for Excised Women." *Res: Anthropology and Aesthetics* 3:15–31.

———. 1983. "The Poisonous Child." *Res: Anthropology and Aesthetics* 6:47–64.

———. 1984. "Speech Made Visible: The Irregular as a System of Meaning." *Empirical Studies of the Arts* 2:127–47.

———. 1987. "*Bamanankan ka gelen.* The Voice of the Bamana Is Hard." *Art Tribal* 2:3–15. Geneva: Musée Barbier Mueller.

———. 1994. *The Making of Bamana Sculpture: Creativity and Gender.* Cambridge: Cambridge University Press.

———. 1996. *The Artfulness of M'Fa Jigi: An Interview with Nyamaton Diarra.* Madison: University of Wisconsin African Studies Program.

Brière, Eloise. 1993. *Le roman camerounais et ses discours.* Paris: Editions Nouvelles du Sud.

Bühnen, Stephen. 1994. "In Quest of Susu." *History in Africa* 21: 1–47.

Bulman, Stephen. 1989. "The Buffalo-Woman Tale: Political Imperatives and Narrative Constraints in the Sunjata Epic." In Barber and de Moraes Farias 1989. Pp. 171–88.

——. 1990. *Interpreting Sunjata: A Comparative Analysis and Exegesis of the Malinke Epic.* Ph.D. diss., University of Birmingham.

——. 1997. "A Checklist of Published Versions of the Sunjata Epic." *History in Africa* 24:71–94.

——. Forthcoming. "Sunjata as Written Literature: The Role of the Literary Mediator in the Dissemination of the Epic." In Austen forthcoming.

Burkhalter, Sheryl. 1992. "Listening for Silences in Almoravid History: Another Reading of 'The Conquest That Never Was.'" *History in Africa* 19:103–31.

*Camara, Seydou. 1974. *Kambili.* Ed. and trans. Charles Bird, Bourama Soumaoro, Gerald Cashion, and Mamadou Kante. Bloomington: Indiana University Linguistics Club.

*——. 1976. *Seyidu Kamara ka Donkiliw: Kambili.* Ed. Bourama Soumaoro, Charles Bird, Gerald Cashion, and Mamadou Kante. Bloomington: African Studies Center.

Camara, Sory. 1992. *Gens de la Parole.* Paris: Karthala (1st ed., Mouton, 1975).

*Cashion, Gerald. 1984. "Hunters of the Mande: A Behavioral Code and Worldview Derived from the Study of Their Folklore." 2 vols. Ph.D. diss., Indiana University.

Charles, Eunice A. 1977. *Pre-Colonial Senegal: The Jolof Kingdom 1800–1890.* Boston: Boston University African Studies Center.

Charry, Eric S. 1992. "Musical Thought, History, and Practice among the Mande of West Africa." Ph.D. diss., Princeton University.

Chatwin, Bruce. 1987. *The Songlines.* New York: Viking.

Cisse, Diango. 1970. *Structures des Malinké de Kita.* Bamako: Editions Populaires.

*Cisse, Diango, and Massa Makan Diabaté [Diabété]. 1970. *La dispersion des Mandeka.* Bamako: Editions Populaires.

Cissé, Youssouf Tata. 1964. "Notes sur les sociétés de chasseurs malinké." *Journal de la Société des Africanistes* 34:175–226.

*——. 1994. *La confrérie des chasseurs Malinké et Bambara: Mythes, rites et récits initiatiques.* Paris: Editions Nouvelles du Sud/Arsan.

*Cissé, Youssouf Tata, and Wa Kamissoko. 1988. *La grande geste du Mali.* Paris: Karthala/Arsan.

*——. 1991. *Soundjata, la gloire du Mali.* Paris: Karthala/Arsan.

Cissoko, Sékéné-Mody, and Kaoussou Sambou. 1974. *Recueil des Traditions Orales des Mandingues de Gambie et de Casamance.* Niamey: CELHTO.

*Clark-Bekederemo, John Pepper. 1991. *The Ozidi Saga, Collected and Translated from the Oral Ijo Version of Okabou Ojobolo.* With a critical introduction by Isidore Okpewho. Washington, DC: Howard University Press.

Conrad, David C. 1981. "The Role of Oral Artists in the History of Mali." 2 vols. Ph.D. diss., School of Oriental and African Studies, University of London.

——. 1983. "Maurice Delafosse and the Pre-Sunjata *Trône du Mande.*" *Bulletin of the School of Oriental and African Studies* 46.2:335–37.

——. 1984. "Oral Sources on Links between Great States." *History in Africa* 11:35–55.

——. 1985. "Islam in the Oral Traditions of Mali: Bilali and Surakata." *Journal of African History* 26:33–49.

——. 1992. "Searching for History in the Sunjata Epic: The Case of Fakoli." *History in Africa* 19:147–200.

——. 1994. "A Town Called Dakajalan: The Sunjata Tradition and the Question of Ancient Mali's Capital." *Journal of African History* 35:355–77.

——. 1995a. "Blind Man Meets Prophet: Oral Tradition, Islam, and *Funé* Identity." In Conrad and Frank 1995. Pp. 86–132.

——. 1995b. "*Nyamakalaya.*" In Conrad and Frank 1995. Pp. 1–23.

——. Forthcoming. "Mooning Armies and Mothering Heroes: Female Power in Mande Epic Tradition." In Austen forthcoming.

*——, ed. and trans. 1989. "'Bilali of Faransekila': A West African Hunter and World War I Hero." *History in Africa* 16:41–70.

——. 1990. *A State of Intrigue: The Epic of Bamana Segu According to Tayiru Banbera.* Fontes Historiae Africanae. Oxford: Oxford University Press and the British Academy.

*——. Forthcoming. *Almami Samori and Laye Umaru: 19th Century Muslim Heroes of the Mande Epic Tradition.* Madison: University of Wisconsin African Studies Program.

*——. Forthcoming. *Epic Ancestors of the Sunjata Era: Oral Traditions from Upper Guinea.* Madison: University of Wisconsin African Studies Program.

Conrad, David, and Humphrey Fisher. 1982. "The Conquest That Never Was: Ghana and the Almoravids, 1076. I. The External Arabic Sources." *History in Africa* 9:21–59.

——. 1983. "The Conquest That Never Was: Ghana and the Almoravids, 1076. II. The Local Oral Sources." *History in Africa* 10:53–78.

Conrad, David C., and Barbara Frank, eds. 1995. *Status and Identity in West Africa: Nyamakalaw of Mande.* Bloomington: Indiana University Press.

Coolen, Michael. 1983. "The Wolof Xalam Tradition of the Senegambia." *Ethnomusicology* 27:477–98.

Cornevin, Robert. 1966. "African Epic Poems and the Living Epic." *Présence Africaine* n.s. 60:134–39.

*Correra, Issagha, ed. and trans. 1992. *Samba Guéladio: Epopée peule du Fuuta Tooro.* Dakar: Université de Dakar/IFAN. Initiations et Etudes Africaines No. 36.

Cosentino, Donald J. 1989. "Midnight Charters: Musa Wo and Mende Myths of Chaos." In *Creativity of Power: Cosmology and Action in African Societies,* ed. W. Arens and I. Karp. Washington, DC: Smithsonian Institution Press. Pp. 21–37.

*Coulibaly, Dosseh Joseph, ed. and trans. N.d. *Récits des chasseurs du Mali: Dingo Kanbili.* Paris: CILF/Edicef.

Coulibaly, Pascal Baba. 1993. "The Narrative Genre among the Bamana of Mali." *Research in African Literatures* 24.2:47–60.

Coupez, A., and Th. Kamanzi. 1962. *Récits historiques Rwanda.* Tervuren: Musée Royal de l'Afrique Centrale. Annales, Sciences Humaines, No. 43.

——. 1970. *Littérature de Cour au Rwanda.* Oxford: Clarendon Press.

Courlander, Harold. 1972. *A Treasury of African Folklore.* New York: Crown Books. Reprinted New York: Marlowe, 1996.

*——. 1978. "Three Soninke Tales." *African Arts* 12:82–88, 108.

*Courlander, Harold, and Ousmane Sako. 1982. *The Heart of the Ngoni*. New York: Crown Publishers.

Curtin, Philip. 1975. "The Uses of Oral Tradition in Senegambia: Maalik Sii and the Foundation of Bundu." *Cahiers d'Etudes Africaines* 25:189–202.

Cutter, Charles. 1967. "The Politics of Music in Mali." *African Arts* 1:38–39, 74–77.

Dalby, David. 1971. "Introduction: Distribution and Nomenclature of the Manding People and Their Language." In Hodge 1971. Pp. 1–13.

*Dantioko, Oudiary Makan, ed. 1985. *Soninkara Tarixinu: Récits historiques du pays Soninké*. Niamey: CELHTO.

*————. 1987a. *Contes et légendes Soninké*. Paris: CILF/Edicef.

*————. 1987b. *Contes Soninke*. Paris: Présence Africaine.

Darbo, Seni. 1976. *A Griot's Self-Portrait*. Banjul: Gambia Cultural Archives.

Delafosse, Maurice. 1911–1912. *Haut-Sénégal-Niger*. 3 vols. Paris: Larose.

*————. 1913. *Traditions historiques et légendaires du Soudan Occidental*. Paris: Publication du Comité de l'Afrique Française.

*————. 1959. "Histoire de la lutte entre les empires de Sosso et du Mande." *Notes Africaines* 83:76–80.

*Dérive, Marie-José, ed. and trans. 1980. "'Bamori et Kowulen': Chant de chasseurs de la région d'Odienné." In *Recueil de littérature mandingue*. Paris: ACCT. Pp. 77–109.

*————. 1982. *Bamori et Kowulen: Chant de chasseurs de la région d'Odienné*. Abidjan: Université d'Abidjan, Institut de Linguistique Appliquée.

*Desplagnes, Louis. 1907. *Le plateau central nigérien*. Paris: Emile Larose.

*Diabaté, Massa Makan. 1970a. *Janjon et autres chants populaires du Mali*. Bamako: Editions Populaires.

*————. 1970b. *Kala Jata*. Bamako: Editions Populaires.

*————. 1975. *L'aigle et l'épervier*. Paris: Jean Oswald.

*————. 1986. *Le Lion à l'arc*. Paris: Hatier.

Diagana, Ousmane. 1990. *Chants traditionels du pays Soninké*. Paris: L'Harmattan.

*Diakhaté, Adramé. 1987–1988. *Le héros brigand maure à travers deux épopées*. Mémoire de maîtrise. Université Cheikh Anta Diop.

Diallo, Thierno. 1972. "Origine et migration des Peuls avant le XIXe. siècle." *Université de Dakar: Annales de la Faculté de Lettres et Sciences Humaines* 2:121–93.

Diawara, Mamadou. 1985. "Les recherches en histoire orale menées par un autochtone, ou L'inconvénient d'être du cru." *Cahiers d'Etudes Africaines* 25:5–19.

————. 1989. "Women, Servitude and History: The Oral Historical Traditions of Women of Servile Condition in the Kingdom of Jaara." In Barber and de Moraes Farias 1989. Pp. 109–37.

————. 1990. *La graine de la parole*. Stuttgart: Franz Steiner Verlag.

————. Forthcoming. "Sunjata and the Others: The Hero and His Paradigm." In Austen forthcoming.

Diawara, Manthia. 1992. "Canonizing Soundiata in Mande Literature: Toward a Sociology of Narrative Elements." *Social Text* 10.2:154–68.

Dieng, Bassirou. 1980. "La représentation du fait politique dans les récits épiques du Kayor." *Bulletin de l'IFAN* 42:857–86.

*————, ed. 1993. *L'épopée du Kajoor*. Dakar and Paris: CAEC/Khoudia.

Dieng, Samba. 1987. "La légende d'El Hadj Omar dans la littérature africaine." *Université de Dakar: Annales de la Faculté de Lettres et Sciences Humaines* 17:27–41.

———. 1989. "L'épopée d'El Hadj Omar: Entre l'oralité et l'écriture." *Université de Dakar: Annales de la Faculté de Lettres et Sciences Humaines* 19:59–69.

Dieterlen, Germaine. 1951. *Essai sur la religion bambara.* Paris: Presses Universitaires de France.

———. 1955, 1959. "Mythe et organisation sociale au Soudan français." *Journal de la Société des Africanistes* 25 (1955): 39–76; 29 (1959): 119–38.

Dieterlen, Germaine, and Youssouf Tata Cissé. 1972. *Les fondements de la société d'initiation du Komo.* Paris and The Hague: Mouton, 1972. Cahiers de l'Homme.

*Dieterlen, Germaine, and Diarra Sylla. 1992. *L'empire de Ghana: Le Wagadou et les traditions de Yéréré.* Paris: Karthala.

Dilley, Roy. 1989. "Performance, Ambiguity and Power in Tukolor Weavers' Songs." In Barber and de Moraes Farias 1989. Pp. 138–51.

*Diop, Samba. 1993. "The Oral History and Literature of the Wolof People of Waalo." Ph.D. diss., University of California, Berkeley, 1993.

Diouf, Mohammedou. 1991. "Invention de la littérature orale." *Etudes Littéraires* 24:29–39.

*Dioum, Abdoulaye. 1977–1978. "Les exploits de Masire Isse Dieye. Mémoire de maîtrise." Thesis, University of Dakar.

Dorson, Richard, ed. 1972. *African Folklore.* New York: Doubleday.

*Doucoure, Lansana, and Mme. Martal, eds. 1970. *L'épopée de Soundiata de Tiemoko Kone.* Niamey: CELHTO.

*Drama, Kandioura, ed. 1981. "Epopée de Naling Sonko (Gabou)." Dakar: IFAN. Paper presented at the conference on Gabou. Dakar.

Drewal, Marguerite. 1991. "The State of Research on Performance in Africa." *African Studies Review* 34.3:1–35.

*Dumestre, Gerard, ed. and trans. 1979. *La geste de Ségou.* Paris: Armand Colin. Classiques Africains. Previously published at the University of Abidjan, Institut de Linguistique Appliquée, 1974. No. 48.

*Dumestre, Gerard, and Lilyan Kesteloot, eds. and trans. 1975. *La prise de Dionkoloni.* Classiques Africains. Paris: Armand Colin.

Dupire, Marguerite. 1970. *Organisation sociale des peuls.* Paris: Plon.

———. 1996. *Peuls nomades.* Paris: Karthala. First printed Paris: Institut d'Ethnologie, 1962.

*Dupuis-Yakouba, A. 1911. *Les Gow, ou chasseurs du Niger.* Paris: Ernest Leroux. Kraus Reprint 1974.

Duran, Lucy. 1995. "Jelimusow: The Superwomen of Malian Music." In Furniss and Gunner 1995. Pp. 197–207.

*Dyao, Yoro. 1912. *Légendes et coutumes sénégalaises.* Ed. Henri Gaden. Paris: Leroux.

Egomve, Elie. 1969. "La littérature orale des fang." *African Arts* 2:14–19, 77–78.

Eno-Belinga, Samuel Martin. 1978a. *Comprendre la littérature orale africaine.* Issy les Moulineaux: Les Classiques Africains (Editions St. Paul).

*———. 1978b. *L'épopée camerounaise: Mvet.* Yaounde: N.p.

———. 1978c. *Introduction à la littérature orale africaine.* Yaounde: N.p.

Enobo-Kosso, Martin. 1969. "Le nom et la personne dans l'épopée." *Abbia* 22:57–63.

Epanya-Yondo, Elolongué. 1966. "La littérature orale Douala." *Abbia* 12/13:73–108.

*——. 1976. *La place de la littérature orale en Afrique.* Paris: La Pensée Universelle.

Equilbecq, François-Victor. 1913–1916. *Essai sur la littérature merveilleuse des noirs, suivi de contes indigènes de l'ouest africain.* 3 vols. Paris: Maisonneuve et Larose.

——. 1974. *La légende de Samba Guélâdio Diégui Prince du Foûta.* Dakar-Abidjan: Nouvelles Editions Africaines.

Faberberg-Diallo, Sonja. 1995. "Milk and Honey: Developing Written Literature in Pulaar." *Yearbook of Comparative and General Literature* 43:67–83.

Faïk-Nzuji, C. 1974. *Kasala: Chant héroique luba.* Lumumbashi: Presses Universitaires du Zaire.

Faliu, Alain. 1980. "Eléments d'histoire du peuplement peul de la vallée du fleuve Sénégal." *Bulletin de l'IFAN,* Series B, 42:257–76.

Ferry, M. P. 1968. "Note sur les cérémonies septennales du Kamablō." *Journal de la Société des Africanistes* 39:183–85.

Fine, Elizabeth. 1984. *The Folklore Text: From Performance to Print.* Bloomington: Indiana University Press.

Finnegan, Ruth. 1970. *Oral Literature in Africa.* Oxford: Oxford University Press.

——. 1977. *Oral Poetry: Its Nature, Significance, and Social Context.* Cambridge: Cambridge University Press; Bloomington: Indiana University Press, 1992.

Foley, John Miles. 1988. *The Theory of Oral Composition: History and Methodology.* Bloomington: Indiana University Press.

——, ed. 1981. *Oral Traditional Literature: A Festschrift for Albert Bates Lord.* Columbus: Slavica.

Frobenius, Leo. 1913. *The Voice of Africa.* 2 vols. London: Hutchison and Co. [originally published as *Und Afrika Sprach,* 2 vols. Berlin: Deutsches Verlagshaus, 1911].

——. 1921. *Spielmannsgeschichten der Sahel. Atlantis VI.* Jena: Eugen Diederichs. Reprint Martin Sändig 1978.

——. 1924. *Dämonen des Sudan: Allerhand religiöse Verdichtungen. Atlantis VII.* Jena: Eugen Diederichs.

——. 1925. *Dichten und Denken im Sudan. Atlantis V.* Jena: Eugen Diederichs.

——. 1973. *Leo Frobenius, 1873–1973; an Anthology.* Ed. Eike Haberland. Wiesbaden: Franz Steiner Verlag.

——, ed. 1971. *African Nights: Black Erotic Folk Tales.* Trans. Peter Ross. New York: Herder and Herder.

Frobenius, Leo, and Douglas C. Fox, eds. and trans. 1983. *African Genesis.* Berkeley: Turtle Island Foundation.

Furniss, Graham, and Liz Gunner, eds. 1995. *Power, Marginality and African Oral Literature.* Cambridge: Cambridge University Press.

Fyle, C. Magbaily. 1979. *Oral Traditions of Sierra Leone.* Niamey: Centre for Linguistic and Historical Studies by Oral Tradition.

Gaden, Henri. 1913. *Le Poular: Dialecte peul du Fouta sénégalais.* Paris: E. Leroux.

——, ed. *See* Yoro Dyao; Sire-Abbas Soh; Mohammadou Tyam/De Ganay, Solange. 1941. *Les devises des Dogons.* Paris: Institut d'Ethnologie.

——. 1995. *Le sanctuaire Kama blon de Kangaba.* Paris: Editions Nouvelles du Sud.

*Geysbeek, Tim. 1994. "A Traditional History of the Konyan (15th–16th Century): Vase Camara's Epic of Musadu." *History in Africa* 21:49–85.

*———, ed. Forthcoming. *Voices from the Upper Niger Valley: Oral Sources from Guinea's Past.* Madison: University of Wisconsin African Studies Program.

Geysbeek, Tim, and Jobba Kamara. 1991. "'Two Hippos Cannot Live in One River': Zo Musa, Foningama, and the Founding of Musadu in the Oral Traditions of the Konyaka." *Liberian Studies Journal* 16:27–78.

Gibbal, Jean-Marie. 1982. *Tambours d'eau: Journal et enquête sur un culte de possession au Mali occidental.* Paris: Le Sycomore.

———. 1984. *Guérisseurs et magiciens du Sahel.* Paris: Editions Métailié.

———. 1994. *Genii of the River Niger.* Trans. Beth Raps. Chicago: University of Chicago Press.

Gleason, Judith, ed. 1994. *Leaf and Bone: African Praise Poems.* Harmondsworth: Penguin.

Glinka, Werner. 1990. *Literature in Senegal.* Berlin: Reimer Verlag.

Gomez, Michael. 1987. "Bundu in the Eighteenth Century." *International Journal of African Historical Studies* 20:61–73.

Goody, Jack. 1972. *The Myth of the Bagre.* Oxford: Oxford University Press.

———. 1977. *The Domestication of the Savage Mind.* Cambridge: Cambridge University Press.

———. 1987. *The Interface between the Written and the Oral.* Cambridge: Cambridge University Press.

———, ed. 1968. *Literacy in Traditional Societies.* Cambridge: Cambridge University Press.

Goody, Jack, and Ian Watt. 1968. "The Consequences of Literacy." In Goody 1968. Pp. 27–68.

Görög-Karady, Veronika. 1994. "Social Speech and Speech of the Imagination: Female Identity and Ambivalence in Bambara-Malinké Oral Literature." *Oral Tradition* 9.1:60–82.

Görög-Karady, Veronika, and Gerard Meyer, eds. and trans. 1985. *Contes bambara: Mali et Sénégal oriental.* Paris: CILF/Edicef.

Görög, Veronika, Diana Rey-Hulman, Suzanne Platiel, and Christiane Seydou. 1980. *Histoires d'enfants terribles.* Paris: G.-P. Maisonneuve et Larose.

Gravrand, Henri. 1983. *La civilisation Sereer: Cosaan.* Dakar: Nouvelles Editions Africaines.

———. 1990. *La civilisation Sereer: Pangool.* Dakar: Nouvelles Editions Africaines.

Greene, Kathryn. 1991. "'Mande Kaba,' the Capital of Mali: A Recent Invention?" *History in Africa* 18:127–35.

Griaule, Marcel. 1948a. "L'arche du monde chez les populations nigériennes." *Journal de la Société des Africanistes* 18:117–26.

———. 1948b. *Dieu d'eau.* Paris: Fayard. English translation, *Conversations with Ogotemmeli.* London: International African Institute, 1965.

———. 1965. *Conversations with Ogotemmeli.* London: International African Institute/ Oxford University Press.

Guèye, Tène-Youssouf. N.d. *Aspects de la littérature pulaar en Afrique Occidentale.* Nouakchott: N.p.

Guillot, René. 1950. *La brousse et la bête.* Paris: Librairie Delagrave.

Hair, P. E. H. 1994. "The Early Sources on Guinea." *History in Africa* 21:87–126.

Hale, Thomas. 1982. "Islam and the Griots in West Africa: Bridging the Gap between Two Traditions." *Africana Journal* 13:84–90.

———. 1990. *Scribe, Griot, and Novelist.* Gainesville, University of Florida Press.

———. 1991. "Can a Single Foot Follow Two Paths? Islamic and Songhay Belief Systems." In *Faces of Islam in African Literature,* ed. K. Harrow. Portsmouth: Heinemann. Pp. 131–40.

*———, ed. 1996. *The Epic of Askia Mohammed.* Bloomington: Indiana University Press.

Hama, Boubou. N.d. *L'histoire traditionelle d'un peuple: les Zarma-Songhay.* [Niamey?].

———. 1964. *Histoire des Songhay.* Paris: Librairie des Cinq Continents.

———. 1968. *Contribution à la connaissance de l'histoire des Peul.* Paris: Présence Africaine. Publication de la République du Niger.

———. 1972. *Contes et légendes du Niger.* 2 vols. Paris: Présence Africaine.

Hamlyn, W. T. 1931. *A Short History of the Gambia.* Bathurst [Banjul]: J. M. Lawani Government Printers.

Hanson, John H. 1996. *Migration, Jihad, and Muslim Authority in West Africa.* Bloomington: Indiana University Press.

Hanson, John H., and David Robinson. 1991. *After the Jihad: The Reign of Ahmad al-Kabir in the Western Sudan.* East Lansing: Michigan State University Press. African Historical Sources No. 2.

Hargreaves, John D. 1966. "The Tokolor Empire of Ségou and Its Relations with the French." In *Boston University Papers on Africa.* Vol. 2: *African History.* Ed. Jeffrey Butler. Boston: Boston University Press. Pp. 125–45.

*Haring, Lee, ed. 1994. *Ibonia: An Epic of Madagascar.* Lewisburg: Bucknell University Press.

Harris, Laura Arntson. 1992. "The Play of Ambiguity in Praise-Song Performance: A Definition of the Genre through an Examination of Its Practice in Northern Sierra Leone." Ph.D. diss., Indiana University.

Hassan, Malam, and Malam Shuaibu. 1952. *A Chronicle of Abuja.* Ibadan: Published for the Abuja Native Administration by the Ibadan University Press.

Hatto, A. T. 1989. "Towards an Anatomy of Heroic and Epic Poetry." In *Traditions of Heroic and Epic Poetry,* ed. A. T. Hatto and J. B. Hainsworth. 2 vols. (1980 and 1989). London: Modern Humanities Research Association. Vol. 2, pp. 145–306.

*Hayidara, Shekh Tijaan, ed. and trans. 1987. *La geste de Fanta Maa.* Niamey: CELHTO.

Henige, David. 1974. *The Chronology of Oral Tradition.* Oxford: Clarendon Press.

Herbert, Eugenia. 1993. *Iron, Gender, and Power: Rituals of Transformation in African Societies.* Bloomington: Indiana University Press.

Hersovits, Melville J. 1938. *Dahomey: An Ancient West African Kingdom.* 2 vols. New York: J. J. Augustin.

Herskovits, Melville J., and Frances Herskovits. 1958. *Dahomean Narrative.* Evanston: Northwestern University Press.

De Heusch, Luc. 1982a. *The Drunken King, or, The Origin of the State.* Trans. Roy Willis. Bloomington: Indiana University Press.

———. 1982b. *Rois nés d'un coeur de vache*. Paris: Gallimard.

Hodge, Carleton T., ed. 1971. *Papers on the Manding*. Bloomington: Indiana University Press; The Hague: Mouton.

Hoffman, Barbara. 1990. "The Power of Speech: Language and Social Status among Mande Griots and Nobles." Ph.D. diss., Indiana University.

———. 1995. "Power, Structure, and Mande *jeliw*." In Conrad and Frank 1995. Pp. 36–45.

Houdas, O., ed. and trans. 1966. *Tedzkiret en-Nisian*. Paris: Maisonneuve. First printed 1913–1914.

Van Hoven, Ed, and Jarich Oosten. 1994. "The Mother-Son and the Brother-Sister Relationships in the Sunjata Epic." In Oosten 1994. Pp. 95–106.

Hulstaert, G. 1978. *Poèmes mongo anciens*. Tervuren: Musée Royal de l'Afrique Central. Annales, Sciences Humaines, No. 93.

———. 1984. *Eléments pour l'histoire mongo ancienne*. Academie Royale des Sciences d'Outre-Mer/Mémoires 48.2.

Humblot, P. 1951. "Episodes de la légende de Soundiata." *Notes Africaines* 52:111–13.

Hunwick, John. 1994. "Gao and the Almoravids Revisited." *Journal of African History* 35:251–73.

Ikiddeh, Ime. 1985. "Ozidi: The Film, the Saga, and the Play." In *Comparative Approaches to Modern African Literature*, ed. S. O. Asein. Ibadan: Department of English, University of Ibadan.

Imperato, Pascal James. 1970. "The Dance of the Tyi Wara." *African Arts* 4.1:8–13, 71–80.

———. 1983. *Buffoons, Queens, and Wooden Horsemen: The Dyo and Gouan Societies of the Bambara of Mali*. New York: Kilima House Publishers.

Innes, Gordon. 1973. "Stability and Change in Griots' Narrations." *African Language Studies* 14:105–18.

*———. 1976. *Kaabu and Fuladu: Historical Narratives of the Gambian Mandinka*. London: School of Oriental and African Studies.

*———. 1978. *Kelefa Saane: His Career Recounted by Two Mandinka Bards*. London: School of Oriental and African Studies.

———. 1985. "Literatures in the Mande and Neighbouring Languages." In Andrzejewski, Pilaszewicz, and Tyloch 1985. Pp. 97–127.

———. 1990. "Formulae in Mandinka Epic: The Problem of Translation." In Okpewho 1990c. Pp. 101–10.

———. ed. and trans. 1974. *Sunjata: Three Mandinka Versions*. London: School of Oriental and African Studies.

*Innes, Gordon, and Bakari Sidibe, eds. and trans. 1990. *Hunters and Crocodiles: Narratives of a Hunters' Bard Performed by Bakari Kamara*. Sandgate: Paul Norbury/Unesco.

Irvine, Judith T. 1978. "When Is Genealogy History? Wolof Genealogies in Comparative Perspective." *American Ethnologist* 5:651–74.

*Jabaté, Kanku Mady. 1987. *L'histoire du Mande*. Collected, translated, and annotated by Madina Ly-Tall, Seydou Camara, and Bouna Diouara. Paris: Association SCOA.

Jablow, Alta. 1984. "Gassire's Lute: A Reconstruction of Soninke Bardic Art." *Research in African Literatures* 15:519–29.

——. 1991. *Gassire's Lute.* Prospect Heights, IL: Waveland Press. First published New York: Dutton, 1971.

Jackson, Michael. 1979. "Prevented Successions: A Commentary upon a Kuranko Narrative." In *Fantasy and Symbol: Studies in Anthropological Interpretation,* ed. R. H. Hook. London: Academic Press. Pp. 95–131.

——. 1982a. *Allegories of the Wilderness.* Bloomington: Indiana University Press.

——. 1982b. "Meaning and Moral Imagery in Kuranko Myth." *Research in African Literatures* 13:153–80.

Jacobs, J., with B. Omeonga and E. Lusandjula. 1961. "Le récit épique de Lofokefoke, le héros des Mbole (Bambuli)." *Aequatoria* 24.3:81–92.

Jansen, Jan. 1994a. "The Dynamics of 'Sunjata': Reports about the Past in Kela (Mali)." In Oosten 1994. Pp. 107–15.

——. 1994b. "The Secret of the Dog that Seized the Soap: Some Observations on Mande Oral Tradition." *St. Petersburg Journal of African Studies* 3:120–29.

——. 1996. "Elle connaît tout le Mande": A Tribute to the Griotte Siramori Diabate." *Research in African Literatures* 27.4:180–97.

——. Forthcoming. "The Jabaté Griots of Kela and the Sunjata Epic: A Preliminary Ethnography." In Austen forthcoming.

Jansen, Jan, and Clemens Zobel. 1996. *The Younger Brother in Mande Kinship and Politics in West Africa.* Leiden: Center for Non-Western Studies.

*Jansen, Jan, Esger Duintjer, and Boubacar Tamboura, eds. and trans. 1995. *L'épopée de Sunjata, d'après Lansine Diabate de Kela.* Leiden: Center for Non-Western Studies.

*Jebaate, Amadu. 1980. "La jeunesse de Soundiata." Ed. and trans. D. Creissels and S. Jatta. *Recueil de littérature mandingue.* Paris: N.p. Pp. 108–25.

Johnson, John William. 1978. "The Epic of Son-Jara: An Attempt to Define the Model for African Epic Poetry." 3 vols. Ph.D. diss., Indiana University.

——. 1980. "Yes, Virginia, There Is an Epic in Africa." *Research in African Literatures* 11:308–26.

——. 1982. "On the Heroic Age and Other Primitive Theses." In *Folklorica: Festschrift for Felix J. Oinas,* ed. E. V. Zygas and Peter Voorheis. Bloomingon: Research Institute for Inner Asian Studies. Pp. 121–38.

*——. 1986. *The Epic of Son-Jara: A West African Tradition.* Text by Fa-Digi Sisókó. Bloomingon: Indiana University Press.

Johnson, John William, Thomas Hale, and Stephen Belcher, eds. 1997. *Oral Epics from Africa: Vibrant Voices from a Vast Continent.* Bloomingon: Indiana University Press.

Joseph, George. 1979. "The Wolof Oral Praise Song for Semu Coro Wende." *Research in African Literatures* 10.2:145–78.

Kaba, Lansiné. 1984. "The Pen, the Sword, and the Crown: Islam and Revolution in Songhay Reconsidered, 1464–1493." *Journal of African History* 25:241–56.

Kagame, Alexis. 1950. *La poésie dynastique au Rwanda.* Mémoires de l'Institut Royal Colonial Belge.

——. 1969. *Introduction aux grands genres lyriques de l'ancien Rwanda.* Butare: Editions Universitaires du Rwanda. Collection "Muntu."

Kamara, Cheikh Moussa. 1970. "La vie d'El-Hadji Omar." Ed. and trans. Amar Samb. *Bulletin de l'IFAN,* Series B, 32:44–135, 370–411, 770–818.

———. 1975. "Histoire du Bondou." Ed. and trans. Moustapha Ndiaye. *Bulletin de l'IFAN*, Series B, 37:784–816.

———. 1978. "Histoire de Ségou." Ed. and trans. Moustapha Ndiaye. *Bulletin de l'IFAN*, Series B, 40:458–88.

*Kamara, Karamogo. 1982. *Griots de Samatiguila*. Ed. and trans. M.-J. Dérive et al. Abidjan: Institut de Linguistique Appliquée.

*Kamissoko, Wa. N.d. *Les Peuls du Manding*. Niamey: CELHTO.

Kane, Moustapha, and David Robinson. 1984. *The Islamic Regime of Fuuta Tooro*. East Lansing: Michigan State University African Studies Center.

Kane, Oumar. 1970a. "Essai de chronologie des *satigis* du XVIIIe siècle." *Bulletin de l'IFAN*, Series B, 32.3:755–65.

———. 1970b. "Samba Gelajo-Jegi." *Bulletin de l'IFAN*, Series B, 32:911–26.

Kanoute, Dembo. 1972. *Histoire de l'Afrique authentique*. Ed. and trans. Tidiane Sanogho and Ibrahima Diallo. Dakar: N.p.

*Kante, Ibrahima. N.d. *L'épopée du Manding*. Ed. and trans. Ahmadou Kaba and Kaimba Kandé. N.p. [Northwestern University Library].

Kante, Nambala. 1993. *Forgerons d'Afrique Noire: Transmission des savoirs traditionnels en pays malinké*. Paris: L'Harmattan.

Kâti, Mahmoûd. 1913–1914. *Tarikh el-fettach ou chronique du chercheur*. Ed. and trans. O. Houdas and M. Delafosse. Paris: Maisonneuve. Reprinted 1981.

Keita, Cheikh M. C. 1990. "*Fadenya* and Artistic Creation in Mali: Kele Monson and Massa Makan Diabaté." *Research in African Literatures* 21.3:103–14.

Kesteloot, Lilyan. 1972. "Actes et valeurs dans l'épopée bambara de Segou." *Canadian Journal of African Studies* 6:29–41.

*———. 1973. "Une épisode de l'épopée bambara de Segou: Bakari Dian et Bilissi." *Bulletin de l'IFAN*, Series B, 35:881–902.

———. 1978a. *Biton Koulibaly, fondateur de l'empire de Segou*. Dakar: Nouvelles Editions Africaines.

*———. 1978b. "Le mythe et l'histoire dans la formation de l'empire de Ségou." *Bulletin de l'IFAN*, Series B, 40.3:578–611.

———. 1987. "La problématique des épopées africaines." *Annales de l'Université de Dakar, Faculté de Lettres et Sciences Humaines* 17:43–53. Reprinted in *Neohelicon* 16; English translation in *African Languages and Cultures* 2.

———. 1991. "Power and Its Portrayals in Royal Mandé Narratives." *Research in African Literatures* 22.1:17–26.

———. 1992. "Myth, Epic, and African History." In *The Surreptitious Speech*, ed. V. Mudimbe. Chicago: University of Chicago Press. Pp. 136–43.

Kesteloot, Lilyan, ed. 1971. *L'Epopée traditionelle*. Paris: Fernand Nathan.

*———, ed. and trans. 1993. *Da Monzon de Segou*. 2 vols. Paris: L'Harmattan. First published in 4 vols. Paris: Fernand Nathan, 1972.

Kesteloot, Lilyan, C. Barbey, S. M. Ndongo. 1985. "Tyamaba, Mythe Peul." *Notes Africaines* 185/186 (January–April):1–72.

Kesteloot, Lilyan, and Bassirou Dieng. 1989. *Du Tieddo au Talibé. Contes et mythes Wolof, II*. Dakar: Nouvelles Editions Africaines/ACCT.

*———. 1997. *Les épopées d'Afrique noire*. Paris: Karthala.

Kesteloot, Lilyan, Bassirou Dieng, and Lampsar Sall. 1983. "L'histoire, le mythe et leurs mystères dans la tradition orale africaine." *Université de Dakar, Annales de la Faculté de Lettres et Sciences Humaines* 13:53–74.

Kesteloot, Lilyan, and Cherif Mbodj. 1983. *Contes et mythes Wolof.* Dakar: Nouvelles Editions Africaines.

Khane, Geneviève. 1984. "La légende de Soundjata et l'archétype de l'enfant orphelin." *Notes Africaines* 181 (January): 1–9.

King, Adele. 1980. *The Writings of Camara Laye.* London: Heinemann.

Knappert, Jan. 1967. "The Epic in Africa." *Journal of the Folklore Institute* 4:171–90.

*———. 1971. *Myths and Legends of the Congo.* London: Heinemann Educational Books.

———. 1983. *Epic Poetry in Swahili and Other African Languages.* Leiden: E. J. Brill.

Knight, Roderic. 1973. "Mandinka Jeliya." Ph.D. diss., University of California, Los Angeles, 1973.

———. 1974. "Mandinka Drumming." *African Arts* 7.4:25–35.

———. 1982. "Manding/Fula Relations as reflected in the Manding Song Repertoire." *African Music* 6.2:37–47.

Konake, Sory. 1973. *Le grand destin de Soundjata.* Paris: ORTF/DAEC.

Konate, Mamadou. 1966. "Une épopée malienne—Da Monzon de Segou." *Abbia* 14/15:171–79.

Koné, A. 1981. "Les mythes dans le récit héroique traditionnel et leur survivance dans le roman africain moderne." *Annales de l'Université d'Abidjan,* ser. D. (Lettres), 14:177–83.

Kotljar, E. Sz. 1983. "Some Aspects of the Development of the Epic Genre. . . . " *Artes Populares* 1:235–38. *Folklore in Africa Today: Proceedings of the Workshop.* Budapest: African Research Project.

Kunene, Daniel. 1971. *Heroic Poetry of the Basotho.* Oxford: Clarendon Press.

———. 1991. "Journey in the African Epic." *Research in African Literatures* 22.2:205–23.

Labatut, R., and S. Labatut. N.d. *Epopées africaines: Morceaux choisis.* Yaounde: Bureau de Recherches Pédagogiques et des Programmes, Ministère de l'Education, de la Jeunesse, et de la Culture.

*Labouret, Henri, ed. 1929. "Livre renfermant la généalogie des diverses tribus noires du Soudan." *Annales de l'Académie des Sciences Coloniales* 3:189–225.

*Lanrezac, H. [1907?]. *Essai sur le folklore au Soudan.* Paris: La Revue Indigene.

*———. 1907. "Légendes soudanaises." *Revue Economique Française* 29:67–619.

De Latour, Eliane. 1984. "Maîtres de la terre, maîtres de la guerre." *Cahiers d'Etudes Africaines* 24:273–97.

Law, Robin. 1980. *The Horse in West African History.* Oxford: International African Institute.

*Laya [Layya], Julde [Juulde, Dioulde]. [1970]. *Anzuru: Traditions historiques de l'Anzuru.* Niamey: Centre Regional de Documentation pour la Tradition Orale.

*———. 1970. *Traditions historiques des ethnies de la région de Dooso (Dosso).* [Niamey]: N.p.

———. 1973. *La voie peule.* Niamey: CRDTO.

———, ed. 1969. *Histoire des Songhay-Zarma.* Niamey: CRDTO.

*Laye, Camara. 1978. *Le maître de la parole.* Paris: Plon. Translated into English by James

Kirkup as *The Guardian of the Word*. New York: Collins, 1980; New York: Aventura, 1984.

Le Pichon, Alain, and Souleymane Baldé. 1990. *Le troupeau des songes*. Paris: Editions de la Maison des Sciences de l'Homme.

Levtzion, Nehemia. 1972. "Was Royal Succession in Ancient Ghana Matrilineal?" *International Journal of African Historical Studies* 5:91–94.

———. 1973. *Ancient Ghana and Mali*. London: Methuen.

Levtzion, Nehemia, and J. F. P. Hopkins. 1981. *Corpus of Early Arabic Sources for West African History*. Cambridge: Cambridge University Press.

Leynaud, Emile, and Youssouf Cisse. N.d. *Paysans Malinke du Haut Niger*. Bamako: Edition Imprimerie Populaire du Mali.

Lord, Albert B. 1976. *The Singer of Tales*. New York: Atheneum. First published Cambridge: Harvard University Press, 1959.

*Ly, Amadou, trans. 1991. *L'épopée de Samba Gueladiegui*. Dakar: IFAN/UNESCO, Editions Nouvelles du Sud.

Ly[-Tall], Madina. 1976. "L'empire du Mali a-t-il survécu jusqu'à la fin du XVIe siècle?" *Bulletin de l'IFAN*, Series B, 38:234–56.

Ly-Tall, Madina. 1977. *Contribution à l'histoire de l'empire du Mali (XIIIe-XVIe siècles)*. Paris: Nouvelles Editions Africaines.

Mage, Eugène. 1980. *Voyage au Soudan occidental (1863–1866)*. Abridged edition. Paris: Karthala.

Magel, Emil A. 1981. "The Role of the *Gewel* in Wolof Society: The Professional Image of Lamin Jeng." *Journal of Anthropological Research* 37:183–91.

Malinowski, Bronislaw. 1954. *Magic, Science, and Religion and Other Essays*. New York: Doubleday.

Makward, Edris. 1990. "Two Griots of Contemporary Senegambia." In Okpewho 1990c. Pp. 23–41.

*Malonga, Jean. 1954. *La légende de M'pfoumou ma Mazono*. Paris: Editions Africaines.

Mané, Mamadou. 1978. "Contribution à l'histoire du Kaabu." *Bulletin de l'IFAN*, Series B, 40:87–159.

Mariko, Keletigi Abdourahmane. 1981. *Le monde mystérieux des chasseurs traditionnels*. Paris: ACCT.

Masonen, Pekka, and Humphrey Fisher. 1996. "Not Quite Venus from the Waves: The Almoravid Conquest of Ghana in the Modern Historiography of Western Africa." *History in Africa* 23:197–231.

Massing, Andreas W. 1985. "The Mane, the Decline of Mali, and Mandinka Expansion." *Cahiers d'Etudes Africaines* 25.1:21–55.

*Mawiri, Ambroisine, and Victor Mbumba. [1985?]. *Epopée Mulombi*. [Libreville, Gabon?]: Editions Vincent de Paul Nyonda.

Mbele, Joseph. 1982. "The Hero in the African Epic." *Africana Journal* 13:124–41.

———. 1986. "Identity of the Hero in the Liongo Epic." *Research in African Literatures* 17:464–73.

McIntosh, Roderick J., and Susan K. McIntosh. 1981. "The Inland Niger Delta before the Empire of Mali: Evidence from Jenne-Jeno." *Journal of African History* 22:1–22.

McIntosh, Susan K., and Roderick J. McIntosh. 1984. "The Early City in West Africa: Towards an Understanding." *African Archaeological Review* 2:73–98.

——. 1993. "Cities without Citadels: Understanding Urban Origins along the Middle Niger." In *The Archaeology of Africa: Food, Metals and Towns*, ed. T. Shaw, P. Sinclair et al. London: Routledge. Pp. 622–41.

McNaughton, Patrick. 1979. *Secret Sculptures of Komo*. Philadelphia: Institute for the Study of Human Issues.

——. 1982. "The Shirts That Mande Hunters Wear." *African Arts* 15:54–58, 91.

——. 1988. *The Mande Blacksmiths*. Bloomington: Indiana University Press.

——. 1995. "The Semantics of *Jugu*." In Conrad and Frank 1995. Pp. 46–57.

Meillassoux, Claude. 1963. "Histoire et institutions du *kafo* de Bamako d'après la tradition des Niaré." *Cahiers d'Etudes Africaines* 4.2:186–227.

——. 1972. "Les origines de Gumbu (Mali)." *Bulletin de l'IFAN*, Series B, 34:268–98.

——. 1975. "Etat et conditions des esclaves à Gumbu (Mali) au XIXe siècle." In Meillassoux 1975. Pp. 221–51.

——. 1978. "Le mâle en gésine, ou De l'historicité des mythes." *Cahiers d'Etudes Africaines* 19:353–80.

——, ed. 1975. *L'esclavage en Afrique précoloniale*. Paris: Maspero.

*Meillassoux, Claude, Lansana Doucoure, and Diaowe Simagha. 1967. *Légende de la dispersion des Kusa*. Dakar: IFAN.

Meillassoux, Claude, and Abdoulaye Sylla. 1978. "L'interpretation légendaire de l'histoire du Jonkoloni (Mali)." In *Fonti Orali*, ed. B. Bernardi, C. Poni, and A. Triulzi. Milan: Franco Angeli. Pp. 347–92.

Meillassoux, Claude, et al. 1968. "Les cérémonies septennales du Kamablō de Kaaba (Mali)." *Journal de la Société des Africanistes* 38:173–88.

Menga, Guy. 1977. *Les aventures de Moni Mambou*. Yaounde: Editions Clé.

Meyer, Gérard. 1987. *Contes du pays malinké*. Paris: Karthala.

——. 1988. *Paroles du soir: Contes toucouleurs*. Paris: L'Harmattan.

*——, ed. and trans. 1991. *Récits épiques toucouleurs: La vache, le livre, la lance*. Paris: Karthala/ACCT.

Miller, Christopher. 1990. *Theories of Africans*. Chicago: University of Chicago Press.

Miller, Joseph, ed. 1980. *The African Past Speaks: Essays on Oral Tradition and History*. Folkestone, England: Dawson; Hamden, CT: Archon.

Misiugin, V., and V. Vydrin. 1994. "Some Archaic Elements in the Manden Epic Tradition: The 'Sunjata Epic' Case." *St. Petersburg Journal of African Studies* 2:98–111.

*Monteil, Charles. 1905. *Contes Soudanais*. Paris: Ernest Leroux. Kraus Reprint 1977.

——. 1915. *Les Khassonké*. Paris: E. Leroux. Kraus reprint 1974.

——. 1929. "Les empires du Mali." *Bulletin du Comité d'Etudes Historiques et Scientifiques de l'Afrique Occidental Française* 12. Reprinted Paris: G.-P. Maisonneuve et Larose, n.d.

*——. 1953. "La légende de Ouagadou et l'origine des Soninké." *Mémoires de l'IFAN* 23:358–409.

——. 1966. "Fin de siècle à Médine." Ed. Vincent Monteil. *Bulletin de l'IFAN*, Series B, 28:82–172.

*——. 1967. "Textes soninké." Ed. Abdoulaye Bathily. *Bulletin de l'IFAN*, Series B, 29:559–98.

——. 1971. *Une cité soudanaise: Djénné*. Paris: Editions Anthropos. First printed 1932.

——. 1977. *Les Bambara de Segou et du Kaarta*. Notes by Jean Bazin. Paris: Maisonneuve et Larose. First printed 1924.

Monteil, Vincent. 1963. "Contribution à la sociologie des peuls (Le 'Fonds Vieillard' de l'IFAN).'" *Bulletin de l'IFAN*, Series B, 25:352–414.

——. 1966. "Le Dyolof et Al-Bouri Ndiaye." *Bulletin de l'IFAN*, Series B, 28:595–636.

——. 1965. "Les manuscrits historiques arabo-africains." *Bulletin de l'IFAN*, Series B, 27:531–42; 28:668–75 (1966); 29:599–603 (1967).

De Moraes Farias, Paolo F. 1974. "Great States Revisited." *Journal of African History* 15.3:479–88.

——. 1989. "Pilgrimages to 'Pagan' Mecca in Mandenka Stories of Origin Reported from Mali and Guinea-Conakry." In Barber and de Moraes Farias 1989. Pp. 152–70.

——. 1992. "History and Consolation: Royal Yorùbá Bards Comment on Their Craft." *History in Africa* 19:263–97.

——. 1993. "The Oral Traditionist as Critic and Intellectual Producer: An Example from Contemporary Mali." In *African Historiography: Essays in Honor of Jacob Ajayi*, ed. Toyin Falola. London: Longman, 1993. Pp. 14–38.

——. Forthcoming. "Praise as Intrusion and Foreign Language: A Sunjata Paradigm Seen from the Gesere Diaspora in Béninois Borgu." In Austen forthcoming.

Morris, H. F. 1980. "East African (The Bahima Praise Poems)." In *Traditions of Heroic and Epic Poetry*, ed. A. T. Hatto and J. B. Hainsworth. 2 vols. (1980 and 1989). London: Modern Humanities Research Association. Vol. 1, pp. 345–76.

*Moser, Rex. 1974. "Foregrounding in the Sunjata, the Mande Epic." Ph.D. diss., Indiana University.

*Mounkaila, Fatimata. 1989. *Le mythe et l'histoire dans la Geste de Zabarkâne*. Niamey: CELHTO.

——. 1993. "Ancestors from the East in Sahelo-Sudanese Myth." *Research in African Literatures* 24:13–21.

Mufuta, Patrice. 1968. *Le chant* kasàlà *des Lubà*. Paris: Julliard.

Muhammad, Akbar. 1977. "The Samorian Occupation of Bondoukou: An Indigenous View." *International Journal of African Historical Studies* 10:242–58.

Munson, Patrick. 1980. "Archaeology and the Prehistoric Origins of the Ghana Empire." *Journal of African History* 21:457–66.

Mve-Ondo, Bonaventure. 1991. *Sagesse et initiation à travers les contes, mythes, et légendes fang*. Libreville: Centre Culturel Français Saint-Exupéry/Université Omar Bongo.

Nassau, Robert. 1969. *Fetichism in West Africa*. New York: Negro Universities Press. First printed 1904.

N'Diaye, Bokar. 1970. *Les castes au Mali*. Bamako: Editions Populaires.

*Ndiaye, Cheikh Mbacké. 1992–1993. "L'épopée orale sereer: La Geste de San Moon Faye." Mémoire de maîtrise." Thesis, University de Dakar.

*N'Diaye, Saki Olal. 1971. "The Story of Malik Sy." Trans. and ed. A. Neil Skinner, Philip D. Curtin, and Hammady Amadou Sy. *Cahiers d'Etudes Africaines* 11.3:467–87.

Ndongo, Siré Mamadou. 1986. *Le Fantang: Poèmes mythiques des bergers peuls.* Paris: Karthala.

Ndoutoume, Daniel Assoumou. 1986. *Du Mvett: Essai sur la dynastie Ekang Nna.* Paris: L'Harmattan.

*Ndoutoume, Tsira Ndong. 1970–1975. *Le Mvett.* 2 vols. Paris: Présence Africaine.

*———. 1993. *Le Mvett: L'homme, la mort, l'immortalité.* Paris: L'Harmattan.

*Ngaïde, Mamadou Lamine. 1981. *Le vent de la razzia.* Dakar: IFAN.

*Ngijol, Pierre. 1980. *Les fils de Hitong.* Yaounde: Centre d'Edition et de Production pour l'Enseignement et la Recherche.

*Niane, Djibril Tamsir. 1960. *Soundiata, ou l'épopée mandingue.* Paris: Présence Africaine.

———. 1972. "Koly Tenguella et le Tekrour." In *Congrès International des Africanistes,* Second Session, Dakar, 1967. Paris: Présence Africaine. Pp. 61–76.

———. 1974. "Histoire et tradition historique du Manding." *Présence Africaine* 89:59–77.

———. 1975. *Le Soudan occidental au temps des grands empires.* Paris: Présence Africaine.

———. [1989?]. *Histoire des Mandingues de l'Ouest.* Paris: Karthala.

———, ed. 1984. *Africa from the Twelfth to the Sixteenth Century.* Vol. 4 of the Unesco General History of Africa. Berkeley: University of California Press; London: Heinemann; Paris: UNESCO.

Norris, Harry T. 1968. *Shinqiti Folk Literature and Song.* Oxford: Clarendon Press.

———. 1972. *Saharan Myth and Saga.* Oxford: Clarendon Press.

———. 1989. "Arabic Folk Epic and Western *Chanson de Geste.*" *Oral Tradition* 4:125–50.

Obama, J. O. 1966a. "Cameroun, Microcosme de la Negritude." *Abbia* 12/13:13–71.

———. 1966b. "La musique africaine traditionelle." *Abbia* 12/13:273–309.

Oinas, Felix J., ed. 1978. *Heroic Epic and Saga.* Bloomington: Indiana University Press.

Okpewho, Isidore. 1977. "Does the Epic Exist in Africa: Some Formal Considerations." *Research in African Literatures* 8:171–200.

———. 1979. *The Epic in Africa: Toward a Poetics of the Oral Performance.* New York: Columbia University Press.

———. 1980a. "Analytical Boundaries in the Oral Narrative." *Bulletin de l'IFAN,* Series B, 42:822–56.

———. 1980b. "The Anthropologist Looks at Epic." *Research in African Literatures* 11.4:429–48.

———. 1981. "The African Heroic Epic: Internal Balance." Instituto Italo-Africano. *Africa* 36.2:209–25.

———. 1983. *Myth in Africa.* Cambridge: Cambridge University Press.

———. 1990a. "The Oral Performer and His Audience: A Case Study of *The Ozidi Saga.*" In Okpewho 1990c. Pp. 160–84.

———. 1990b. "Towards a Faithful Record: On Transcribing and Translating the Oral Narrative Performance." In Okpewho 1990c. Pp. 111–35.

———, ed. 1990c. *The Oral Performance in Africa.* Ibadan: Spectrum Books.

———. 1992. *African Oral Literature: Backgrounds, Character, and Continuity.* Bloomington: Indiana University Press.

Olivier de Sardan, Jean-Pierre. 1975. "Captifs ruraux et esclaves impériaux du Songhay." In Meillassoux 1975. Pp. 99–134.

———. 1982a. "Le cheval et l'arc." In Bazin and Terray 1982. Pp. 189–234.

———. 1982b. *Concepts et conceptions Songhay-Zarma: Histoire, culture, société.* Paris: Nubia.

———. 1984. *Les sociétés Songhay-Zarma.* Paris: Karthala.

———, ed. and trans. 1976. *Quand nos pères étaient captifs: Récits paysans du Niger.* Paris: Nubia.

Olney, James. 1975. "Of *Griots* and Heroes." *Studies in Black Literature* 6:14–17.

Ong, Walter J. 1983. *Orality and Literacy.* London: Methuen.

Oosten, Jarich, ed. 1994. *Texts and Tales: Studies in Oral Tradition.* Leiden: Center for Non-Western Studies.

Opland, Jeff. 1989. "The Structure of Xhosa Eulogy and the Relation of Eulogy to Epic." In *Traditions of Heroic and Epic Poetry,* ed. A. T. Hatto and J. B. Hainsworth. 2 vols. London: Modern Humanities Research Association. Vol. 2, pp. 121–44.

———. 1983. *Xhosa Oral Poetry.* Cambridge: Cambridge University Press.

———. 1987. "World Epic: On Heroic and Epic Traditions in Oral and Written Literature." *Comparative Criticism* 8:307–20.

Pageard, Robert. 1961a. "La marche orientale du Mali (Segou-Djenne) en 1644." *Journal de la Société des Africanistes* 31:73–81.

———. 1961b. "Soundiata Keita et la tradition orale." *Présence Africaine* 36:51–70.

———. 1962. "Contribution critique à la chronologie historique de l'ouest africain." *Journal de la Société des Africanistes* 32:91–132.

Pâques, Viviana. 1953. "L'estrade royale des Niaré." *Bulletin de l'IFAN* 15:1642–54.

———. 1954a. *Les Bambara.* Paris: Presses Universitaires de France.

———. 1954b. "Bouffons sacrés du cercle de Bougouni." *Journal de la Société des Africanistes* 24:63–110.

———. 1956. "Les 'Samake.'" *Bulletin de l'IFAN,* Series B, 18:369–90.

———. 1977. *Le roi pecheur et le roi chasseur.* Strasbourg: Travaux de l'Institut d'Anthropologie de Strasbourg.

Park, Mungo. 1907. *The Travels of Mungo Park.* Ed. Ronald Miller. London: Dent. Reprinted 1954.

Paulme, Denise. 1976. *La mère dévorante.* Paris: Gallimard.

*Pepper, Herbert, ed. 1972. *Un Mvet de Zwè Nguéma: Chant épique fang.* Ed. P. and P. de Wolf. Classiques Africains. Paris: Armand Colin.

Perinbam, B. Marie. 1972. "Trade and Society in the Western Sahara and the Western Sudan: An Overview." *Bulletin de l'IFAN,* Series B, 34:778–801.

———. 1986. "Islam in the Banamba Region of the Eastern Beledugu, c. 1800 to c. 1900." *International Journal of African Historical Studies* 19:637–57.

Person, Yves. 1963. "Les Ancêtres de Samori." *Cahiers d'Etudes Africaines* 4.1:125–56.

———. 1968-1975. *Samory: Une révolution Dyula.* 3 vols. Dakar: IFAN.

———. 1981. "Nyaani Mansa Mamudu et la fin de l'empire du Mali." In *Le sol, la parole, et l'écrit: Mélanges offerts à Raymond Mauny.* Paris: Société Française d'Histoire d'Outre-Mer. Pp. 613–51.

Pickett, G. D., trans. 1965. *Sundiata: An Epic of Old Mali.* London: Longmans. (See Niane 1960.)

Pollet, Eric, and Grace Winter. 1971. *La société Soninké (Dyahunu, Mali)*. Brussels: Editions de l'Université de Bruxelles.

*Prost, A. 1956. "Légendes Songay." *Bulletin de l'IFAN* 18:188–201.

Quinn, Charlotte. 1972. *Mandingo Kingdoms of the Senegambia*. Evanston: Northwestern University Press.

Quiquandon, F. 1892. "Histoire de la puissance mandingue." *Bulletin de la Société de Géographie Commerciale de Bordeaux,* Second Series, 15:305–18, 369–87, 401–29.

Raffenel, Anne. 1856. *Nouveau voyage au pays des nègres*. 2 vols. Paris: Imprimerie de Chaix.

Recueil de littérature manding. N.d. Paris: ACCT.

Riesman, Paul. 1986. "The Person and the Life Cycle in African Social Life and Thought." *African Studies Review* 29:71–138.

Roberts, Mary Nooter, and Allen F. Roberts. 1996. *Memory: Luba Art and the Making of History*. New York: Museum for African Art.

Roberts, Richard L. 1980. "Production and Reproduction of Warrior States: Segu Bambara and Segu Tukolor." *International Journal of African Historical Studies* 13:389–419.

Robinson, David. 1971. "The Impact of Al-Hajj 'Umar on the Historical Traditions of the Fulbe." *Journal of the Folklore Institute* 8:101–13.

———. 1985. *The Holy War of Umar Tal*. Oxford: Clarendon Press.

———. 1991. "An Approach to Islam in West African History." In *Faces of Islam in African Literature*, ed. K. Harrow. Portsmouth: Heinemann, 1991. Pp. 107–29.

Robinson, David, Philip Curtin, and James Johnson. 1972. "A Tentative Chronology of Futa Toro from the Sixteenth through the Nineteenth Centuries." *Cahiers d'Etudes Africaines* 12:555–92.

Roche, Christian. 1970. "Les trois Fode Kaba." *Notes Africaines* 128 (October):107–11.

De Rop, A. 1956. "L'épopée des Nkundo: L'original et la copie." *Kongo-Oversee* 24:170–78.

———. 1964. *Lianja: L'épopée des Móngo*. Brussels: Academie Royale des Sciences d'Outre-Mer/Mémoires, Classe des Sciences Morales et Politiques. N. S. 30.1.

———. 1974. "La littérature orale Mongo: Synthèse et bibliographie." *Cahiers du CEDAF* 2:1–36.

*———. 1978. *Versions et fragments de l'épopée Mongo*. Brussels: Académie Royale des Sciences d'Outre-Mer. Classe des Sciences Morales et Politiques. N. S. 45.1.

*De Rop, A., and E. Boelaert. 1983. *Versions et Fragments de l'épopée Mongo: Nsong'a Lianga*. Part 2. *Etudes Aequatoria* 1. Mbandaka, Zaire.

Rouch, Jean. 1953. *Contribution à l'histoire des Songhoy*. Dakar: Mémoires de l'IFAN 29:138–259.

*———. 1978. *La Chanson de Fara Makan*. Documents presented to the SCOA conference in Niamey.

———. 1989. *La religion et la magie songhay*. 2nd ed. Brussels: Editions de l'Université de Bruxelles. First published Paris: PUF, 1950.

al-Sa'di, Abd al-Rahman [es-Sa'di Abderrahman]. 1981. *Tarikh es-Soudan*. Ed. and trans. O. Houdas. Paris: Maisonneuve et Larose. First printed 1900.

Sadji, Abdoulaye. 1985. *Ce que dit la musique africaine*. Paris: Présence Africaine.

Saint-Père, J.-H. 1925. *Les Sarakollé du Guidimakha.* Paris: Emile Larose. Publications du Comité d'Etudes Historiques et Scientifiques.

Samaké, Maximin. 1988. "*Kafo* et pouvoir lignager chez les Banmana: L'hégémonie gonkòròbi dans le Cendugu." *Cahiers d'Etudes Africaines* 28:331–54.

Sanankoua, Bintou. 1990. *Un empire peul au XIXe siècle.* Paris: Karthala/ACCT.

Sar, Samba Ndaw. 1980a. "Prédestination, héros et gumbala: L'exemple de Samba Gelaajo Jeegi." *Demb ak Tey* 6:12–23.

*———, ed. 1980b. "Les circonstances de la naissance de Samba." *Demb ak Tey* 6:94–98.

*Sare, Ougoumala. [1974?]. *La guerre entre Ndje Fara Ndje et Hambodedjo Hammadi.* Niamey: CELHTO/OUA.

Sarr, Mamadou. 1976. "L'empire du Ghana." *Etudes Maliennes,* special issue, 16:1–132.

———. 1978. "La genèse des féodalités peules." *Etudes Maliennes,* special issue, 25:1–94.

*Sauvageot, Serge. 1981. "Le testament politique de Monzon: Texte bambara." In *Le sol, la parole, et l'écrit: Mélanges offerts à Raymond Mauny.* Paris: Société Française d'Histoire d'Outre-Mer. Pp. 289–95.

*Sawse, Ali, and David Ames. 1972. "The Lion of Manding." In Courlander 1972. Pp. 71–78.

Schapera, Isaac. 1965. *Praise Poems of the Tswana Chiefs.* Oxford: Clarendon Press.

Scheub, Harold. 1985. "A Review of African Oral Traditions and Literature." *African Studies Review* 28:1–72.

Seydou, Christiane. 1972. "Trois poèmes mystiques peuls du Foûta-Djalon." *Revue des Etudes Islamiques* 40:141–85.

———. 1973. "Panorama de la littérature peule." *Bulletin de l'IFAN,* Series B, 35:176–218.

———. 1976. *Contes et fables des veillées.* Paris: Nubia.

———. 1977a. *Bibliographie générale du monde Peul.* Niamey: Institut de Recherches en Sciences Humaines. Etudes Nigériennes No. 43.

———. 1977b. "La devise dans la culture peule: Evocation et invocation de la personne." In *Langage et cultures africaines,* ed. G. Calame-Griaule. Paris: Maspero. Pp. 187–264.

———. 1982. "Comment définir le genre épique? Un exemple: L'épopée africaine." In *Genres, Forms, Meanings: Essays in African Oral Literature,* ed. Veronika Görög-Karady. *Journal of the Anthropological Society of Oxford,* Occasional Papers. Pp. 84–98.

———. 1983. "A Few Reflections on Narrative Structures of Epic Texts: A Case Example of Bambara and Fulani Epics." *Research in African Literatures* 13:312–31.

———. 1987a. "Les hérauts de la parole épique." In *Kalevala et traditions orales du Monde,* ed. Jocelyne Fernandez-Vest. Paris: Editions du CNRS. Pp. 449–66.

———. 1987b. "La notion de parole dans le dialecte peul du Mâssina (Mali)." *Journal de la Société des Africanistes* 57:45–66.

———. 1987c. *Des preux, des belles, des larrons. Contes du Mali.* Paris: Nubia.

———. 1989. "Epopée et identité: Exemples africains." *Journal des Africanistes* 58:7–22.

———. 1992. "Jeu de pions, jeu des armes: Le combat singulier dans l'épopée peule." *Cahiers de Littérature Orale* 32:63–99.

*———, ed. and trans. 1972. *Silâmaka et Poullôri.* Classiques Africains. Paris: Armand Colin.

*———, ed. and trans. 1976. *La geste de Hambodedio ou Hama le rouge.* Classiques Africains. Paris: Armand Colin.

———, ed. 1991. *Bergers des mots.* Paris: Classiques Africains.

Shelton, Austin. 1968. "The Problem of Griot Interpretation and the Actual Causes of War in Sonjata." *Présence Africaine* 66:145–62.

*Sidibe, Bakari. 1980. *The Battle of Kansala, Recited by Sana Kuyate.* Banjul, Oral History and Antiquities Division, 1980. Paper presented at the conference on Gabou. Dakar.

*Sidibe, Fodé Moussa Balla. 1984. "Deux récits de chasse banmana: 'Ndoronkelen' et 'Bani Nyenema.'" Master's thesis, University of Dakar.

*Sidibe, Mamby. 1959. "Soundiata Kéita, héros historique et légendaire." *Notes Africaines* 82 (April):41–50.

Smith, Pierre. 1970. "La Forge de l'intelligence." *L'Homme* 10:5–21.

———. 1974. "Des genres et des hommes." *Poétique* 19:294–312.

———. 1979. "Naissances et destins: Les enfants de fer et les enfants de beurre." *Cahiers d'Etudes Africaines* 19:329–52.

Soares, Benjamin F. 1997. "The Spiritual Economy of Nioro du Sahel." Ph.D. diss. Northwestern University.

*Soh, Sire-Abbas. 1913. *Chroniques du Fouta Senegalais.* Ed. and trans. Maurice Delafosse and Henri Gaden. Paris: Leroux.

Sonko-Godwin, Patience. 1986. *Ethnic Groups of the Senegambia Region: Social and Political Structures.* Banjul: Government Printers.

———. 1988. *Ethnic Groups of the Senegambia Region: A Brief History.* 2nd ed. Banjul: Sunrise Publishers.

*Soumare, Mamadou. 1987. *Wagadu-Biida und Kagoro.* Published dissertation. Marburg: Philipps-Universität.

*Soumare, Mamadou, and Diarra Sylla. N.d. *Documents du Colloque de Niamey.* Paris: Fondation SCOA.

Sow, Abdoul Aziz. 1993. "Fulani Poetic Genres." *Research in African Literatures* 24:61–77.

Sow, Alfa Ibrahim. 1966. *La femme, la vache, la foi.* Classiques Africains. Paris: Armand Colin.

———. 1968. *Chroniques et récits du Fouta Djallon.* Paris: Editions Klincksieck.

Sow, Ibrahima. 1982. "Le monde des Subalbe (vallée du fleuve Sénégal)." *Bulletin de l'IFAN,* Series B, 44:237–320.

Spear, Thomas. 1981. "Oral Traditions: Whose History?" *History in Africa* 8:165–81.

Stoller, Paul. 1978. "The Word and the Cosmos: 'Zarma Ideology' Revisited." *Bulletin de l'IFAN* 40:863–78.

———. 1989. *Fusion of the Worlds: An Ethnography of Possession among the Songhay of Niger.* Chicago: University of Chicago Press.

Stoller, Paul, and Cheryl Olkes. 1987. *In Sorcery's Shadow.* Chicago: University of Chicago Press.

Stone, Ruth. 1988. *Dried Millet Breaking: Time, Words, and Song in the Woi Epic of the Kpelle.* Bloomington: Indiana University Press.

Suret-Canale, Jean. 1988. *Essays on African History.* Trenton: Africa World Press.

*Sy, Amadou Abel. 1978. *Seul contre tous.* Dakar and Abidjan: Nouvelles Editions Africaines.

*———. 1980. *Le geste tiedo.* Doctoral thesis, Université Cheikh Anta Diop, Dakar.

Tamari, Tal. 1991. "The Development of Caste Systems in West Africa." *Journal of African History* 32:221–50.

———. 1993. "Relations symboliques de l'artisanat et de la musique." In *Jeux d'Identités: Etudes comparatives à partir de la Caraïbe,* ed. M.-J. Jolivet and D. Rey-Hulman. Paris: L'Harmattan. Pp. 217–34.

———. 1995. "Linguistic Evidence for the History of West African 'Castes.'" In Conrad and Frank 1995. Pp. 61–85.

*Tandina, Ousmana Mahamane. 1983–84. "Une épopée Zarma. Wangougna Issa Korombeïzé Modi ou Issa Koygolo 'Mère de la science de la guerre.'" Thèse de troisième cycle sous la directions de Lilyan Kesteloot. Université de Dakar, FLSH, DLM. 1983–84.

*Tautain, L. 1895. "Légende et traditions des Soninké." *Bulletin de Géographie Historique et Descriptive* 9/10:472–80.

Tauxier, Louis. 1937. *Moeurs et histoire des peuls.* Paris: Payot.

———. 1942. *Histoire des Bambara.* Paris: Paul Geuthner.

Tedlock, Dennis. 1983. *The Spoken Word and the Work of Interpretation.* Philadelphia: University of Pennsylvania Press.

Tegnaeus, Henri. 1950. *Le héros civilisateur.* Stockholm: Viktor Petterson.

Terray, Emmanuel. 1988. "Tradition, légende, identité dans les Etats précoloniaux de la boucle du Niger." *Cahiers d'Etudes Africaines* 28:5–11.

Thompson, Robert Farris. 1984. *Flash of the Spirit.* New York: Vintage Books.

*Thoyer-Rozat, Annik, ed. and trans. 1978. *Chants de chasseurs du Mali.* 3 vols. Vols. 1 and 2 contain texts by Mamadu Jara, vol. 3 by Ndugace Samake. Paris: N.p. Vols. 1 and 2 reprinted Paris: L'Harmattan, 1995.

*———. 1986. *Nyakhalen la forgeronne . . . par Seyidou Kamara.* N.p.

*Tiki a Koulle a Penda, Pierre Celestin. 1987. *Les merveilleux exploits de Djeki La Njambe.* 2 vols. Douala: Editions College Libermann.

Towo-Atangana, Gaspard. 1965. "Le Mvet: Genre majeur de la littérature des populations Pahouines." *Abbia* 9/10:163–79.

Tradition historique peul. 1974. [Ed. Youssouf Tata Cissé?]. [Niamey?]: CELHTO.

Traore, Dominique. 1947. "Makanta Jigi, fondateur de la magie soudanaise." *Notes Africaines* 35 (July):23–25.

———. 1947. "Samaniana Bassi." *Notes Africaines* 34:1–3.

Traore, Issa Baba. [1962?]. *Un héros: Koumi-Diosse.* Bamako: Edition de la Librairie Populaire du Mali.

Traore, Karim. 1994. "Relevance and Significance of the Sunjata Epic." In Oosten 1994. Pp. 79–94.

*Trilling, Alex. 1980. "A Sourcebook on the Fall of Kansala and the Life of Janke Waali." Banjul, Oral History and Antiquities Division, 1980. Paper presented at the conference on Gabou. Dakar.

Turnbull, Colin M. 1972. *The Mountain People.* New York: Simon and Schuster.

*Tyam, Mohammadou Aliou. 1935. *La vie d'El Hadj Omar: Qacida en Poular*. Ed. and trans. Henri Gaden. Paris: Institut d'Ethnologie, 1935.

Vail, Leroy, and Landeg White. 1991. *Power and the Praise Poem: Southern African Voices in History*. Charlottesville: University Press of Virginia, and London: James Currey.

Vansina, Jan. 1962. *L'évolution du royaume rwanda des origines à 1900*. Brussels: Academie Royale des Sciences d'Outre-Mer. Mémoires No. 26.

———. 1964. *Le royaume Kuba*. Tervuren: Musée Royal de l'Afrique Central. Annales, Sciences Humaines, No. 49.

———. 1966. *Kingdoms of the Savanna*. Madison: University of Wisconsin Press.

———. 1983. "Is Elegance Proof? Structuralism and African History." *History in Africa* 10:307–48.

———. 1985. *Oral Tradition as History*. Madison: University of Wisconsin Press. (First edition 1965.)

Vidal, J. 1924. "La légende officielle de Soundiata." *Bulletin du Comité d'Etudes Historiques et Scientifiques de l'Afrique Occidentale Française* 7:317–28.

*Vieillard, Gilbert. N.d. *Récits peuls du Macina, du Kounari, du Djilgodji*. Ed. Eldridge Mohammedou. Niamey: N.p.

*———. 1931. "Récits peuls du Macina et du Kounari." *Bulletin du Comité d'Etudes Historique et Scientifique de l'Afrique Occidentale Française* 14.1:137–56.

*Wade, Amadou. 1964. "Chronique du Wâlo sénégalais (1186?–1855)." Ed. V. Monteil. *Bulletin de l'IFAN*, Series B, 26:440–98.

*Wamenka, N'Sanda. 1992. *Récits épiques des Lega du Zaire*. 2 vols. Tervuren: Musée Royal de l'Afrique Central. Annales, Sciences Humaines, Nos. 135–36.

*Watta, Oumarou. 1985. *The Human Thesis: A Quest for Meaning in African Epic*. Ph.D. diss., State University of New York at Buffalo.

*———. 1993. *Rosary, Mat and Molo: A Study in the Spiritual Epic of Omar Seku Tal*. New York: Peter Lang. American University Studies in Theology and Religion.

Westley, David. 1991. "A Bibliography of African Epic." *Research in African Literatures* 22.4:99–115.

Wilks, Ivor, Nehemia Levtzion, and Bruce Haight. 1986. *Chronicles from Gonja*. Cambridge: Cambridge University Press. Fontes Historiae Africanae Series Arabica 9.

Womersley, Harold. 1984. *Legends and History of the Luba*. Los Angeles: Crossroads Press.

Wright, Donald. 1972. "Kaabu and Niumi." Paper presented to the conference on Manding studies. London.

———. 1977. *The Early History of Niumi*. Ohio University, Center for International Studies. Africa Series No. 32.

———. 1978. "Koli Tengela in Sonko Traditions of Origin." *History in Africa* 5:257–71.

———. 1979. *Oral Traditions from the Gambia*. Vol. 1: *Mandinka Griots*. Athens: Ohio University Center for International Studies.

———. 1980. *Oral Traditions from the Gambia*. Vol. 2: *Family Elders*. Athens: Ohio University Center for International Studies.

———. 1987. "The Epic of Kelefa Sane as a Guide to the Nature of Precolonial Senegambian Society—and Vice Versa." *History in Africa* 14:287–309.

———. 1991. "Requiem for the Use of Oral Tradition to Reconstruct the Precolonial History of the Lower Gambia." *History in Africa* 18:399–408.

Zahan, Dominique. 1960. *Sociétés d'initiation bambara: Le N'domo, le Kore.* Paris: Mouton.

———. 1963. *La dialectique du verbe chez les Bambara.* Paris: Mouton.

———. 1974. *The Bambara.* Leiden: Brill.

De Zeltner, Franz. 1913. *Contes du Sénégal et du Niger.* Paris: E. Leroux.

Zemp, Hugo. 1966. "La légende des griots malinké." *Cahiers d'Etudes Africaines* 6:611–42.

*Zouber, Mahmoud Abdou, ed. and trans. 1983. *Traditions historiques Songhoy.* Niamey: CELHTO.

Zumthor, Paul. 1990. *Oral Poetry.* Trans. Kathryn Murphy-Judy. Minneapolis: University of Minnesota Press. First published as *Introduction à la poésie orale.* Paris: Editions du Seuil, 1980.

INDEX

Italicized locators refer to illustrations.

STEPHEN BELCHER is co-editor with John William Johnson and Thomas A. Hale of *Oral Epics from Africa: Vibrant Voices from a Vast Continent.*